IN PLACE OF GODS AND KINGS
Authorship and Identity in the *Relación de Michoacán*

CYNTHIA L. STONE

UNIVERSITY OF OKLAHOMA PRESS : NORMAN

To my parents, Reynold L. and Ann E. Stone

Library of Congress Cataloging-in-Publication Data

Stone, Cynthia L., 1962–
    In place of gods and kings : authorship and identity in the Relación de Michoacán / Cynthia L. Stone.
       p. cm.
    Includes bibliographical references and index.
    ISBN 978-0-8061-5763-4 (paper)
    1. Relación de Michoacán. 2. Indians of Mexico—Mexico—Michoacán de Ocampo—History. 3. Tarasco Indians—History. 4. Michoacán de Ocampo (Mexico)—History. 5. Michoacán de Ocampo (Mexico)—Antiquities. I. Title.

    F1219.1.M55 S76 2004
    972'.37—dc21

00-064844

The paper in this book meets the guidelines for permanence and durability of the Committee on Production Guidelines for Book Longevity of the Council on Library Resources, Inc. ∞

Copyright © 2004 by the University of Oklahoma Press, Norman, Publishing Division of the University. All rights reserved. Paperback published 2017. Manufactured in the U.S.A.

All rights reserved. No part of this publication may be reproduced, stored in a retrieval system, or transmitted, in any form or by any means, electronic, mechanical, photocopying, recording, or otherwise—except as permitted under Section 107 or 108 of the United States Copyright Act—without the prior written permission of the University of Oklahoma Press. To request permission to reproduce selections from this book, write to Permissions, University of Oklahoma Press, 2800 Venture Drive, Norman OK 73069, or email rights.oupress@ou.edu.

Contents

List of Illustrations	v
Preface	vii
Acknowledgments	ix
Introduction: Mapping Identities	3
1. Reconstructing a Multistaged Project: The Escorial Manuscript	16
2. Transparent Silences: The Friar-Compiler	43
3. Writing in Pictures: The *Caracha* (Scribes-Painters)	74
4. Remapping the Lake Pátzcuaro Basin: The *Petámuti* (High Priest)	111
5. The Many Faces of Don Pedro Cuiníarángari: The Indigenous Governor	154
Glossary	223
List of Abbreviations	227
Notes	229
Works Cited	293
Index	313

Illustrations

PLATES

Following page 80
1. Presentation of the manuscript to Viceroy Don Antonio de Mendoza
3. Alliance between the Uacúsecha and Huréndetiecha
24. Petámuti's address to the assembled lords and caciques
27. Genealogy of the principal Uacúsecha lords
33. War as a means of "feeding" the gods
38. How the commoners ~~marry~~ \used to marry/
42. Omens prefiguring the Spanish conquest
44. Arrival of the conquistadors in the Lake Pátzcuaro Basin

Following page 187
2. Ceremony of Equata cónsquaro
4. Magical warfare by Taríacuri
[Note: Plates 5–8 of Escorial Ms. C.IV.5 are not included.]
9. Infidelity of Taríacuri's wife
10. Sacrifice of warriors from Curínguaro
11. Gift of the sacred arrows
12. Poverty of Hiripan and Tangaxoan
13. Immorality of Curátame II and virtue of Hiripan and Tangáxoan
14. Taríacuri's advice to Hiripan, Tangáxoan, and Hiquíngaje
15. Surrender of the islander Zapíuátame to Tangáxoan
16. Debauchery of Curátame II and penance of Hiripan, Tangáxoan, and Hiquíngaje
17. Gift of an obsidian blade representing the god Curícaueri
18. Execution of Curátame II by order of his father, Taríacuri
19. Dream apparitions of the gods Curícaueri and Xarátanga
20. Fall of the town of Itzíparámuco
21. Hiripan's fall from a rotten tree
22. Taríacuri's division of the future kingdom in three parts
23. Uniting all the 'jewels' of the kingdom in one place
25. Execution of Tamápucheca by order of his father, Taríacuri

26. Beheading of a lord of Curínguaro by a female relative of Taríacuri
28. Officials in the cazonci's government I
29. Officials in the cazonci's government II
30. Priests and guardians of the temples
31. Preparations for a surprise attack on an enemy village
32. Captain general's address to the assembled troops
34. Mourning those who die in war
35. Cazonci's administration of justice
36. Choosing a successor for a dead cacique
37. How the lords married among themselves
39. Burial ceremony of a cazonci
40. Choosing a new ruler
41. Inauguration ceremonies
43. Mexica embassies to the cazonci Zuangua
45. Transfer of the diocese from Tzintzuntzan to Pátzcuaro (Beaumont)
46. Map of the Lake Pátzcuaro Basin (Beaumont)
47. Ceremony of Equata cónsquaro (Beaumont)
48. Hand 1, Prologue and first five chapters of part two
49. Hand 2, Remaining leaf of part one
50. Hand 3, Chapters six to thirty-five, part two
51. Hand 4, All of part three
52. Hand 5, The principal corrector

FIGURES

1. The earth goddess from the viewpoint of the celestial gods and those of the underworld — 94
2. The four quadrants: gods of the right-hand and left-hand sides of the cosmos — 94
3. Primary diagonal separating the realms of the male solar deities and female lunar deities in both their visible and invisible aspects — 95
4. Genealogy of the principal Uacúsecha lords — 124

MAPS

1. Michoacán — 2
2. The Lake Pátzcuaro Basin — 5

Preface

I was brought up in a family in which words mattered. Not just the surface meaning of words, but their potential to draw us into parallel symbolic universes. Evenings would typically find each of us ensconced in couch, armchair, or bed, lost in fictional reveries—from detective novels and diaries to eighteenth-century British masters. One of my earliest memories is the sound of my father's voice reading us children the adventures of Huck Finn or the Hobbit until finally, no longer able to match the words to any sense whatsoever, we would drift off to sleep.

So when I received as a gift some years ago a copy of a controversial bilingual children's book by the Zapatista revolutionary Subcomandante Marcos (see, for example, *The New York Times*, March 3 and 10, 1999), I opened it with delight, anticipating the joy of sharing a new treasure with my daughter. *La historia de los colores* tells the story of how colors came into the world and how the gods made one bird in particular, the macaw, their guardian. And because it does so through both prose and pictures, it gives form and substance to the abstract notion that words and colors—the way we think and the way we see—are intimately connected to one another. As old Antonio, the narrator of the story within a story, puts it in his closing remarks: "And that was how the macaw took hold of the colors, and so it goes strutting about just in case men and women forget how many colors there are and how many ways of thinking, and that the world will be happy if all the colors and ways of thinking have their place" (Marcos [1996]1999).

This concept of writing in color has a clear historical precedent in the ancient Mesoamerican tradition of recording important cultural information in pictographic books or codices. Indeed, the colonial-era practice of including pictures in compilations of indigenous traditions, such as the *Relación de Michoacán*, can be attributed, in no small part, to the first impulse of the recently conquered peoples of New Spain, when asked to provide information about their ancient customs and beliefs, which was to make drawings whose meaning they would then expound upon verbally for the benefit of the missionary-compilers.

In *La historia de los colores*, there is no clear dividing line between myth and history. The story is not set in the time of the first creation, that is, of "the first ones, the seven gods who gave birth to the world, the very first ones," but rather in an era when much of the ancient knowledge about the origin of things had already been forgotten. The gods of this later era, it turns out, were much like human beings: prone to quarrel, especially when bored; easily tired after physical exertion; capable of bleeding when struck on the head by a rock or of losing their sight after staring too long at the earth from on high; careless in the manner in which they flung the colors from the top of a ceiba tree.

In the act of flinging the colors, they painted the world as we know it today. Thus, the innovation introduced into a formerly black-and-white world by the gods' discovery of red, green, brown, blue, yellow, and all the myriad combinations derived therefrom, coincides with the beginning of recorded history. The cosmic energy unleashed, moreover, is a type of lovemaking that adds a touch of happiness to an otherwise gray existence. In short, the above parable—originally included by Subcomandante Marcos in a communiqué issued on October 27, 1994, to the Mexican people—synthesizes many motifs at the core of Mesoamerican religious traditions: the notion of a dynamic universe in a constant state of flux, characterized by the periodic irruption of the sacred into everyday life; the sacrifice required of those who aspire to leave their mark upon the world in an enduring way, as well as the benefits that accrue to all as a result of such sacrifice; the central place of trees and birds, and of plants and animals generally, within the cosmic order.

This book is an attempt to elucidate the connections between such ideas and the incipient process of transculturation exemplified in the *Relación de Michoacán*. By establishing analogies I am not positing exact equivalences between the ideology of the Zapatistas and that of the indigenous contributors to the collaborative project commenced on the shores of Lake Pátzcuaro in the 1530s and '40s. Rather, I am inviting the reader to tag along as I attempt to construct plausible scenarios for understanding the mind-set of the particular historical individuals involved, who also happen to embody larger historical processes. In this way the renegotiation of identities and alliances described in the pages of this book speaks to our continuing need to come to terms with the past, as well as with the value of those who paint pictures and tell stories on the margins of official discourse.

Acknowledgments

This study of the textual dynamics of the *Relación de Michoacán* was made possible, to a considerable degree, by the groundbreaking research of two professors with whom I was fortunate enough to study at the University of Michigan in the late 1980s—Rolena Adorno and Walter D. Mignolo. Adorno began her comprehensive study of Felipe Guamán Poma de Ayala's *Nueva corónica y buen gobierno* at a time when it was still considered the largely incoherent ravings of a semiliterate peasant. Especially germane to chapter three of this book, her various analyses of the Guamán Poma drawings provide a theoretical framework for articulating the connections between prose and pictures in colonial-era manuscripts. Her more recent writings on Bartolomé de las Casas and Álvar Núñez Cabeza de Vaca further elucidate that vast web of discursive formations where alliances were forged between Spaniards and Indians in the wake of conquest.

My debt to Walter D. Mignolo derives from his systematic efforts, within the context of colonial Spanish-American studies, to formulate alternatives to Eurocentric definitions of literature as belles lettres and writing as exclusively alphabetic. Not only has this approach allowed for the inclusion within the literary canon of an ever-greater number of manuscripts from the period, it has also opened the floodgates to a wealth of new strategies for articulating the present-day relevance of texts from the past.

I would also like to take this opportunity to offer thanks to a number of other professors, colleagues, and friends who have been instrumental in bringing this project to fruition. To Gene Bell-Villada and Antonio Jiménez at Williams College, for motivating me to change my major from psychology to Spanish. To Norma Klahn and Flor María Rodríguez Arenas at Columbia University, for introducing me to the chronicles and *relaciones* of the Spanish-American colonial period. To the members of my dissertation committee at Michigan: Rolena Adorno (dissertation director), Walter D. Mignolo, Charles Fraker, and Bruce Mannheim, for their support and advice. To Nina Gerassi-Navarro, for her friendship and for having introduced me to the experience of intellectual inquiry as a shared endeavor. To my colleagues at the College of the Holy Cross, especially Isabel Álvarez-Borland and Karen Turner, and at other colleges and universities, particularly Shahzad Bashir, Raquel Chang-Rodríguez, Bradley Levinson, and Marysa Navarro, who have read and offered commentary on the material contained in this book prior to its publication. To Rolena and the late David Adorno, above all, for their unstinting support, guidance, and encouragement at every stage throughout my professional career.

My contacts with fellow scholars specializing in prehispanic and colonial Michoacán began with a fortuitous encounter at the Real Biblioteca del Escorial in the summer of 1991 with Armando M. Escobar Olmedo. While on sabbatical leave in Mexico during the fall of 1999, moreover, I was fortunate to receive commentary on various aspects of my work from scholars at the Universidad Michoacana de San Nicolás de Hidalgo in Morelia and the Colegio de Michoacán in Zamora, including Felipe Castro Gutiérrez (who was on leave from the Universidad Nacional Autónoma de México), Moisés Franco Mendoza, Agustín Jacinto Zavala, Pedro Márquez Joaquín, Francisco Miranda Godínez, Cristina Monzón García, Cayetano Reyes García, Hans Roskamp, Gerardo Sánchez Díaz, and J. Benedict Warren. Special thanks are due J. Benedict Warren and Helen Perlstein Pollard for their many suggested revisions of the manuscript as outside reviewers for the University of Oklahoma Press, as well as J. Benedict and Patricia S. Warren for graciously hosting me and my family during the aforementioned visit to Michoacán.

The archival research that has gone into the making of this study, although not extensive if judged by the norm among historians, is central to the metaphor of the Escorial manuscript as palimpsest that is developed in the first two chapters. My evidence concerning modifications made to the drawings as well as last-minute suppressions and additions in the hand of the principal corrector was gathered during visits to the Escorial during the summer of 1991. Father Alonso Teodoro Turiezno, O.S.A. was most helpful in facilitating access to the manuscript and related documents. This trip was partially funded by a Horace Rackham Dissertation Fellowship from the University of Michigan. Another opportunity for conducting research, at the Centro de Documentos Históricos Microfilmados in Tiripetío, Michoacán, during in the summer of 1993, was made possible in part through a Batchelor (Ford) Summer Faculty Fellowship from the College of the Holy Cross. The cost of an eight-page color insert was subsidized through a 1998 Research and Publication award from Holy Cross.

I wish to express my gratitude to Patrimonio Nacional de España, as proprietor of Escorial Ms. C.IV.5, for permission to reproduce the drawings that appear in this study. All Craine and Reindorp plates are reprinted from *The Chronicles of Michoacán*, translated and edited by Eugene R. Craine and Reginald C. Reindorp, copyright © 1970 by the University of Oklahoma Press. The remaining plates are reprinted from the edition of the *Relación de Michoacán* by Moisés Franco Mendoza, copyright © 2000 by the Colegio de Michoacán and Gobierno del Estado de Michoacán. I would also like to thank the staff of the Archivo General de la Nación (Mexico City) and the John Carter Brown Library at Brown University for their permission to use the Beaumont "maps."

This project has gone through several incarnations. It began as a 1992 doctoral dissertation entitled *Fragile Coalitions*. A substantially expanded and rewritten version was cited by Hans Roskamp 2000 and James Krippner-Martínez 2001 as *Mapping Identities*, which was the working title of the manuscript then in the process of being edited by the University of Oklahoma Press. Complications over the reproduction of the drawings of the Escorial manuscript subsequently led to a delay in the production process which, while not of my volition, has provided me with an opportunity to incorporate some of the additional research published in the interim.

Finally, I would like to thank my husband, Donald N. S. Unger, a fellow believer in the value of words, for helping me to hone my skills as a writer, for keeping his faith in me as a teacher and scholar, and for enduring with me the joys and tribulations of shared parenting. Last but not least, to our daughter, Rebecca: there are some things, as all parents know, that words are simply inadequate to express.

In Place of Gods and Kings

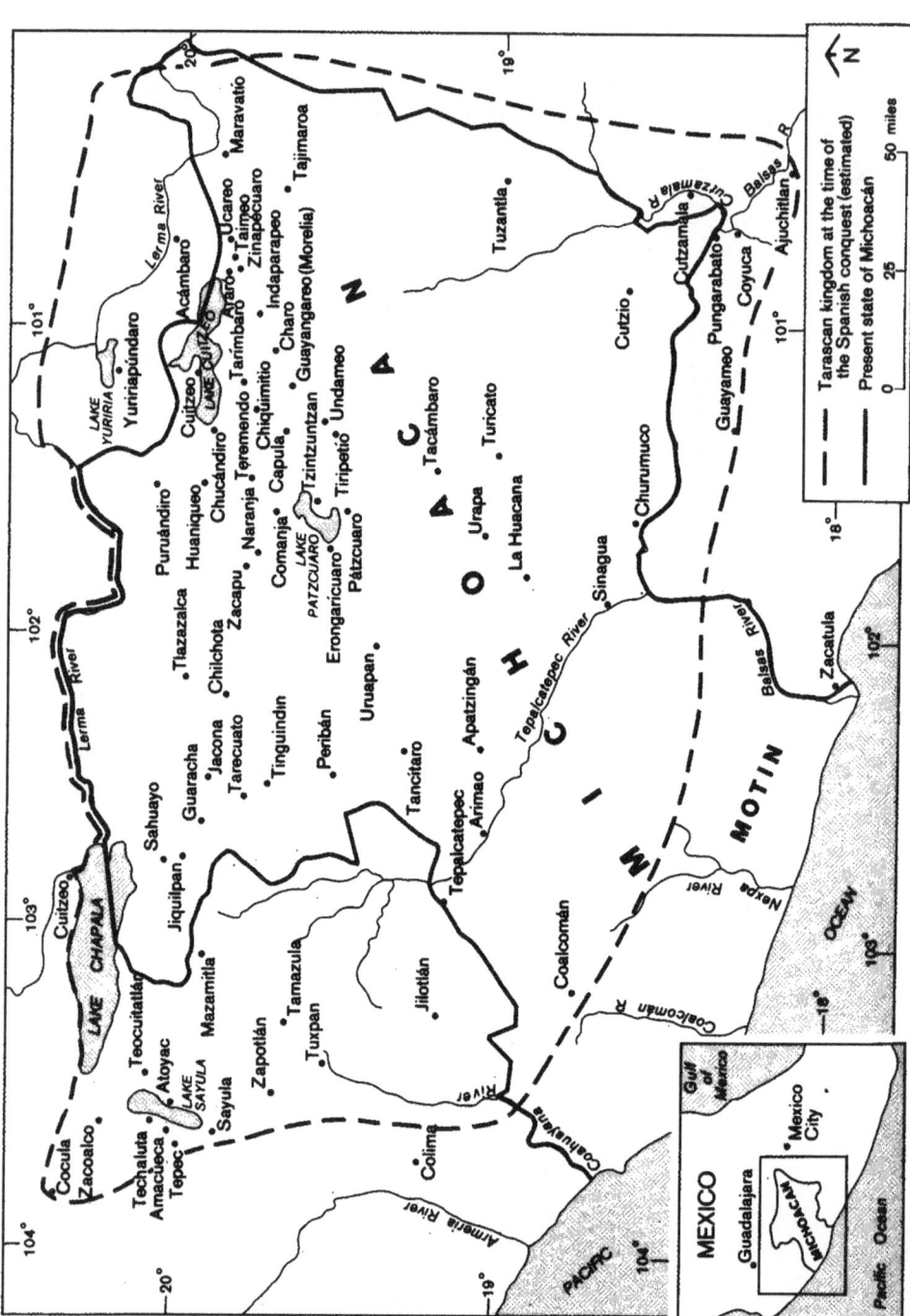

MAP 1. Michoacán (Reprinted from Craine and Reindorp, map drawn by John Rav.)

INTRODUCTION

Mapping Identities

If I were to begin this book about the *Relación de Michoacán* in the usual way, I would structure my introductory remarks around the figure of the friar-compiler, the barefoot Franciscan in plate 1 (color section), who offers an open book, presumably the completed manuscript, to the man who commissioned it—the first viceroy of New Spain, Don Antonio de Mendoza. I would begin with this image linking the ideal of missionary fervor with the goal of service to the Spanish crown. I would highlight, moreover, all that is known about the friar, beginning with his name— Jerónimo de Alcalá,[1] the first part of which evokes a tradition of biblical exegesis beginning with Saint Jerome, the second, the site of one of the great centers of learning and translation in sixteenth-century Castile.[2]

But the story I have chosen to tell is not centered on the figures of the friar-compiler and viceroy. Nor is it centered on the other representatives of secular and religious authority pictured in plate 1: namely, the indigenous governor, Don Pedro Cuiníarángari,[3] who provides his perspective on the Spanish conquest of Michoacán; and the anonymous *petámuti* (high priest) and other *curáecha* (elders), whose oral testimonies recount the adventures and way of life of the early settlers of the region and their descendants.

The temptation to focus on one set of bodies or another, to separate out the traces left by the acts of transcription and translation from the voices of oral tradition, to counterpoise two sets of cultural values defined in opposition to each other, is an impulse that has defined the fields of colonial and postcolonial studies to a considerable degree. Yet it is a mode of operation that proves insufficient to the task I have set for myself in this book: the creation of a space for the *Relación de Michoacán* and other culturally mixed texts within the corpus of colonial Spanish-American literature.

To that end, I have chosen to focus on the metaphor of place as a means of representing the text as a whole, for it suggests a common surface upon which each of the mostly anonymous participants in the production of the *Relación de Michoacán*, as well as its many readers, have inscribed their own responses, an intersection for a wide range of human interests and motivations from colonial times to the present. This layering process applies to the text as palimpsest and also, in a more general sense, to all humanmade and natural environments. As Keith Basso has observed with respect to his ethnographic fieldwork among the Apache: "place-making is a way of constructing history itself, of inventing it, of fashioning novel versions of 'what happened there'" (1996, 6). Thus, although no two individuals are linked to a given place through identical needs and memories, their interactions with it are conditioned by its physical attributes as well as by the stories they have told or heard tell about it. The mapping of identities thereby accomplished binds people together through the power of the senses and imagination, allowing for the coexistence of multiple points of view, no matter how contradictory.

In the case of the *Relación de Michoacán*, as of many texts from the colonial period, the weight of collective anonymity is greater than the weight of personalized authorship. This dynamic is especially pronounced in those works whose perceived deficits and/or excesses vis à vis modern literary norms are such that they resist easy categorization. The negative impact on the artistic worth generally accorded a text lacking a clearly defined author or one in which the points of view of colonized and colonizer are woven together is not to be underestimated. At the same time there is a growing body of scholarship that turns the above value judgment on its head by exploring the ways marginalized cultures "metaphorize the dominant order" (Certeau [1980] 1984, 32), reconfiguring their own traditions in response to changing circumstances.[4]

This process of "refunctionalization" or "remythification," as Alfredo López Austin dubs the creative response of the indigenous peoples of Mesoamerica to the imposition of Christianity beginning in the early sixteenth century, is fraught with ideological contention, since it can be difficult to pin down the standard for comparison or degree of individual variation in any given case. Still, the theoretical model I have employed assumes a framework within which change occurs, much as the contours of a community shape the experiences of its members and, in the process, are themselves transformed.

What are the places that serve as a locus for the mapping of identities analyzed in this book? One such place is the physical manuscript itself, the sole surviving copy of which is housed in the Real Biblioteca del Escorial outside Madrid. A second is the Lake Pátzcuaro Basin, whose mountains, shores, and human settlements serve as the backdrop for the stories

MAP 2. The Lake Pátzcuaro Basin (Based on a map by Cynthia L. Stone)

narrated in the *Relación de Michoacán*. It is a region that formed the core of the fourfold kingdom ruled by the *cazonci* or supreme ruler of Michoacán at the time of the Spanish conquest and that continues to play a major role in the collective imaginary of the state's present-day inhabitants.

THE ESCORIAL MANUSCRIPT

Listed in the first catalogue made of the library's holdings about 1600, Escorial Ms. C.IV. 5 is marked throughout by the twin extremes of insufficiency and excess. To begin with, it is missing all but a leaf of part one, on the principal gods and religious ceremonies of Michoacán. The current binding, accomplished after the removal of the remainder of this section, the transposition of parts two and three, and the addition of a number of loose leaf drawings, suggests the handiwork of a custodian who felt compelled to establish some semblance of order for the purposes of preservation and cataloging. Further evidence of inconsistent care or vigilance is provided by four stubs, at least two of which appear to have been cut out of the manuscript at some point after it was bound; the location of the cut-out leaves between folios 8–9 and 48–49 suggests they might have contained drawings of the women who served in the palace of the cazonci and of the cazonci's treasure (Escobar Olmedo 2001, 30); it is unclear what may have been on the missing parts of the two cutouts between folios 60'3 and 60'4 (Hidalgo Brinquis 2001, 70).[5]

If the physical integrity of the manuscript has been compromised by the above deletions, transpositions, and additions, it should be noted that the document that made its way to Philip II's monastery palace sometime in the sixteenth century was by no means pristine or complete at the time of its arrival. On the contrary it was already characterized by numerous repositionings, emendations, erasures, and blank spaces for drawings that were never completed, as well as by a multiplicity of hands that had left their marks upon it at various stages in the compilation process. Regarding the latter, plates 48–52 provide samples of four distinct hands responsible for copying over the prose portions of the manuscript as well as a fifth identified as the hand of the principal corrector.[6] The plates in the color section and following chapter 5, moreover, contain reproductions of most of the forty-four colored pen-and-ink miniatures that accompanied the prose chapters and that were drawn by an indeterminate number of *caracha*.

The basic bibliographic information that can be gleaned from a perusal of the Escorial manuscript likewise tends to strike modern sensibilities as either too much or too little. The title, for example, is customarily abbreviated, since the one given on the frontispiece is of a typical colonial-era length:

> Relaçion de las çerimonias y rrictos y poblaçion y governaçion de los yndios de la provinçia de mechuacan hecha al yllustrisimo señor don antonio de mendoça virrey y governador desta nueva españa por su magestad real catolica imperial (1)[7]

> [Account of the ceremonies and rites and settlement and government of the Indians of the province of Michoacán made for the Illustrious Lord Don Antonio de Mendoza viceroy and governor of this New Spain on behalf of his Royal Catholic Imperial Majesty][8]

As for evidence regarding the time frame in which the manuscript was compiled, although there are a handful of clues, it has proven difficult to determine definitive dates for the initiation of the project. References to contemporaneous events are scattered throughout the text, but differences of interpretation persist. My own reading of the available data suggests that some of the indigenous testimonies were transcribed as early as 1538 and that the manuscript was delivered to Viceroy Mendoza in late 1541.[9]

The bibliographic conundrum that has generated the most speculation to date, however, does not involve the title of the manuscript or its dates of compilation, but rather the identity of the friar-compiler. Indeed, the history of textual interpretation of the Escorial manuscript can be traced back to the musings of the anonymous commentator who penciled in the suspicion that the author may have been Bernardino de Sahagún.[10] I will treat other speculations on the subject in greater detail in chapter two. Suffice it to say at this point that the lack of an autographic copy has complicated efforts to categorize, contextualize, and, by extension, fully appreciate the literary value of the Escorial manuscript.

The ethnohistorical significance of the manuscript, in contrast, has been widely recognized since the early nineteenth century, at which time several well-known antiquarians had full or partial copies made, now located in the New York Public Library (Obadiah Rich collection); Library of Congress (Peter Force collection); Archivo de la Real Academia de la Historia (Juan Bautista Muñoz collection); Biblioteca Nacional de Madrid (Pascual Gayangos collection); Bibliothèque Nationale de Paris (Brasseur de Bourbourg collection); and Milan Public Library (Francisco del Paso y Troncoso collection). At least one of these manuscript copies was probably produced as early as the late 1700s by scriveners in the employ of Juan Bautista Muñoz, who was empowered by Charles III to search out "relevant documentation in the archives and libraries of Spain" for his history of the Indies (Brownrigg 1978, vii).[11]

It was not until 1869, however, when a paleographic version by Florencio Janer was printed in Madrid as volume 53 of the *Colección de documentos inéditos para la historia de España*, that the Escorial manuscript's potential to reach a wider audience began to be tapped in earnest.[12] The initial task of dissemination was aided by the efforts of several eminent nineteenth-century historians who summarized its contents in their writings, including Brasseur de Bourbourg (1857–59), Payno (1869), Orozco y Berra (1880), Chavero and Riva Palacio (1882–83), Francisco del Paso y Troncoso ([1887]1888), and Francisco Plancarte y Navarrete (1889).[13] Subsequent editions, totaling seven to date in Spanish (León 1903; Tudela 1956; Miranda 1980 and 2001; Cabrero 1989; Franco Mendoza 2000; Escobar Olmedo 2001), not including reprints and abridged versions, and one translation each in English (Craine and Reindorp 1970), French (Le Clézio 1984), and Japanese (Mochizuki 1987), have done much to raise the profile of the work and to encourage its study from the perspectives of a variety of disciplines, especially history, linguistics, anthropology, and archaeology.[14]

Among the many individuals who have devoted a significant portion of their scholarly endeavors to the interpretation of the Escorial manuscript, special note must be made of the two founding fathers of Michoacán studies in this century, Nicolás León and Eduardo Ruiz. Echoes of the polemic between these two figures—the former of whom was primarily concerned to validate the text by inserting it within a scriptural tradition originating in the colonial period; the latter, to explore its connections to folklore and legend—can still be heard in ongoing debates involving the relative weight that should be attributed to documentary as opposed to popular sources.[15]

A third key interpreter at the turn of the century was the German linguist and ethnohistorian Eduard Seler, whose wide-ranging interests in Mesoamerican cosmology led him devote an extensive monograph to the ancient beliefs and customs of the indigenous inhabitants of Michoacán.[16] This focus was further developed at mid-century by the famous Cardenista activist José Corona Núñez,[17] who was wont to establish one-on-one equivalencies between the gods and ceremonies described in the Escorial manuscript and the better-known central Mexican pantheon and related religious beliefs.[18]

The number of scholars who have made significant contributions over the past few decades defies summary classification. Those whose writings I have mined extensively in this book include: J. Benedict Warren,[19] whose meticulously documented history of the events that transpired in Michoacán from 1521 to 1530 draws heavily on the version of the conquest articulated by the indigenous governor in part three of the Escorial manuscript; Helen Perlstein Pollard,[20] who explores the parallels between archaeological and ethnohistorical materials from the region; Francisco Miranda,[21] who has greatly contributed to increasing the accessibility of the text through his editorial efforts; Alfredo López Austin,[22] who has helped to elucidate several important dimensions of the story told by the petámuti, such as the notion of sacred kingship; and Jean Marie G. Le Clézio,[23] who has synthesized in his own writings many of the central poetic features of the work, especially those related to shamanic rituals and practices.[24]

The above distinguished cast of characters notwithstanding, the *Relación de Michoacán* has yet to realize its potential for leaving an indelible mark on the literary landscape both inside and outside of Mexico. What remains to be done is, paradoxically, to articulate more fully the universal in the particular—the process whereby the characters who populate the pages of the Escorial manuscript, as they once did the shores of Lake Pátzcuaro, speak to widespread human concerns—highlighting the points of contact, as well as disjunctions, between their stories and those of other peoples who belong to other places.

THE LAKE PÁTZCUARO BASIN

One advantage of centering this book on the metaphor of place is that it combines both the vertical and the horizontal—the stances of an observer looking up at the night sky and of an individual who moves through a landscape suffused with the light of day. The lived experience of those who inhabit a particular environment, such as the Lake Pátzcuaro Basin, is made up of the intertwining of these two spatial dimensions.

What is visible in the daylight—natural phenomena such as trees, rock formations, mountains, rivers, and humanmade structures such as houses, places of worship, roads—suggests one point of comparison for the stories contained in the Escorial manuscript. Like the narratives recounting the wanderings of the Aztecs or Mexica in search of their promised land, history in the *Relación de Michoacán* weaves together sequences of foundational moments identified with one or more characters, sites, and events.

Each toponym mentioned in the narrative is endowed with multi-layered symbolism. Uayámeo, for instance, is both the site of the first settlement in the area by the Uacúsecha—the ruling dynasty at the time of the Spanish conquest—and also the setting, many years later, for the *pueblo-hospital* (community devoted to charitable pursuits) founded by the first bishop of Michoacán, Don Vasco de Quiroga. Another oft-mentioned locale is the hill in Pátzcuaro where, long ago, four rock formations were found in the shape of the ancestor gods, upon which temples to the god Curícaueri were built and upon whose ruins, in turn, a cathedral was being constructed at the time of compilation of the Escorial manuscript. Tzintzuntzan, for its part, is encoded in the text as the location where a ball court and steam bath dedicated to the goddess Xarátanga had once stood, a wild place that the Uacúsecha took it upon themselves to restore to its former grandeur, eventually transforming it into the capital of the *iréchequa*, or fourfold kingdom.

A second common denominator of lived experience involves the act of looking up at the night sky, especially when the observer is far removed from sources of artificial light. The work of pioneering astronomers such as Anthony F. Aveni (1975; 1977; 1980) has galvanized discussion in recent decades around recurring patterns related to the configuration of the stars and planets from a Mesoamerican viewpoint, especially those that correlate with important agricultural and life cycles. One such constant involves the coincidence between the beginning of the rainy season and the passage of the sun across the zenith (Aveni 1980, 40–42).[25] Other, more generally observable, phenomena include the correlation between the phases of the moon and the female menstrual cycle and the contrapuntal relationship between the daily movement of the sun from east to west and the trajectory of the moon over the course of a complete lunation, during which it waxes in the western part of the sky and wanes in the east.

Like the Popol Vuh, the sacred book of the Quiché Mayas, which was transcribed in alphabetic letters circa 1554, the *Relación de Michoacán* can be tentatively read as a blueprint for interpreting the symbolic significance of the movement of the stars and planets. From this perspective the interactions among the various characters who appear in the text constitute a veritable storehouse of archetypes and patterns that echo cosmological principles and are capable of infinitely varied recombinations. In order to perceive this sacred dimension, however, one must temporarily set aside a no-less-compelling tradition of textual interpretation that stresses the unique historical nature of the various characters and events described therein.

The ongoing debate among Mesoamericanists over whether to emphasize unity or diversity, continuity or change, follows a similar pendulum-like motion, with advocates alternately focusing on generic principles that have remained constant over the long duration versus individual peculiarities that correspond to a shorter time frame. My own stance vis à vis this polemic seconds the opinion expressed by Alfredo López Austin ([1994] 1997, 4–12): namely that, at this stage of the game, it is important to push against the boundaries of what is considered appropriate for purposes of comparison.

I would add to this call for greater experimentation, moreover, the caveat that the ability to engage in metaphorical flights of fancy is precisely one of the areas in which those trained in literary analysis can best contribute to this interdisciplinary discussion. To be sure, we must take care to ground our readings in plausible interpretations of the literal meaning of the text at hand; but this sort of two-pronged approach, combining sensitivity to nuance with an appeal to concrete example, is a hallmark of the profession.

Almost fifty years ago, Ángel María Garibay K. led the battle to recognize the literary value of the oral traditions of the Nahuas of the central valley of Mexico as they had been transcribed around the time of the Spanish conquest. The benefits that have accrued to the study of the indigenous cultures of Mesoamerica in general have been great. What remains suspect in certain circles, however, is the act of drawing analogies across culture groups and time periods.[26] And yet such imaginative speculation is at the heart of the literary enterprise, which contributes, at its best, to fostering a heightened sense of the bonds that unite all human beings, no matter how dissimilar. Granted, not all analogies are well founded, but the crux of the issue has more to do with the need for precise and judicious implementation than with faulty methodology per se. As Ivan Šprajc has observed, the power of analogies is their capacity to engender innovative hypothesis; their limitation that, without corroborating evidence, they cannot serve to establish anything definitively (1996, 14).

The need for caution is augmented, in the case of the *Relación de Michoacán*, for several reasons: (1) the sole surviving manuscript is a translation into Castilian with only isolated words and phrases in indigenous languages;[27] and (2) research to date on the prehispanic archaeology and history of Michoacán is limited compared to that on other areas of Mesoamerica. The experimental nature of this study, however, is its primary strength. Whatever the ultimate validity of the various hypotheses proposed, my hope is that they will contribute to extending the discussion in fruitful directions.

MULTIPLE AUTHORSHIP

All the compilations of indigenous traditions ascribed to the missionaries of sixteenth-century Mexico were collaborative enterprises in which the particular Franciscans, Dominicans, Augustinians, or Jesuits involved presided over a more or less numerous group of informants, translators, scribes, and painters. Unlike those whose missionary activity was focused on central Mexico, however—such as Andrés de Olmos; Toribio de Benavente "Motolinía"; Bernardino de Sahagún; Pedro de los Ríos; Diego Durán; and Juan de Tovar[28]—the friar-compiler of the *Relación de Michoacán* processed the indigenous customs and beliefs of the region through more than one linguistic and cultural filter: his native Castilian and also Nahuatl—the language of the Spaniards' principal indigenous allies. This systematic privileging of Nahuatl as an indigenous lingua franca is especially pronounced in the writings of members of the Franciscan order, since they, as the first to arrive in New Spain, dominated evangelization in the viceregal capital and its immediate environs.[29]

A corollary of the above dynamic is that missionaries such as Sahagún are more easily able to temper their condemnation of heathen practices with a heavy dose of appreciation for the cultural achievements of their spiritual charges. There are, no doubt, many reasons for the greater emphasis placed by the friar-compiler of the Escorial manuscript on the lack of "reason" to be found in Michoacán within the figurative darkness of "idolatry." The shadow cast by the Franciscan promotion of Anahuac as the model for all things "Indian," however, clearly plays a part in the above equation.[30]

The problem, of course, is that the friar-compiler's prejudices have become our own. So long as our gaze remains fixed on the barefoot Franciscan, we are left with little guidance from the self-appointed interpreter who promises to orient us as we cross the threshold into a strange new world, few clues to help in articulating a larger context within which to appreciate what we find there.

One way out of the bottleneck represented by this denial of the symbolic value of the indigenous traditions of Michoacán, however, is to refuse to accept, à la Michel Foucault ([1969] 1972, 215–37) and Roland Barthes (1977, 142–48), the Romantic-European notion of the unitary author. The issue of multiple authorship is as crucial to this book as that of mapping identities, for it is only when we set aside the exclusive identification of the friar as author that we can begin to perceive the complex textual dynamics of the *Relación de Michoacán*: the layering of oral, pictorial, and alphabetic traditions; the traces of earlier manuscript drafts in the sole copy that has been found to date; the efforts to shape the final product in such a way as to edit out politically sensitive material; the struggle between competing viewpoints within the text, which have led, in turn, to contrary currents of interpretation.

Each of the chapters of this book approaches the above project from a different angle. Chapter one stresses the claim to authorship in the name of political authority, with a focus on Viceroy Mendoza and his role in commissioning the Escorial manuscript in the late 1530s. Also highlighted are a number of hypotheses regarding the dissemination of fragments, alternate drafts, or manuscript copies during the colonial period, authorship of which has been attributed, over the years, to a variety of individuals, from Don Antonio Huitziméngari (the son of the last cazonci of Michoacán) to the Augustinian and Jesuit rivals of the early Franciscans of the region.

Chapter two puts the accent on the contributions of the friar-compiler, and it is here that I explore in detail the notion of authorship that he articulates in his prologue. One of my reasons for avoiding references to the friar by name throughout this book is that I see his decision to remain anonymous as more than simply an act of Christian humility. It is also an important part of his editorial strategy, which aims to foreground the roots of the text in oral tradition in order to more easily disavow the claim to truth of the pagan belief system expressed therein.

This second chapter focuses on the disjunction between the contributions of the friar and those of the indigenous participants, especially insofar as they can be reconstructed through an analysis of last-minute changes made to the manuscript by the hand of the principal corrector—who is almost certainly the friar-compiler. In this way I show how all editions to date, by assuming that the definitive version must be the "corrected" one, have—however unintentionally—privileged the voice of the European missionary and thereby obscured a fuller appreciation of the contributions of the indigenous participants.

The final three chapters collectively redefine the role of the caracha, petámuti, and Don Pedro Cuiníarángari (who served as indigenous governor from 1530 to 1543) as additional authors in the sense of their being active contributors to the production of textual meaning, each with a distinctive vision of the project as a whole.

My analysis of the colored pen-and-ink drawings in chapter three seeks to underscore one of the aspects of the text negated by the friar-compiler and by many modern commentators as well—its links with the Mesoamerican tradition of writing in pictures and, by extension, with the sacred dimensions implicit in such writing. Through analogy with some of the principal metaphors that serve to structure the prose narrative, I show how the drawings partake of their own form of symbolic language. Thus, spatiotemporal position becomes the equivalent of grammar, and the greater or lesser use of indigenous versus European pictorial conventions in the representation of particular figures, an indication of the lexical mixing common throughout the Americas.[31]

In my reading of the oral performance of the petámuti in chapter four, I view his words as directed primarily to the indigenous peoples who survived the early ravages of conquest, rather than to the colonial authorities. His discourse, humorous in parts, is peppered with references to familiar landmarks, to the ancestors of the various members of his audience, to a shared set of knowledge and experiences. With the exception of the relatively infrequent commentary provided by the friar-compiler, there are few concessions to the uninitiated. At the same time the petámuti does not draw a sharp distinction between pre- and postconquest Michoacán. He notes the presence of church bells and other evidence of recent missionizing and colonizing efforts in the same breath with which he speaks of the marks of earlier foundational moments that draw their force from the divine power attributed to springs, rocks, and mountains. This remapping of identities weaves together past, present, and future, time and space, the lives of gods and mortals. The petámuti's prophetic call to remain faithful to tradition does not seek to codify it once and for all, but rather exemplifies how it must be constantly transformed in response to changing circumstances.

Finally, in chapter five I analyze the uneasy tension between political expediency and political advocacy that characterizes the perspective of Don Pedro Cuiníarángari. This prototypical colonial-era "cultural broker" (Hinderaker 2002) exemplifies the ambivalence that lies at the heart of many attempts to construct a pluralistic identity for the Americas. Opportunistic traitor or faithful messenger, portly buffoon or eloquent orator, exemplary Christian or champion of traditional values—the many faces that have been attributed to this indigenous governor over the centuries are here presented as all prefigured within Cuiníarángari's own account of the events that transpired in Michoacán from 1519 to 1530.

For those who espouse a version of cultural *mestizaje* grounded in the myths of the Mexican Revolution, it is his similarity to La Malinche as paradigmatic traitor that stands out most clearly. For those who seek to elucidate the links between colonial-era figures and present-day advocates for greater indigenous political and cultural autonomy, his story can be read in tandem with Bartolomé de las Casas's critique of the injustices of colonial rule. For all those interested in recasting familiar stories in order to define more actively the role of indigenous participants, his narrative implicitly undermines essentialist models of cultural authenticity by highlighting the masks worn by conquered and conqueror alike.

My ultimate goals are to assist the readers of the *Relación de Michoacán* in training their ears to pick up the distinctive modulations of the voices of the friar, the petámuti, the indigenous governor, and the other informants and their eyes to perceive symbolic patterns in the drawings made by the caracha. Parts of what each of these contributors has to say may strike present-day readers as odd or offensive, but there is much of value to be unearthed through the systematic excavation of the various strata. Indeed, the full measure of their contributions cannot be taken without a keen awareness both of our own cultural and temporal distance from the viewpoints expressed by the various participants and also, conversely, our common humanity.

1

RECONSTRUCTING A MULTISTAGED PROJECT

The Escorial Manuscript

> Antiquities are history defaced, or some remnants of history which have casually escaped the shipwreck of time.
> —*Francis Bacon*

The fortuitous nature of the materials that escape the "shipwreck of time," as Bacon observes in the above quote, is worth pondering by those engaged in historically based studies, however interdisciplinary.[1] Indeed, many of the erroneous assumptions made today about colonial-era manuscripts result from a too-narrow vision of scholarly production and reception in the age ushered in by the voyages of Columbus.

In an effort to avoid such an overly restricted focus, I would like to begin by situating the *Relación de Michoacán* in the context of manuscript compilation and dissemination from the sixteenth to eighteenth centuries. My general overview of how the missionary-compilers of New Spain went about researching the antiquities of the peoples they had come to convert is complemented by an analysis of clues contained in the Escorial manuscript itself regarding the way in which it was assembled.

I have also cast a relatively wide net in my subsequent discussion of points of contact between the Escorial manuscript and other texts from the colonial period that touch on the customs of the indigenous inhabitants of Michoacán. These include the writings of the historian Francisco Cervantes de Salazar ([1566] 1985, 781–809); a lost manuscript by Don Antonio Huitziméngari, indigenous governor of Michoacán from 1545 to 1562 (mentioned in Escobar [1729] 1970, 124); a treatise on marital practices by the Augustinian Alonso de la Veracruz ([1556] 1988, 277–312); a *littera annua* (annual letter addressed to the provincial superior) by the Jesuit Francisco Ramírez ([1585] 1959, 2:492–96); Antonio de Herrera y Tordesilla's general history of the Indies ([1601–15] 1934–57; dec. 3, bk. 3, ch. 10); and some pictures copied by the Franciscan Pablo Beaumont from an ancient painting on a *tira,* or long strip of paper, belonging to a man named Cuiní ([ca. 1778] 1985–87, 2:30, 42, 59, 138).

I hypothesize that the production of multiple drafts by the friar-compiler of the *Relación de Michoacán* and his indigenous assistants circa 1538–41, of which the Escorial manuscript is the only one known to have survived, did more to assure the circulation of the material it contained over the course of the colonial period than has been generally recognized. The extant remnants of this multistaged project, and the traces of it that can be extrapolated from related texts, provide a glimpse of what the complete enterprise was all about. Like the ruins of the great Mesoamerican city of Teotihuacan, whose surviving structures provide little indication of the vibrant hues with which they were once decorated, efforts to reconstruct the work of the participants in the making of the Escorial manuscript must, of necessity, leave something to the imagination.

A touchstone against which to measure the influence of the *Relación de Michoacán* from colonial times to the present is a letter from the first viceroy of New Spain, Don Antonio de Mendoza, to the first official chronicler of the Indies, Gonzalo Fernández de Oviedo y Valdés,[2] dated October 6, 1541. In the letter Mendoza expresses confidence that a definitive account of the things of Michoacán, due in large part to his own efforts, will soon come to rival popular descriptions of the customs and life-style of the inhabitants of the central valley of Mexico:

> La relación de las cosas desta tierra yo he procurado de sabello muy particularmente, e hallo diversas opiniones; porque como había muchos señores en cada provincia, cuentan las cosas de su manera. Yo las ando recogiendo e verificando, y hecho, os lo enviaré; porque me paresce que sería cosa muy vergonzosa que os enviase yo relación y que me alegásedes por auctor dello, no siendo muy verdadera. Y lo de aquí no es tan poco que no podáis hacer libro dello, e no será pequeño; porque aunque Montezuma e Méjico es lo que entre nosotros ha sonado, no era menor señor el Cazonzí de Mechuacán, y otros que no reconoscían al uno ni al otro. (Oviedo [1537–48] 1959, 4:252–53; bk. 33, ch. 52)

> [I have very especially sought to become familiar with the account of the things of this land, and I find diverse opinions; because, since there were many lords in each province, they tell things in their own manner. I am in the process of gathering and verifying

[these *relaciones*] and once I am finished [collecting the material], I will send it to you. Because I believe it would be a shameful thing for me to send you a *relación*, and have you give my name as author, if it were not very truthful. And what I have here is not so negligible that you cannot make a book of it, and it will not be a little one. For although the names of Moctezuma and Mexico are those that resound among us, the cazonci of Michoacán was no lesser lord, nor were others who recognized no other sovereign than themselves.][3] (my trans.)

Among the *relaciones*, or oral testimonies, that Mendoza was in the process of collecting, he mentions with special enthusiasm one from the province of Michoacán. The interest sparked by the tales of Moctezuma and México-Tenochtitlan, he implies, will now be rivaled by a "truthful" account of the cazonci, lord of Michoacán. The material collected, he assures Oviedo, is substantial. All it requires is for him to finish "verifying" the accuracy of the testimonies of the indigenous nobles.

Certainly, such an enthusiastic endorsement must be seen, to a considerable degree, as advance propaganda for a manuscript Mendoza had himself commissioned. No less noteworthy, however, is the subsequent lack of explicit mention made of the project by Mendoza or, indeed, by any of his contemporaries, in the available documentary record.

This book grew out of my desire both to see the *Relación de Michoacán* live up to Mendoza's initial expectations and to understand why it has not yet done so, in spite of the many valuable studies that have been devoted to it since its publication in 1869. While I harbor no illusions that this particular analysis will magically remove the remaining obstacles to a fuller appreciation of this complex and multifaceted text, I am convinced that, before another wave of scholarly attention can examine it productively, it is necessary to bring into sharper focus the context in which it was produced.

THE MODEL ESTABLISHED BY FRAY ANDRÉS DE OLMOS

The methodology employed by the friar-compiler of the *Relación de Michoacán* cannot be understood in isolation from that of other sixteenth-century missionaries in New Spain who were similarly involved in recording indigenous traditions.[4] While the identities of some of these compilers are well known, others have passed into oblivion. The large number of manuscripts produced anonymously is not surprising if one considers that it was common among religious writers at the time to emphasize service to their order, to the Spanish crown, and to God over their own personal accomplishments.

For instance Fray Toribio de Benavente "Motolinía," the youngest of the famous twelve Franciscan "apostles" who arrived in Mexico in 1524, requested that his name not be given as author if his work were published; rather, it should "be said to be [by] a friar minor and no other" ([1541] 1979, 8; my trans.).[5] The virtue of humility was especially emphasized among members of the Order of Friars Minor, whose founder was celebrated for his childlike simplicity and voluntary embrace of a life of poverty. In New Spain, it was the Franciscans who initiated the investigation of indigenous traditions, typically at the urging of their religious superiors and/or secular officials. Rather than personal glory, the primary goal of these missionaries was the evangelization of the indigenous population, a task that could only be achieved through the collective endeavors of numerous individuals. And, since most of them were known to each other personally, it is to be expected that they drew heavily on each other's methods and materials.

This process began formally in 1533, when Fray Andrés de Olmos was commissioned by Martín de Valencia, the Franciscan custodian of New Spain, and Sebastián Ramírez de Fuenleal, the president of the Second Audiencia, to begin researching the "antiquities" of the Nahuatl-speaking peoples of México-Tenochtitlan, Texcoco, and Tlaxcala. Motolinía, who widened the scope of investigation to include other indigenous groups, was an inveterate traveler, exploring as far south as Nicaragua and as far north as the land of the Huastecs (Baudot [1976] 1983, 247–319). Sahagún, who like Olmos taught at the Colegio de Santa Cruz in Tlatelolco, undertook the most comprehensive study of Nahua life and customs, overseeing the compilation of over a dozen manuscripts on the subject between 1547 and 1585. His ambitious plan, never fully realized, entailed sifting through and organizing this material into separate columns for the testimony in Nahuatl, its translation into Castilian, and accompanying pictures plus editorial commentary (León-Portilla 1999, 10). Another Franciscan, Diego de Landa, wrote an account of the traditions of the Mayas of Yucatán in 1566. By the latter part of the century, these friars were joined by members of other religious orders, such as the Dominicans Pedro de los Ríos and Diego Durán and the Jesuit Juan de Tovar.[6]

In the chronicles of the Franciscan Order, it is Olmos who is credited with developing the model for researching indigenous traditions used by the early missionaries of Mexico. As Jerónimo de Mendieta remarked toward the end of the sixteenth century, he was the "the fountain from which all the streams that treat of this material have emanated" ([1573–1604] 1997, 1:180; prologue to bk. 2).

Olmos's methodology was as follows. First, he gathered together as many of the pictographic codices, or "picture books," as he could find—those that had survived the fury of the early years of book burning and destruction of religious artifacts. Then, based on the testimony of old men, survivors of the conquest who were well versed in the traditional forms of knowledge, he set about to decipher the contents of these books and interpret them for a European audience.

According to Mendieta, the original manuscript and three or four copies were then sent to Spain, so that when Bartolomé de las Casas requested a copy in the 1540s, Olmos was only able to provide him with a summary based on the *memoriales* or rough drafts that had remained in his possession. Although most of Olmos's lengthy opus is no longer extant, various anonymous manuscripts such as the *Historia de los mexicanos por sus pinturas*, *Codex Tudela*, and *Histoire du Mexique* have been attributed to him. Olmos also included a collection of *huehuetlatolli* (traditional oral discourses) in his Nahuatl grammar of 1547.[7]

From the above description of the work of Olmos a pattern emerges that was to be repeated, albeit in modified form, by later sixteenth-century compilers of indigenous traditions. The pattern includes the use of pictographic codices and/or other pictorial materials, the transcription and translation of oral testimonies from members of the indigenous nobility, the organization of this material into book form, and the addition of commentary or supplementary information by the friar-compilers.

This basic model was followed in all the works cited above, although the relative weight given to any particular component varies considerably. Thus, in some cases the oral testimony of the indigenous nobles predominates; in others more weight is given to personal observations or commentary by the friars. While some manuscripts are bilingual, the majority are in Castilian with a sprinkling of indigenous terminology. In some cases these manuscripts consist essentially of pictographs with alphabetic writing as a gloss on the drawings; at the other end of the spectrum are those that do not include drawings, although the information they contain may be based at least in part on pictorial sources.

THE ESCORIAL MANUSCRIPT AS PALIMPSEST

Due to the relative paucity of explicit information concerning the making of the *Relación de Michoacán*, the reconstruction of the compilation process depends largely on physical evidence derived from the Escorial manuscript. The clues provided by the anonymous friar, for instance, are less extensive than those of some of his fellow missionary-compilers: namely, a few comments about his reasons for undertaking the project; some clarifications regarding matters of style and translation; the attribution of certain sections to one informant or another; and a few references to dates of compilation. This reserve on the part of the friar-compiler is compounded by the fact that there is no unequivocal mention made of the project in other sixteenth-century sources except for the aforementioned letter by Viceroy Mendoza. Moreover, the lack of success to date in unearthing earlier drafts of the Escorial manuscript—a state of affairs that contrasts markedly with the well-documented stages of the Sahaguntine project—further complicates the reconstruction process.

In the absence of multiple manuscripts representing distinct chronological moments, the need to highlight the multilayered dimension of the text as palimpsest becomes more pronounced. The advantage of the palimpsest metaphor is that it translates a temporal concept—successive stages of production—into a spatial one—overlapping layers of graphic signs. In other words it provides a model for explaining how a number of individuals could have left their marks on the same manuscript at different points in time. Thus, although the notion of palimpsest does not adequately convey the nature of the *Relación de Michoacán* as an enterprise grounded as much in oral as in written tradition, for the purpose of this chapter the emphasis on the materiality of the book as artifact is appropriate.

Fortunately, there is no lack of additions, emendations, lacunae, and inconsistencies in the Escorial manuscript. These "imperfections" convey a wealth of information. Consider, for example, the relative functions of the five hands identified in plates 48–52, the first four of which correspond to copyists, the fifth to the principal corrector.[8] The latter, at some point before the manuscript was shipped to Spain, went through it systematically using a distinctive colored ink and made numerous changes: filling in blank spaces left by the copyists, presumably when they had trouble reading the draft from which they were working; changing spelling; modifying word choice; eliminating repetitions; rewriting chapter titles covered over by drawings; crossing out certain phrases and inserting others.

Evidence regarding the making of the *Relación de Michoacán* can also be gleaned from the dual nature of the Escorial manuscript—its juxtaposition of prose and pictures. As will be discussed in greater detail in chapter two, the frontispiece is invaluable for the information it provides on the various participants. Once again, however, the bulk of the data results directly from the unpolished nature of the manuscript, from what is missing or not fully integrated into the structure put in place by the copyists.

Immediately apparent are the nine blank spaces for drawings that were never completed, the majority of which are located at the end of part three. Since the scribe responsible for this section anticipated the inclusion of additional pictures, it follows that he must have had some prior knowledge of what the painters would be contributing to the manuscript during the subsequent stage of production.

The procedure followed in part two, in contrast, suggests that the majority of the pictures located there were included as an afterthought: they are either squeezed into blank spaces at the ends of chapters or painted over the original titles, which were whited out to make room for them. In some cases the excess of pigment applied has led to cracks that allow some of the original titles to show through, as on plates 15, 16, 19, located on folios 113, 116, 122.

A third type of relationship between prose and pictures is exemplified by several full-page drawings (plates 27-30,44 [27, 44 in color section]; folios 140, 5, 9, 46, respectively) that are structurally separate from the alphabetic narrative and that may correspond to an earlier stage in the compilation process. The paper used for some, if not all, of these drawings is also different from that utilized in other parts of the manuscript. Curiously, the blank pages that derive from the same sheet as plate 27 (folios 141–43) contain the description of a Nahua calendar wheel attributed to Motolinía. (In addition to my own examination of Ms. C.IV.5, the source for the above physical description is Hidalgo Brinquis 2001.)

I postulate that, like Olmos and Sahagún, the friar-compiler of the *Relación de Michoacán* began his investigation based on drawings that served to elicit the initial oral testimonies. The resulting drafts (which have been lost) could then have been used in the elaboration of a questionnaire or outline designed to generate more detailed information on the subjects of greatest interest to the colonial authorities: indigenous forms of government; rules of succession; administration of justice; tribute collection; marital and burial ceremonies; methods of waging war. Significantly, all but one of the chapters explicitly related to the above topics are grouped together at the beginning of part three; of the structurally separate drawings, three include alphabetic glosses in the hand of the principal corrector (plates 28–30).

According to this scenario, as the friar inquired about the names or functions of the various individuals pictured in the drawings provided by his original informants, he jotted down the answers provided—in the indigenous language and/or Castilian—directly above or to the side of the figures.[9] This argument is particularly compelling if one compares the full-page drawings of the priests and officials who served in the cazonci's government with the prose chapters that are situated immediately after them in the Escorial manuscript.

Consider the figure glossed bilingually as "piruqua vandari"/"mayordomo de mantas y algodon" in the picture, and whose responsibilities are described at greater length in the accompanying prose chapter:

> ay otro llamado pirovaqua vandari que tiene cargo de rrecoger todas las mantas que da la gente y algodon para los tributos y este todo lo tiene en su casa y tiene cargo de rrecoger los petates y esteras de los oficiales para las neçesidades de comun. (174)

> [There is another [official] named *pirúuaqua uándari* who is in charge of collecting all the mantles given by the people and cotton for tribute. He keeps it all in his house and is in charge of collecting the *petates* and mats from the officials for general use.]

The above prose passage reads like a straightforward listing of the principal attributes of the members of the group located to the immediate left of the cazonci in the drawing, the foremost of whom is holding a "mantle" (that is, a measure of cloth), with skeins of cotton at his feet. It is as if the friar-compiler had decided at the last minute to insert into the completed manuscript the original drawing that had served to elicit the oral testimony.

The comparison between prose and pictures is also interesting for the light it sheds on other aspects of the production process. It is noteworthy, for instance, that the transcriptions of the name of the indigenous official described above do not coincide exactly in the two locations; to wit, a syllable is missing in the pictorial notation. Based on other sixteenth-century sources, the prose version turns out to be more accurate.

Gilberti, for instance, translates *piriuaqua* as "thread," while *uándari* may be the nominal form of *uándani*, "to multiply" (Márquez Joaquín 2000, 714). One plausible explanation for this discrepancy is that the friar's indigenous assistants corrected his use of their language in much the same way he proofed their spelling errors in Castilian.[10]

The possibility that some of the drawings of the Escorial manuscript may have been modeled on preexisting pictorial prototypes is also suggested by similarities between another picture containing alphabetic writing (plate 2; folio 61) and one of the colored drawings or "maps" reproduced in the eighteenth century by Pablo Beaumont (plate 47). Beaumont's source for this drawing was a sixteenth-century tira made of palm leaf owned by a "descendant of the nobles or first caciques" of Tzintzuntzan, the capital city at the time of the Spanish conquest ([ca. 1778] 1985, 2:30, 390; my trans.); Hans Roskamp dubs it the *Tzintzuntzan codex* (1998a and 2000). Both pictures show the petámuti overseeing the judgment and punishment of those called *uázcata* (accused criminals), with *angámecha* (those who wear lip plugs), representing the four parts of the iréchequa, observing the ritual seated on three-legged stools while smoking tobacco pipes.

The framing of this picture in the Escorial manuscript provides the context of enunciation for the petámuti's oral performance recounting the rise to power of the ruling Uacúsecha, the written form of which takes up most of part two. The resemblance to a portion of the *Tzintzuntzan codex* and the glosses in alphabetic writing in the hand of the principal corrector indicate that, like the full-page drawings, either it or a prototype may have been used at an earlier stage in the compilation process as a basis for eliciting the accompanying oral testimony.[11]

A final observation relates to the process of relocation of chapters once the transcription of the verbal descriptions had been accomplished. In general the voices of the various informants are kept separate in the Escorial manuscript: the petámuti's narrative, in part two; the indigenous governor's account of the Spanish conquest, at the end of part three; the collective voice of the elders, in the chapters describing forms of government and customs.

One of the exceptions to this rule is the account of Governor Cuiníarángari's marriage to a woman from the cazonci's house. Although it is located at the beginning of the section dedicated to marital ceremonies, it contains a number of references to the arrival of the conquistadors that suggest it may have been cut out of Cuiníarángari's primary narrative and relocated. The drawing that ostensibly accompanies this account (plate 37) actually corresponds to the following chapter, a more generalized description of marital practices among the indigenous elite.

In this case it would appear that, while the copyists anticipated the inclusion of certain pictures based on a previously agreed-upon plan for ordering the various parts of the narrative, the painters were working from an earlier pictorial draft or outline that followed a different order. Thus, the *carari*, or scribe-painter, responsible for this picture could easily have failed to take into account the additional prose chapter inserted into the section on marital ceremonies. This "mistake" would have led him to copy the first drawing under the title corresponding to the description of Cuiníarángari's marriage, leaving the following pictorial space blank. Indeed, this is precisely what occurred in the Escorial manuscript, as can be observed on folios 24 recto and 25 verso (pp. 207 and 210 in Tudela 1956).

There are other inconsistencies that shed light on the textual dynamics of the *Relación de Michoacán*, the analysis of some of which can be found in the notes to this chapter. In general the methodology that can be reconstructed from a study of the physical evidence contained in Escorial Ms. C.IV.5 demonstrates that, in terms of the complexity of operations characterizing most early colonial compilations of indigenous traditions, it is exemplary. These operations include the glossing of pictures, the transcription and translation of oral testimonies, their division into chapters, the insertion of editorial commentary, the production of a clean copy, the inclusion of additional drawings, and the making of final corrections. The Escorial manuscript may not be as polished or complete as some of its counterparts, but it is no less multilayered.

POLITICS AND AUTHORSHIP

In his 1541 letter to Oviedo, Mendoza—as if torn between conflicting imperatives—hints at his discomfort with the notion of accepting responsibility for a text that depends too heavily on a single group of informants. Couched in the rhetoric of authorship, his words tentatively lay claim to the relaciones from Michoacán and other outlying provinces, whetting the chronicler's appetite for the promised manuscripts and articulating a context in which the material contained therein can be published for a European audience. The "diversity of opinions" among the indigenous peoples of New Spain, although it complicates the elaboration of a definitive account of "the things of this land," is presented in a positive light insofar as it points to the existence of independent kingdoms beyond the sphere of influence of the Aztecs or Mexica.

Mendoza—whose great-grandfather, Íñigo López de Mendoza, the Marqués de Santillana, and brother, Diego Hurtado de Mendoza, were among the most important literary figures of their times—was no neophyte with respect to Renaissance standards for establishing "truthfulness."[12] Thus, his trepidation suggests that his desire to promote knowledge of the pagan antiquities of New Spain was tempered by the realization that to do so effectively he must assure their presentation in a morally appropriate framework.[13]

The issue is one of politics as much as of scholarship. In keeping with his family's tradition of pursuing jointly the two vocations of arms and letters, Mendoza's literary ambitions cannot be separated from his larger political objectives. At the time he wrote this letter, Mendoza was actively engaged in rivalry with Hernán Cortés over the allegiance of the Spaniards resident in the colony and their indigenous allies. Only two years previously he had personally organized an expedition, headed by his close friend Francisco Vásquez de Coronado, to the northern frontier of New Spain to discover a kingdom called Cíbola, which, it was rumored, far surpassed the empire conquered by Cortés in wealth and splendor.[14]

Mendoza's concern with the way in which the names of the cazonci and other indigenous lords were being "eclipsed" by that of Moctezuma can thereby be seen to mirror his political ambitions at the time. Subsequently, with the outbreak of the Mixtón War in 1541, followed by the consolidation of power in the viceregal capital and shattering of illusions about the fabulous seven cities of Cíbola, the incentive to gain greater recognition for less familiar indigenous groups, and for the northwestern provinces in particular, was correspondingly reduced.

As viceroy, one of Mendoza's tasks was the promotion of a pan-indigenous identity, the imposition of the unitary concept of "Indian" on a diverse population unaccustomed to collaboration across political jurisdictions. This unifying strategy comes through strongly in some of the characterizations of the Mixtón War by the Spaniards' indigenous allies. For instance Don Francisco de Sandoval Acazitli, lord of Chalco, tells of a great victory dance in which "all the nations of the diverse provinces danced, wearing their weapons, their shields and clubs; they all danced, without any part remaining that did not dance" (CDHM [1858–66] 1971, 2:318; my trans.). The act of dancing together is indicative here of the process of reforging identities and alliances based on their new shared status as vassals of the Spanish crown.[15]

The dynamics at work are not too different from the efforts of the modern Mexican state to more fully assimilate marginalized groups within a common national project centered in the capital, efforts that run counter to movements advocating greater regional autonomy and the preservation of local traditions. In Mendoza's advice to his successor, Luis de Velasco, he speaks of how his initial preconceptions regarding the resident Hispanic as well as indigenous populations blinded him to what he ultimately came to see as his primary responsibility as viceroy; namely, to maintain the cohesion of the body politic above all else. Ten years after his 1541 letter to Oviedo, the problematic side of the diversity he had initially promoted had come to take precedence in his mind. "There are so many opinions and viewpoints and so diverse, that it is not to be believed," he confesses to Velasco. "I could swear that I find myself more new and confused regarding the government of [this land] now than at the beginning" (CDII 1866, 6:510; my trans.). Over time, Mendoza had evidently come to better appreciate the strategic importance of a strong centralized authority.[16]

The significance of Mendoza's post-1541 decision to concentrate on Mexico City at the expense of the provinces is hard to overestimate. The present state of scholarship on early colonial Michoacán is simply one example of the degree to which the national capital continues to dominate the cultural imagination. Because of this legacy, any attempt to define a space in which to evaluate the Escorial manuscript free from the shadow of Anahuac must first articulate the ways in which both the moment of production and the history of interpretation of the text are permeated by the presence of México-Tenochtitlan.[17]

From the first moments of contact between the Spaniards and the peoples of Michoacán, the latter were seen in relation to those who had been encountered earlier—the Taino and other Arawaks of the Caribbean, the Mayas of Yucatán, and especially, the Nahuas of the central plateau of Mexico. This dynamic is manifested on a linguistic level in the Escorial manuscript in the large number of words of Nahua, Taino, and Mayan origin—*ají, areito, cacalote, cacao, cacaxtle, cacique, caimán, canoa, charchuy, chichimeca, chontal, ciuatlan, colima, cuitlateca, cuyuacan, cu, hamaca, hibueras, huzizilzi, iguana, jalisco, jical, jicalan, macegual, maguey, maíz, mastil, matlalzingas, mechuacan, naca, naguas, naguatato, ocote, otomí, papa, patol, petaca, petate, sabana, tamal, tameme, tianguis, tomate, tototl, tuza, tuzantlan, yácata, zacatula, zapotlan*—that are integrated into the narrative in a sort of lingua franca shared by all the early Spaniards of Mexico.[18]

The double filter of Castilian and Nahuatl that characterized almost all interactions between the colonial authorities and peoples of outlying provinces is immediately apparent to anyone familiar with primary sources from the period. Judicial documents inevitably record the presence of an interpreter called a *naguatato* (a corruption of *nahuatlato*—speaker of Nahuatl), regardless of the specific indigenous language being translated. In the case of Michoacán, a multiethnic state composed of sizable communities of Nahuas, Matlazincas, and other linguistic groups distinct from the ethnic majority, most of these interpreters were recruited from among the local indigenous population, for there were enclaves of Nahuatl speakers in the capital city of Tzintzuntzan as well as in numerous other locales.[19]

The presence of Nahuas in the elaboration of the Escorial manuscript is suggested by both internal and external evidence. It is noteworthy, for instance, that the province is consistently referred to by its Nahuatl designation, Michihuahcan—from *michin*, fish, *-huah*, possessive suffix, *-can*, locative suffix—literally, "place of the owners of fish" (Martínez Baracs 1997, 161–62); the spelling Michoacán is the one that has survived in modern usage. The city of Tzintzuntzan (from the regional word for hummingbird, *tzintzuni*), is likewise referred to in the text as "la cibdad de mechuacan," while the city of Ihuatzio (from *hiuatsi*, or coyote) is dubbed "cuyuacan," a variant of the modern spelling Coyoacán (from the Nahuatl *coyoaque*, Spanish *coyotes*). Other evidence includes references in the *Relación de Michoacán* to the continuous presence of Nahua communities in the Lake Pátzcuaro Basin since ancient times and to nahuatlatos as principal lords and interpreters in the court of the cazonci both before and after the Spanish conquest. This state of affairs is amply confirmed by other colonial-era documents.[20]

In the Escorial manuscript, Nahuatl vocabulary is used for everything from common household items—*jical* instead of *urani* for gourd—to the name of the nomadic hunters whose rise to power in the Lake Pátzcuaro Basin is recounted in part two of the Escorial manuscript; they are collectively referred to by the Nahuatl plural *chichimeca* (Anglicized version, Chichimecs). This pervasiveness makes it extremely difficult to avoid using cultural categories of Nahua origin as a reference point for a study of the *Relación de Michoacán*.

Ultimately, whether such linguistic mixing is more a result of the intended audience of the manuscript or of the longstanding participation of nahuatlatos in the local power structure is less relevant to this book than the fact that it has become an integral part of the historical record. Indeed, a great deal of the ink that has been expended with reference to the cultural production of early colonial Michoacán involves polemics originating in the search for more autochthonous equivalents to the Hispanicized or Nahuatlized terminology previously in use.

Thus, the term *cazonci*, used in the Escorial manuscript and other primary sources from Michoacán to refer to the supreme indigenous ruler, is generally preferred by modern scholars to the word of choice among colonial-era chroniclers, the unequivocally Nahuatl *caltzontzin*. One proposed etymology is that of Mauricio Swadesh, who translates *katz-o-n-si* as "the one with shaved head" (cited in López Sarrelangue 1965, 32). Others, however, consider *cazonci* to be a corruption of *caltzontzin*, a hypothesis supported by its absence from any of the sixteenth-century dictionaries compiled in Michoacán as well as the plethora of words of Nahuatl origin in the Escorial manuscript and other local documents from the period. The definition of *autochthonous* in this context is problematic, nevertheless, given the multilingual composition of the local population.[21]

The precise meaning of *caltzontzin* is also subject to debate. According to some, it means "great lord of infinite palaces." Others assert it is a pun on *cazonci* that combines the Nahuatl term for old sandal with a suffix indicating a person of high standing and political influence.[22] The insulting connotations of the second derivation are largely to blame for the heated nature of the resulting controversy, which is similar in intensity to that surrounding the term *tarasco*, the English translation of which is Tarascan.

According to the *Relación de Michoacán*, which is the most frequently cited source for this opinion, *tarasco* is both a misnomer and an insult. It derives from the local word for in-law, *tarascue*, and it came into use after the first Spaniards to visit Michoacán made concubines of the daughters of the indigenous nobles who had been given them for wives (247).[23] A contrary tradition traces the origin of *tarascos* to a local deity called Taras, whose name may be a partial corruption of the indigenous word for idol, *tharés*.[24]

The search for alternatives to the controversial *tarasco* (the Hispanicized plural form of which is *tarascos*) has tended to coalesce around the word *purépecha*, widely used by most present-day speakers of the indigenous language and by those scholars who draw upon oral as well as written traditions. The problem is that, in the sixteenth century, *purépecha* was generally translated as the equivalent of the Nahuatl *macehualtin*—that is, "commoners"—and, by extension, "language of the common people." Although *purépecha* (variously spelt *phurhépecha* or *p'urhépecha*) is widely accepted in a modern context, its use is more problematic when applied generically to the indigenous peoples of Michoacán at the time of the Spanish conquest. Some argue that, as in the case of *macehualtin*, it functioned in certain contexts as a shorthand for "people" in general, since the destiny of all humans was to pay homage to the gods (see, for instance, López Austin 1994, 101). Others prefer the narrower definition of *purépecha*, as it reinforces how the social structure of preconquest and early colonial Michoacán, far from constituting a single egalitarian community, was complex and highly differentiated in terms of both social class and cultural origin.²⁵

A third option is represented by sources such as the *Relación de Tiripetío* [1580], which is based on testimony provided by the elders of that city to their local *corregidor* (crown official in charge of the indigenous population):

> La lengua que hablan estos naturales se llama, en su vulgar, [TZIN]TZUNTZA NABU VANDAUA [*sic*]; nosotros le llamamos lengua *tarasca*. Llamábanle [así] ... porque su rey de *Mechoacan* tenía su asiento y cabecera en un pu[ebl]o desta provincia, que se dice *Tzintzontza*. (Acuña 1987, 340–41)
>
> [The language spoken by these natives is called, in their vernacular, *tzintzuntza anapu uandaqua*; we call it Tarascan. They called it thus ... because the king of Michoacán had his palace and the seat of his government in a town of this province, which is called Tzintzuntzan.]²⁶ (my trans.)

The city of Tzintzuntzan, as previously noted, is commonly referred to in colonial-era documents as Mechuacan or some variant thereof. The designation "city and province of Michoacán" became especially widespread after the capital was officially recognized by Charles V in 1534 and granted its own coat of arms. An alternate toponym, Uchichila—a Hispanicized corruption of Huitzitzilan, which is the literal Nahuatl translation of Tzintzuntzan—is also frequently encountered.

I have opted to follow the use established by the Escorial manuscript, the dictionaries of Gilberti and Lagunas, and the writings of the Jesuit missionary Francisco Ramírez. This position represents a compromise of sorts, combining the term *tzintzuntza anapu uandaqua* with one of the names of Nahuatl origin used to refer to Tzintzuntzan. Thus, the capital city and its subject towns, the province as a whole, the native language, and the indigenous peoples are all referred to as the city/province/language/peoples of Michoacán.²⁷

To return to the issue of the active promotion or lack of promotion of the *Relación de Michoacán* by Mendoza, if the Escorial manuscript was prepared as a presentation copy for the viceroy, it would likely have been turned over to him in late October 1541 when he stopped in the area on his way to put down the indigenous rebellion in the vicinity of Guadalajara that has since come to be known as the Mixtón War (one of the most serious challenges to Spanish rule during the early colonial period) (Aiton 1927, 137–58). In this context the incomplete nature of the Escorial manuscript appears as more than merely accidental, becoming a metaphor for the constant interruptions implicit in life on the frontier.

Mendoza's ambivalence regarding the claim to "truthfulness" of the oral testimonies of the indigenous informants is echoed in the delicate balance that characterized the need, on the part of the colonial authorities, to foment better relations with recently conquered groups whom they did not fully trust in order to prevent wide-scale indigenous rebellions. The tendency throughout the colonial period to alternately promote and suppress research into indigenous customs and beliefs can be attributed, in considerable degree, to the uneasy coalition between a small group of ruling Spaniards and the masses of newly converted peoples whose ways of thinking they only vaguely understood.

Significantly, the role of the Spaniards' indigenous allies from Michoacán was decisive in the resolution of the Mixtón conflict. At the head of five thousand warriors, Governor Cuiníarángari participated in the attack of June 24, 1541, under the direction of Pedro de Alvarado, the famous conquistador of Guatemala. Alvarado was fatally wounded in the attempt. It took a force of some five hundred Spaniards and fifty thousand indigenous allies to route the last of the rebels encamped on the mountains of Mixtón, Nochistlán, and Cuiná (Aiton 1927, 149–55). Several months later, Cuiníarángari and Fray Jerónimo de Alcalá—the compiler of the *Relación de Michoacán*—accompanied Mendoza into battle (Warren 1971, 322–25). The presence of Alcalá was not unusual, for it was customary at the time for missionaries to serve as intermediaries with the rebellious indigenous population in addition to providing spiritual solace for the Spanish soldiers and their recently Christianized allies.

In his 1541 letter, Mendoza downplays the importance of the indigenous rebellion, stating that he is going in person, "not so much because of the trouble the Indians are causing us, but because of some disagreement that resulted between the captains I had there" (Oviedo [1537–48] 1959, 4:253; my trans.). This mild statement contrasts markedly with his somber pronouncement outside the rebel stronghold at Mixtón a few months later: "in this victory [consists] the loss or gain of all New Spain" (Tello [ca.1650] 1968, 3:314; bk. 2, ch. 139; my trans.). The eagerness with which Mendoza was awaiting the completion of the relaciones he had commissioned from the various provinces appears to have dissipated in the symbolic gap between these two remarks. It would take the viceroy several years to recover from the aftermath of his overconfident assessment of Spanish military and political strength. Indeed, the delay in responding with requisite force to the 1541 rebellion is one of the chief accusations brought against him by Francisco Tello de Sandoval, the inspector sent to investigate his performance, in a *residencia* (judicial review of tenure in office) that was not definitively resolved in Mendoza's favor until 1548.[28]

While the available documentation suggests that Mendoza was slow to recognize the potential dangers of the Mixtón rebellion, shortly thereafter he was to make his mark as a consummate political strategist in terms of the dual mandate to foster collaboration with the indigenous peoples, especially the nobility, while simultaneously reinforcing the ultimate authority of the Spanish crown. On one hand, he created an order of indigenous knights, or *caballeros tecles*, to reward those nobles of proven loyalty to the Spaniards, bestowing upon them the controversial privileges of carrying swords and riding horseback. He also advocated the continuation of local customs regarding tribute collection, artisan guilds, and election of indigenous governors and caciques. On the other hand, he was capable of using all the means at his disposal, including enslavement, throwing rebels to the dogs, and execution of prisoners en masse, to punish those with the temerity to prefer their ancient way of life to the new Christian dogma.[29]

The compilations of indigenous traditions, which Mendoza initially commissioned with an eye to strengthening his political position in relation to Cortés, appear to have taken on a somewhat different cast for him after the Mixtón War. The relative weight given to their value as a publicity tool (versus their value as aids in the implementation of a policy of limited negotiation with the indigenous elite) would have shifted, with a corresponding increase in the incentive to control their dissemination. These works include not only the *Relación de Michoacán* (ca. 1541), but also the *Codex Mendoza* (ca. 1542)—a pictorial record of the succession of rulers of México-Tenochtitlan, the tribute paid to Moctezuma by subject towns, and the educational and reward systems regulating passage from birth to old age—plus other assorted manuscripts on practices governing the awarding of special titles and the inheritance of land rights. Even after his appointment as viceroy of Peru, Mendoza continued to recognize the importance of bridging the transition between indigenous and colonial rule, commissioning a work by Juan de Betanzos on Inca history and customs in 1551, the year before his death.[30]

The relative openness to promoting "diversity" that characterized Mendoza's early years as viceroy is a good starting point for a discussion of the legacy of the *Relación de Michoacán* because it helps to explain both the motivation behind its production and the reasons for its subsequent marginalization. Unfortunately, in terms of what happened to the actual physical text, this line of inquiry leads to a dead end, for although Oviedo included the viceroy's letter in book 33 of his history of the Indies, compiled between 1537 and 1548, there is no indication that he ever received the manuscript in question or summarized any part of it.[31]

To complete the history of the Escorial manuscript during the colonial period, we need to reformulate the task at hand—to approach the body of available evidence from a different angle. The key is to recognize that the trajectory of the *Relación de Michoacán* is not synonymous with that of the presentation copy entrusted to the viceroy's control. Similarly, the literary fortunes of the Escorial Ms. C.IV.5, which lay forgotten for centuries in Philip II's monastery palace, are only one facet of the larger question of the possible reverberations that the project initiated by Mendoza and the friar-compiler had upon the work of their contemporaries.

Consider the case of an early colonial writer from New Spain, the historian Francisco Cervantes de Salazar, who—like the viceroy—harbored an ambition to remedy the general lack of knowledge in Europe regarding the cazonci and Michoacán. In his *Crónica de la Nueva España* he goes some distance in that direction, incorporating information from several sources, including an extensive account by Francisco Montaño, one of the first Spaniards to visit the region. He ends, moreover, with the following intriguing comment:

> Y porque de las cosas de Mechuacán hablaré más largo cuando tenga recogidas las Memoriales y papeles de aquella provincia, cerca del Cazonci por ahora no diré más . . . ([1566] 1985, 809; bk. 6, ch. 28)

> [And because I will speak more at length on the things of Michoacán when I have collected the rough drafts and papers of that province, I will say no more at present about the cazonci . . .] (my trans.)

So far as we know, Cervantes de Salazar did not follow through on the above promise, but his reference to memoriales or rough drafts from Michoacán provides a glimpse of what may have happened to some of the earlier copies whose existence we previously deduced from a physical analysis of the Escorial manuscript.

In the same passage in which Cervantes de Salazar speaks of these papers, he boasts of his friendship with the cazonci's younger son, Don Antonio Huitziméngari, who spent several years at the viceregal court under the auspices of Mendoza and served as indigenous governor of Michoacán from 1545 to 1562:

> Dexó el Cazonci dos hijos, los cuales aprendieron Gramática y nuestra lengua castellana, y el mayor, habiendo tenido el señorío de su padre algún tiempo, murió sin dexar hijos y subedióle [sic] el segundo, que se decía Don Antonio, a quien yo muy familiarmente traté. Era grande amigo de españoles, muy querido y obedescido de los suyos, muy bien enseñado en la fee católica; presciábase de tener muchos libros latinos, los cuales entendía muy bien. Era muy gentil Escribano y especialmente en castellano escrebía con mucho aviso una carta, y no menos en latín. (id.)

> [The cazonci left two sons, who learned Latin Grammar and our Castilian tongue. The elder, having ruled the domain of his father for a while, died childless; the second, whose name was Don Antonio, and with whom I was very intimately acquainted, succeeded him. He was a great friend of Spaniards, much loved and obeyed by his people, very well educated in the Catholic faith. He prided himself on having many books in Latin, which he understood very well. His penmanship was very fine and especially in Castilian he wrote a most noteworthy letter, no less so in Latin.][32] (my trans.)

According to the chronicles of the Augustinian order, Huitziméngari studied philosophy, theology, Christian doctrine, fine arts, sciences, and various languages (Latin, Greek, Hebrew, and Castilian) at the school of advanced studies in Tiripetío, founded by Fray Alonso de la Veracruz in 1540.[33]

This same Veracruz—one of the most eminent scholars to take up residence in the New World, a former student and colleague of Vitoria and Soto—is the author of a work entitled *Speculum coniugiorum*, published in Latin in 1556. A treatise on the universality of marriage and difficulties facing missionaries who must decide on the legitimacy of diverse marital practices, it uses customs prevalent in Michoacán to exemplify and test the arguments presented. Indeed, in the attempt to understand the local language and customs, the maestro Veracruz is said to have benefited from the assistance of his pupil, the aforementioned Huitziméngari.[34]

Another Augustinian, the chronicler Matías de Escobar, credits the younger son of the cazonci with having written a lost treatise on the "royal genealogy of the Tarascan kings." From the existence of this vanished text he concludes that "Peru is not the only [nation] to produce an Inca Garcilaso . . . for Tiripetío created another son of kings who wrote, perchance with tears of blood," many things concerning his gentile origins (Escobar [1729] 1970, 124; ch. 14; my trans.).

These connections between early colonial writers who refer to the history and customs of Michoacán and the indigenous nobleman Huitziméngari point to fundamental differences between the way in which information was disseminated and authorship determined in the sixteenth to eighteenth centuries versus the modern age. In general the availability of published works and the notion of creative genius were much less significant during this period than the practices of manuscript circulation and scholarly patronage.

In other words we cannot assume, when Escobar speaks of the younger son of the cazonci as the author of a lost history of preconquest Michoacán, that he is referring to some work fundamentally different from the *Relación de Michoacán*. Perhaps Don Antonio Huitziméngari participated directly in one or more of the stages of elaboration of the Escorial manuscript. Even if he did not, however, the fact that he subsequently assumed the position of highest indigenous authority in the region would have conferred upon him some claim to authorship over manuscripts of indigenous origin bequeathed to him in his capacity as governor.

Of the several drafts of the *Relación de Michoacán* produced from about 1538 to 1541, it is likely that at least one remained in the possession of the indigenous nobility. That these papers included a transcript in the language of Michoacán focusing, among other things, on marital ceremonies is suggested by analogies between Veracruz's treatise and the Escorial manuscript.

The order of presentation of the bulk of the material is virtually identical: first, a general account of arranged marriage among the nobility; then, a description of the same among commoners, followed by a discussion of the practice of marrying for love (Veracruz [1556] 1988, 304–12;

pt. 2, art. 2). Veracruz also includes an explanation of the procedure for obtaining a divorce that echoes the Escorial manuscript, although he treats this topic separately from the others (pt. 2, art. 5).[35]

The two texts are particularly close with respect to the subject of arranged marriage, with direct parallels between both quoted dialogue and auxiliary description. For instance, in the Escorial manuscript the indigenous priest advises the bridegroom:

> si notares a tu muger de algun adulterio dexala mansamente y enbiala a su casa sin azelle mal que no hechara a nadie la culpa sino a si misma si fuere mala. (212)

> [If you notice your wife committing adultery, let her go peacefully and send her to her [parents'] house without doing her harm, for she will not blame anyone but herself if she is bad.]

The corresponding passage in the *Speculum coniugiorum* reads:

> Si mulierem tuam in adulterio deprehenderis, relinque eam, et mitte in domum propriam, pacifice, sine hoc quod ei iniuriam inferas, quia poenitentia ducta, dolebit. (Veracruz 1556, 315; pt. 2, art. 2)

> [If you chance upon your wife committing adultery, sever your connection with her and allow her to go to her own house, peacefully, without inflicting injury upon her, because led by penance, she will be sorry.] (my trans.)

Likewise, both works describe events subsequent to the formal exchange of gifts among commoners in a similar fashion:

> antes que llegase a ella ni la conoçiese carnalmente yva quatro dias por leña para los ques y la muger varria su casa y vn gran trecho del camino por donde entravan a su casa. (214–15)

> [Before [the husband] would join with [the wife] or have carnal relations with her, he would go four days in search of firewood to burn in the temples and the wife would sweep the house and a good stretch of the road leading to the house.]

> Sponsus quatuor diebus continuis ibat in montem antequam carnaliter iungerentur sponsus et sponsa, ligna, quae cremabantur in templus idolorum, et sponsa verrebat domum et magnam partem

viae, qua perveniebat sponsus in domum sponsae. (Veracruz 1556, 315; pt. 2, art. 2)

[Before the husband and wife would unite carnally, during four straight days the husband would go to the mountain and bring back firewood that was burned in the temples of the idols, and the wife would sweep the house and a good part of the road along which the husband would come to the house of the wife.] (my trans.)

In one of his prefaces to the *Speculum*, Veracruz affirms that he wrote the first draft in 1546 (1556, 657), a time frame consistent with the hypothesis that he had some version of the *Relación de Michoacán* at his disposal. While his inclusion of several expressions in the indigenous language may reflect firsthand experience interviewing local residents about traditional marital ceremonies, another plausible explanation is that he was working—in collaboration with Huitziméngari—from a transcription in that language also utilized by the compiler of the Escorial manuscript. This latter possibility is supported by minor divergences between the two texts consistent with varying interpretations of the material being translated.[36]

Another indication that some version of the *Relación de Michoacán* was still in circulation in that province well after 1541, when the Escorial manuscript was presumably presented to Mendoza, is provided by the littera annua of the Jesuit Francisco Ramírez to his superiors in Castile, dated April 4, 1585. Paragraphs 42–48 contain the most complete description that has been found to date of the preconquest religious and cosmological beliefs of the peoples of Michoacán.

Although evidence that this account was excerpted from a draft or copy of the missing part one of the Escorial manuscript is by no means definitive, several details point to that conclusion. The language of the Ramírez description, for example, echoes the impersonal use of the third person—"deçian," "tenian"—by the friar-compiler of the *Relación de Michoacán* in those sections attributed to the collective voice of the "elders of the city of Michoacán."

In addition, both texts manifest similar word choice: "fabulas" when referring to indigenous oral traditions; "y estos eran" to introduce a sequence of nouns (i.e., different categories of sacrificial victims or accused criminals). They use similar spelling, moreover, for the names of the gods Curita Caheri ("curiti caheri" in Ramírez; "curita caheri" or "curitacaheri" in the Escorial manuscript) and Cueráuaperi ("cueravaperi" in the former; "cueravaperi," "cuerauaperi," or "cuerabaperi" in the latter)—

no small coincidence at a time when there was no fixed orthography for Castilian, much less for the indigenous languages of the New World.

There is even an explicit reference to similar content, for the anonymous compiler of the Escorial manuscript alludes to the fact that part one contained a description of how the gods made the first human beings from ash—one of the central tenets of indigenous belief according to the Ramírez littera annua. Finally, one should not assume that when the text refers in the first person singular to the process of gathering indigenous testimonies, it necessarily implies that Ramírez himself was the compiler. In accordance with the conventions of the time, he is as likely to have been quoting without attribution from one of his sources.[37]

As mentioned previously, Oviedo did not include the anticipated material on Michoacán in his history of the Indies; however, a subsequent official chronicler, Antonio de Herrera y Tordesillas, was fortunate in having at his disposal a number of documents pertaining to the things of that province. Many of the passages he includes in his *Historia general*, compiled from 1596 to 1601, are taken directly from extant sections of Cervantes de Salazar, but Herrera also provides a brief account of preconquest religious beliefs that does not appear in that source.

According to this version, the first human beings were made of mud or clay; those of ash and "certain metals" came later. Also noteworthy is the enumeration of similarities to Christian doctrine—the belief in a single God (named Tucúpachá), a final judgment, heaven and hell, a flood whose end was signaled by a hummingbird carrying a branch, and a man who built "a wooden thing like an ark" (dec. 3, bk. 3, ch. 10). In spite of references to these common elements, the general tenor of the description is decidedly negative, with repeated allusions to the cruel practice of human sacrifice and the frightful aspect of the indigenous priests.

In contrast to the Ramírez letter, there are few readily documented coincidences in content and presentation between Herrera's discussion of religion in Michoacán and the surviving portions of the Escorial manuscript. Since Herrera, as *cronista mayor de Indias* (royal chronicler of the Indies), had access to materials from the Real Biblioteca del Escorial, it is tempting to imagine him as the individual responsible for removing the missing leaves of part one before the manuscript was bound. Pending further archival research, however, all that can be said definitively is that the circumstantial evidence is inconclusive on this point.[38]

Those readers familiar with the religious chronicles of New Spain may be wondering why, in the course of the above analysis of possible relationships between the Escorial manuscript and other colonial-era writings on Michoacán, I have yet to mention the voluminous and distinguished literary production of the early Franciscans. The official chronicles of the order, by the likes of Jerónimo de Mendieta, Juan de Torquemada, Alonso de la Rea, Isidro Félix de Espinosa, and Pablo de la Purísima Concepción Beaumont, are replete with glowing descriptions of the accomplishments of their brethren; indeed, this promotional dimension is one of their defining characteristics.[39] Much of our knowledge regarding the research methodology of Olmos, Motolinía, and Sahagún into Nahua "antiquities," of Landa among the Mayas, and of the work of the linguists Gilberti and Lagunas among the indigenous peoples of Michoacán is drawn from these works, many of which enjoyed widespread circulation among their contemporaries.[40]

The answer, quite simply, is that with one notable exception there is no mention of the *Relación de Michoacán* in these works. The most likely explanation for such silence is that it was unavailable for consultation by the official chroniclers of the Franciscan order, who lacked even the minimal data necessary to infer its existence. In accordance with this hypothesis, after the Escorial manuscript was shipped to Spain the remaining drafts or copies in circulation may have fallen into the hands of the Augustinians and Jesuits who, far from being motivated by a desire to promote Franciscan accomplishments, were actively engaged in competition with them for the allegiance of the new converts.[41] It is telling, in this regard, that Ramírez follows his discussion of preconquest religion and cosmology with a brief aside exalting the missionary fervor of the first bishop of Michoacán, Vasco de Quiroga, and denigrating the efforts of the early Franciscans (paragraphs 50–55).[42]

This simple picture of neglect of the *Relación de Michoacán* due to interreligious rivalry is complicated, however, by the fact that Motolinía, one of the primary Franciscan compilers of indigenous antiquities, has the additional distinction of being the only colonial author whose use of the *Relación de Michoacán* has been established unequivocally to date (Warren 1971 and 2000; Stone 1994). A comparison of Motolinía's *Memoriales* and the Escorial manuscript demonstrates that he excerpted an entire chapter, on the burial ceremony of a cazonci, to which he added a number of modifications, and that he also summarized some isolated information on marital customs (Motolinía [ca.1536–43] 1996, 411–16, 438, 451). Since these sections of the *Memoriales* were compiled from about 1536 to 1543, it is possible that Motolinía was able to consult the presentation copy of the *Relación de Michoacán* in Mexico City or its environs before it was physically removed from New Spain. This hypothesis is supported by a physical analysis of Escorial Ms. C.IV.5, one gathering of which contains both a picture from the *Relación de Michoacán* (plate 27, color section) and an unrelated calendar wheel attributed to Motolinía.

Insofar as information from the Escorial manuscript was disseminated among the intellectual elite of the colonial period, credit must be given above all to Motolinía, for his excerpts were subsequently reelaborated in the works of numerous chroniclers including Las Casas, Gómara, Mendieta, Torquemada, La Rea, Escobar, Espinosa, and Beaumont.[43] Interestingly, Motolinía does not mention the name of the fellow Franciscan from whom he borrowed the material related to Michoacán. Most of the above writers, if they give their source for these fragments at all, attribute authorship to Motolinía or to the nearest person on the chain of literary borrowings originating with him.

In this case the incentive to exalt the achievements of the members of his order appears to have been superseded by the convention of valuing the process of reelaboration of primary materials over the act of compilation per se. Thus, Motolinía affirms, in a 1555 letter to Charles V:

> Tres o cuatro frailes hemos escrito de las antiguallas y costumbre [sic] que estos naturales tuvieron, e yo tengo lo que los otros escribieron, y porque a mí me costó más trabajo y más tiempo, no es maravilla que lo tenga mejor recopilado y entendido que otro. (Motolinía [1541] 1979, 217)
>
> [Three or four of us friars have written of the antiquities and customs held by these natives, and I have what the others wrote. Since it cost me more effort and time, it is not to be wondered at that I have compiled and understood it better than any other.] (my trans.)

The implication is that "fieldwork" alone is not sufficient to enable one to understand and contextualize what has been gathered; it takes time and cognitive distance to "digest" the "raw" material—a metaphor that still enjoys currency today.

As in Mendoza's comments regarding the need to verify the testimony of the indigenous informants of the *Relación de Michoacán*, the above remarks by Motolinía suggest that the prevailing prejudices of the era favored the "effort and time" involved in commenting on and reorganizing such testimonies to fit into European-based categories over that spent transcribing and translating them. Presumably, the farther one could remove the material from its source in oral and pictorial tradition, the more prestige the resulting text would be accorded. The flip side of this foregrounding of the role of the editor is the way in which the relatively "unprocessed" nature of the *Relación de Michoacán* is encoded as a mark of inferiority, an invitation for a better qualified individual—in age, learning, political connections—to intervene and recast the material in more presentable form for the outside world.

CONCLUSION

A complex web of scholarly and political preferences appears to account for the relatively modest literary status accorded the Escorial manuscript from colonial times to the present. Caught in the "cross fire" between Mendoza and Cortés, between the Franciscans and other religious orders, between the forces of centralization and those favoring greater regional autonomy, between the impulse to simultaneously promote and suppress the continuation of indigenous traditions, between the goals of laboring anonymously in the service of God and of publicizing the work of one's brethren, between recording the peculiarities of indigenous modes of expression and recasting them to better fit sixteenth-century European norms, the *Relación de Michoacán* has yet to emerge clearly. My intention is to facilitate the process of clearing the air: to clarify the major points of debate; to situate the project in the context of the historical period in which it was produced; and to suggest possible connections to other works that have also survived, more or less intact, the ravages of time.

One facet of the discrepancy between the prestige accorded the Escorial manuscript as ethnohistorical source and the relative paucity of critical studies on its textual dynamics has to do with canon formation and the forces determining literary taste. Ironically, the *Relación de Michoacán* is closer in many ways to present-day tendencies to interweave multiple points of view than to the hierarchical appeal to truth as authority prevalent during the colonial period or the scientific rationalism of the nineteenth and early twentieth centuries. In this sense the very deficiencies of the Escorial manuscript, when judged against the standards set by much previous scholarship, become its greatest assets.

It is noteworthy that the indigenous testimonies recorded in the Escorial manuscript exceed the objectives set by the friar-compiler to a significant extent. This excess is intentional to a degree, for the friar acknowledges the benefits of a relatively unmediated text for the purpose of introducing new missionaries to their future charges (3–7). But it is also unintentional, as evidenced by a belated attempt to bring aspects of the indigenous testimony into line with the friar's stated objectives. The time constraints under which the Franciscan compiler and his indigenous collaborators were operating are also an important factor. In many ways the Escorial manuscript is a hurried and imperfect work. Yet it is this very incompleteness that allows us, over four centuries later, to more easily perceive the inner contradictions of the text, to tease apart the loose threads in order to reconstruct its textual dynamics.

Those who measure the Escorial manuscript against the more rigorous scholarly bent of the Sahagún project—the checking of the testimony of different groups of informants against each other; the inclusion of the testimony in Nahuatl in the final manuscript; the separation between the voices of the indigenous informants and the editorial commentary—are bound to be disappointed. There are also those who have attempted to read it through the prisms of *indigenismo* or Franciscan millenialism, albeit largely unsuccessfully.[44] I propose that the problem stems, in no small part, from overestimating the contributions of the friar. The singularity of the *Relación de Michoacán* lies precisely in the way in which the voices of the indigenous nobles come across with such intensity, rivaling, even overpowering, that of the missionary-compiler. Consequently, it is possible to discern not only the general outlines of the project as envisioned by the friar and viceroy, but also the agendas of the petámuti and indigenous governor; not only the efficacy of the spoken and written word, but also the potency of a tradition of writing through pictures personified in the caracha. It is to the contributions of each of these participants that we will turn in the following chapters.

2

Transparent Silences

The Friar-Compiler

> Writing is that neutral, composite, oblique space where our subject slips away, the negative where all identity is lost, starting with the very identity of the body writing.
>
> —*Roland Barthes*

The first person to hazard a guess concerning the identity of the friar-compiler of the *Relación de Michoacán* simply penciled in Fray Bernardino de Sahagún's name the Escorial manuscript. The opinion expressed by this anonymous commentator does not hold up to scrutiny, however, since Sahagún never worked as a missionary in Michoacán nor studied the indigenous language.[1]

Another early speculator on the subject was José Mariano Beristain de Souza, who cites Fray Martín Jesús de la Coruña—the first Franciscan guardian of Michoacán—as author of a work fitting the description of the Escorial manuscript in his *Biblioteca hispanoamericana septentrional*, published in 1816–21. In spite of the numerous problems with this hypothesis, it remained in force for some time, most recently in Georges Baudot's study of the work of the early Franciscan compilers of New Spain ([1976] 1983).[2]

Another candidate over the years has been Fray Maturino Gilberti, author of the first published dictionary in the language of Michoacán ([1559] 1989). This attribution, however, is also based on an erroneous assumption, in this case an equivocation regarding the date of publication of Gilberti's *Diálogo de doctrina cristiana*—1559 is the correct date, not 1539.[3]

The most recent development is J. Benedict Warren's well-documented article on the subject in 1971. Since then, most scholars have agreed that the evidence regarding the identity of the friar-compiler points to a relatively obscure Franciscan by the name of Jerónimo de Alcalá who died shortly after the project's completion.[4]

The quote from Roland Barthes cited in the epigraph, however, does not refer to the identity of the writer as historically verifiable individual, but rather to the nature of writing itself as an inherently unstable activity—the inscription within a matrix of signs of a subject who disappears at the very moment of enunciation. To write, in this sense, is to lose one's individuality, to locate oneself within a vast "tissue" consisting of all that has been and will be written.

The anonymity embraced by the friar-compiler of the *Relación de Michoacán* is not as far from this semiotic web as it might initially appear to be. To give up one's individuality in pursuit of the greater glory of God is clearly not the same as Barthes's avowal of the death of the "Author-God" (1977, 146). And yet both gestures express the futility of the search for meaning, in the most profound sense, within the confines of the individual ego.

In the case of the friar, the manner in which he deflects attention away from himself has the additional benefit of allowing him to exercise editorial control out of the limelight—to lay claim to a measure of responsibility for the text without endorsing any of the pagan views expressed therein. The concept of multiple authorship advanced in this chapter can thus be seen to have as much to do with negation as with affirmation.

Indeed, some of the most revealing evidence regarding the friar's vision comes from the silences in the *Relación de Michoacán*, from what is left out or suppressed in the Escorial manuscript. A close textual analysis discloses many cracks in the surface of the text—places where contradictory systems of meaning coexist or where the original message has been modified by a later hand. These inconsistencies or lacunae (in the case of information that is conspicuously absent) point to the work as the product of many hands and voices; a weaving together of various textual functions and levels; an amalgam of bits and pieces derived from individuals with varied interests, points of view, and political agendas.[5]

Over the course of four and a half centuries, the ink used in the Escorial manuscript has faded. Each time one of the copyists sharpened his pen or dipped it in the inkwell, his handwriting became darker, and as the pen became duller and the ink was consumed, the marks on the page became progressively lighter. Still, it is possible to see in the original manuscript those places where a different hand (that of the principal corrector), using a distinctively colored ink, has modified a word or letter, inserted additional information, or changed the position of a chapter title. Significantly, in spite of this layering of different systems of meaning, in all editions of the *Relación de Michoacán* to date it is the version corresponding to the hand of the principal corrector (that is, the friar-compiler) that has been privileged in the body of the text.

This privileging of the hand of the friar may appear, at first glance, to be at odds with the editorial strategy outlined by the anonymous Franciscan in his prologue, dedicated to Viceroy Mendoza, in which he presents himself as a mere "interpreter" committed to translating the testimony of the indigenous informants in as literal and unobtrusive a manner as possible:

> yllustrisimo señor esta escritura y rrelaçion presentan a vuestra señoria los viejos desta çibdad \de michuacan/ y yo tanbien en su nonbre no como avtor sino como ynterpete dellos en la qual vuestra señoria vera que las sentençyas van sacadas al propio de su estilo de hablar y yo pienso de ser notado mucho en esto mas como fiel ynterpete no he quesido mudar de su manera de dezir por no corronper sus sentençyas. . . . a esto digo que yo sirvo de ynterpete destos viejos y haga cuenta que ellos lo cuentan a vuestra señoria yllustrisima y a los letores dando rrelaçion de su vida y çerimonias y gouernaçion y tierra. (6)
>
> [Illustrious Sir, this writing and relation is presented to Your Lordship by the elders of this city \of Michoacán/, and I also in their name, not as its author, but rather as their interpreter. In which [work] you will observe that the sentences are translated according to their own style of speech. And although this may appear odd to the reader, as a faithful interpreter I have not wished to change their manner of speaking so as not to corrupt their sentences. . . . That said, I repeat that I serve as interpreter for these elders, and that you are to imagine they are speaking directly to Your Lordship and to the readers, telling of their life and ceremonies and government and country.]

The friar's partial disavowal of authorship—his goal of making his own contributions to the text transparent—is expressed in the decision to de-emphasize the processes of transcription and translation, most notably by changing relatively little in the "manner of speaking" of the indigenous informants. Another strategy involves the weaving together of the indigenous testimony and the editorial commentary. Although the content of some passages marks them as undoubtedly representative of the voice of the friar, the attribution of other words and phrases is open to interpretation. Thus, while Francisco Miranda, in his editions of the *Relación de Michoacán*, attributes to the Franciscan compiler a lengthy description of colonial-era construction in Pátzcuaro on the site of the ruins of some indigenous temples, in chapter four I characterize the same passage as a central component of the petámuti's oral performance.[6]

Ironically, the way in which the friar cedes authorship to the indigenous informants does not undermine his sense of cultural superiority, for they are identified exclusively with the "lesser" authority of oral as opposed to literary tradition. When the friar instructs Mendoza and, by extension, the other readers of the text, to imagine the elders speaking directly to them through his transparent body, he underscores his humility, his willingness to renounce the title of author in spite of the great effort he acknowledges he has put into the project. At the same time he concedes, with a wink to the readers, that they will probably find the language of the translation "odd," thereby evoking his similarity to them in terms of educational background and expectations about conventions of proper literary style. In a typically ethnocentric gesture, the forging of a bond between reader and editor is contingent upon the construction of an "other" who is unfamiliar with both literature, in the sense of books made up of *litterae*, or letters, and the rules governing proper speech—the very definition of a barbarian according to the ancient Greeks.[7]

The friar's symbolic exclusion of the indigenous peoples of Michoacán from the world of writing is echoed in plate 1 (color section), the most European-style pictorial composition in the Escorial manuscript and the one most marked by repositionings and concealments, suggesting that the anonymous compiler probably had a greater hand in determining its final form than that of the other drawings. In plate 1 (color section), the pictorial space is divided between two kinds of authority—the higher authority of the book, corresponding to the representatives of the church and crown, and the lesser authority of the spoken word, corresponding to the oral informants.

The book, the thematic center of the composition, is held by the friar and viceroy. Significantly, the indigenous painters and the copyists, who had primary responsibility for creating the text as artifact, are not depicted. The actual hands that wielded the pens and brushes in the making of the Escorial manuscript are thus marginalized from both the prose and the pictorial descriptions of the process of production.[8]

This silence regarding the participation of the other indigenous contributors to the Escorial manuscript, with the sole exception of the oral informants, contrasts markedly with the attitude of another early compiler of Mesoamerican traditions, Fray Bernardino de Sahagún. In the prologue to book two of the *Florentine codex*, Sahagún makes a point of foregrounding the role played by his many assistants:

> el primer cedaço, por donde mjs obras se cernjeron, fueron los de tepepulco: el segundo, los del tlatilulco: el tercero, los de mexico: y en todos estos escrutinjos, vuo gramaticos colegiales. El principal y mas sabio, fue antonjo valeriano vezino de azcaputzalco: otro poco menos, que este fue alonso vegerano, vezino de quauhtitlan: otro fue martin Jacobita . . . otro pedro de san buenauentura, vezino de quauhtitlan: todos espertos en tres lenguas, latina, española y indiana. Los escriuanos, que sacaron de buena letra, todas las obras, son: Diego de grado, vezino del tlatilulco, del barrjo de la conception. Bonifacio maximjliano, vezino del tlatilulco, del barrjo de sanct martin. Matheo seuerino, vezino de suchimjlco, de la parte de vllac. (Sahagún [1577–80] 1950–82, 13:55)

> [The first sieve through which my works were sifted was the people of Tepepulco; the second, the people of Tlatilulco; the third, the people of Mexico. And in all these scrutinies there were grammarians from the College [of Santa Cruz in Tlatilulco]. The principal and wisest one was Antonio Valeriano, a native of Azcaputzalco; another, a little less so, was Alonso Vegerano, a native of Quauhtitlan. Another was Martín Jacobita, [then rector of the College, a native of the district of Santa Ana in Tlatilulco] . . . another was Pedro de San Buenaventura, a native of Quauhtitlan. All were expert in three languages: Latin, Spanish, and Indian. The scribes who copied all the work in a good hand are Diego de Grado, native of the district of la Concepción in Tlatilulco; Bonifacio Maximiliano, native of the district of San Martín in Tlatilulco; Mateo Severino, native of Xochimilco, near Ullac.] (trans. Anderson and Dibble)

The care with which Sahagún credits the participation of his indigenous assistants and copyists is related to the link between his project and the colegio mentioned in the above quote of Santa Cruz in Tlatelolco. Founded in 1536 exclusively for the sons of the native elite (although some commoners were surreptitiously substituted by resistant parents for their own children), it served as a testing ground to determine both the intellectual capacity of the newly colonized peoples and their suitability for the priesthood.

In this experiment, initiated under the auspices of many prominent members of colonial society, including the first viceroy, Antonio de Mendoza, and the first bishop, Juan de Zumárraga, Nahuatl was defined as the indigenous language par excellence; Sahagún refers to it simply as "Indian." Although the test was soon acknowledged by the Franciscans to be a failure in terms of the goal of training a corps of native priests, it laid the groundwork for a literary renaissance in early colonial Mexico that drew upon the talents of several generations of indigenous scholars familiar with both the culture of their ancestors and the new Spanish elite.[9]

The central role played by the Colegio de Santa Cruz in the initial wave of Franciscan evangelization gave it a prominence that would not be accorded any other educational institution founded by the members of that order in New Spain. Thus, although there is evidence that the Franciscan monastery in Tzintzuntzan, founded in 1526, included a school for the instruction of indigenous youth in reading, writing, and Christian doctrine,[10] the possible role of these multilingual nobles as assistants in the compilation of the Escorial manuscript remains a mystery.

Ironically, the polemical nature of the Colegio de Santa Cruz may be partly responsible for the explicit mention made by Sahagún of its graduates. During the majority of his years in New Spain (1529–90), Sahagún dedicated himself to defending the colegio and the intellectual capacity of the indigenous peoples it benefited from the attacks of skeptics and detractors. Not only did he serve periodically as teacher there over a span of fifty-odd years, he also organized his compilations of Nahua antiquities in such a way as to demonstrate "the talents and skills these native Mexicans possessed in the time of their unbelief and . . . the vices and virtues which were considered as such among them" ([1577–80] 1950–82, 13:74; bk. 10, ch. 27; trans. Anderson and Dibble).[11] He even goes so far as to bemoan the general decline in educational and moral rigor among the local population in the wake of the Spanish conquest (ibid., 74–77).

The friar-compiler of the *Relación de Michoacán*, in contrast, is more committed to crediting the early missionaries and Mendoza with bringing the light of faith and reason to a people immersed in the darkness of idolatry than to highlighting the more enlightened aspects of their preconquest way of life. Thus, he extrapolates from the presumed lack of a writing system among the indigenous peoples of Michoacán a supposed incapacity for abstract reasoning and the exercise of virtue:

apenas se vera en toda esta escriptura vna virtud moral mas çerimonias y ydolatrias y borracheras y muertes y guerras ~~que~~ yo no he hallado otra virtud entre esta gente si no es la liberalidad que en su tienpo los señores tenian por afrenta ser escasos y digo que apenas ay otra virtud entre ellos porque avn nonbre propio para ninguna de las virtudes tienen donde pare*z*\ç/e que no las obravan porque para dezir castidad se a de dezir por rrodeo en su lengua y asi de otras virtudes como es templanza caridad justiçia que avnque tengan algunos nonbres no las entienden como caresçia esta gente de libros. (4)

[One will scarcely observe in this entire work any moral virtue, only ceremonies and idolatries and drunken feasts and deaths and wars. Indeed, I have found only one virtue among this people, [and that is] generosity, for under their system the nobles considered it an affront to be stingy. And I say there is hardly any other virtue among them, for they even lacked proper names for the virtues, from which it would appear that they did not practice them. For in order to say chastity one has to say it in a roundabout way in their language, and the same is true of other virtues like temperance, charity, justice. For even though they may have some words, they do not understand them, since this people had no books.]

On a first reading, what emerges most strongly from this line of reasoning is the lack of cultural sensitivity of a friar incapable of recognizing that there is no exact parallel between languages for the definition of virtues and vices. If one judges a culture based on a system of values not of its own making, it will obviously appear inadequate. As a select group of missionaries, including Sahagún and Las Casas, was beginning to realize, the crux of the matter was the need to establish the cultural and linguistic parameters within which it would become possible to make valid comparisons.[12]

Nevertheless, it should not be surprising that the friar-compiler of the *Relación de Michoacán* was not as philosophically oriented or sophisticated as some of his fellow missionaries who had dedicated their lives to defending the indigenous peoples from those who questioned the latter's moral and intellectual integrity. The battle this young catechist was fighting is framed by him in rather narrow terms, but in this he was typical of many of his brethren. A short saying, included by Fray Juan Baptista de Lagunas in his 1574 grammar of the indigenous language of Michoacán, gives a taste of prevailing attitudes among most missionaries in the field. For those interested in remembering how to pronounce the language correctly, Lagunas advises they commit to memory the following aide-mémoire:

> [Los indios de Michuacan] no tenian diction que començasse en B, y ansi no tenian Baptismo. En D pues no tenian ni conoscian a Dios. En F, pues no tenian Fe. En G, pues no tenian gracia. En I, pues carescian de la verdadera justicia. En L, pues no tenian \en vso/ ley de natura, ni de scriptura, ni de gracia. En R, porque carescian de regimiento regla y razon pues tan tyranica y cruel y ciegamente biuian. (Lagunas [1574] 1983, 29)

> [The Indians of Michoacán had no words beginning in B, and thus they had no baptism; in D, because they did not have or know God; in F because they had no faith; in G, because they had not grace; in I, because they lacked true justice; in L, because they had \in practice/ no natural, written, or God-given law; in R, because they lacked regulation, rule, and reason, for they lived so tyrannically, cruelly, and blindly.] (my trans.)

It is important to bear in mind that neither Lagunas nor the friar-compiler of the *Relación de Michoacán* is necessarily impugning the intellectual capacity of his charges in a racial or genetic sense. Rather, they are pointing to what they see as missing components in their cultural apparatus and using these "deficiencies" as a justification for exalting the benefits that have supposedly accrued to the indigenous peoples as a result of their evangelization and newly acquired political status as vassals of the Spanish crown. The highly partisan nature of this line of reasoning is underscored by the contrast with other early colonial sources that provide close equivalents to Christian virtues such as humility, charity, chastity, justice, and temperance in the indigenous language of Michoacán.[13]

It is also important to note that the underlying premise in the above remarks—the superiority of Christianity over paganism—does not negate the recognition by many missionaries, especially those who dedicated long hours to learning indigenous languages, that it was necessary to meet potential converts at least partway in order to convince them of the benefits of changing their ancient customs and beliefs. The 1533 order to Fray Andrés de Olmos, the first to begin researching Nahua antiquities in central Mexico, is typical in this regard, for it contains in embryonic form the three main arguments, each drawing upon the authority of a different church father, that underlay the work of the friar-compilers.

Olmos is charged with preserving the memory of indigenous traditions, "as many things of other Gentiles are noted and remembered" (Mendieta [1573–1604] 1997, 1:179; prologue to bk. 2; my trans.).[14] The focus here is on the role of the early missionaries as intellectuals. They had come to convert the peoples of the New World to Christianity, but they were also guardians of the knowledge of their own societies and, as such, interested in learning about the traditions of others.

A favorite authority cited for this purpose was Saint Jerome, who, in the prologue to the Latin Vulgate, mentions how the search for wisdom took such men as Pythagoras, Plato, and Apollonius far from their native lands:

> es vn dicho muy ~~trillado~~ \comun/ que dize que naturalmente desean todos saber y para adquerir esta çiençia se consumen muchos años rrebolviendo libros y quemandose las çejas y andando muchas provinçias y deprendiendo muchas lenguas por ynquirir y saber como hizieron muchos gentiles como lo rrelata y cuenta mas por estenso el bienaventurado sant hieronimo en el prologo de la blibia [*sic*]. (3)

> [As the saying goes, everyone naturally desires knowledge, and to acquire this science many years are spent leafing through books, burning eyebrows, traversing provinces, and learning many languages for inquiry and knowledge, as was done by many Gentiles, as the blessed Saint Jerome relates and tells of more extensively in the prologue to the Bible.][15]

The above quote, from the prologue to the *Relación de Michoacán*, is interesting because it suggests that one of the things that inspired the friar-compiler to come to the New World was the appeal of learning about faraway peoples and places. This spirit of adventure and intellectual inquiry may not have predisposed him to approve of the things he found there, but it was clearly an important stimulus in getting him to devote the time and effort necessary to research and record indigenous traditions.

In addition to the desire to preserve knowledge of the indigenous past for posterity, the 1533 order to Olmos suggests a more immediately practical reason for recording these traditions: to better refute evil and foolhardy practices, thereby demonstrating the superiority of Christianity over indigenous religions. As the experience of the Mixtón War was to demonstrate in 1541–42, it was dangerous to underestimate the power that the indigenous priests could still exercise over a nominally Christian population by combining an appeal to the ancient gods with military successes against the Spaniards.[16]

The mandate to learn about pagan traditions in order to better combat them stemmed from the authority of Saint Augustine, who admitted to having been powerfully drawn to the stories of Greek and Roman gods in his youth. As Sahagún reminded his readers in the prologue to book three of the *Florentine codex*:

> No tuuo por cosa superflua, nj vana el diujno Augustino, tratar, de la theologia fabulosa de los gentiles, en el sexto libro de la ciudad de Dios. Porque, como el dize; conocidas las fabulas y ficciones vanas que los gentiles, tenjan cerca de sus dioses fingidos pudiesen facilmēte darles a entender, que aquellos no erā dioses, nj pudian dar cosa njnguna que fuesse prouechosa a la criatura racional. (Sahagún [1577–80] 1950–82, 13:59)

> [The divine Augustine did not consider it superfluous or vain to deal with the fictitious theology of the gentiles in the sixth Book of the City of God, because, as he says, the empty fictions and falsehoods which the gentiles held regarding their false gods being known, [true believers] could easily make them understand that those were not gods nor could they provide anything that would be beneficial to a rational creature.] (trans. Anderson and Dibble)

According to Sahagún, the desirability of presenting the teachings of Christianity in such a way as to maximize their appeal to the indigenous peoples of New Spain was an important consideration and one that necessitated an in-depth understanding of the languages and ways of thinking of the people one was trying to convert. A thorough knowledge of indigenous rhetorical strategies was also indispensable if missionaries were to present the Christian message in an authoritative and convincing manner and thus compare favorably with the eloquence of the local priests.

The importance of learning about non-Christian traditions takes on a special urgency in the writings of Sahagún, for he also believed that, unbeknownst to most friars, pagan practices were continuing in New Spain under the guise of Christianity. The difficulties involved in differentiating these idolatrous acts from more "innocent" practices, however, were enormous. Not only did one need to recognize the symbolic value of countless seemingly insignificant practices, it was also necessary to understand the complicated calendrical system, the dates on which different festivals traditionally occurred, and the potential association of a particular saint with an indigenous deity as a means of keeping the native religion alive.

Although the friar-compiler of the *Relación de Michoacán* does not go into as much detail as Sahagún regarding the theological justifications for his work, nor does he explicitly address the incipient mixing of Christian and indigenous traditions, it is clear that he also conceived of his manuscript as a sort of training manual for new missionaries in the field. Thus, part one, on the gods and religious ceremonies of the peoples of Michoacán, is specifically addressed to "the religious who are in charge of their conversion" (7). The importance of this function is underscored by the fact that, in spite of the loss of all but one leaf of this section, there is still plenty of information on religion scattered throughout parts two and three.

Moreover, one of the areas in which the friar-compiler is most prone to make an exception and draw attention to his own role in the elaboration of the text is the use of language among the indigenous peoples of Michoacán, another crucial element in the training of new missionaries. Thus, when he mentions the tendency of his informants to speak in questions in order to signify negation, or points out that their language has more nouns than Castilian, or explains their use of metaphors, he is testifying both to his linguistic interest and to his dedication to the principle of teaching Christianity in the indigenous language. This concession to the culture of the conquered, one of the centerpieces of the early years of missionary activity in New Spain, reflects sensitivity to the need to better understand and communicate with the conquered peoples in order to effect their conversion.[17]

The third major incentive for researching indigenous traditions expressed in the 1533 order to Olmos is the mandate to record any "good" things that may be found. As the Jesuit José de Acosta was to assert toward the end of the century:

> generalmente es digno de admitir que lo que se pudiere dejar a los indios de sus costumbres y usos (no habiendo mezcla de sus errores antiguos) es bien dejallo, y conforme al consejo de San Gregorio Papa, procurar que sus fiestas y regocijos se encaminen al honor de Dios y de los santos cuyas fiestas celebran. (Acosta [1590] 1962, 318; bk. 6, ch. 28)

> [It is generally worthy of note that that which can be left to the Indians of their customs and uses (so long as there is no mixture of their ancient errors), it is good to let stand and, in accordance with the advice of Saint Gregory, the pope, endeavor to make their feasts and celebrations redound to the glory of God and of the saints whose feasts they are celebrating.] (my trans.)

The notion that those customs "untainted by idolatry" should be preserved is at the heart of initiatives undertaken by many colonial officials, including Mendoza, to adapt certain indigenous political and economic structures to Christian and Spanish ends.[18]

That this was more a short- than a long-term strategy is implicit in the metaphor Saint Gregory uses of the climber who gradually leaves the past behind as he reaches for the highest peaks.[19] The ultimate goal, as the friar-compiler of the *Relación de Michoacán* makes clear in his prologue—in spite of a token reference to preserving "the good things they had in their time" (4)—is to "implant faith in Christ, and polish and adorn this people with new customs, fashioning them anew if possible as men of reason following [in the way of] God" (3). The cultivation of natural reason, by the introduction of "superior" European ideas and technologies (such as books and alphabetic writing), culminates in the supreme gift of faith in the one true God and the possibility of eternal salvation through the mechanism of divine grace.[20]

It is this vision that informs many of the modifications made by the hand of the principal corrector to the Escorial manuscript. I am not particularly concerned here with such emendations of a purely practical nature as the filling in of blanks left by the copyists or the repositioning of chapter titles to create space for additional drawings. And, while many changes of a stylistic nature are interesting as reflections of the transfer of the text from an oral to a written register[21] or, in the case of grammatical and spelling errors, as indications of the possible sociocultural origin of the copyists,[22] they are not my focus either. Rather, my goal is to explore the significance of those corrections that are directly related to the production of textual meaning.

These latter emendations tend to coalesce around several key topics; these topics, in turn, correlate with information that can be gleaned from other primary sources regarding the kinds of tensions that existed between the Spanish authorities and indigenous nobles around the time of compilation of the Escorial manuscript. First, there is the attempt to conceal evidence that might call into question the character and success of the Franciscan missionary enterprise in Michoacán in the 1520s and 1530s. The continuation of idolatrous practices and the ongoing influence of the indigenous nobles as priests fall under this category.

Also of interest is the friar's silence regarding Vasco de Quiroga, bishop of Michoacán from 1538 to 1565, who is credited in many contemporary sources with convincing the indigenous peoples, in his capacity in 1533 as an *oidor* (royal judge), to return to their villages and cooperate with the Franciscans.[23] At issue is not so much the physical presence of Quiroga in the province in the 1530s, which was, admittedly, much more belated and intermittent than that of the Franciscans at the time. Rather, it is the contrast between, on one hand, the central role he plays in other texts from the period—including (as I argue in chapter four) the petámuti's oral performance in part two of the *Relación de Michoacán*—and, on the other, the lack of a place accorded Quiroga in the vision articulated in the prologue by the friar-compiler, who highlights instead the role of the Franciscans and Viceroy Mendoza.

The continued political authority of the indigenous nobles is another area of suppressed tension in the Escorial manuscript. Although the friar admits this was a problem in the past, especially around the time of the execution of the cazonci by Nuño de Guzmán, the picture he paints of the present, since the arrival of Mendoza, is unequivocally enthusiastic. According to the friar, the moral and political authority of the viceroy (and, by extension, the Spanish crown) is now undisputed in the eyes of the indigenous peoples. This interpretation, however, is called into question by references scattered throughout the text, many of them partially modified or erased, suggesting the continuation of service to the indigenous lords and recognition of their authority.

These two threads of religious and political friction combine in a third category of omissions and modifications that originate in inconsistencies between the friar's attempt to prove the superiority of the Spanish and Christian way of life and the testimonies of the indigenous elders, who tend to look more favorably on the past and to situate moral and spiritual decline in the present, beginning with the arrival of the Spaniards. An interesting twist on this dynamic involves the appropriation, by the indigenous nobles, of Christian symbols of spiritual and temporal power in order to convince a European audience of their ability to govern themselves.[24] The friar-compiler, in contrast, tends to underscore the distance they have yet to travel along the path to self-sufficiency and, consequently, their need for missionaries to instruct them in the Christian faith and benevolent leaders like Mendoza to demonstrate for them the advantages of enlightened European government.[25]

THE HIDDEN FRONTISPIECE

As in other parts of the Escorial manuscript, it is possible to identify more than one layer of meaning in the frontispiece, corresponding to different stages in the production process. If one holds the drawing up to the light, one can perceive at least three major pictorial changes: (1) at some point after the initial version was completed, a figure located behind the viceroy was obscured by the addition of a tapestry or screen; (2) Don Pedro Cuiníarángari's right arm was lowered from a raised position, with hands apparently joined in prayer, to a rather awkward outstretched position, with palm raised; and (3) the lower torso of the friar-compiler was modified in such a way as to move him from a seated to a standing position.

The prominent place accorded this picture on the title page, immediately preceding the prologue, marks it as a site where one might expect the disjunction between the expectations and agenda of the friar who supervised its production and the indigenous carari who carried out his orders to be particularly pronounced. It is also likely that the carari simultaneously felt pressured to complete his work to the satisfaction of Cuiníarángari and the other indigenous nobles.

My hypothesis is that the first version of the frontispiece, modeled on European prototypes of the so-called "presentation miniature,"[26] was executed according to the specifications of both the Franciscan compiler and indigenous nobles. Subsequently, however, after the friar had composed his prologue, he charged the painter with making additional modifications in order to bring the drawing more fully into line with his stated objectives.

The key to the motivation that inspired these changes is the catalogue of virtues and vices mapped out by the anonymous compiler in his prologue, according to which missionaries like himself represent the theological virtues of faith, hope, and charity, while Mendoza is seen as exemplifying the cardinal (or moral) virtues of prudence, justice, temperance, and fortitude. The friar-compiler frames this discussion as a prayer to God, praising Him for providing the indigenous peoples with exemplary religious and political leaders capable of bringing them to spiritual and moral plenitude:

y permite nuestro señor que como les provee de rreligiosos que dexando en castilla sus ençerramienctos y sosiego espiritual les ynspira que pasen a estas partes y se abajen no solamente a predicalles segun su capaçidad mas avn de enseñales las primeras letras y no solamente esto mas avn abaxarse a su poquedad de ellos y hazerse a todos todas las cosas como dize el apostol san pablo de si ansi les prouee cada dia quien les muestre las virtudes morales como proueyo en vuestra yllustrisima señoria para la administraçion y governaçion y rregimiento deste nuevo mundo. (4–5)

[And as Our Lord God has provided them with religious, who leaving behind in Castile their cloisters and spiritual peace, are inspired by Him to come to these parts and lower themselves, not only to preach to [this people] according to their capacity, but even to teach them to read and write, and not only this, but also to lower themselves to their humble condition and become everything for everyone, as the Apostle Saint Paul says of himself, so He provides them each day with someone capable of showing them the moral virtues, as he foresaw in your Illustrious Lordship for the administration and government and legislation of this New World.]

This image of the selfless New World apostles, lowering themselves to the level of the Indians in order to preach to them and teach them to read and write, is implicitly contrasted, in another passage from the *Relación de Michoacán*, with that of the morally bankrupt and weak-willed natives, unable to resist a life of debauchery without the assistance of the friars:

de tan duros como estaban se ablandaron y dexaron sus borracheras y ydolatrias y çirimonias y bavtiçaronse todos y cada dia ban aprobechando y aprobecharan con el ayuda de nuestro señor. (264)

[From being extremely stubborn, they softened, and relinquishing their drunken feasts, idolatries, and ceremonies, they were all baptized. Each day they show improvement and will continue to do so with the help of Our Lord.]

There is no distinction made between those indigenous peoples who resisted evangelization and those who actively collaborated with the friars. They are all presented as initially resistant and subsequently more favorably disposed—the implication being that this change of heart was due to divine intervention through the medium of the Franciscans rather than to an internal power struggle between indigenous factions in which the path of voluntary conversion gradually gained adherents.

The portrait of the Franciscans in the prologue as the exclusive bearers of the gifts of faith, hope, and charity is thereby contrasted with the anonymous compiler's implied opinion of Cuiníarángari and the other indigenous nobles who collaborated with him on the *Relación de Michoacán*. On one hand, in order to justify the work as a whole, he insists on the reliability of their testimony; moreover, as a missionary, he is clearly committed to the notion of the importance of their eternal salvation in the eyes of God. On the other, he asserts that they are incapable on their own of excelling at anything other than "ceremonies, idolatries, drunken feasts, deaths, and wars" (4).

This paternalistic view of the indigenous nobles is potentially contradicted, however, by the initial version of the frontispiece, in which Cuiníarángari is the only figure shown with his hands together, as if in prayer. Ironically, the appropriation of a Christian symbol by an indigenous noble can be read as potentially threatening to one of the very missionaries responsible for his conversion.

This "misallocation" of a powerful symbol of Christian faith, according to the aforementioned catalog of virtues and vices, is exacerbated by the friar's pose in the original frontispiece. In the typical presentation miniature, the author or translator of the manuscript kneels before his patron, holding the bound volume in outstretched hands. The latter, generally seated on a throne or ornate chair to the far left or right of the pictorial space, gestures toward the work or symbolically receives it in his or her hand.

If one holds the Escorial manuscript up to the light, one can see how, in the hidden frontispiece, many of these details are echoed, except that the friar appears to be seated opposite the viceroy rather than kneeling before him. Not only does this violate an important European pictorial convention, it also flies in the face of the celebrated dedication of the early Franciscans to the vows of obedience and voluntary poverty. In the chronicles of the order, self-effacement and physical hardship are equated with saintliness, and the fact that a friar habitually went barefoot or dressed in a rough habit is recorded with particular care. Clearly, the compiler of the *Relación de Michoacán* was concerned about such matters, for he did not sign his name to the manuscript, preferring to remain anonymous; he also explicitly notes the great humility required of those who choose to become missionaries in the New World; moreover, he is pictured barefoot in the frontispiece.

Why the indigenous painter subsequently changed the friar's posture from a sitting to a standing position, rather than a kneeling one is unclear. One potential hypothesis is that in New Spain, beginning with Cortés, the highest colonial official always made a point of deferring to the spiritual authority of the barefoot friars.[27] In any case the censored posture is another potential indication that the anonymous compiler was determined to put the accent on his spiritual status, rather than his temporal power.

The prevailing image of Mendoza that has survived to the present is one of a wise and benevolent viceroy much beloved by the people of New Spain, both Spaniards and Indians. This is also clearly the view espoused by the friar-compiler of the *Relación de Michoacán*, one of whose central theses is the transformative effect of Mendoza's presence on all sectors of colonial society:

> vuestra señoria paresçe ser electo de dios para la governaçion desta tierra para tener a todos en paz para mantener a todos en justiçia para oyr a chicos et\y/ grandes para desagraviar a los agraviados y bien esta la prueva clara pues el aposento de vuestra señoria esta patente a chicos y grandes y todos se llegan con tanta confiança a la presençia de vuestra señoria y\que/ quitando sus rrecreaçiones y pasatienpos de señor da avdiençia todo el dia hasta la noche a vnos y a otros que avn hasta los rreligiosos estamos casi admirados de la constançia de vuestra señoria. (5)

> [Your Lordship appears chosen by God for the government of this land, to keep everyone in peace, to provide justice for all, to listen to the humble and the grand, to set right those who have been wronged. And the proof of this is clear, for Your Lordship's chamber is open to the lowly and the great. Such confidence do they show in the presence of Your Lordship who, sacrificing lordly recreations and pastimes, gives audience all day and into the night to one and all, that even we religious are almost astonished by the constancy of Your Lordship.]

This idealized portrait of a benign and peaceful rule under Mendoza is contrasted with the period of armed conflict under Cortés and Nuño de Guzmán:

> y podemos dezir de vuestra señoria que haze mas en sustentar y conservar lo conquistado que fue en conquistallo de nuevo porque en

lo primero fue trabajo de algunos dias y en esto trabajo de muchos años en el primero se alaba la animosidad del coraçon en vuestra señoria se alaba la beninidad para con todos ~~y~~ el gran talencto que vuestra señoria tiene para rregir la prudençia en todas las cosas la afabilidad para con todos no perdiendo la autoridad y grauedad que el ofiçio rrequiere el çelo para que se plante en esta gente nuestra rreligion cristiana. (5)

[And we can say of Your Lordship that you do more in sustaining and preserving that which was conquered than was done in conquering it for the first time. For the former was a task of a few days and the latter work of many years; in the first one admires the fearlessness of heart, in Your Lordship your mercy towards all, your great talent in governing, your prudence in all things, your affability toward all, never losing the authority and gravity that your office requires, your zeal in implanting our Christian religion in this people.]

In this quote Mendoza's virtues of prudence and fortitude—with the latter's twin correlates of patience and magnanimity—are counterposed to the pride and ambition of his predecessors. Thus, although the friar expresses some admiration for the "fearlessness of heart" engendered by such passions, he censures, by opposition, the concomitant evils of violence and discord.

Even more explicit is the contrast with the supposedly tyrannical form of government prior to the arrival of the Spaniards. According to the friar, the indigenous peoples view Mendoza as a savior, since they no longer need fear for their lives at the hands of their former leaders:

que avn solas las palabras de vuestra señoria tienen por mandamienctos viendo como vuestra señoria los trata y como los conserva y tiene a todos en tanta paz y tranquilidad lo qual no asi tan façilmente se haçia en su ynfidelidad porque por la ~~mayor~~\enor/ desobediençia que tenian a sus señores les costavan las vidas y heran sacrificados. (5–6)

[Such that even the words of Your Lordship they take as commandments, seeing how Your Lordship treats them and how he preserves them, and keeps them all in such peace and tranquility. All of which was not so easily accomplished in their infidelity, because the \slight/est disobedience towards their lords would cost them their lives and they were sacrificed.]

In the view of the anonymous compiler, there is no room for uncertainty regarding two of the central polemics of his day: the debate over which of the various rivals for political supremacy in New Spain—Cortés or Mendoza—was most worthy;[28] and the question of the advantages conferred upon the indigenous peoples by Christianity and Spanish rule.[29]

The scribe who was responsible for copying the prologue in a clear hand made a rather curious error when he reached the above passage. Rather than writing "the slightest [*menor*] disobedience towards their lords would cost them their lives and they were sacrificed," he began to write "the greatest [*mayor*] disobedience," caught the error, and corrected it before continuing on with the sentence. In a later revision of the manuscript, the hand of the principal corrector reinforced this "correction" with his characteristic colored ink. This inconsistency, a relatively minor example of the text's "stuttering in its articulation" (Hulme 1986, 12), remains as another potential indication of the distance between the friar's vision in the prologue and the views presented in other parts of the text, where the indigenous judicial system does not appear exceptionally rigorous according to the standards of the time.[30]

As for the third example of censorship in the frontispiece—the figure hidden behind a brocade tapestry or screen—I propose that it potentially undermines the idealized vision of Mendoza's viceregal government outlined above. Although the figure is difficult to make out in its entirety, over the years some of the green paint concealing it has worn off and, if one looks closely, it is possible to make out a red tunic, the outlines of a head (the hair is drawn in ink, not colored), and a hand at the level of the viceroy's shoulders.

What makes this individual particularly compelling is his similarity in terms of size, clothing, and hairstyle to the sons of the cazonci—Don Francisco Taríacuri and Don Antonio Huitziméngari—pictured in plate 27, color section;[31] as well as his location on the far right of the pictorial space. Here I will argue for the meaningful character of position in pictorial space.[32]

In a large percentage of the drawings (twenty out of a total of forty-four), the right-hand side is reserved for the figure of the cazonci or some other representative of temporal authority, either alone or accompanied by advisors. See, for instance, plates 18, 25, and 26, in which the founder of the empire, Taríacuri, seated at right, issues commands that are executed at left.[33] In plates 13 and 40, it is the cazonci's empty chair, or *uaxántsiqua*, that occupies this position, a sign that the seat of power is temporarily empty due either to a death or dispute over succession.[34] In three additional drawings (plates 9, 16, 20), this pattern is reversed, indicating some sort of disturbance in the natural or moral order.[35]

It follows that whether or not the hidden figure located behind the viceroy is meant to represent one of the sons of the cazonci, it is likely to represent someone in a position of authority. It also appears to have been a person whose presence was perceived to subvert the meaning that the anonymous friar-compiler considered appropriate for the frontispiece. Given the exalted representation of Mendoza in the prologue, the great honor and esteem in which he is purportedly held by the indigenous peoples of New Spain, any suggestion that this authority is conditional upon an alliance with someone else is clearly unacceptable. In spite of a wealth of contradictory evidence, the final version of the frontispiece leads the reader to believe that the indigenous peoples, after less than twenty years of Spanish rule, no longer demonstrate loyalty toward the former ruling dynasty.

There are more examples of revisions and partial erasures in the Escorial manuscript. Not all of them, however, are equally significant. At times a copyist will appear to have lost his place, skipping several lines before becoming aware of the error and crossing out the mistake. At other times one can see how a later hand, using a different colored ink, has modified the spelling of a word ("diçiendo" > "diziendo"), resolved an abbreviation ("sa⸺" > "sauer") or substituted one synonym for another ("trillado" > "comun"). Other modifications, however, fall into clearly defined patterns related to the friar-compiler's attempt in the prologue to emphasize a definitive break with indigenous tradition since the arrival of Mendoza. I would like to turn next to these textual stutterings and the hidden conflicts they expose.

CENSORING THE USE OF THE PRESENT

My argument is based on the cumulative effect of numerous small details that may appear insignificant: minor inconsistencies between different parts of the text; the modification of words or phrases in one context, but not in another; traces of a hand that discretely attempts to bring the testimony of the indigenous nobles into conformity with that of the friar-compiler.

The predominant strategy used by the friar when confronted with potential areas of conflict is to locate the problem exclusively in the past; the contrary evidence is then modified in order to conceal it from the reader. Consider the way in which he both admits and denies the existence of tensions between members of his own religious order and the indigenous priests. In a lengthy passage detailing some of the common misconceptions once held by the local population concerning the Spaniards, he relates that certain "priests and sorcerers" spread the word among the people that the Franciscans were dead men come to life, that their habits were winding sheets, that at night their flesh would disintegrate and they would go as skeletons to the underworld where they kept their wives (265). Another rumor supposedly spread by the indigenous priests was that the friars were baptizing children with blood, which is why so many died (265). The missionary compiler goes on to assure the reader that these misconceptions have since disappeared; the more flattering notion that the missionaries were born without mothers is the only one, he claims, that still lingers. According to this view, the Franciscans have successfully overcome the challenge to their authority represented by the indigenous priests.

Meanwhile, other passages from the Escorial manuscript leave open the question of the continued power and influence of these native religious leaders, especially when key words and phrases are partially modified by a later hand. These suppressions take the form of "corrections" of the original version of the manuscript. Their interpretation, nevertheless, is complicated by the way in which the friar's commentary is blended with the testimony of the indigenous informants and also by the fact that not all the emendations can be attributed to him, for the indigenous nobles also had a stake in concealing the continuation of certain practices from the colonial authorities. Whoever is responsible for the change of meaning in any particular passage, however, it almost always signals some residue of unresolved conflict between the different parties involved in the compilation of the Escorial manuscript.

Regarding the priests known as *curízitacha* or *cuirípecha*, for example, in the original version their duties are recorded in the present—they are in charge of maintaining the incense burners at night and the pyres at the appointed times: "tienen cargo de poner ençienso en vnos braseros de noche y pilas en sus tienpos" (181). These same priests now bring sedge and cypress branches for the Christian "fiestas," the text adds. In other words, the old order coexists with the new. During a subsequent revision of the manuscript, this message was modified—the verb *tener* was changed from the present to the imperfect: "*tenian* cargo de poner ençienso en vnos braseros de noche y pilas en sus tienpos" (emphasis added). The new meaning erases the temporal ambiguity regarding these ceremonies; it suggests that the old order has been completely replaced by the new.

The account of the activities of the priests known as *hirípacha* is modified in a similar manner. In the original version they are said to be in charge of saying certain prayers and spells while burning incense: "tienen cargo de haçer vnas oraçiones y conjuros con vnos olores llamados andamuqua" (182). In the corrected version this passage is changed to: "*tenian* cargo de hazer vnas oraçiones y conjuros . . ." (emphasis added). In this case a subsequent comment, in the imperfect in both versions, appears to have been added by the friar during a previous stage in the compilation process. It consists of an explanation regarding the traditional setting for these supplicatory fires: "*ardian* alli quando *avian* de yr a las guerras" (emphasis added). Here the use of the present evokes the voice of the indigenous informants; the use of the imperfect, the framing of this testimony by the friar-compiler; and the change from present to imperfect, the suppression of the difference between these voices and privileging of the point of view of the friar.

The close association between prehispanic religious beliefs and the exercise of war presented particular difficulties for the Spanish authorities, since the conquistadors' armies tended to be composed in large part of indigenous allies who still conceived of war as a means of "feeding," or paying homage to, their gods. The friar-compiler implicitly resolves this difficulty in his prologue by relegating it to the past, as something that would only have occurred under the administrations of Cortés and Nuño de Guzmán (264).

If one looks closely at those places in the text that refer to war or idolatrous practices, however, one again finds a fluctuation between the use of the present and imperfect, as well as a systematic attempt to cover up the traces of this fluctuation. Thus, in part two one finds the correction:

> tiene\ia/ esta gente costunbre quando sacrifican alguno de partille por las casas de los papas y alli hazian la salba a los dioses y comian aquella carne los saçerdotes. (57)

> [This people have \had/ a custom when they sacrifice someone to divide him up among the temples. There they would make a salve to the gods and the priests would eat that meat.]

In this case someone (either the principal corrector or the scribe) caught the first inadmissible use of the present—"have" but missed the second—"sacrifice." The final part of the excerpt—"There they would make . . ."— probably corresponds to the voice of the friar, who adds a reference to cannibalism, one of the favorite rationales used by Europeans to justify the conquest of the New World.[36]

The implicit contrast between the violent and idolatrous behavior of the indigenous nobles and the equally violent, yet ultimately "beneficial," behavior of the conquistadors lies at the heart of many texts from the early colonial period. One of the most graphic pictures of the Escorial manuscript (plate 33, color section) shows the gods Xarátanga and Curícaueri (or priests dressed as their earthly representatives) looking on while indigenous warriors capture prisoners, tearing out the hearts of men and women, burning houses and temples, plundering precious objects made of gold, securing additional prisoners by their necks with a long rope.

According to the title of this chapter, the picture represents something that happened *before* the conquest: "quando metian alguna poblacion a fuego y sangre" (197). Nevertheless, as in other parts of the *Relación de Michoacán*, if one looks closely, the contrast between the old order and the new is not so clear. The Mesoamerican concept of sacrifice comes across so vividly in this picture, the viewer is swept into the action with such force, that it is difficult not to perceive it as something familiar to the indigenous painter, as much a part of present reality as of the past.[37]

The passages in the Escorial manuscript concerning marital ceremonies also contain numerous instances of verbs in the present that have been discretely changed to the imperfect. Since indigenous taboos against incest were different from those held by the Spaniards, the friars had to decide how to deal with cases of marriage that violated Christian precepts and then be consistent in their application of these standards. In Michoacán, for instance, an uncle could marry his niece, but a nephew could not marry his aunt. A man could marry his wife's sister if the wife died, or his dead brother's former wife. He could also marry an older woman and then marry her daughter later, once she had grown up. As this last example suggests, polygamy was relatively common, especially among the indigenous nobles (Tudela [1541] 1956, 217–18; Pollard 1993, 55–59).

In theory none of these practices were permitted to continue under Spanish rule. But the difficulties involved in imposing a Christian conception of marriage on a foreign people in their native land made this an extremely delicate issue. The missionaries could attempt to prohibit any further violation of Christian precepts. But what about those cases in which the "offending" practice dated from before the Spanish conquest?[38]

The issue of polygamy was especially sensitive, since it formed part of the fundamental structure of native society and intimately affected the lives of the indigenous nobles who served as intermediaries with the colonial authorities. Significantly, one of the prophesies mentioned by the Zacatec priests who incited the peoples of Nueva Galicia to revolt during the Mixtón War was that the men would once again have many wives and those who listened to the friars and were content with only one wife would die. The problem, as Fray Antonio Tello put it, was that the indigenous peoples loved their wives and children too much, and they were consequently so resistant to the notion of monogamy that the missionaries were sometimes forced to dissemble and wait for a more opportune moment to insist on this fundamental point of Christian doctrine (Huerta and Palacios 1976, 207).[39]

Two of the most prominent examples of modification of the present tense in relation to marital practices in the Escorial manuscript occur in the chapter titles. Thus, in the original title of the chapter on illicit marriages—"de los que se casan por amores" (215)—the verb is changed to "used to marry"/"se cassauan," as if to suggest that the friars were somehow better able to control the impulses of youthful passion than the indigenous priests. A few pages later, there is another reference to clandestine marriages in the present, but this one is not "corrected" in the final version.[40]

Plate 38 represents a typical marriage between commoners. Before consummating the marriage, the woman sweeps the road in front of the house to assure good fortune, while the man goes to the mountain for firewood to burn in the temple in honor of the gods. The original title of this chapter reads: "de la manera que se casa la gente baxa" (213). During a subsequent revision it was changed to "se cassaua," thereby suggesting that such superstitious and idolatrous customs were no longer in practice in Michoacán. A few pages later the friar-compiler admits, nevertheless, that some of the poorer people continue to refuse Christian marital rites (217). This pattern of both admitting and denying the continuation of indigenous practices makes sense if one considers the dual objectives of the friar-compiler, who needed to convince the readers of the success of the missionary enterprise and also of the need for greater economic and political support. Thus, he implies that, if only there were more resources available, the friars would be able to bring the few remaining idolaters within the Christian fold.[41]

A similar process of obfuscation is evident in those passages that refer to the continued economic and political authority of the indigenous nobles. Again, the friar-compiler admits there was a problem in this area in the past:

despues que vinieron a esta provinçia españoles estubo el cazonçi algunos años y mando la çibdad de mechuacan y todavia tenian rreconoçimiento los señores de los pueblos que hera su señor y le syrbian secretamente. (267)

[After the Spaniards came to this province, the cazonci was alive a few years. He ruled the city of Michoacán and the lords of the towns still recognized him as their lord, serving him secretly.]

This admission is mild if one compares it with other documents from the period, such as the legal records from the trials of the cazonci, Cuiníarángari, and other principal lords (Scholes and Adams 1952). During his visit to Michoacán in 1528, the inspector Juan de Ortega reportedly said that the lords of that province deserved to die a thousand deaths for their disloyalty to the Spanish crown. Among the charges the cazonci and other nobles faced were ordering the deaths of abusive Spaniards (some sixty to seventy were killed around that time, according to Ortega), refusing to turn all their gold and silver over to the encomenderos, and continuing to receive tribute and other services from their former subjects (Warren 1985, 124–36).

The response of Cuiníarángari to these charges will be examined in chapter five. At this point, suffice it to say that a close reading of the Escorial manuscript indicates that these difficulties, which ultimately led to the torture and execution of the cazonci in 1530, do not appear to have been completely resolved some ten years later, at the time of compilation of the Escorial manuscript. Unlike the references to indigenous priests and idolatrous practices, however, the continuation of indigenous forms of government is not always marked as problematic. Rather, these practices are encoded in the text in a variety of ways.

Consider the first chapter of the section devoted to this topic, which describes the duties of officials in charge of various trades and categories of tribute, namely: textiles, agriculture, construction, stone masonry, hunting deer and rabbits, hunting ducks and pheasants, fishing with nets, fishing with hooks, chile peppers, grains, beans, honey, maguey wine, animal pelts, featherwork, firewood, drums, carpentry, precious metals, cotton war doublets, bows and arrows, shields, maize, canoes, paddling, spying, messages, war banners, feeding the cazonci's wild animals, medicine, painting, ceramics, sweeping, garlands, and trading. Many of these officials and a few others not mentioned in the prose description are represented pictorially in plates 28 and 29.

The title of this chapter reads: "De la gobernaçion que \tenia y/ tiene esta gente entre si" (173). The original title speaks of indigenous forms of government in the present. The final version, without striking out the use of the present, adds the same verb in the imperfect. Thus, the form of indigenous government under Spanish rule is defined, in the "corrected" version of the Escorial manuscript, as a mixture of the old system and the new.

If one looks closely at the way the various officials are described, a number of distinct patterns become apparent. While some duties are marked as potentially problematic by a later hand, others are let stand in the present tense or rendered exclusively in the imperfect. Thus, some officials are defined as no longer in existence and others as continuing to perform similar functions, metaphorically bridging the gap between indigenous and colonial rule.

For example, the officials known as *ocánbecha*, in charge of taking the census, directing public works projects, and collecting tribute, are described in the present in both versions. The same is true of the official known as *pirúuaqua uándari*, in charge of textiles. The characterization of others, such as the *cacari* (stonemason), *cuzuri* (curer of hides), *pucúriquari* (woodcutter), *paricuti* (paddler), *uaxánoti* (messenger), and *urani atari* (painter of gourds), is in the imperfect, but followed by comments explicitly affirming their continued existence. As observed in chapter one, the continuation of these particular duties (tribute collection, organization of labor, the work of indigenous artisans) was sanctioned, even actively fomented, by the viceregal government.[42]

Other activities, however, are marked by the hand of censorship. *Acháecha*, for example, is one of the terms used to refer to the indigenous lords. The Escorial manuscript describes their duties as follows:

> ay\via/ otros llamados achaecha que heran prinçipales que de contino aconpañavan al caçonçi y le tenian palaçio. (173)
>
> [There are \were/ others called *acháecha* who were principal lords and constant companions of the cazonci who made up his court.]

In this case the mixture of imperfect and present (corresponding to the testimony of the friar-compiler and the indigenous informants, respectively?) was deemed unsuitable by someone during a subsequent perusal of the manuscript (the handwriting and ink used to make the emendation resemble those of the copyist for this section), at which time the initial verb was changed to the imperfect.

This correction is reminiscent of another of the complaints brought against the cazonci during his trial—that he was keeping the principal lords, from the towns controlled by the Spanish encomenderos, in his court in Tzintzuntzan. The cazonci countered by pointing out that these lords formed part of his personal retinue, that they had been raised as a part of his household (Scholes and Adams 1952, 21). The potential for conflict in this case is clear: between indigenous forms of government and Spanish claims and expectations; between the system of personal service enjoyed by the cazonci and the claims of the encomenderos to exclusive control over the personal service, as well as the material wealth, of the inhabitants of the towns under their jurisdiction.

Another official, in charge of making cotton doublets for war, is originally described in both the present and the imperfect, but in the final version, only in the imperfect: "avia otro llamado chereri\n/guequa\vri/de\i/putado para hae\z/er jubones de algodon para las guerras con gente que tiene\ia/ consigo e prençipales" (177).

Several of the corrections in this sentence involve orthographic modifications or clarifications of one kind or another.[43] The replacement of "tiene" by "tenia," however, changes the meaning of the entire passage. From the category of officials who are depicted as somehow bridging the gap between present and past, it is converted to the category of those whose practices are presumably no longer in existence. The specific verb modified, moreover, has to do with the way in which certain people and principal lords would traditionally form part of the retinue of this *cherénguequauri*, or maker of cotton war doublets.

Another example involves the *uarucha*, or fishermen who use nets. They are described as: "pescadores de rred que tienen\ian/ cargo de traer pescado al cazonçi y a todos los señores" (175). In the original version they are characterized as still bringing fish to the indigenous nobles; in the "corrected" version, this activity is relegated to the indigenous past. The message communicated by this change? Theoretically at least, the uarucha now render exclusive service to their Spanish masters.

Other potential areas of tension that can be observed in the Escorial manuscript have to do with treasure and other kinds of material wealth. The feather workers, or *usquarecucha*, for example, are depicted as keeping many brightly colored birds in the towns where they live:

avia otro llamado vzquarecuri diputado sobre todos los plumajeros que labravan de pluma los atavios de sus dioses y hazian los plumajes para vaylar todavia ay estos plumajeros estos tienen\ian/ por los pueblos muchos papagayos grandes colorados y de otros papagayos para la pluma y otros les trayan pluma de garças otros otras maneras de pluma de aves. (176)

[There was another named *usquarecuri* in charge of all the feather workers who used to make the ornaments for the gods. They used also to make the plumes for the dances. These feather workers still exist; they have \used to have/ many large red parrots in the towns and other varieties of parrots for their feathers. Other people would bring them heron feathers, still others all manner of feathers from different birds.]

The continued existence of these feather workers is not marked as problematic. The fact that they still possess precious feathers, however, conflicts with the right of the encomenderos to the material wealth of the towns under their jurisdiction, and perhaps for this reason it was subsequently modified.

Even more potentially inflammatory was the suggestion that the indigenous people were still in possession of gold, silver, and precious jewels. This was another of the accusations that eventually led to the death of the cazonci and the torture of other prominent lords, including Cuiníarángari. It is not surprising, therefore, that the passage describing the duties of the head treasurer is similarly marked by the hand of censorship:

avia otro que hera thesorero mayor diputado para guardar toda la plata y oro con que haç\z/ian las fiestas a sus dioses y este tiene\ia/ diputados otros pre\i/nçipales con gente que tiene\ia/ la cuenta de aquellas joyas. (176)

[There was another who was head treasurer in charge of guarding all the silver and gold with which they made festivals for their gods. This [official] is \was/ in charge of other principal lords with people who keep \kept/ a record of those jewels.]

What is censored is the suggestion that some part of the cazonci's treasure was still in existence at the time of compilation of the Escorial manuscript and that the head treasurer continued to exercise authority in this capacity. Again, one wonders who was responsible for the suppression of this information in the final manuscript. It may have been the friar-compiler, concerned to hide from the reader inconsistencies with his idealized portrait of the colonial authorities as in complete control of the indigenous population. On the other hand, it may have been one of the copyists, interested in countering suspicions as to the degree of resistance to Spanish rule.

The reader may object to the above interpretation of editorial corrections as censorship on the grounds that the oral testimony of the indigenous nobles featuring verbs in the present does not necessarily constitute evidence of the continuation of such activities nor support for them among the local population. As hypothesized in chapter one, the pictures accompanying the section on the cazonci's officials may actually have preceded and served as a point of departure for the written text. If so, it is possible that, as the friar pointed to each of the officials pictured, the indigenous informants simply recited their names and duties. The friar-compiler wrote the names in alphabetic writing directly on the pictures and then he, or perhaps an assistant, transcribed the brief descriptions given by the indigenous informants. In the translation, the initial descriptions of the informants would thus be in the present; the commentary added later by the compiler, in the imperfect.

What this model alone does not explain, however, is the fluctuation between the use of present and imperfect in the testimony attributed to the indigenous informants, even if one discounts, as much as possible, the commentary added by the friar. Why are some types of uses of the present not marked by a later hand, while others are consistently modified? At issue is not the presence of the present or imperfect per se, but rather the *suppression* of the former in certain instances and not in others.

CONCLUSION

Webster's Third New International Dictionary (unabridged version) includes among the definitions of *transparent:* "having the property of transmitting light without appreciable scattering so that bodies lying beyond are entirely visible"; and "free from pretense or deceit." Both definitions are evoked by the friar in his prologue when he counsels Mendoza and the other readers to metaphorically "see through" him in his role as interpreter. The implication is that his own agenda is relatively simple and straightforward. He wants to provide as accurate a portrait as possible of the peoples of Michoacán in order to assist new missionaries and policy makers interested in their conversion to Christianity and adaptation to a Hispanic system of government.

As we have seen in this chapter, however, the editorial strategy the friar pursues is not as "invisible" nor as "free from pretense" as he would have us believe. In those cases where a relatively unmediated presentation of indigenous ways contradicts his vision for the work as a whole, he does not hesitate to shape the verbal or pictorial testimony to his own ends. The same can be said of the indigenous participants who, in spite of their diverse agendas, also had a compelling interest in presenting themselves in the best possible light.

At times these various imperatives come into overt conflict. Thus, the chapter originally entitled "como alçaron otro rey . . ." (245)—"How They Proclaimed Another King . . ."—is changed to "como alçaron otro *señor*..."—"How They Proclaimed Another *Lord* . . ." (emphasis added). Although in other, less prominent, parts of the manuscript the use of the word *king* to refer to the cazonci is not censored (206, 228, 230), here the suggestion that an indigenous ruler is somehow equivalent to a European one is explicitly rejected. Even the latter term—*señor*—was determined around the time of compilation of the Escorial manuscript to be overly exalted by the Spanish crown. A royal decree of 1538 specifically prohibits its use in reference to the indigenous peoples, thereby officially downgrading their leaders' status to that of mere caciques and *principales* (*Recopilación* bk. 6, title 7, law 5).[44]

Other examples of disjunctions between the interests of the friar and indigenous participants include the aforementioned passages in the prologue that refer to their lack of virtue and general immorality, a charge that is repeated more than once (4, 185), as well as more specific accusations of wanton behavior and corruption. For example, in one of the sentences in which the use of the present is not modified, the indigenous lords are described as given to drunkenness and licentiousness (61). Moreover, the friar accuses those ocánbecha who are still in charge of collecting tribute of surreptitiously keeping some of it for themselves (174).

These internal inconsistencies notwithstanding, the agendas of the colonial authorities and indigenous nobles overlapped on a number of important issues; otherwise, the production of a work like the *Relación de Michoacán* would not have been possible. Most notably, both the friar and the nobles had a stake in ingratiating themselves with Viceroy Mendoza and maligning Nuño de Guzmán, who in the course of his tenure as president of the First Audiencia had made enemies among missionaries, Spanish officials, and the native population alike.[45] Moreover, all parties to the making of the *Relación de Michoacán* were concerned to put a positive face on recent evangelization efforts, albeit often in strikingly different ways, as will be explored at greater length in the final two chapters.

To return to the question of the most productive way to read the Escorial manuscript, the tendency to emphasize the idealism of the early missionary-compilers, to the exclusion of other motivating factors, strikes me as inadequate. Granted, there are no shortages of heroes and villains. One thinks of Sahagún, seventy years old, barely able to hold a pen, copying his manuscripts in a hand so shaky as to be almost illegible because his religious superiors had denied him the funds with which to hire a copyist. There is also a spirit of intellectual inquiry and scientific curiosity—the desire to record for posterity the achievements of the most advanced indigenous civilizations before the last knowledgeable survivors died from the effects of war, famine, slavery, old age, or disease.

Nevertheless, it is difficult to cast the youthful friar-compiler of the Escorial manuscript in the role of a great scholar and intellectual and even harder to fit him into the mold of unitary author. What is left, if one is to take seriously the challenge to integrate the *Relación de Michoacán* into the corpus of ethnohistorical writings by the early missionaries of Mexico, is to show that his contributions are unique because they are relatively minimal. In the history of interpretation of this text, one of the most persistent mistakes has been to attribute too many of its exceptional features to the friar. For instance, the millenialism ascribed to him by Georges Baudot is more convincingly read, as I argue in chapter four, as a function of a different sort of messianic fervor originating in the oral performance of the petámuti.

Though the friar may have served as the final screen through which everything was sifted and as a controlling presence during every stage of the compilation process, the narratives in the *Relación de Michoacán* draw much of their force from the storytelling abilities and pictorial imagination of his indigenous collaborators. Indeed, only when the friar's contributions to the Escorial manuscript are contextualized as one voice and one hand among many does it become possible to appreciate the text for what it is, rather than focusing on the ways it fails to measure up to the standards set by later missionary-compilers.

3

WRITING IN PICTURES

The *Caracha* (Scribes-Painters)

> La puerta es para que cualquiera pueda entrar y es por donde entran las visiones.
>
> —*Ernesto Cardenal*

The goal of this chapter is to sketch out a strategy for reading the drawings of the *Relación de Michoacán* based on the assumption that they collectively embody a coherent system of meaning complementary to the prose portions of the text yet capable of standing alone in and of themselves.[1] When the drawings are viewed in this light, their interpretation not only adds to our understanding of the oral tradition, but also vice versa. Far from fulfilling a purely ornamental function as mere illustrations, the work of the caracha constitutes a fundamental component of the text on a par with the contributions of the friar-compiler and the indigenous elders who provided the oral testimony.

Among the ancient Nahuas, writing was referred to as *in tlilli, in tlapalli* or the black, the red (Boone 2000), 35. Theirs was a philosophy of writing that highlighted the importance of color in determining textual meaning. Another characteristic of Mesoamerican writing systems is the complementarity between pictographic and oral traditions. Two concepts usually defined in opposition to each other in the western European tradition—the graphic transcription of oral narratives and the graphic representation of visual phenomena—are conflated into one category under the aegis of the *tlacuilo* or scribe-painter—the Nahua equivalent of the carari of Michoacán.[2]

In the *calmecac*—the specialized school for the training of priests in Aztec Mexico—the pupils learned to memorize the songs, poems, and speeches of their ancestors with the assistance of the painted codices. As a *cuicapicqui,* or Nahua poet, explains:

Yo canto las pinturas del libro,
lo voy desplegando,
soy cual florido papagayo,
hago hablar los códices,
en el interior de la casa de las pinturas. (cited in León-Portilla 1996, 42)

[I sing the pictures of the book,
As I turn its pages,
I am like a flowering parrot,
I make the codices speak,
In the interior of the house of paintings.] (my trans.)

A similar complementarity between spoken words and visual images is one of the defining characteristics of modern motion pictures, but it is not normally associated in the Western tradition with reading and writing, the book as artifact, nor with cultural literacy in an academic, as opposed to a popular, sense.

Another feature of Mesoamerican writing is the way it is permeated by religious symbolism and thereby plays a central role in facilitating communication between gods and mortals. Thus, while alphabetic writing, as represented above all in the printed word, is generally considered one of the underpinnings of modern secular democratic institutions, those in charge of reading and writing the pictographic codices tended to be priests who belonged to a highly trained and specialized elite. Note the parallels with the European manuscript tradition prior to the invention of the printing press: the role of monks as guardians and transmitters of esoteric knowledge; the ritualized public reading of sacred texts at designated times; the importance of illumination as a function of textual meaning.

The ritual significance of prehispanic codices applied as well to the materials from which they were made. Paper made from the bark of a ficus (wild fig) or other tree belonging to the Moraceae family, sprinkled with the blood a penitent would obtain by piercing his or her own tongue and earlobes, was a common sacrificial offering from those eager to gain the favor of the gods. Other forms of paper were made from deerskin and maguey or cotton fiber, all of which have multiple sacred connotations in Mesoamerica.[3]

References to pictorial writing and to the ritualistic use of paper are less numerous for Michoacán than for some other areas of Mesoamerica during the colonial period, but they are still fairly common. A serpent-butterfly made of paper, worn by a priest during a special ceremonial dance, is mentioned in the one surviving folio related to indigenous religious ceremonies in Escorial Ms. C.IV.5 (9). A little flag made of paper is also described as part of the attire worn by captives destined to be sacrificed to the gods (160). In other parts of the text, paper and writing are closely associated with the role of messenger known as uaxánoti and the indigenous judicial system.

Thus, Don Pedro Cuiníarángari describes how the cazonci sent him to the house of a rival noble named Timas with a letter containing a death sentence against the latter (262). Plate 35, which accompanies a chapter on the administration of justice, similarly shows a messenger exchanging a piece of folded paper or cloth with an indigenous judge, presumably containing information related to the crimes and/or sentences of those being punished at left. Another drawing, plate 29, depicts a group of messengers identified in Castilian as *carteros* (letter carriers), the foremost of whom is holding an object resembling a letter on a stick. If one holds the Escorial manuscript up to the light, one can see that this "letter" was originally represented as a large crumpled paper (or perhaps a crudely drawn folded tira) like that in plate 35.[4]

The evidence from other sources from Michoacán also suggests a strong correlation between painting, letter writing, map making, and the administration of justice. One of the first Spaniards to visit the area, Francisco Montaño, related that the governors of the towns sent pictures of him and his companions to the cazonci showing how they traveled, what they ate, how they slept, and the arms and clothes they were wearing (Cervantes de Salazar [1566] 1985, 786; bk. 6, ch. 15). After the death of the cazonci, the indigenous peoples of the region often submitted pictures as evidence in Spanish courts. The residents of Tzintzuntzan, for instance, brought a complaint against the corregidor Juan Alvarez de Castañeda in 1533 in the form of a painting made on two "mantas" (cloths). In 1535 the inhabitants of the towns around Lake Pátzcuaro presented a painting demonstrating that several encomenderos had stolen their lands (Escobar Olmedo 1989, 88–89, 143). In 1549 Bishop Quiroga was sent a feather painting representing the communities of the Lake Pátzcuaro Basin (León [1903] 1984, 319). And Pablo Beaumont, author of an eighteenth-century history of Michoacán, copied a multisectional painted tira, related to events that took place in the sixteenth century, from an indigenous elder by the name of Cuiní ([ca. 1778] 1985, 2:30, 138).[5] Hans Roskamp, whose valuable study of colonial-era pictographic materials from the region is the most comprehensive to date, lists a total of nineteen surviving originals or copies of codices, *lienzos* (painted sheets of cloth), titles, and coats of arms, including the drawings of the *Relación de Michoacán* and the Beaumont "maps" (1998a, 75, 283–87).[6]

As for linguistic references, several of the indigenous terms listed in the 1559 dictionary of Fray Maturino Gilberti suggest that the inhabitants of Michoacán practiced a form of "writing in pictures" (Martínez Baracs 1997, 122). These include: *carani* (to write or to paint); *carari* (scribe or painter); *ambéngaricuni* or *ambétanstani* (to erase what is written); *siranda* (book or paper or letter); *sirunda* (ink); *sirútzeti* (something bound in the form of a book).

The contrary evidence consists of: (1) the observation made by colonial-era witnesses, most notably the friar-compiler of the *Relación de Michoacán*, that the Indians of the province lacked "books";[7] (2) the absence of surviving prehispanic prototypes, in contrast to those from areas such as central Mexico, Oaxaca, Yucatan, and Guatemala;[8] and (3) preliminary studies of the iconography of ceramic design style, which suggest a relatively low level of standardization in terms of decoration and few links with pictorial manuscripts from the region.[9]

Even if one assumes the controversial position that some form of "picture writing" was well established in Michoacán at the time of the Spanish conquest, its links to the ruling Uacúsecha elite remain problematic. Roskamp, for instance, hypothesizes that it may have been developed by the local Nahuatl-speaking population (1998a, 31–32, 284), in which case it probably constituted a specialty subordinated to the needs of the state, but not generally practiced by the cazonci or those of his ethnic group.

It is not essential for the purposes of this book to posit the existence of a full-fledged independent writing system in prehispanic Michoacán. As mentioned in the introduction, the crux of the matter is the extent to which the drawings under consideration can be shown to echo indigenous conceptual categories manifested in other artistic media, such as oral tradition, as well as the viability of positing analogies with pictographic materials produced by culture groups from other regions.

If sufficient parallels can be established between the prose and pictures of the Escorial manuscript, it follows that the two textual components operate on a par with one another in their ability to provide a window into the ways of thought of the inhabitants of the Lake Pátzcuaro Basin circa 1538–41, especially the indigenous nobility. Insofar as the analysis of the pictures suggests links with pictorial sources from other areas of

Mesoamerica, moreover, they can be seen to partake, however indirectly, of a longstanding and widespread tradition of "writing in pictures."

It is important to note that some steps have already been taken in the direction of validating the significance of the pictures as text. Recent editions have included high quality full-color illustrations as well as analyses of them by Hans Roskamp (2000), Nuria Salazar Simarro (2000), Juan José Batalla Rosado (2001), and Francisco Miranda Godínez (2001). My contribution to this discussion highlights the notion of spatiotemporal organization as a sort of pictorial grammar that aids in elucidating the relationships among the individual icons in a given composition.

In contrast to the prevailing view in the western European tradition, according to which artistic value and utilitarian function are defined in inverse proportion to each other, for the caracha of Michoacán writing and painting were not mutually exclusive activities. It follows that it is not enough to inquire as to the literal meaning of a particular composition; its symbolic structure and links with other systems also need to be understood. Moreover, a necessary precondition for this task is the articulation of a sufficiently broad definition of writing to allow for the making of comparisons.

Fortunately, a good deal of progress has been made in the above areas in recent years within the field of Mesoamerican studies. The pioneering work of Joaquín Galarza, for instance, has been instrumental in articulating the system used by the Nahua tlacuilo to construct "word pictures." Among his major insights is the recognition that the larger pictorial scenes in central Mexican codices function in a similar manner to the smaller name and place glyphs that have long been understood to represent discrete phonemes. Other scholars, such as Ferdinand Anders, Maarten Jansen, and Luis Reyes García, have made significant contributions to elucidating the multiple connections between surviving pictographic codices and related oral testimonies in Nahuatl, Mixtec, and Castilian that were transcribed during the early colonial period.

Recent debates concerning the definition of writing are also germane to this discussion. Over the past few decades, scholars such as Elizabeth Hill Boone and Walter D. Mignolo have done much to deconstruct the notion that alphabetic writing is the inevitable culmination of a unidirectional evolutionary process.[10] If one defines writing, in the most general sense, as "the making of visible marks on some kind of material, in accordance with a set of preestablished conventions, in order to communicate relatively specific ideas,"[11] it follows that it is associated with multiple functions, some of which may resemble the features considered of primary importance in the Western tradition (i.e., the ability to reconstruct a message verbatim), while others may not (such as the use of color and other visual cues to add multiple layers of symbolic meaning). The existence of any overlap at all is significant, however, for it suggests that the drawings of the *Relación de Michoacán* are at least partially analogous to an alphabetic prose narrative.

According to Boone and Mignolo, a writing system like that of the Nahuas, which contains a mixture of pictographic and more abstract ideographic signs, will not always evolve in the direction of maximizing the arbitrary relationship between signifier and signified. Still, there is no consensus at present among those who specialize in the categorization of writing systems as to how to classify those that are not unequivocally phonetic. Of the three best-known Mesoamerican varieties, the more abstract Maya hieroglyphs tend to be less controversial than the more highly pictorial Mixtec and Aztec scripts.

Pictographic signs are those that can be readily identified as representing some object from the material world, such as the sun, an eagle, or water. Ideographic signs put the accent more consistently on the metaphorical connotations or other related attributes of the objects represented. Thus, an eye may represent a star; a stylized circle, the concept of marketplace; an A-shaped "trapeze-and-ray" sign, an abstract notion like year.[12]

Both pictographic and ideographic signs can be used to represent discreet phonemes, syllables, or the sounds of complete words. The placename Huexotzinco, for instance, is represented in the codices Boturini and Mendoza by a willow (*huexotl* in Nahuatl) emerging from the lower portion of a human body (*tzintli*). Since *tzin* is a homonym for "small" or "new" in Nahuatl, this word picture of a willow with human buttocks and legs yields a toponym meaning "the smaller or more recently founded Huexotla" (Dibble 1971, 329–30).

The tendency to dismiss nonexclusively phonetic notational systems as either not writing at all or not "full writing" (Gelb [1952] 1963, 12) and to assume that the pictographic end of the spectrum represents at best a primitive or incipient form of writing has clear implications for the analysis of the surviving colonial-era pictorial documents from Michoacán. Indeed, the parallels between the dominant paradigms about writing in our own time and those that informed the literary works of the early missionaries of the New World are striking.

When the friar-compiler of the *Relación de Michoacán* speaks of the lack of understanding of the moral virtues among the indigenous peoples of the region, for example, he draws an analogy between the absence of words for abstract concepts like chastity, temperance, charity, and justice in their vocabulary and their lack of books (4). The implication is that the sort of knowledge contained in European-style books is markedly different from, and inherently superior to, a knowledge that is grounded in the materiality of the physical universe, just as the use of abstract words is indicative of more highly developed rational and moral faculties than the simple naming of everyday objects.[13]

But what if moral properties are considered to be contained within physical objects? If, indeed, they are seen as inseparable from them? In the categorization of notational systems, this would mean that rather than drawing an absolute distinction between pictographic and ideographic signs, the former would tend to contain the latter within themselves. An arrow would thus represent an arrow, but it might simultaneously serve as a shorthand for those attributes associated with the Chichimec virtues of bravery, self-sacrifice, and expert marksmanship, as well as with the warriors and solar deities who incarnate these ideals.[14] As in poetry, the literal and metaphoric are one.

I chose the example of an arrow because there is a memorable episode in the *Relación de Michoacán* in which the Uacúsecha hero Taríacuri, while still in a relatively powerless position vis à vis rival ethnic groups in the Lake Pátzcuaro Basin, sends some arrows to the lords of Curínguaro as their portion of the booty of rich plumes, gold, silver, and precious stones that he and his warriors have obtained from raids on the people of the *tierra caliente*, or hot country. The elderly messengers from Curínguaro are told by Taríacuri that the green arrows are long green plumes; the blue arrows, turquoise necklaces; the white arrows, silver; the yellow arrows, gold; the red arrows, rich parrot feathers; and the variously colored obsidian arrowheads, cloth, maize, beans, and other "seeds."

The young lord Huresqua and his brothers react indignantly when they receive this message, for they can see with their own eyes that, instead of valuable tribute items, Taríacuri has sent them only painted arrows. Following the advice of their sister, the prototype of the unfaithful wife in the *Relación de Michoacán*, they break the arrows and throw them on the fire. When their elderly father, Chánshori, hears what has happened, he is much troubled, for he fears that the arrows must have some divine properties—that they are, in other words, more than they seem to be.[15]

This episode occurs towards the end of a series of anecdotes about Taríacuri that collectively demonstrate his skill at deceiving rival lords as to the true meaning of important symbolic items. Previously, he had

Drawings of the Escorial Manuscript

PLATE 1. Presentation of the manuscript to Viceroy Don Antonio de Mendoza (Reprinted from Franco Mendoza [ca. 1541] 2000, 322.)

PLATE 3. Alliance between the Uacúsecha and Huréndetiecha (Reprinted from Franco Mendoza [ca. 1541] 2000, 358.)

PLATE 24. Petámuti's address to the assembled lords and caciques (Reprinted from Franco Mendoza [ca. 1541] 2000, 526.)

PLATE 27. Genealogy of the principal Uacúsecha lords (Reprinted from Franco Mendoza [ca. 1541] 2000, 546.)

PLATE 33. War as a means of "feeding" the gods (Reprinted from Franco Mendoza [ca. 1541] 2000, 589.)

Plate 38. How the commoners ~~marry~~ \used to marry/ (Reprinted from Franco Mendoza [ca. 1541] 2000, 615.)

Açotado y Rey en la gra deSudios ani übern y lagos gacu figo aña
—onges don Guelles la nobes que don fraydo defas entradas y lagaca
A todos el que concgonea nan cobrado cenavos y cusavase con lo das aqu
llos uno guesa queadian sido Desupadec y andando el tienpo le ny
tran en su caso lo trâsi usos de ozeriques y sn oteas

Delos aqueros que tubo esta gente y sueños an
tes que viniesen los españoles a esta provincia

PLATE 42. Omens prefiguring the Spanish conquest (Reprinted from Franco Mendoza [ca. 1541] 2000, 640.)

PLATE 44. Arrival of the conquistadors in the Lake Pátzcuaro Basin (Reprinted from Franco Mendoza [ca. 1541] 2000, 665.)

succeeded in getting the lords of Taríaran, Curínguaro, and Xaráquaro to eat human flesh that was not properly sacrificed. The implication is that these deceptions are what eventually turn the gods against his rivals, thereby setting the scene for the subsequent rise to power of the Uacúsecha.[16]

What this story is telling us is that the meaning of an arrow, or of anything else for that matter, is highly context dependent and that the ability to accurately read the divine attributes of everyday objects is a requirement for those who seek to govern. Significantly, it is the elderly Chánshori who recognizes the prophetic import of the broken arrows; and, in spite of his apprehension for his descendants, he cannot help laughing at the ingeniousness of the deception:

> Yo que soy viejo he oido esto ya hahora me huelgo de no aver muerto por oyr esto. (89)
>
> [I, who am old, I have heard this, yes. Now I rejoice to have not died in exchange for hearing this.]

Chánshori's reaction validates the right of the Uacúsecha to rule based on the skill at reading, or interpreting, signs that constitutes part of Taríacuri's legacy to them.

Taríacuri's skill at reading signs is consistent with the Nahua conception of the *tlamatini* (wise man) as one "who can 'look' at the sky or at the painted books and interpret them to tell stories based on [the] discerning of signs" (Mignolo 1995, 104). It is also reminiscent of the shamanic inner vision according to which magical transformation is the primary means of achieving transcendence. As Markman and Markman observe, perhaps the most essential form of this transformation is that it "does not require abandoning one state for another but allows them all to exist simultaneously" (1989, 142).

As mentioned above, the layering of symbolic meanings is a defining characteristic of Mesoamerican pictographic writing in general, with its use of color, gesture, and other visual cues to generate multiple metaphorical associations. The drawings of the *Relación de Michoacán* differ from the pictographic compositions of Nahua origin, however, in that there are fewer overt indications as to which pictorial elements are functioning in any given context as symbols, since they are all highly representational. There does not appear to be anything analogous to common central Mexican glyphs like the blue speech scroll, for instance, which consistently identifies the speaker of a ritual discourse.

On the other hand, another typical device for indicating speech among the Nahuas, a pointing finger, is found repeatedly in the drawings of the *Relación de Michoacán*, often in association with individuals who are issuing commands. Thus Taríacuri, pictured in his palace at the right in plate 18, is clearly the one responsible for ordering his eldest son's death, according to the carari responsible for that drawing. This motif is also frequently found in pictures that correspond to prose passages with lengthy ritual speeches, like that of the captain general in plate 32 who is addressing the assembled warriors. At times the pointing finger can also provide information about the topic of a conversation, as in plate 42 (color section) where the two priests at lower left point upward to the various omens foretelling the Spanish conquest.

Rather than the combination found in central Mexican codices of the stylized speech scroll and the pointing finger (a visual metaphor whose meaning is transparent even to the uninitiated), the drawings of the *Relación de Michoacán* manifest a decided preference for the latter type of sign, to the exclusion of more nonrepresentational ones. Ironically, these pictures are difficult for outsiders to read in large part because they seem so obvious, so banal, so devoid of exotic peculiarities.

This lack of depth is only apparent, however. Once one begins to look for the conceptual possibilities inherent in the recurring pictorial motifs of the *Relación de Michoacán*, it is not difficult to find verbal and visual clues to assist in decoding them. And, although in some ways they closely parallel European iconography, in other ways they are markedly different.

Consider plate 27 (color section), which shows Iréticátame (here spelled Thicatame), the mythical founder of the Uacúsecha dynasty, lying at the base of a tree on whose branches are perched the various lords who succeeded him. A meandering red line connects each lord's hand to that of his successor as head of of the Uacúsecha; or, in some cases, younger sibling, for the brothers Uápeani II-Pauácume II and Zétaco-Aramen ruled jointly. When more than one lord share the same branch (i.e., Uápeani II and Pauácume II), it may be because they are dual founders of the same lineage. When the line of succession splits (i.e., Uápeani II-Pauácume II to both Zétaco-Aramen and Taríacuri), so does the red line that represents it.[17]

The carari responsible for painting this picture provides us with a blueprint for reading the symbolism of a large number of related icons. Clearly, the tree is the dynasty; the founder is the tree's roots; each bough represents a separate lineage or branch of the family tree; the last cazonci, Tzintzicha Tangáxoan (executed by Nuño de Guzmán in 1530) is the crown of the tree; Taríacuri—the main subject of the petámuti's epic history—is situated at its midpoint.[18]

Moreover, it appears to be an oak tree, for each of the lords is in a seat resembling an acorn cup, a shape reminiscent of the uaxántsiqua that can be observed in many pictorial representations from Michoacán. Indeed, the lords are sitting in acorn cups because they *are* acorns—that is, the fruit of the tree, a visual metaphor underscored by their green clover wreaths that echo the crisscross pattern of the woody cup. At the same time the wreaths are evocative of leaves, in which case the lords can be understood to represent both acorns and trees, descendants of kings and progenitors of future kings.[19]

The meandering red line connecting the lords is like the sap that flows from one successor to the next. It is also that which guides the reader in the proper temporal progression by showing how to move through the pictorial text.

The multiple overlapping metaphors can be summarized as follows. The founder is the one who dreams (note that Iréticátame is the only one whose eyes are closed); he is the *áxame,* or sacrificer responsible for feeding the gods (note the characteristic sacrificial knife in his left hand); he is the roots of the oak tree. The successors are the branches of the tree; they are those who sit in the uaxántsiqua, those who provide nourishment; they are the seeds of future lineages. The red line is the divine lifeforce of the Uacúsecha; it is the connection between those who rule and the gods, the dynamic principle set in motion by the reading of the text.[20]

In order to identify a corpus of visual metaphors with specific regional characteristics in the drawings of the *Relación de Michoacán,* it is important to establish that the above icons, when they appear in other pictures, tend to maintain the same meaning. In plate 27 (color section) the analogy between humans and oak trees is relatively explicit. In other drawings it is not so clear. How one interprets the meaning of any given tree depends on both pictorial and oral narrative context.

Thus, in plate 9, the tree at whose base Taríacuri is unsuccessfully attempting to dream also appears to be a metaphor for the branch of the Uacúsecha that rose briefly to prominence under Taríacuri, only to lose political authority with the transfer of the capital to Tzintzuntzan during the reign of Tsitsíspandáquare. If Taríacuri were not sitting at the tree's base, if the roots were not visible, and if the oral narrative did not present his behavior as an attempt to advance the fortunes of his descendants by establishing direct contact with the gods, the symbolic reading of this icon would not be warranted. Since trees or poles are also the means by which the gods descend from the heavens to earth (112), there is an implied correlation between the concepts of divine intervention in human affairs and the founding of a strong dynasty capable of maintaining clear channels of communication with the celestial gods.

The same theme is echoed in plate 19, which shows Taríacuri's "nephews" Hiripan and Tangáxoan similarly engaged in an attempt to attract the attention of the gods.[21] In this case their efforts are more successful, and we see the gods Curícaueri at right and Xarátanga at left prodding them awake in their dreams. Does it follow that the various trees depicted in this drawing represent different dynasties? Possibly, but not necessarily so.

The fact that a tree is incorporated into a landscape setting should not be interpreted as indicating that it does not also have some deeper symbolic meaning, as in plate 9. On the other hand, one cannot assume that all trees are equally significant when they appear in the drawings of the *Relación de Michoacán*. The trees in plate 19 may simply serve—as in a Renaissance European painting—to evoke the setting for Hiripan and Tangáxoan's dreams, which occurred at the base of mountains covered with oak trees on the shores of Lake Pátzcuaro.

For humanmade objects like the uaxántsiqua, the symbolic import is more consistent, irrespective of narrative context. It is safe to assume that a person sitting on a uaxántsiqua is in a position of authority. This is due in part to the function of such auxiliary items as social symbols. The wearing of a lip plug, or *angámequa*, for instance, always indicates some kind of official status in the drawings of the *Relación de Michoacán*, for only those angámecha chosen by the cazonci to represent their respective "lineages" were allowed to wear them.[22]

When an angámecha is sitting on a uaxántsiqua in the *Relación de Michoacán*, it can be interpreted as a good omen, for he is fulfilling his proper role. If a uaxántsiqua is empty, it is potentially a portent of disaster, for it means that the iréchequa is deprived of the acorn, of nourishment, of a future. In plate 13, for example, the seats of both Taríacuri and his eldest son, Curátame, are empty, as are the bowls of food behind them. In an adjoining room the son attacks his father, another clear reference to a violation of the natural order of things.

In another drawing, plate 40, the uaxántsiqua is temporarily unoccupied due to the death of previous ruler. This state of affairs is analogous to the metaphor of a house devoid of smoke that is mentioned in the prose narrative as a synonym for great sadness and deprivation:

> ... que estando los señores en casa ponen mucha leña en los hogares y se lebanta mucho humo lo qual no es ansi muriendo que todo esta deshierto y oscuro como niebla. (226–27)
>
> [... for when the lords are at home, they place a lot of firewood on the hearths, which gives rise to much smoke. [But] it is not thus when they die, for all is deserted and dark as fog.]

Firewood is consistently encoded in the *Relación de Michoacán* as a metaphor for tribute; smoke, as one of the primary means of maintaining a link between the heavens and earth, gods and mortals. The image of the empty uaxántsiqua can thus be seen to tie in with a whole series of cultural metaphors that play on the connections between humans and living wood, deadwood and tribute, smoke and life-sustaining nourishment (in both a material and spiritual sense), fire and political legitimacy.

One of the advantages of reading the drawings of the *Relación de Michoacán* in tandem with the prose passages is that it greatly extends the number of available cultural motifs that can be gleaned from each of them separately. In terms of the ability to generalize from the information thus obtained, moreover, it is fortunate that both the oral testimonies and pictorial compositions are based on the contributions of more than one individual. The multiple authorship of the drawings can be inferred from the wide variety of styles apparent in such recurrent motifs as the standing figure, the seated figure, the three-quarter profile, and the thatched roof.[23]

An icon rendered by different painters, yet which has similar symbolic connotations, can be more readily assumed to represent a culturally shared rather than a personally idiosyncratic world view. As Alfredo López Austin explains:

> In many ways, cosmovision may be compared to grammar, the work of everyone and of no one, a product of reason but not of consciousness, coherent and possessing a unifying nucleus that increases its radius to the degree that it is restricted to social sectors that are more homogeneous. All of this is true because a cosmovision is not the result of speculation but of practical daily relationships. ([1994] 1997, 9)

Insofar as the caracha of the Escorial manuscript share the values of the indigenous community in which they were raised, the "grammar" expressed in their compositions will echo prehispanic prototypes, a state of affairs that does not necessarily preclude their having been influenced by European cultural traditions as well.

Indeed, some of the symbolic associations found in the drawings of the *Relación de Michoacán* correspond quite closely to Western pictorial models. The notion of a family tree, for instance, is a commonplace. A somewhat less obvious parallel in plate 27 (color section) is the way in which those lords who died violently are depicted with the instruments responsible for their deaths—Iréticátame with a lance in his side, Tzintzicha Tangáxoan engulfed in flames. Such symbolism is highly evocative of Christian iconography in which saints are typically represented with the instruments of their martyrdom.

These parallels are interesting, for they suggest an incipient blending of analogous European and indigenous traditions—a nascent form of transculturation—with the ruling lineages of the early colonial period at the vanguard of this process. As we have seen in previous chapters, this principle is at the heart of the methodology employed in the making of the *Relación de Michoacán*. In the prose passages the voices of the indigenous informants and the friar-compiler tend to be combined within the same sentence. In the drawings European and indigenous pictorial conventions coexist in such a way that it not always easy to tell them apart.[24]

Within the general parameters of this overlapping of cultural conventions, it is important to note that the forty-four drawings of the *Relación de Michoacán* exhibit a fairly wide range in their degree of indigenous versus European pictorial influence. At the more Europeanized end of the spectrum is the frontispiece, with its individuation of the facial features of the viceroy and friar; ample use of shading to create the illusion of three-dimensionality; and encoding of size according to the principles of proportionality (the book is smaller than the friar and the viceroy who hold it) and relative distance from the viewer (the viceroy is smaller than the friar because he is farther away). That these techniques are only imperfectly realized does not minimize the significance of the fact that the carari responsible for this drawing both was familiar with Western pictorial conventions and considered them more appropriate for the representation of certain figures—the friar and viceroy and, to a lesser extent, the indigenous governor—than for the less-Hispanicized native priests.

At the other end of the spectrum is plate 33 (color section), with its circular distribution of largely free-floating figures, a partial example of what Donald Robertson calls "scattered-attribute space" ([1959] 1994, 61). Here the color, rather than being graduated to show texture, is applied in flat washes. The size of the figures, moreover, is not so much a function of proportionality or distance from the viewer as of symbolic or narrative significance.

The burning buildings, in accordance with Mesoamerican pictorial conventions, represent conquered communities, while the humans with their hearts torn from their chests represent sacrificial victims. Both are more or less equally important as symbols of war, which is the subject of this particular composition. The fact that real buildings are proportionately larger than the humans who inhabit them is irrelevant to the system of representation exemplified by this drawing. Moreover, rather than attempting to establish a fixed external viewpoint for the viewers, with the various pictorial figures arranged in accordance with a theoretical vanishing point (the key to the technique of linear perspective developed during the European Renaissance),[25] plate 33 (color section) encourages the viewers to perceive the events depicted from multiple positions simultaneously.[26]

The majority of the drawings of the *Relación de Michoacán* fall roughly midway between these two extremes, with some movement toward creating an illusion of three-dimensionality and the incorporation of figures into a landscape setting, but also a clear tendency to suggest multiple perspectives and to repeat standard leitmotifs with few attempts at individualization.

Within this dual structure, repetition is often a function of the juxtaposition of culturally divergent techniques to communicate analogous ideas.[27] Thus, in plate 27 (color section), the banners bearing the names of the lords in alphabetic writing help the Spanish-speaking readers identify the various Uacúsecha lords. For those readers familiar with indigenous symbolism, the position on the oak tree and other pictorial details associated with the various lords serve a similar function. Curátame II is easy to identify, because he is holding the club with which he was killed in accordance with his father's orders. Those lords who excelled at "feeding" the gods through their prowess in war are shown carrying bow and arrow. These sorts of narrative tags are handy mnemonic devices. Like the Homeric "rosy-fingered dawn," they are the fundamental building blocks with which the epic histories and pictorial compositions of the indigenous peoples of Michoacán are constructed.

The early missionaries of New Spain were quick to recognize the pedagogical value of the Mesoamerican familiarity with reading and writing in pictures. Those responsible for the evangelization of Michoacán were no exception. As Pablo Beaumont explains:

> Como habían advertido estos benditos padres que los indios tarascos usaban como los demás naturales de esta Nueva España, de símbolos y pinturas para tratar de todas las cosas . . . hacían pintar en varios lienzos de metl o pita, o de palma, en unos, los artículos de la fe; en otros, los diez mandamientos de la ley de Dios, los siete Sacramentos, y demás cosas importantes de la doctrina cristiana. ([ca. 1778] 1985, 2:139; bk. 2, ch. 18)

> [Since these saintly fathers had observed that the Tarascan Indians, like the other natives of this New Spain, used symbols and pictures to treat of all things . . . they had them paint on various pieces of cloth made of maguey or pita fiber, or of palm leaves; on some, the articles of the faith; on others, the ten commandments of the law of God, the seven sacraments and other important things in Christian doctrine.] (my trans.)

By providing the indigenous painters of New Spain with some rudimentary instruction in European pictorial techniques, or at least access to models on which they could base their own drawings such as woodcuts from printed books or illuminated manuscripts, the Franciscans and other friars hastened the process of transculturation. For a brief period of time during the sixteenth and seventeenth centuries, a bicultural form of literacy flourished among a certain sector of indigenous society, with pictures and alphabetic writing juxtaposed as part of the same narrative compositions.

Ironically, it was those prehispanic codices whose religious symbolism was most immediately apparent that elicited from the early missionaries both the greatest expressions of horror and the greatest acknowledgment of their value as depositories of cultural knowledge more or less on a par with European books. The friars' Christian sensibilities were enormously offended at the sight of painted Maya, Mixtec, and Nahua screenfolds covered with dried human blood. Many of these books, folded accordion-style and stored in temples and other sanctuaries, were destroyed in bonfires or secreted away by those in charge of preserving the ancient ways for posterity.

In Michoacán, in contrast, references to picture writing in colonial-era sources tend to emphasize its more prosaic nature: the recording of judicial sentences, of boundaries between communities, of strategic military information. For the friar-compiler of the *Relación de Michoacán,* such "primitive" forms of record keeping were hardly worthy of mention. There is certainly no indication that the early missionaries of Michoacán considered these representational paintings a threat to their evangelical activities in the way that Fray Andrés de Olmos viewed the codices of central Mexico or Fray Diego de Landa those of Yucatan.[28]

As in other areas of Mesoamerica, however, the act of writing in pictures was also a sacred activity in Michoacán, one intimately related to the process of maintaining intact vital channels of communication between gods and mortals. "Aqui pues an de benir los dioses del çielo"/"Here, then, the gods of the sky will come" (193), says the captain general in plate 32 as he stands before a circular map drawn in the earth with five houses on its rim, another house some distance away, and long, wavy lines radiating outwards from the circle, between which are located rows of sticks. He continues:

> . . . donde esta la traza del pueblo que avemos de conquistar aqui donde ay leña para los fuegos en quatro partes donde an de benir las aguilas rreales que son los dioses mayores y las otras aguilas pequeñas que son los dioses menores y los gabilanes y alcones y otras abes muy ligeras de rrapiña llamadas tintivapeme aqui nos faboresçeran los dioses del çielo. (193)
>
> [. . . where the outline of the town we are to conquer is located. Here where the wood for the fires is arrayed in four parts, where the golden eagles who are the elder gods, the other smaller eagles who are lesser gods, the hawks and falcons and other light birds of prey called *tíntivápeme* are to come. Here the gods of the sky will favor us.]

In this passage writing is a means of invoking the gods, of erasing the boundary between earth and sky, as much as it is a component of basic military strategy.[29]

In the remainder of this chapter I will argue for the way the work of the caracha created the forty-four drawings of the *Relación de Michoacán* constitutes a sacred activity, a gateway to the realm of the spirits. The visions contained therein are apparent for all to see, as in the quote from Ernesto Cardenal's poem cited at the beginning of the chapter. First, however, the "door" that provides access to them must be identified.

WRITING THE COSMOS

The original inspiration for this book comes from the pioneering work of Rolena Adorno on the drawings of Felipe Guamán Poma de Ayala's *Nueva corónica y buen gobierno* (Adorno 1979, 1981, 1986, 1989, 2001; see also López-Baralt 1979, 1988, 1990). In my search for a similar colonial text with both prose and pictures that had yet to be incorporated into the canon of colonial Spanish-American literary studies, I came upon the *Relación de Michoacán* and, from the beginning, was convinced that the key to understanding the drawings was to unlock the secret of their spatio-temporal organization.

Adorno builds on the iconographic studies of Erwin Panofsky and B. A. Uspensky, as well as on descriptions of Andean territorial organization by Tom Zuidema, Nathan Wachtel, and Juan Ossio among others. She thereby demonstrates how the Andean concepts of upper and lower, or hanan and hurin, structure the interpretation of the four hundred pen-and-ink drawings.

The *mappa mundi* of Tawantinsuyu, variously spelled Tahuantinsuyo (Quechua for "the land of the four parts or corners"), included by Guamán Poma in his text provides a blueprint for filling in the symbolic associations attributed to figures located in each of five primary spatial positions. The center is "the position of preferred value" (Adorno 1986, 89), corresponding to the place occupied in the mappa mundi by Cuzco, the Incan capital. The center left (*hanan*) corresponds to Chinchaysuyu, associated with the concept of descent through the male line. The center right (*hurin*) corresponds to Collasuyu, which is related to the concept of matrilineal descent. This primary male-female opposition is structured along a diagonal axis running from lower left to upper right. A second diagonal, which intersects with the first, further defines those qualities associated with above center (the location of Antisuyu, home of the fierce jungle people, whose "barbarous" customs contrast with the "civilized" demeanor of the Chinchays) and below center (the position occupied by Cuntisuyu, an arid coastal region, whose poverty contrasts with the wealth of Collasuyu).

Unfortunately, there is no such clearly labeled mappa mundi in the surviving pictorial texts from early colonial Michoacán. Instead, there is a story that fulfills an analogous function and which is recounted in the 1585 littera annua from the Jesuit Francisco Ramírez to his superiors in Castile. As I argue in chapter one, sections 42 to 48 may have been copied verbatim from some earlier version of the missing part one of the

Escorial manuscript. In any case, much of the metaphorical language found therein echoes images contained in the prose and pictures of the *Relación de Michoacán*.

In the Ramírez letter the creation of all living things is described as having emanated from the womb of a goddess positioned facedown:

> ... que tenía la cabeza hacia poniente, y los pies hacia oriente, y un brazo a septentrión, y otro a meridión y el dios del mar la tenía de la cabeza y la madre de los dioses de los pies y otras dos diosas, una de un brazo y otra de otro, porque no cayese. (Ramírez [1585] 1959, 494)

> [... who had her head pointed west and her feet pointed east, one arm to the north and the other to the south. The god of the sea held her by the head and the mother of the gods by the feet and another two goddesses, one by one arm and one by the other, so that she would not fall.][30] (my trans.)

In several passages from the *Relación de Michoacán*, the center and four directions are similarly evoked through the custom of making a "salve to the gods" by sprinkling maguey wine, blowing tobacco smoke, or wafting incense towards the heavens, the four directions,[31] and the underworld before eating or performing a religious ceremony (17, 28, 188; plates 2, 31).[32] Although the specific deities invoked and the order of invocation vary depending on the ritual context, the right-hand side is consistently identified with the north and the left-hand side with the hot country to the south of Lake Pátzcuaro.[33]

Rudolf van Zantwijk has identified three basic numerical schemata in Mesoamerica: the duality of masculine and feminine; the triptych of underworld, earth, and sky; and the quadruple sectors on the horizontal earth (1985, 22). The inhabitants of Michoacán at the time of the Spanish conquest do not appear to have deviated substantially from the standard pattern. Although some have questioned whether dualism was as fundamental a category in this region as in other parts of Mesoamerica (Pollard 1991),[34] my analysis of the Escorial manuscript suggests that it was indeed central to their world view. There appears to be a general consensus, moreover, regarding the indigenous division of the cosmos into three main parts when projected along a vertical axis: the sky—inhabited by several categories of deities occupying distinct levels; the surface of the earth; and the underworld—which was similarly subdivided into various sublevels.[35] Each of these planes, when projected along a horizontal axis, was then organized into various compartments or "houses," typically associated with the numbers four or five.[36]

The surface of the earth, for instance, is customarily referred to in the *Relación de Michoacán* as "the four parts of the world" (35, 159, 173), an expression translated by Gilberti as *thámbengarani* (*thamu* means four)— a regional equivalent of the Andean Tawantinsuyu ([1559] 1989, 127). To engage in battle, in metaphorical terms, is to play "on the earth's back" (35), for the plains, valleys, and mountains are, respectively, the flat, concave, and convex contours of the backside of the earth goddess, who lies facedown, suspended between sky and underworld.

The act of making war is further described in the prose portions of the *Relación de Michoacán* as an occasion when the celestial gods, the sun, and the gods of the four parts of the world watch from on high: "jugaremos en las espaldas de la tierra y beremos como nos miran de lo alto los dioses çelestes y el sol y los dioses de las quatro partes del mundo" (35), say the lords of Curínguaro to the Uacúsecha when they feel their authority is being challenged by these relative newcomers to the Lake Pátzcuaro Basin. In other words, while human beings play out their lives on the goddess's back, the stars and planets, as well as the deities corresponding to the four corners of the earth, gaze down upon her.

Plate 33 (color section), previously analyzed in terms of its greater use of indigenous versus European pictorial conventions, can be seen to contain a visual equivalent of these metaphors. The various components of the cosmos are defined, on one hand, by the >-shaped lines emanating from the pictorial center to the upper and lower left corners, where the gods Xarátanga and Curícaueri (or their earthly representatives) survey the carnage. The other side of the pictorial space is defined by a mirror image in the shape of a <, the upper leg of which is formed by the figure of a man being dragged by his feet toward upper right; the lower leg, by a circular rope to which eight captives are bound by the neck.[37]

The wavy lines, reminiscent of both the meandering red line connecting the Uacúsecha lords to their successors in plate 27 (color section) and the wavy lines emanating from the rim of the circle drawn in the earth in plate 32, can thus be interpreted figuratively as channels of communication between the earth and heavens. The symbolic figures aligned along this > shape are being sacrificed to the gods of the sky. In a similar fashion those figures who make up the < shape are destined to be sacrificed to the gods of the underworld. The prose passages of the *Relación de Michoacán* describe how the latter, who were killed with clubs, were then dragged by their feet "a los heruaçales donde los comian los adyues y auras y bueytres y eran dedicados aquellos al dios del ynfierno"/"to weed-choked fields where they were eaten by coyotes, buzzards, and vultures; these were dedicated to the god of the underworld [which was called *cumíechucuaro*]" (158).[38]

In short, the wavy lines, like the man being dragged by the feet, the circular rope, the sacrificial victims with their hearts torn from their chests, and the cauldron filled with human body parts, constitute pictorial references to one of the central tenets of Mesoamerican religious belief—the necessity of feeding the gods in order to guarantee the continued stability of the universe and social order. According to this world view, the survival of the gods and of the celestial bodies they represent is dependent upon the efforts of human beings who "feed" them through such offerings as agricultural products, penitential bloodlettings, and animal and human sacrifices. Gods and mortals are bound together through the principle of reciprocity in a ritual dance that maintains the balance of the cosmos.[39]

When analyzed spatially in tandem with the Ramírez earth goddess metaphor, plate 33 (color section) can be interpreted as representing the horizontal plane of the surface of the earth—a flat, two-dimensional view of the goddess—upon which is superimposed a three-dimensional model of the cosmos evoked by the lines flowing from the center upward to the heavens at left and downward to the underworld at right. In other words, the pictorial left-of-center corresponds to the earth goddess facedown, as seen from the perspective of the celestial gods Curícaueri and Xarátanga (shown at far left), while the pictorial right-of-center corresponds to the earth goddess faceup, as seen from the perspective of the gods of the underworld. (For a visual exemplification of this symbolic organization, see figure 1.)

In directional terms, the west is here the pictorial center, conceived of as the head of the earth goddess, who lies facedown with her legs to the east (the pictorial left) and also face up with her legs again to the east (the pictorial right). Because she is facing in opposite directions, in both projections her right hand points downward, signifying north, and her left hand points upward, signifying south.[40] The north is the realm of the firstborn gods, the eagles and other birds of prey who accompany the sun on its daily journey. The south is the realm of the Uirámbanecha, the stars who form the entourage of the moon. (This latter dynamic is illustrated in figure 2.)[41]

Because gold was considered the excrement of the sun (152), the gold disks and lip plugs in plate 33 (color section) can be considered

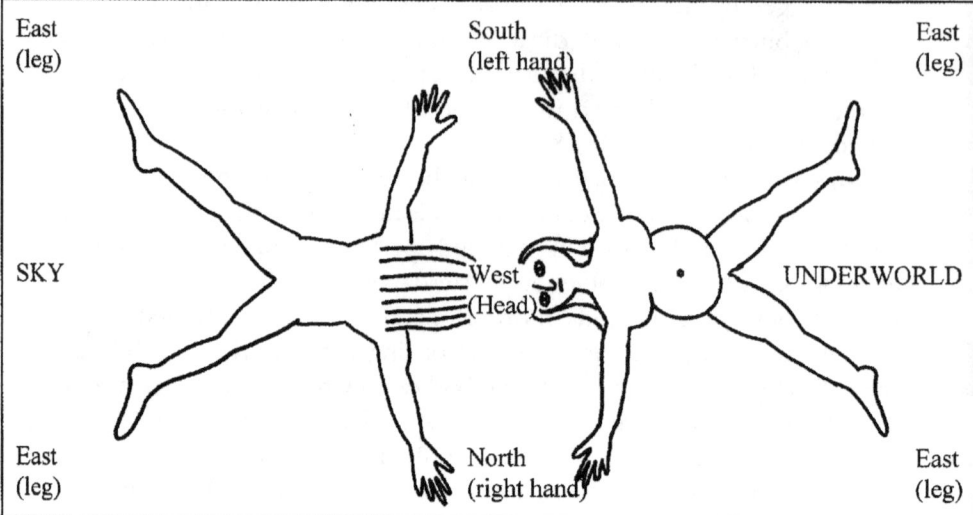

FIGURE 1. The earth goddess from the viewpoint of the celestial gods and those of the underworld (Drawing by Cynthia L. Stone.)

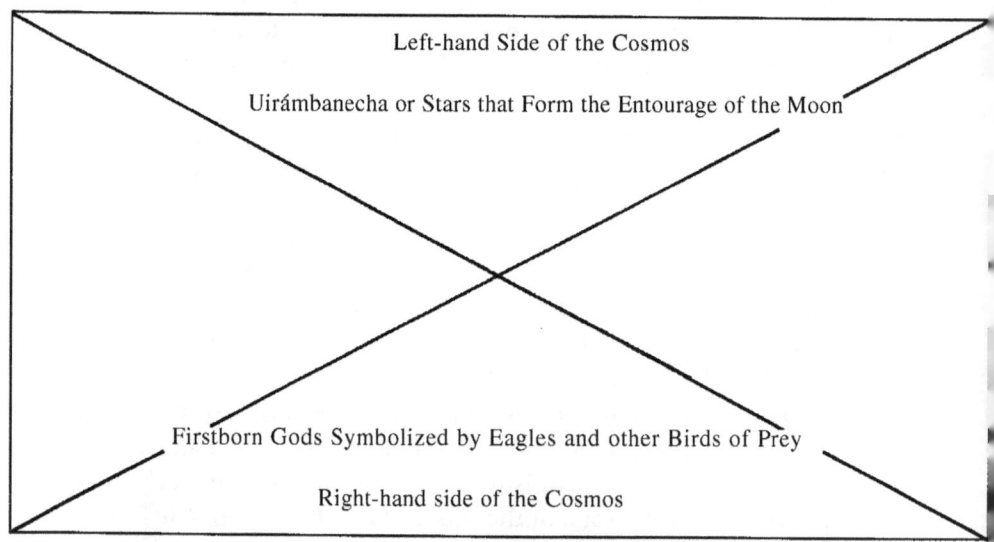

FIGURE 2. The four quadrants: gods of the right-hand and left-hand sides of the cosmos (Drawing by Cynthia L. Stone.)

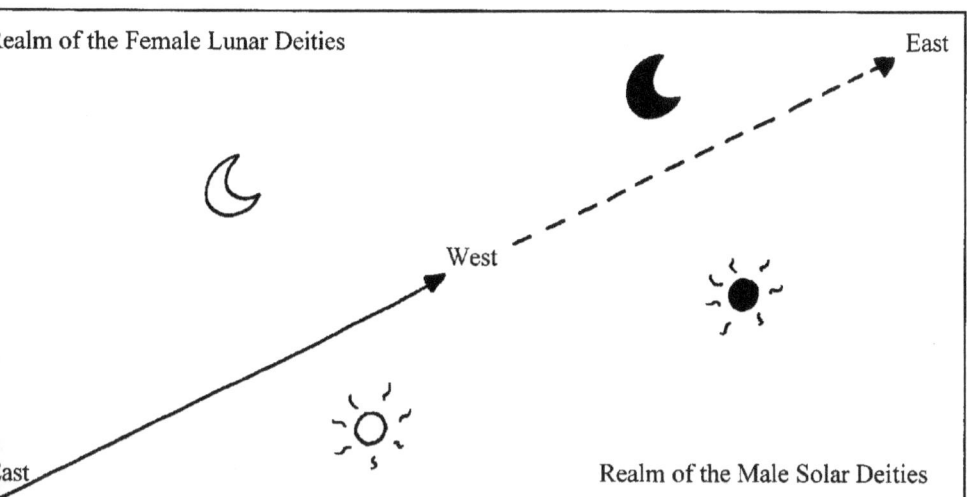

FIGURE 3. Primary diagonal separating the realms of the male solar deities and female lunar deities in both their visible and invisible aspects (Drawing by Cynthia L. Stone.)

attributes of the solar deity Curícaueri (the pouches may represent a numerical quantity; in central Mexican codices a similar-style purse stands for the concept of eight thousand). The male sacrificial victims at lower left are also associated with the sun as patron deity of the Chichimec hunters who reside on the northern boundaries of the iréchequa (fourfold kingdom) and from whom the Uacúsecha lords trace their patrilineal descent. In the symbolic grid represented by figure 3, the solar gods, whose multiple manifestations are predicated upon the prior existence of Curícaueri, "he who is fire,"[42] travels along a diagonal trajectory from lower left to upper right, during the first half of which they are located in the sky and the second half in the underworld. This primary diagonal separates the realm of the male solar deities from that of the female lunar deities, which explains the appearance of a Chichimec warrior bearing bow and arrow at upper right. The moon, in contrast, resides in the heavens at night and in the underworld during the day. Thus, the female sacrificial victims at upper left, wearing the characteristic wraparound skirt or *siríhtaqua* (Anawalt 1981, 87), are associated with the nighttime appearance of moon goddesses such as Xarátanga in the sky.

If this grid is superimposed on the other drawings of the *Relación de Michoacán*, it becomes apparent that the primary diagonal tends to define complementary pairs such as female/male (plates 8, 12), subject/ruler (plates 6, 14), tributary town/ceremonial center (plates 17, 20), captive/captor (plate 15), island/mainland (plates 3, 4), wrongdoer/judge (plates 2, 18, 25, 35), immorality/virtuous behavior (plates 13, 16), loss of authority/gain of authority (plates 10, 11, 26), younger brother/firstborn son (plates 19, 27, color section). Often a given drawing will combine several of the above dualities, as in plate 15, where the concepts of island/mainland, captive/captor, and subject/ruler are all represented pictorially, with the more privileged position in each case located below the primary diagonal.[43]

In order to explicate more fully the symbolic import of any particular composition, however, one must first understand how the cosmological principles expressed in plate 33 (color section) are partially transformed when seen from different perspectives. In plate 3 (color section), for example, the point of view is not that of the gods of the sky and underworld watching their mortal creations "play on the earth's back," thereby providing the divine sustenance that maintains the balance of the cosmos, but rather of the humans who inhabit the Lake Pátzcuaro Basin.

The episode in the petámuti's oral narrative that accompanies this drawing tells of events leading up to the birth of Taríacuri, son of a Uacúsecha lord and the daughter of a fisherman from the island of Xaráquaro. To narrate the life of Taríacuri is also to tell the story of the symbolic union of the male and female lines of descent, the former related to the cult of the sun and fire god Curícaueri, associated with the nomadic Uacúsecha or Eagle Chichimecs; the latter, to the cult of the moon and water goddess Xarátanga, associated with the Huréndetiecha, the original inhabitants or sedentary fisherfolk of Lake Pátzcuaro.[44]

Although at first glance the two gods do not appear to be depicted in this drawing, they are nevertheless present in allegorical form. The rivulets of blood on the steps of the pyramid refer to the concepts of sacrifice and fertility. This is a common motif in pictorial manuscripts of central Mexican origin as well, where its meaning is frequently underscored through the appearance of a human figure at the pyramid's base who has been ritually sacrificed (see, for instance, the Nuttall and Vienna codices as well as the drawings of Sahagún's *Primeros memoriales*).

In plate 3 (color section) the motif of the bloody stairs defines a symbolic relationship of reciprocity between the Huréndetiecha of the island of Xaráquaro and their patron lunar goddess Xarátanga. According to Cristina Monzón García and Andrew Roth Seneff (1999), the word for girl or maiden in the indigenous language of Michoacán is *yurítsqueri*, a compound made up of *yuritsi* (person who bleeds or menstruates) and *queri* (one who climbs or arrives).[45] In this two-way channel of communication, the pyramid stairs lead upward to the sky, from the perspective of mortals (whose blood assures the regularity of the lunar cycles), and downward from the heavens, from the perspective of the moon (who regulates female menstruation).[46]

The second manner in which Xarátanga is alluded to in plate 3 (color section) is through the four waterfowl, three of them with fish in their mouths, who frolic in the waters of the lake. The sacred number four is a reference to the elements of water and earth and those deities associated with them, such as Cueráuaperi, with her fourfold female retinue of white clouds, yellow clouds, red clouds, and black clouds (9).[47] Significantly, Xarátanga is referred to in the pages of the *Relación de Michoacán* as having four priests, as opposed to the five priests identified with Curícaueri (192).

Waterfowl, moreover, are one of the tribute items destined "para los sacrifiçios de la diosa xaratanga"/"for the sacrifices of the goddess Xarátanga" (175). The Huréndetiecha fisherfolk sustain the goddess through their ritual sacrifices just as she sustains them by providing them with fish and crops and children.

According to the translation of José Corona Núñez, Pátzcuaro literally means "lugar de la Negrura, de la Niebla"/"place of Blackness, of Fog" (1993, 47).[48] As such, it is a metaphor for death, as we saw previously in relation to the image of the cold, foggy house devoid of smoke; in particular, it stands for the watery paradise that is the final resting place of those who die by drowning—the equivalent of Tlalocan among the Nahuas.[49] In pictorial terms the waters of Lake Pátzcuaro constitute a mirror image of the principle of reciprocity symbolized by the pyramid steps; instead of connecting the earth and sky, however, they lead to and from the underworld.

While water is associated with Xarátanga and the underworld, the opposing male element of fire is personified through the Uacúsecha lords at lower right, one of whom symbolically bears the sun god Curícaueri on the back of his tunic, pictured as a red circle surrounding a bull's eye with lines radiating out from the circle like rays. The allegorical appearance of Curícaueri in the "sky" at lower right balances the reference to Xarátanga at upper left. Although it is daytime for the Uacúsecha lords, it is nighttime for the fisherman, who is using a net rather than a hook, a method employed during the night according to the oral narrative (27).

Other qualities associated with the human figures are also revealing. The perpendicular lines on the fisherman's cheeks indicate his advanced age (another common motif in early colonial pictorial manuscripts from Mesoamerica, such as the Florentine and Mendoza codices). The lip plugs of the Uacúsecha indicate they are angámecha (official representatives), while the clover wreaths evoke their status as heads of lineages (those who sustain the mother goddess Cueráuaperi) and their braids of red deerskin evoke their descent from Chichimec hunters. Finally, the manner in which the fisherman and Uacúsecha point toward each other indicates that they are engaged in dialogue.

If this drawing were a spoken discourse, the blood flowing down the pyramid stairs, the pointing fingers, and the fish-eating waterfowl would be verbs, each symbolizing a different relationship of reciprocity. The nouns that are symbolically joined together through these various syntheses include man and woman, day and night, sun and moon, fire and water, hunting and fishing, youth and elder, principal lord and commoner.

As in plate 33 (color section), the primary dividing line in this drawing is a diagonal that runs from lower left to upper right, with those qualities and elements of the material world associated with the male solar deities positioned below the diagonal and those associated with the female lunar deities above it. The female side is shown at night, the male side during the day, for neither is visible to mortal eyes at all times, since they both figuratively reside part of the time in the underworld.

This union of opposites is expressed in the petámuti's oral narrative through the prophesy of the rise to power of Curícaueri, made possible through the alliance between the Huréndetiecha and Uacúsecha:

> ... porque curicaueri a de conquistar esta tierra y tu pisaries por la parte la tierra y por la otra parte el agua y nosotros tanbien por vna parte pisaremos el agua y por la otra la tierra y moraremos en vno tu y nosotros. (29)

> [... because Curícaueri is destined to conquer this land. Then will you walk with one foot on land and the other on water; and we also will walk with one foot on water and the other on land. [Thus] will we live as one, you and us.]

Once again we have the motif of the two bodies that are mirror images of each other. In this case, however, they are the bodies of the moon and sun, respectively, the former walking with her left foot on land and right foot on water, the latter with his right foot on land and left foot on water.

Because this scene is viewed from the perspective of Xarátanga's people, who dwell at upper left, and Curícaueri's people, situated at lower right, we see a cross section of the earth goddess that reveals only those parts of her visible from the earth's surface. The center has shifted in such a way, moreover, that the primary diagonal is here formed by the waters of Lake Pátzcuaro—another symbolic entrance to the underworld—rather than by the orbit of the sun on its daily journey from east to west and back again, as in plate 33 (color section).

In plate 3 (color section) Lake Pátzcuaro is encoded as a privileged locus of power from the point of view of human beings—the symbolic center of the iréchequa. The manner in which the fisherman is positioned, with the base of his canoe touching the mainland and the tip of his paddle the island shore, converts him into a metaphorical bridge for the Uacúsecha lords who, through him—or, more precisely, his absent daughter—gain access to the domain of the original inhabitants, the locus of female power and the cult of the moon goddess Xarátanga. Significantly, the source of sacred power upon which the Uacúsecha will build their future empire is predicated upon the displacement of women from the center. The female principle symbolized by Xarátanga is pictured, but it is a man rather than a woman who serves as her earthly representative.[50]

To summarize what has been gleaned so far regarding the spatio-temporal organization of the drawings of the *Relación de Michoacán*, both plate 33 (color section) and plate 3 (color section) evoke similar cosmographic principles, but from different perspectives. The first is oriented primarily along a vertical axis; it locates the viewers in such a way that they are gazing down and up on the various activities taking place on earth. The second is more horizontally structured, in accordance with the viewpoint of those located on the surface of the earth rather than in the sky or underworld.

Not all the drawings correspond to these two models, however. Consider plate 32, which combines a bird's-eye view of the earth (at pictorial left) with a close-up of one particular segment (at pictorial right). This reading is reinforced by the overt content of the two scenes. The left side includes a circular map, or *curúzetaro* (189), of the territory to be conquered, complete with instructions as to the routes of access—represented as long, wavy lines—to be taken by the various squadrons whose warriors are arrayed in concentric circles around it. The numbers of squadrons that will take each path are indicated by the sticks laid out between the lines of the map. The footprints show the direction in which they will travel.

What the right side of the pictorial space reveals is a close-up of a portion of the map—a concrete example of the strategic principles depicted at left. At lower right several squadrons of warriors are following their designated paths, in the process encircling the villages. Meanwhile, a few warriors pretend to run away in order to lure the people from their houses (that is, communities). Here the footprints show the path taken by the people who will be ambushed by the warriors lying in wait for them, as exemplified by the motif of the club-wielding figure grabbing a captive by the hair. The man with a plant on his head is a spy; he is setting fire to a house or village—a frequent shorthand for conquest in Mesoamerican pictographic codices.[51]

Other drawings that manifest this dual organization include plate 22, which also contains a curúzetaro, drawn by the elderly Taríacuri to show his "nephews" and younger son how they are to divide the future kingdom into three parts. In Taríacuri's tripartite division of the kingdom, the cities of Tzintzuntzan, Ihuatzio, and Pátzcuaro are each represented at left as a mound of earth with a rock on top. On the curúzetaro or map side of the pictorial space, the squadrons of warriors are represented by rows of sticks, while at right a few actual warriors are shown in the process of obtaining "food" for the gods, thereby fulfilling Taríacuri's prophetic design.

This correspondence between the elements of the material universe and those signs that function as symbolic equivalents of them—the circle is a territory, the houses are communities, the wavy lines are paths, the sticks of firewood each represent a squadron of warriors—echoes the way in which the lives of mortals parallel the movements of the stars and planets. Although, in the more complete cosmography outlined in plate 33 (color section), the right side of the pictorial space corresponds to the domain of the underworld and the left to the realm of the sky, in the majority of the drawings of the *Relación de Michoacán* with an actual (or implied) perpendicular line down the middle, only one of the two spiritual realms is pictured.

Thus, plate 31 is structured by means of the primary opposition sky/earth, with a priest praying to the celestial gods at left and a scene from the subsequent military campaign at right. Plate 23, in contrast, is divided between the two realms of earth/underworld, with a battle scene pictured at left and the place where the booty thereby obtained is guarded—a treasure house on an island in Lake Pátzcuaro, symbolic entryway to the watery underworld—at right.[52]

Those pictures divided into three segments are more likely to correspond structurally to the complete triptych of sky/earth/underworld. Consider plate 39, a drawing whose temporal progression—the order in which the various scenes are meant to be read—can be deduced from the accompanying prose passage. The subject matter is the burial ceremony of a cazonci, who is pictured sick in bed at upper left. His dead body is then carried in a ceremonial procession, after which the servants who will accompany him in the afterlife are clubbed to death and his remains ritually cremated. Finally, the ashes are buried at the foot of the main *yácata* (pyramid). Here the "earth" is symbolically represented in the box at upper left; the "underworld," in both the lower register and the upper right corner; and the "sky"—evoked through the motif of the pyramid whose stairs reach upward to the heavens—in the box at top center. The principle of movement, of narrative progression, follows the shape of a spiral, a symbolic equivalent of the theme of death and resurrection exemplified in the prose chapter.[53]

It is not enough, in other words, to superimpose the symbolic grid of the cosmos onto a particular composition; one must first determine which elements of the universe are depicted and from what perspective. One of the clues in making these determinations is what Robertson describes as the greater or lesser use of "scattered-attribute space" as opposed to the grounding of individual figures in a "landscape setting."

The subject matter of a given composition is also key. Plate 33 (color section) concerns the "feeding" of the gods of the sky and underworld through the acts of ritual sacrifice associated with war. It is not surprising, therefore, that it contains one of the most complete blueprints for the way the cosmos is structured and differing values assigned to spatial position.

The thematic focus of plate 3 (color section), in contrast, involves relationships among human beings. Again, a two-way dynamic is established, with the same basic value positions as in plate 33 (color section). But in this case what we are viewing is portrayed from the perspective of the Huréndetiecha who live on the island of Xaráquaro and the Uacúsecha who inhabit the mainland. As a consequence, the pictorial center is not the west coast—the place where the sun dips under the horizon—as in plate 33 (color section), but Lake Pátzcuaro, where the symbolic union of the patron gods of these two major groups first occurred.

Another important consideration is whether or not the pictorial space is divided into segments. In those drawings organized in multiple parts, one can expect to find some combination of the following: a top-down perspective identified with the sky; a horizontal perspective aligned with the earth; and a bottom-up perspective associated with the underworld. Because the events occurring on earth are prefigured in the relative positions of the celestial bodies, to gaze down from on high is the spatiotemporal equivalent of the acts of map making and formulating military strategy (plates 22, 32), of prophesy (plate 22), and of prayer (plate 31). In this way space and time are conflated and spatial position becomes another way of encoding the direction in which a pictorial narrative is meant to be read.

THE DOOR AS SPIRITUAL BOUNDARY

Now that we have outlined a preliminary theory for reading the models of spatiotemporal organization that collectively define the pictorial language used by the caracha, let us explore a little further the way in which symbolic connections are established between earth, sky, and underworld in the prose and pictures of the Escorial manuscript. There are many interconnected systems of metaphors that refer to the vertical *axis mundi*[54] linking gods and mortals, but none is more prevalent than the notion of the door as spiritual boundary.

When the lords of Itzíparámuco decide to abandon their village for fear of the Uacúsecha, their leader declares:

> que se abra la puerta por mi pueblo de yziparamucu que yo con mi gente estauamos hechos vna çerca y pared muy gruesa con que esta atada la puerta. (139)

> [let the door be opened by way of my town of Itzíparámuco. For I with my people were formed a fence and very thick wall with which the door is tied.]

On one level he is referring, as the friar-compiler of the *Relación de Michoacán* explains, to "the doors they use in their houses made of planks tied with cords" (139). In this sense, the act of opening a door is equivalent to the removal of part of a thick wooden fence or wall located on the dividing line between political jurisdictions.[55] Not coincidentally, Itzíparámuco is described as a subject town of the lords of Curínguaro, situated strategically on the border separating their domains from those of the rival Uacúsecha.

And yet on a deeper level, corresponding not to the surface of the earth but to the vertical axis mundi linking "the four parts of the world" to the domains of the gods, this act is also a sign of the imminent incursion of the spiritual realm into the political conflict being played out between rival Chichimec dynasties. The gods have weighed the relative merits of the two groups and they are about to take sides. To open the door, in this more spiritual sense, is to allow for the uncontrolled irruption of the sacred into daily life. The role of ritual is precisely the opposite. When properly enacted, it serves to ensure that the gods will look favorably upon the enactor—that is, they will make their appearances on schedule or undertake surprise incursions somewhere else.

In the drawings of Escorial Ms. C.IV.5, the doors of houses almost always appear in conjunction with a head of lineage who guards the entrance to a dwelling or domain. See, for instance, plate 4 (where both a male and a female figure are seated facing doors) as well as plates 10, 28, 36, and 41. It follows that a door left opened or unguarded, especially when it appears along with an empty uaxántsiqua (plates 7, 13, 20, 37, 40), is a sign of a violation of one of the most sacred duties of a ruler. An unprotected door is like an invitation to the gods to destroy one's family or community.

We have seen how Pátzcuaro is symbolically encoded in the *Relación de Michoacán* as "the door to paradise, through which [the] gods would descend and ascend" (35).[56] Caves similarly serve as metaphorical doors to the underworld.[57] In plate 16, for example, Taríacuri's younger son and "nephews" are engaged in penitential fasting at the entrance to a cave. Meanwhile, Taríacuri's elder son Curátame II, who has taken over from his father in the latter's old age, neglects his duties as spiritual guardian of the kingdom through excessive drinking. For those familiar with indigenous symbolism, there is no question as to whose lineages are destined to prosper.[58]

The flip side of the image of the cave is that of the mountain as gateway to the sky. The *angámucuracha*, or mountain deities, associated with the communities clustered around its base, are the grandfathers (*curáecha*) who stand (*aŋá*) at the mouth or door (*mu*).[59] Other translations of the suffix *mu* include shore—as of a river or lake, or border—as of a town or piece of cloth (Swadesh 1969, 40; Friedrich 1971b, 15, 87). All these images, when they occur in pictorial form, are potential references to that subliminal zone that constitutes a sort of permeable boundary line between the realms of gods and mortals.

Pyramids are similar to mountains in that they also serve to establish a symbolic link between sky and earth. The act of climbing a mountain to keep watch and gather firewood to burn to the gods (plates 4, 5, 9, 13, 19) is equivalent to climbing the stairs of a pyramid, which is a sign, in turn, of both a virtuous life-style and political ambition.[60]

Those who seek the favor of the gods in this way and are successful will be visited in their dreams by the deity they are attempting to conjure.

To do so is potentially dangerous, however, for one must be in a position to reciprocate. This dynamic explains why Taríacuri, incensed at his beloved younger son and "nephews" for building a temple to Curícaueri before obtaining the requisite number of sacrificial victims for its dedication, shot an arrow at them (the theme of plate 17).

One of the favorite stories of the last cazonci, Tzintzicha Tangáxoan, concerned a lord of Queréquaro named Carócomaco who kept pestering the god Querenda angápeti to give him riches and political power: "Where did he miss an opportunity to sleep? Did he not sleep on all the mountain ranges in order to have some sort of dream?" (112). In this manner Carócomaco metaphorically climbed the stairs of the god's pyramid step by step. But the political fortunes of his descendants were short-lived, for he did not lay down deep roots through virtuous behavior and cultivation of the visionary faculties required of those chosen by the gods to be their earthly representatives.[61]

In short, the door as spiritual boundary offers potential leaders an entryway to the celestial realm and a means of furthering the interests of their successors. Yet those who try and fail at such a task run the risk of experiencing the adverse side of this dynamic as a catastrophic reversal of fortune.[62]

THE CENTER AS MOVEMENT

The motif of the center is linked in Mesoamerican symbology with the notion of the synthesis of opposites that sets the cosmos in motion as well as with the crossroads as a metaphor for instability. The Nahua referred to this principle as *ollin*, or movement, represented pictorially by two intersecting sticks in the shape of a diagonal cross. Ollin is the sign that presides over the fifth sun or creation, the universe inhabited by the indigenous peoples of Mesoamerica at the time of the Spanish conquest, and whose end was prophesied to come about through earthquakes.[63]

The translation of *ollin* in the indigenous language of Michoacán, according to José Corona Núñez (1986, 115), is *manóuapa* (movement), the name as well of one of the incarnations of Venus. Significantly, the god Manóuapa is referred to in the *Relación de Michoacán* as the son of Xarátanga and Curícaueri (257). As such, his identification with the center takes on the added meaning of a symbolic link or "door" between female and male, night and day, water and fire.[64]

The door as metaphor has both positive and negative associations. When the inhabitants of Itzíparámuco "open the door" by deserting their village, they convert the center as locus of virtuous power and authority into a site of instability, immorality, and disorder. The drawing accompanying this episode in the petámuti's narrative, plate 20, depicts a fork in the road where two sets of footprints meet. This may be interpreted as a graphic representation of the principle of manóuapa or synthesis of opposites. Below is an *ojo de agua* (spring) atop a rock formation, the sign of a human settlement from the perspective of the gods of the underworld, much as the circular base of a mountain represents a cluster of communities as seen from above.[65]

The motif of the unstable center often corresponds in the drawings of the *Relación de Michoacán* to a violation of one or more of the spatiotemporal patterns described above. The role of women, moreover, is key in this regard. In general the motif of the woman in the center—unless she is being punished in accordance with accepted judicial practices as in plates 2 and 35—tends to correspond to negative value judgments of some kind as well as to the theme of a major disturbance or transformation in the cosmic order.

Compare the women standing at center in the negatively encoded Itzíparámuco drawing (plate 20) with the positively charged plate 3 (color section), where the fisherman's daughter is conspicuously absent from her father's canoe. Of the two women pictured in plate 20, the larger is the goddess Auícanime;[66] the other is the wife of one of the lords of Itzíparámuco to whom the goddess has sold a type of mole or gopher in exchange for some eggs. As in the story of the sacred arrows, however, the surface meaning is deceptive; for the rodent, a symbol of death, turns out to be the woman's own infant son, who is shown cooking in the pot at left. When the husband discovers what has happened, he shoots his wife in the back with an arrow, an act he later regrets. The reaction of his father, the chief, is to underscore the prophetic nature of the transformation of the future heir from one who eats into one who is cooked/eaten.[67]

Another example is provided by plate 9, where Taríacuri's unfaithful first wife from Curínguaro appears at center being fondled by two of her kinsmen. The house lying on its side at right is a further indication that the subject matter of this drawing involves a perversion or violation of sorts.

Even when the woman at center is performing an act that will redound to the benefit of the Uacúsecha, she nevertheless functions as a harbinger of death and destruction. Plate 26 depicts a female relative of Taríacuri who has just beheaded Cando, one of the lords of Curínguaro, by enticing him to commit adultery with her. This image constitutes a pictorial rendition of the metaphorical expression *no cuché hepu hucárixacan,* which the friar-compiler of the *Relación de Michoacán* translates as "no tenemos cabeças con nosotros"/"our heads are not with us" (6). The end of the hegemony of the Chichimec dynasty established at Curínguaro is rendered symbolically through the image of a headless body or, given the linguistic ambiguity inherent in the Spanish word *tronco*, a tree whose crown has been cut off. As the alphabetic narrative puts it: "quedo solo su cuerpo hecho tronco" (164); that is: "only the trunk of his body remained," and/or "only his body remained, made [into the] trunk of a tree" (i.e., one that will no longer produce living branches).

The motif of the woman at center is also helpful in decoding ways in which the caracha subtly allude to their subordinate status in relation to the Spaniards, even in drawings that supposedly represent preconquest events. By using the symbolic associations contained in the drawings previously analyzed as a reference point, one can begin to perceive how certain scenes are encoded by the caracha as the inverse of what is proper, as examples of an upside-down world.

Consider plates 37 and 38, both from part three of the *Relación de Michoacán*. In plate 37 the inauspicious symbol of the woman standing at center is combined with the ill omen of an empty uaxántsiqua. Although the cazonci is guarding his domain at right, the lords of those dynasties allied with the ruling Uacúsecha are not portrayed in as positive a manner. Perhaps it is for this reason that the cazonci has decided to strengthen his alliance with them by marrying off "one of his daughters or sisters" (208). This mixing of ethnicities, although capable of yielding positive results (as in the case of Taríacuri), is also a portent of change in the cosmic and social order that can lead to disaster if not properly controlled.

In plate 38 (color section), we again see a woman standing at center, a negative sign once again reinforced by the motif of the crossroads or fork in the road. According to the prose narrative that accompanies this drawing, it was customary for the husband to go to the mountains in search of firewood to burn in the temples for four days before consummating a marriage. The smoke from these fires would rise to the heavens as a promise to the celestial gods that he would fulfill his responsibilities to them if they took notice and watched over him and his family. Similarly, the wife would sweep the path before their home for four days, thereby symbolically acting out the ritual importance of maintaining the channels of communication open between husband and wife, gods and mortals—that is, free of obstructions in the form of improper or immoral behavior.[68]

As discussed in chapter two, however, the alphabetic narrative can also be interpreted as referring to the manner in which commoners still married some sixteen years after the Spanish conquest of the region. Not only is there a fluctuation between the use of verbs in the imperfect and present, but some of the latter are censored by the hand of the principal corrector—in all likelihood the friar-compiler—suggesting that he was sensitive to criticism that certain "idolatrous" practices were continuing after the nominal conversion of the native population to Christianity.[69]

In the drawing the "good" husband appears at upper right and the "good" wife at center, performing the rituals described above. The potential difficulties of marriage are represented by the lower branch of the fork in the road, the path taken by the "bad" wife or adulteress mentioned at the end of the prose narrative,[70] her shoulders covered by a garment classified by Patricia Anawalt as most likely a European-style shawl (1981, 89). Here the standard spatiotemporal pattern of symbolic values is inverted. In contrast to the majority of drawings in the *Relación de Michoacán*, in plate 38 (color section) it is daytime above the primary diagonal running from lower left to upper right and nighttime below. Even more significantly, since this is a drawing about what constitutes proper and improper behavior, the standard locus of immorality as opposed to virtue is reversed, with the "good" conduct occurring above the diagonal and the "bad" below.

The use of a shawl in this drawing suggests a correlation between adultery and European cultural influence. Ironically, the more ample clothing imposed by the friars in order to abolish the "scandalous" custom of women exposing their bare breasts, rather than encouraging greater modesty is here encoded as allowing them to more easily conceal their identity under cover of darkness and thereby escape detection for bad behavior.[71]

Another spatiotemporal pattern is inverted in plate 42 (color section)—the one involving the proper alignment of the sky in relation to the earth. In this drawing, which accompanies the chapter on the prophesies foretelling the Spanish conquest, the gods of the four parts of the world appear in a circular formation at right, corresponding to a prophetic vision seen by a woman possessed by the spirit of the goddess Cueráuaperi. The view as it would appear from the surface of the earth, meanwhile, is shown at left: a crumbling pyramid, at the foot of which a petámuti and an áxame (sacrificer) point upward to the various omens.

The relative position of the two realms is thus given as earth|sky rather than the previously established norm of sky|earth.

Again, the reversal of the standard pattern can be considered the equivalent of a negative value judgment on the part of the carari responsible for this drawing, an indication that these are sinister omens heralding the coming of a time of great sadness, disorientation, and deprivation. As in the pictorial representation of the abandonment of Itzíparámuco, plate 42 (color section) tells the story of a major transformation in the cosmic order. In this case it is not only the lords of certain ruling dynasties whose world is being turned upside down, but rather the lives of all the peoples represented by the assembled deities: the blue-green gods of the center; the red gods of the east; the yellow gods of the north; the white gods of the west; and the black gods of the south.

And yet, in spite of the traumatic upheaval expressed through the above motifs, plate 42 (color section) is not devoid of hopeful signs. Indeed, one of the visual messages that comes across most powerfully involves the parallels between the two realms corresponding to earth and sky: The petámuti replicates the gesture and insignia of the messenger god Curita caheri; the stance of the áxame is almost a mirror image of that of the woman. There is also a clear correlation between the shape of the pyramid at upper left and the mountain covered with trees at upper right, as well as between the placement of the offerings of food and drink at lower right and the bloody stairs perpendicularly opposite. Because the two realities echo each other, the implication is that the disruption heralded by the Spanish conquest and evangelization cannot fundamentally subvert the relations of reciprocity that define life. Although the temples may be torn down, their spiritual counterparts, the mountains, will remain. Similarly, the human sacrifices represented by the flowing blood may cease, but food and drink and other offerings to the gods will retain their sacred connotations.

Certainly, one interpretation of this portion of the *Relación de Michoacán* could emphasize the fatality of events, the inevitable demise of indigenous religious practices and beliefs, the futility of resistance. I am more convinced, however, by scholars such as Miguel León-Portilla (1992b, 227–29) and Miguel Pastrana Flores (1999), who see in these omens an attempt to make sense of the conquest in accordance with traditional conceptual categories, a strategy of adaptation, not capitulation. Thus, although the persecution of overt displays of indigenous religious belief presented a major challenge to keeping the channels of communication between gods and mortals open and functioning, it was not necessarily an insurmountable one, given the penetration of the sacred into all aspects of daily life.

CONCLUSION

As mentioned in chapter two, the caracha are noticeably absent from the frontispiece of the Escorial manuscript. There are at least two ways to read this absence. On one hand, it implies that their contributions to the making of the Relación de Michoacán were secondary at best. The power of writing is hereby converted into the exclusive purview of the friar and viceroy, those who hold the book in their hands, while it is symbolically erased from the world of the indigenous peoples.

But if one looks at the drawings as together constituting a coherent narrative, it becomes clear that the caracha have not been erased from the Escorial manuscript; they have simply been relocated. Certainly, they do not play a central role in the colonial bureaucracy, as the frontispiece would lead us to believe. But in the representation of the government of the cazonci in plate 28, a drawing depicting not just one particular administration, but the entire iréchequa in symbolic form, they occupy a privileged position—the pictorial center. In this sense they are encoded as guardians of the axis mundi, the ones responsible for controlling the sacred channels of communication between gods and mortals.

There are nine caracha in all, the foremost of whom is holding a pen or brush, with a container of ink or black paint by his side. The Spanish translation of *caracha* is here given as *pintores*, putting the accent on their status as painters to the exclusion of their related function as writers. But this alphabetic gloss—a later addition in the hand of the principal corrector—is one of the few concessions to a European point of view. Although the cazonci's palace partially anchors the figures portrayed in a landscape setting, the various groups of officials are mostly free-floating. Since there is no attempt to individualize them through unusual facial features or other identifying marks, it can be assumed that they are not meant to represent specific people but rather eternal principles manifested in human form.

In the bottom portion of this drawing (below the cazonci and his palace), the spatiotemporal organization exemplified by plate 33 (color section) has been rotated ninety degrees. Those agricultural and fishing practices associated with the matrilineal ancestors and hot country to the south are located below an imaginary diagonal running from lower right to upper left; those associated with the meat-eating, mountain-dwelling, woodcutting Chichimecs are situated above the diagonal. One way to interpret this arrangement is that the cazonci and his palace correspond to the "earth" and the groups of officials to the "sky"; there is no indication that a negative value judgment should be attached to this rotation.

My reading of plate 28 highlights the central position of the caracha in the symbolic organization of the fourfold kingdom, which, in turn, echoes the sacred structure of the cosmos. These cosmic principles, moreover, serve as the basis for determining the spatiotemporal organization of the drawings to a greater extent than the European conventions of pictorial representation that coexist alongside them. The "language" spoken by the caracha may incorporate a good deal of European "vocabulary," but its basic "grammatical structure" remains decidedly non-European.

The extent to which the caracha of the *Relación de Michoacán* should be credited with inventing a new type of "writing in pictures" is unclear. Perhaps, as hypothesized in chapter one, prehispanic prototypes existed for some of the drawings contained in the Escorial manuscript. Even if they did not, however, there can be no doubt that these deceptively simple compositions have much to tell us about the profound and sacred dimensions of everyday life.

With the coming of the Spaniards, many of the rituals that served to maintain the balance of the cosmos were disrupted. The dance of the serpent-butterfly made of paper—the serpent representing the vertical axis mundi, the butterfly's wings, the four parts of the world—would have been increasingly difficult to reenact in the traditional way.[72] This same paper, however, when manufactured in accordance with European standards, could still serve as a symbolic representation of the cosmos, as we have seen through the above analysis of the drawings of the *Relación de Michoacán*. By reproducing the principles of reciprocity that, according to indigenous tradition, govern all human and divine relationships, the caracha, through the act of writing in pictures, symbolically reestablished their links with the gods, giving them new life under colonial rule.

4

REMAPPING THE LAKE PÁTZCUARO BASIN

The *Petámuti* (High Priest)

> Myths, and the characters whose stories they are, live in the quiet of mountains and valleys, forests and meadows, rocks and springs, until someone comes along and thinks to tell them. They have other hiding places too, inside the language we use every day, in the names of the places where they happened, or the names of trees or days on the calendar.
>
> —*Dennis Tedlock*

In the stories told in part two of the *Relación de Michoacán* there is an obsessive attention to matters of dress, of genealogy, and of place.[1] At times in the narrative the petámuti (for he is the principal storyteller) addresses his listeners directly, reminding them of previous events that had taken place "here in Pátzcuaro" (42, 108), referring to the contemporary descendants of the characters whose adventures he is relating (14, 42, 146, 155–58) or expounding upon the origin and significance of important markers of ethnic, professional, and social status.

In stark contrast to the opinion of the friar-compiler, for whom these stories are practically devoid of moral content, consisting almost entirely of "ceremonies, idolatries, drunkenness, deaths, and wars" (4), for the petámuti the narrative woven from these details serves as a moral compass, a living tapestry of familiar landmarks in which past, present, and future coexist and mutually illuminate one another, a repetition of the divine act of creation heralded by the sound of the conch-shell trumpet.[2]

During important ritual functions the petámuti stands in place of the cazonci, who stands in place of the god Curícaueri. The high priests' oral performance on the occasion of the final day of the feast of Equata cónsquaro[3] would last from noon to sunset, at the end of which each would declare, "now I have fulfilled my obligation to the cazonci in what I had to tell you; for these words are his" (157). The oration progresses in tandem with the movement of the sun, ending with an exhortation to all those congregated in the patio of the royal palace to follow in the footsteps of their ancestors—to be who they should be—followed by a graphic demonstration of the punishment awaiting those who violate the sacred trust, no matter how illustrious their family origin.

The word for royal palace in the indigenous language of Michoacán is *iréchequaro*,[4] a term that adds the locative suffix *rho* to *iréchequa*, which means kingdom.[5] Thus, the royal palace stands symbolically for the conglomerate of communities who owe tribute to a common *irecha* (king) and, by extension, to his patron god. This political organization, moreover, is modeled on the structure of the *thámbengarani* ("four parts of the world"), itself a reference to the ordering of the cosmos in terms of "the four stars which form the pillars of the palace porch" of the god Tucúpachá (Boyd 1969, 11).[6] Within this interlocking web of territorialities, events taking place on earth echo ancient cosmogonic myths, and the laws governing politics mirror those of the heavens.

The place where the petámuti delivers his oral performance is of crucial importance to the argument advanced in this chapter, which rejects the friar-compiler's framing of part two of the *Relación de Michoacán* as a ceremony frozen in time, a story repeated verbatim by the high priests from one generation to the next, bearing little or no relation to events in the wake of the Spanish conquest and evangelization of the region. The transcription of the oral testimony into alphabetic characters and its subsequent translation into Castilian may have destined this particular version of the traditional story to become the one most widely disseminated in our age, but the petámuti's testimony was clearly not recorded in prehispanic times, nor should his contribution to the Escorial manuscript be judged as if it were delivered in the form of a written text.[7]

And yet, if the petámuti's presentation of the past, with its focus on the lives of the earliest Uacúsecha settlers of the Lake Pátzcuaro Basin, is simultaneously oriented toward the exigencies of the colonial present, why has this dimension not been more apparent to the many modern readers of the manuscript since its publication in 1869? Moreover, if there is comparatively little in the way of colonial-era references in the stories he relates, what is the evidence upon which such an interpretation can be built?

This chapter attempts to answer the above questions by reframing the petámuti's narrative in spatial terms. In this geographic/prophetic reading, space is the dimension that erases the distinction between past, present, and future. As Dennis Tedlock observes in the quote cited in the epigraph above, traces of the stories consecrated by oral tradition remain hidden in the place-names and natural environment of the peoples whose identities have been forged through them. As we have seen in chapter three, oak trees in the *Relación de Michoacán* may stand for dynasties. Eagles (*uacúsecha*) are symbols of the sun's rays and of the people of Curícaueri. Even the proper names of many of the characters in the petámuti's narrative are inextricably linked to the natural elements and the landscape populated by their descendants. Corona Núñez translates Taríacuri as "priest of the wind" (1988, 75).[8] It is still today the name of a mountain (variously spelled Tariácuri, Taríacuri, and Tariaqueri) located west of present-day Tzintzuntzan, which was built on the ruins of the indigenous capital at the time of the Spanish conquest (Pollard 1993, 29).[9]

Viewed in these terms, the real protagonists of part two of the *Relación de Michoacán* become the rocks, springs, trees, and mountains of the Lake Pátzcuaro Basin, along with their inhabitants (both human and nonhuman, mortal and immortal). And the evidence that can be drawn upon to substantiate the interpretation of particular passages expands to include all the legends surrounding the places mentioned in the text from prehispanic times to the present.

For example the first bishop of Michoacán during the colonial period, Don Vasco de Quiroga, is not mentioned by name in the Escorial manuscript. And yet he is central to the argument proposed in this chapter, since he is repeatedly invoked through reference to the pueblo-hospital of Santa Fe de la Laguna that he founded on the northeastern shores of the lake during his first visit to Michoacán (23–26, 242), as well as the episcopal palace and cathedral that he was in the process of building in Pátzcuaro in 1538–39 (34), the fountain he is said to have miraculously "discovered" there on the site of a previous Uacúsecha settlement (34), and the bell he ordered transferred from Tzintzuntzan to Pátzcuaro during the relocation of the diocese (34).

Quiroga, like Taríacuri before him, left his mark upon the landscape of the region in an enduring way because he played the role of an organizer and visionary on a grand scale during a time of great uncertainty. At issue in this chapter is not so much what Quiroga was like in a historical sense (his litigiousness is as legendary as his idealism) as the way in which the stories told about him, culled from a variety of sources, echo the stories told by the petámuti in the *Relación de Michoacán* about earlier foundational figures who symbolically reestablished the iréchequa centered in the Lake Pátzcuaro Basin. In this dynamic, the articulation of his role in local affairs by the petámuti and other indigenous leaders in the wake of the Spanish conquest is more important than Quiroga's perspective regarding his own legacy.

As the petámuti stood, circa 1538–39, most likely in the ruins of the patio of the royal palace that represented the sacred organization of the fourfold kingdom, he symbolically reenacted for his audience the successive disbandings and regroupings that his people had experienced through the ages, each preceded by omens, each centered on a different capital, but all still partially visible, still tangible to those listeners familiar with the contours of previous settlements, the names of mountains and forests. His final remarks challenge the assembled lords and caciques to return to the life-style of an earlier and more ascetic age, when the capital of the iréchequa was at Pátzcuaro—the place where Quiroga was in the process of transferring his diocese; the place from which the petámuti was speaking. It is a message consistent with the life-style led by the Christian converts at Quiroga's community of Santa Fe de la Laguna, who wore simple, natural-colored clothing, sang God's praises at dawn and dusk, practiced rigorous penance, worked the fields, and shared the proceeds of their labor through the principle of collective ownership.[10]

But before going into greater detail regarding the connections between the legends surrounding Quiroga and the symbolic import of certain key events and places mentioned in the petámuti's narrative, it will be helpful to spell out the meaning of some of the expressions used as a sort of metaphorical shorthand by him in his opening and closing remarks to the assembled lords and caciques of the realm. It is only by elucidating his use of formulaic language that one can begin to perceive how his oral performance bridges the gap between prehispanic past and colonial present, how it potentially serves to articulate for his listeners a way for them to stay true to their roots while adapting to the exigencies of a new era.

MORAL PRECEPTS AND DIVINE LAMENTATIONS

In the friar-compiler's introductory remarks to part two of the *Relación de Michoacán*, he succinctly sums up what he considers the most relevant information to be distilled from the petámuti's lengthy oral narrative:

> lo que se colige desta ystoria es que los anteçesores del caçonçi vinieron a la postre a conquistar esta tierra y fueron señores della estendieron su señorio y conquistaron esta probinçia que estava primero poblada de gente meg\x/icana naguatatos y de su misma

lengua que pareze que otros señores vinieron primero y avia en cada pueblo su caçique con su gente y sus dioses por si. (15)

[What can be gathered from this story is that the ancestors of the cazonci arrived to conquer this land later [than the other inhabitants] and became lords over it. They extended their sovereignty, conquering a province originally populated by Mexicans, [that is] Nahuatl speakers, and [by] others [Purépecha] who shared their same language. Thus it would appear that other lords established themselves first and that in each town there was a cacique with his people and their own gods.]

The focus here is on the supposed political illegitimacy of the cazonci and his descendants based on the principle of territorial first rights—a familiar theme in the chronicles and relaciones of the colonial period. If the Spaniards were relative newcomers to the region, the argument tended to go, so were many of the indigenous lords they were replacing—at least from the point of view of the earliest settlers, who had been conquered by them in the more or less distant past.[11]

The friar-compiler's pragmatic reading of the events recounted by the petámuti puts the emphasis on the temporal reconstruction of a clear line of succession in which sequential waves of immigrants occupy the position of a regional nobility, with the Uacúsecha as the most recent conquerors. It is a reading that parallels the tendency to emphasize the outsider status of the ex-Chichimec ruling dynasties of central Mexico at the time of the Spanish conquest in contrast with that of the more sedentary descendants of the ancient civilizations of Tula and Teotihuacan.[12]

The manner in which the petámuti sums up what he has to say in the *Relación de Michoacán*, on the contrary, puts the accent on a more metaphorical dimension in which there is no *one* definitive interpretation. In the remarks with which he frames his narrative, what comes across most strongly is the moral, spiritual, and pedagogical functions of telling stories about the past—not just the narrow legalistic function. The boundaries between poetry and prophecy become blurred as the bard articulates, in first person, the will of the gods.[13]

When I first read the petámuti's final speech in part two of the *Relación de Michoacán*, I thought there must be an error in the manuscript at the point where he is speaking about the great personal sacrifices endured by the founders of the principal lineages of the Uacúsecha. A detailed enumeration of the trials they endured—the many varieties of wild plants they ate instead of tortillas; their coarse clothes and wooden lip plugs; the primitive stone axes with which they gathered firewood; the maguey-spike earrings worn by their wives and mothers—ends with the following enigmatic pronouncement: "that is how they multiplied the towns and dwellings and stole clothing and food for *me* from [our] enemies" (157; italics added).

What is the reason for this irruption of a first-person pronoun into the speaker's account of events from the past? And why would the petámuti be the recipient of the spoils of war?

In order to formulate an answer to these questions, it is necessary, first, to take a careful look at the way the traditional role of petámuti is characterized in various parts of the narrative. Consider the drawing that accompanies the final chapter of the petámuti's epic history (plate 24, color section), in which the high priest is shown carrying a staff or lance ("bordon o lanza" in the Spanish translation) topped by a diamond-shaped arrowhead and circular turquoise gemstone with skirt of multi-colored feathers.

The name for this ritual object in the language of Michoacán is most likely the translation given by Gilberti for "vara real" (royal staff): *iréchequa tsiríquarequa* ([1559] 1991, 544).[14] For that is precisely what it is—a symbolic representation of the iréchequa, uniting the arrowhead, symbol of the gods of the hunt (Heyden 1988), with the blue gemstone and multi-colored feathers associated with his "younger brothers," the Tirípemencha, who are gods corresponding to the center and four directions. According to this metaphoric system, one can surmise, the turquoise stone stands for the blue-green waters of Lake Pátzcuaro; the yellow feathers for the lands to the north; the red feathers for the eastern provinces; the white feathers for the pacific coastal region; and the black feathers for the hot country to the south.

When placed in the context of his symbolic function during the ceremony of Equata cónsquaro, the petámuti's use of a first-person pronoun in the above passage begins to make sense. It is as if, by carrying the staff, he has become magically possessed by the spirit of the gods that reign over the heavens and earth. He speaks in their voice because he has merged with the divine essence.[15]

In the case of the petámuti and other ritual bearers of the iréchequa tsiríquarequa, they cease to be embodiments of Curícaueri as soon as their role in a particular ceremony comes to an end. The cazonci, in contrast, serves at all times as an earthly manifestation of his patron god (173). That is why, upon receiving a message, the head of the Uacúsecha was wont to say: "that which you have come to say is not told to me but to Curícaueri, who is here present" (16). When betrayed, he would state: "this affront has not been done to me, but to Curícaueri" (69). Even his *ireri*, or first wife, was metaphorically referred to as a gift bestowed not upon him, but upon Curícaueri (15, 67), for whom she was expected "to make blankets and offerings . . . and food" (16, 65). Once the head of the Uacúsecha had attained sovereign status over all the peoples of the region, he presumably would have simultaneously fulfilled the role of earthly representative of the gods of the fourfold kingdom, those collectively termed Tirípemencha.

This interpretation is bolstered by additional pictorial and testimonial evidence from the *Relación de Michoacán*. Only those priests who are functioning as embodiments of the cazonci, who are specifically designated by him to speak in his stead in a ceremonial context, are shown carrying the iréchequa tsiríquarequa. Thus, the alphabetic narrative makes clear that the petámuti in plate 2 is supervising the execution of justice "by mandate of the cazonci" (13). The priests in plates 36 and 37 are sent by the cazonci to outlying communities in order to, respectively, install a new cacique in power and perform a wedding ceremony between one of the cazonci's women and a lord from an allied group (203–10).[16] When the iréchequaro (royal palace) is metaphorically empty during the search for and coronation of a successor, it is the petámuti who speaks for Curícaueri in lieu of the cazonci (plates 40, 41).[17]

What, then, are we to make of the fact that at least two of the indigenous priests depicted in plate 1 (color section) are carrying similar feather-topped spears? In 1538–41 the last cazonci, Tzintzicha Tangáxoan, had been dead for more than eight years; his sons, still too young to assume the responsibilities of leadership, had yet to take the place of their father. During this period of symbolic emptiness of the iréchequaro, those who speak for Tirípeme Curícaueri (14), temporarily filling the void left by the death of the earthly representative of the solar god and the sacred fourfold kingdom, are those who carry the iréchequa tsiríquarequa. These are the elders or curáecha (literally, grandfathers), whom the friar-compiler mentions in his prologue as the authoritative depositories of collective memory.

Interestingly, there are three indigenous priests pictured in plate 1 (color section), although the third is only partially visible. This number is reminiscent, in the story told by the petámuti, of the three elders named Chupítani, Nuriuan, and Tecaqua who counsel the rulers of the Uacúsecha regarding their responsibilities and who serve as messengers to the lords of other dynasties (39, 43, 70, 78, 83, 91, 97, 103, 127).[18] They are the ones who advise the original founders of Pátzcuaro, the lords Uápeani II and Pauácume II, to beware of their in-laws, the Huréndetiecha from the island of Xaráquaro, because the latter are planning to ambush them in alliance with the snake Chichimecs of Curínguaro. And, when their words go unheeded, it falls to them to redeem their lords' bodies in exchange for gold and precious feathers and to bury them at the foot of the temple to Curícaueri (39–43). Later, these three elders are instrumental in preparing Taríacuri, then little more than a child, for his future role as the founder of a realm that will eventually surpass in grandeur all cultural centers in the region within recent memory.[19]

The advice the elders give Taríacuri returns insistently to three primary obligations: to "feed" the gods, especially Curícaueri, by burning as much "firewood" as possible at the temples dedicated to them; to "sacrifice [his] ears"; and to "remember to avenge the insults" inflicted upon his paternal ancestors (43–44). Let us examine in detail each of these exhortations, for they constitute the core of the moral vision advocated by the petámuti under Spanish rule.

First, it should be noted that, in accordance with the metaphor of "feeding" the gods analyzed in chapter three, war is only one component of the Uacúsecha lord's responsibility to promote "service" to the gods among all the peoples under his protection.[20] Moreover, while his primary obligation is to his own patron god, that does not free him from the imperative to sustain as abundantly as possible the religious cults associated with other groups as well: "Gorge with firewood all the gods that be" (44), the elders instruct Taríacuri.

As discussed previously, "firewood" is shorthand for a number of related concepts. To begin with, it refers to the kindling used to maintain the sacred fires to Curícaueri. In this sense "firewood" is the symbol of masculinity par excellence in the *Relación de Michoacán*. While the "good" wife in plate 38 replicates the actions of the goddess Xarátanga, one of whose functions is to sweep away impurities (Corona Núñez 1992, 27), the "good" husband in the same chapter is a replica of the solar god Curícaueri—he who makes possible the burning of the sacred fires.[21] According to the value system exemplified by this metaphorical language, a man devoid of religious devotion, who does not fear the gods and neglects the proper performance of ritual, violates the natural order of things. That is why every wrongdoer (*uázcata*) was said to have disobeyed the cazonci's command to bring "firewood" for the temples, whether the particular crime was spying for the enemy, desertion in time of war, black magic, adultery, chronic indolence, drunkenness, or sodomy (11–12).

"Firewood" is also shorthand for tribute. Thus, the elders' admonition to Taríacuri to be constantly alert for ways of finding "firewood" can be understood as a mandate to be vigilant in searching for potential sources of revenue. This obligation does not only hold true for those who currently hold the position of irecha; on the contrary, it is the duty of all potential leaders to lay the groundwork for future greatness by fomenting relationships of reciprocity, not only with the gods, but also with their fellow mortals.

In several passages from the *Relación de Michoacán*, for example, the Uacúsecha lords are described as actively promoting economic exchanges with neighboring groups. Literally, they are said to "bring firewood" (24, 97).[22] Clearly, many varieties of tribute are metaphorically subsumed under this heading including, of course, firewood itself.[23] Plate 28 shows the most important ones: cotton textiles, agricultural products (most notably maize and maguey wine), feathers, hides, quarried rock and minerals, fish, game, and kindling.

Finally, "firewood" can be understood as a metaphorical reference to human beings as living wood that, in death, serves to light the fires of the heavens, thereby maintaining the cosmos in motion. The most dramatic sacred mandate to be inferred from this analogy, and the one most dwelt upon in both colonial and modern interpretations of Mesoamerican traditions, is the requirement that rulers periodically engage in "flower wars" to obtain sacrificial victims for important ceremonial occasions. Several passages from the *Relación de Michoacán* refer to this practice (127–28, 229–30). Still, it is noteworthy that references to the smoke from ritual bonfires as a means of whetting the appetite of the gods for the spoils of war, thereby motivating them to intercede on one's behalf, are considerably more frequent (15, 35, 46, 137, 143, 182, 187, 193, 229). This practice ties in with both the custom of burning "olores" (scents) as a form of prayer and the manner in which many of the indigenous priests depicted in the *Relación de Michoacán* carry elaborate gourds inlayed with turquoise on their backs, filled with little balls of tobacco and incense.

Regarding the symbolic significance of the ritual items worn by the petámuti and other high priests, if the iréchequa tsiríquarequa (royal staff) designates the power invested in them by Tirípeme Curícaueri via his earthly representative the cazonci, the turquoise-encrusted gourds are representative of their responsibilities towards the Purépecha commoners, whose welfare they are charged with safeguarding. That is why the priests known as *cúritiecha*, the foremost of whom is the petámuti, were said to "carry all the people upon their backs" (181). The residue left over from the burning of these "pelotillas" of tobacco and incense (186) was a constant reminder of those four "little balls of ash" (212) from which the first human beings were said to have been created.

In short, one of the theological principles underscored through this system of symbolic equivalences is the function of the petámuti and other cúritiecha as guardians of the common good. The cazonci and his Uacúsecha relatives who served as *áxamencha*, or sacrificers (181), were similarly charged with carrying the "people" upon their backs through the metonymy of the tobacco-filled gourd (110, 187). By overseeing the burning of "firewood" and "scents" in the temples, these guardians of the sacred trust thereby assured the constant regeneration of the lineages (the living branches) under their charge.

To return to the other two mandates articulated by the elders for Taríacuri, the second one—the obligation to "sacrifice the ears"—is shorthand for serving as an example to one's subjects by excelling in the performance of ritual penance. Although, as representatives of the gods, the heads of dynasties enjoyed access to a wide range of privileges and luxuries, the petámuti makes it abundantly clear that those lords who overindulged in earthly delights did so at their own peril. Nobles were expected to routinely and profusely sacrifice to the gods blood drawn from their earlobes, tongue, and other soft tissues by piercing them with maguey spikes; to fast and stay awake at night praying, especially during religious holidays; and to periodically abstain from sexual relations.[24]

The contrast between the exemplary behavior of Taríacuri and his followers in this regard, and the lack of religious fervor among the rulers of neighboring communities, is the central theme of a number of episodes from part two of the *Relación de Michoacán*. In one, two lords from Itzíparámuco (a subject town of Curínguaro) pledge to accompany Taríacuri into the mountains to "sacrifice [their] ears" (70), but instead remain behind in his palace, where they indulge in a drunken orgy with Taríacuri's first wife. Other emotionally wrenching episodes, concern Taríacuri's decision to kill two of his own sons (including his firstborn) because they have not been sufficiently self-sacrificing. The elder son, Curátame, is repeatedly encoded in the story told by the petámuti as the paradigm of those with a penchant for debauchery (92, 100–106, 122–23, 131–34). The younger son, Tamápucheca, in contrast, is described as a brave and worthy Uacúsecha warrior. Nevertheless, through no fault of his own, he is redeemed as a war captive by his maternal relatives after being consecrated to the gods, and so must be executed (159–60). The lesson to be learned from these parables is clear. In order to preserve the common good, a ruler must be prepared to perform (like the biblical Abraham) the ultimate sacrifice: to voluntarily offer up his own children, his own lifeblood, as "firewood" to the gods if their continued existence would be harmful to the "tree" as a whole; to actively nurture a different "branch" at the expense of his own direct descendants if that is the will of the gods.

The final charge transmitted to Taríacuri by the three elders—to "remember . . . the insults" suffered by his paternal ancestors in order to "avenge" them—is repeatedly evoked in connection with the notion of survival. As the elders put it: "in all these places [where your paternal ancestors were murdered] you [too] can be killed if you do not become who you are meant to be and do not listen to what we have to say" (43–44). Since the lord stands metonymically for his subjects (15), I assume what is meant here is not just personal survival, but the preservation of the entire community. The problem with Taríacuri's father and uncle is that they were not sufficiently "discerning" (39, 41); in other words, they did not possess the vision and experience necessary to correctly interpret present circumstances through comparison with past events. That is why, the petámuti suggests, they were outwitted by their enemies. The ultimate "revenge," from this point of view, is survival; and the best guarantee of achieving this goal is to learn how to "remember" from those whose primary occupation is to serve as the living depositories of oral tradition.

Again, Taríacuri functions as the prototype for how a lord is expected to go about acquiring this wisdom and experience. In pursuit of the goal of "remembering," the story told by the petámuti illustrates, personal effort can prevail even in the absence of direct intervention by a particular god on a given lord's behalf. Thus, Taríacuri is never graced with a prophetic dream or vision during his many penitential vigils at the base of trees on the mountains overlooking the Lake Pátzcuaro Basin.[25] Yet he never fails to consult with the elders before undertaking an important endeavor, and he always listens to their advice and follows it to the last detail. Even his name, if indeed it means "priest of the wind," identifies him as an expert at the art of prophecy, of giving voice to the will of the gods of all the "four parts of the world" (35, 159, 173).

Along these lines, it is significant that several additional symbolic items worn by the petámuti during his recitation of the oral history of his people are explicitly cited as accouterments of the priests of the goddess Xarátanga, from whom Taríacuri is descended on his maternal side

(47–49). The "headdress made of string" (32, 110, 113, 232), for instance, appears to be a general attribute of the Huréndetiecha and their allies, for it contrasts with both the "leather headdress" identified with the pure-blooded Chichimec lords and their gods (39, 53, 136, 137, 191) and with the "cloverleaf garland" worn in homage to Cueráuaperi (158, 221, 232, 234–35).

The petámuti's most distinctive symbolic item, however, is the *uanduqua*, translated as "tenazuelas" or "tenazillas" (little pincers) in the *Relación de Michoacán*.[26] This golden pectoral is shaped like the valves of a conch shell, with additional spirals curling upward on each side, providing a symbolic representation of the same shell in cross-section. In addition to the ceremony of Equata cónsquaro (plates 2, 24, color section), other contexts in which the uanduqua is pictured in the Escorial manuscript are drawings depicting: the omens foretelling the Spanish conquest (plate 42, color section); ritual preparations prior to the launching of an attack on an enemy village (plate 31); the arrival of the Spaniards in the Lake Pátzcuaro Basin (plate 44, color section). The symbolic significance of the shell it resembles is underscored in another drawing, moreover, through the representation of several musicians playing conch-shell trumpets as part of the funeral procession accompanying the body of a dead cazonci prior to his cremation (plate 39).

According to José Corona Núñez, in Mesoamerican symbology the conch shell is related to the concepts of birth and matrix (1988, 21–22). As a musical instrument, its sounding prefigures the future resurrection of the cazonci, who dies, like the sun (or, in Greek and Roman mythology, the phoenix), only to rise again from the ashes. The prophecies recounted by the priest who wears the uanduqua in plate 42 (color section) similarly herald the end of the prehispanic era and the dawn of a new Christian age in which there will be only one "cantar" (one poem, one manner of singing) throughout all the ends of the earth (234).[27]

When the petámuti rises to his feet to tell the "cantar" or epic history of his people, he is also acting as prophet, his voice an echo of the words of the creator gods at the beginning of time, his breath like the sound of the wind as it circles back and forth through the spirals of history. Within the confines of the conch shell, space and time are conflated, for as the story advances it repeats the same patterns incessantly, adding ever more layers of meaning to the same basic structure.[28]

The mournful sound of the conch-shell trumpet is evoked thematically in the petámuti's opening and closing remarks to the assembled lineages, through the motif of the gods lamenting their fate:

vosotros los del linaje de nuestro dios curicaueri que aveis venido los que os llamais eneami y çacapuhireti y los rreyes llamados vanacaze todos los que teneis este apellido ya nos av[. . .]os juntado aqui en vno donde nuestro dios tirepeme curicaueri se quiere quexar de vosotros y a lastima de si. (14)

[You who belong to our god Curícaueri who have come, you who are called Enéani and Zacapu hireti and the kings called Uanácaze, all you who share this name: We have come together here at this time, in the place where our god Tirípeme Curícaueri desires to air his grievances against you and where he bemoans his fate.]

The three Uacúsecha lineages the petámuti mentions by name in the above quote are presumably the ones founded by Taríacuri's son Hiquíngaje and by the two sons of Zétaco and Aramen named, respectively, Hiripan and Tangáxoan (see figure 4).

Hiquíngaje inherited his father's seat in Pátzcuaro. Hiripan, for his part, was graced with a vision from Curícaueri, who instructed him to build a temple on the site of Ihuatzio. And Tangáxoan, the paternal great-grandfather of the last cazonci, Tzintzicha Tangáxoan, was visited in his dreams by Xarátanga, who complained that her pyramid in Tzintzuntzan had been reduced to ruins and that it would fall to him to restore it. Based on other evidence in the *Relación de Michoacán* such as the positioning of the squadrons of warriors from the three capitals when the cazonci would go to war—Ihuatzio "in the middle of" Tzintzuntzan and Pátzcuaro (148)— it is my hypothesis that the lineage called Enéani or Enéami consisted of the surviving descendants of Hiquíngaje; those named Zacapu hireti, of the direct descendants of Hiripan; and the "kings called Uanácaze," of the heirs of Tangáxoan.[29]

Given that most of Hiquíngaje's sons were either executed (allegedly because of their immoral life-style) or, in one instance, killed by lightning (165), it is not surprising that in his concluding remarks the petámuti concentrates on the exemplary life-style of Hiripan and Tangáxoan, the founders of the two most powerful Uacúsecha lineages at the time of the Spanish conquest. Still, it is striking that he does not mention Taríacuri in his summing-up commentary.

One explanation for this disjunction between the body of the oral performance (whose protagonist is Taríacuri) and the closing remarks (which focus on Hiripan and Tangáxoan) has to do with the notion of "official history" as a means of reinforcing the authority of the ruling elite.

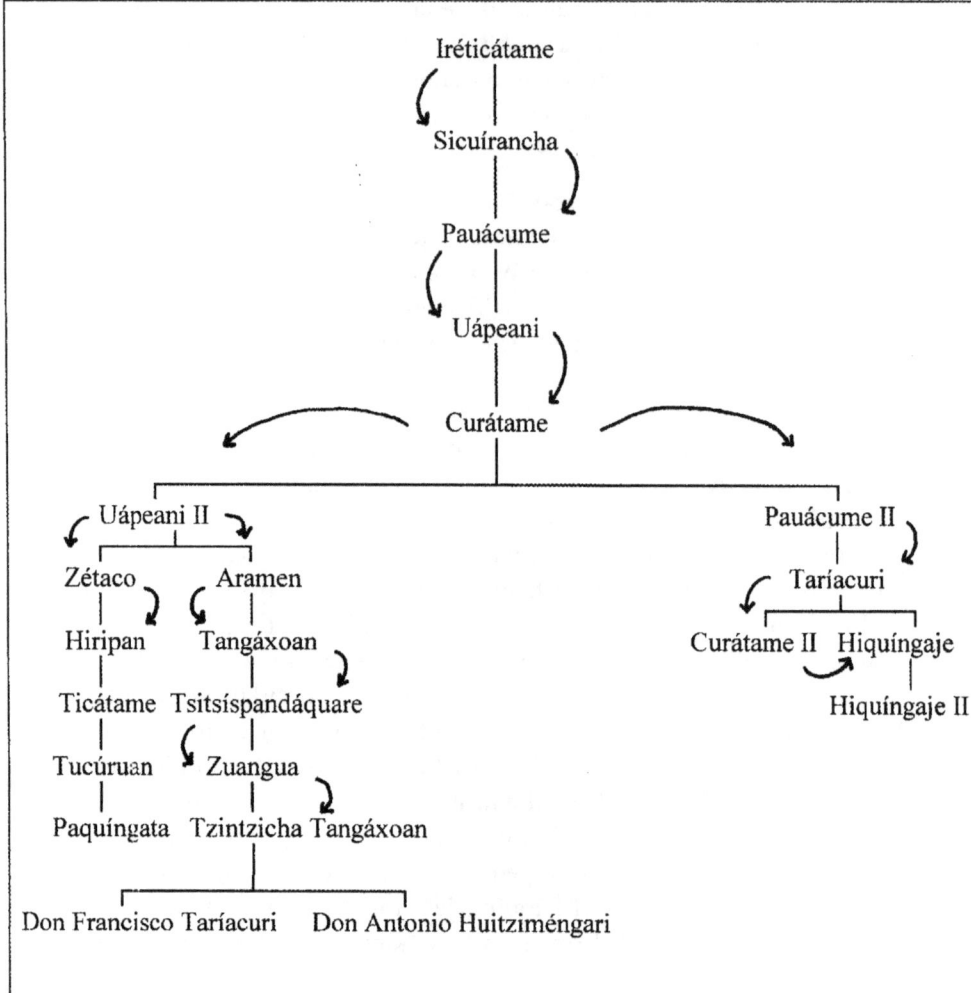

FIGURE 4. Genealogy of the principal Uacúsecha lords. The curved lines represent political succession as head of the Uacúsecha. (Chart by Cynthia L. Stone.)

From this purely instrumental point of view, the stories told by the petámuti can be interpreted as a justification for the preeminence of the Uanácaze, followed by the Zacapu hireti and Enéani lineages, at the time of the Spanish conquest.

The defenders of this position among modern-day commentators are sometimes referred to as advocates of the "Tzintzuntzanist" orientation of the *Relación de Michoacán* (Martínez Baracs 1989, 106). The most frequently cited ethnohistorical evidence upon which this interpretation is based includes: (1) the use of the terms "city" and "province" of Michoacán throughout the Escorial manuscript to refer to Tzintzuntzan; (2) the consistent designation of Pátzcuaro as a "barrio" or subject town of Tzintzuntzan; and (3) the fact that the Franciscans and Viceroy Mendoza became engaged in a series of lengthy legal battles with Quiroga beginning in the 1540s regarding the best location for the diocese, buttressed by testimony from indigenous nobles concerning how they were forced by Quiroga to abandon their capital.[30]

It is not difficult to flesh out this argument with additional evidence from the *Relación de Michoacán*. The petámuti's testimony recorded in part two, and not just the contributions of the friar-compiler in his role as editor and translator, can be convincingly read as a self-serving rationalization on the part of the Uacúsecha, a reinterpretation of local history that justifies the indigenous status quo and the preeminence of the lords of Tzintzuntzan.

A few examples from the stories related by the petámuti will suffice to suggest the basic contours of this reading. After the fathers of Hiripan and Tangáxoan are murdered by the Islanders of Xaráquaro, the two young "orphans" are reduced to eating scraps of food discarded by others in the marketplace (92–93; plate 12).[31] The future benefits for their descendants that accrue from these early hardships are here prefigured in accordance with the symbolic system alluded to in the mandate to "sacrifice the ears." Later episodes reinforce this foreshadowing of the advantageous position of the Zacapu hireti and Uanácaze, including one in which Hiripan and Tangáxoan are described as taking pity on the young Hiquíngaje and feeding him all their toasted corn while the three cousins are engaged in ritual fasting at the mouth of a cave (124–25; plate 16).

A rationale for the dominant position of the Uanácaze within the triple alliance, meanwhile, is provided by the story of the death of Taríacuri's eldest son, Curátame. Of the three founders of the principal lineages at the time of the Spanish conquest, it is Tangáxoan who demonstrates his superior bravery by wielding the club that dispatches Curátame to the other world, thereby metaphorically "feeding" the gods of the underworld (plate 18). Moreover, even though Hiripan is the eldest, and so at first seems predestined to occupy the favored position, the enigmatic reference to his accidental fall from a tree rotted by "woodworm or earthworms" (144–45; plate 21) reads like a moral parable foreshadowing the fall from power of his descendants.[32]

In spite of the internal coherence of the above reading, my hypothesis is that it is not sufficient to account for certain key passages from part two of the *Relación de Michoacán*, nor does it exhaust the symbolic associations implicit in the petámuti's use of metaphorical language. On the contrary, the Tzintzuntzanist position follows a logic similar to that sketched out by the friar-compiler in his summary, according to which the petámuti's narrative reads as a story about political legitimacy (or, rather, the lack thereof). Although this is certainly an important dimension of the rationale behind the elaboration of the Escorial manuscript for all its contributors, I argue that it should not be emphasized to the exclusion of other readings that put the accent more firmly on the ethical and spiritual dimensions of the text.[33]

An alternative explanation for the focus on Hiripan and Tangáxoan in the petámuti's concluding remarks is the role these two characters play in the oral performance. Unlike Taríacuri, who embodies both masculine and feminine attributes (much like Quiché Maya day-keepers, who are referred to as "mother-fathers"), Hiripan and Tangáxoan are consistently encoded in the narrative as pure Chichimecs, archetypal hunters who owe their allegiance exclusively to the male solar god Curícaueri.

In the episodes from part two of the *Relación de Michoacán* that describe the lives of Hiripan and Tangáxoan as children, the narrative returns obsessively to the notion that it is not their destiny to be farmers. Each time they try to make a living by tending the fields or looking after the children of the various uncles who give them shelter, they are unable to follow through on these responsibilities. Instead, they feel compelled to climb the mountains in search of "firewood" to burn in the temples (94–97). In this version of the classic Mesoamerican morality tale, the burning of firewood takes on the symbolic connotations of the ball game that reenacts the symbolic course of the sun, moon, and stars on their daily journey through the heavens.[34] Another key component of this reading is Hiripan and Tangáxoan's performance of ritual penance at the mouth of a cave, which echoes the struggles of the heroes of the Popol Vuh with the lords of Xibalbá—the Quiché Maya underworld.[35]

Even a seemingly minor observation made by the three elders Chupítani, Nuriuan, and Tecaqua regarding the great beauty of the young Hiripan and Tangáxoan (97)[36] is significant in this alternate reading. The fact that this beauty was an inner attribute and not a result of fashion or a pampered upbringing is underscored when Hiripan observes that he has a "round head, which is not [characteristic] of valiant men" (145). As the friar-compiler explains, this is a reference to the local custom whereby nobles flattened the heads of their children with boards. Tangáxoan, in response, laments that he is even worse off, having "small feet and [a] skinny body," both of which can be understood as references to beauty as a function of being well nourished.

Again, the petámuti is directing the attention of his listeners to the moral and spiritual value of his narrative by highlighting that true beauty does not come from riches or surface embellishments, but from their opposites—the overcoming of adversity and the rejection of ostentatious displays of wealth and status. The narrative construction of Hiripan and Tangáxoan as archetypes adds another dimension to the petámuti's oral performance. It also suggests something about his audience—that the specific thrust of his final remarks may be a function of his addressing a group made up disproportionately of young men.

There are other analogies with the Popol Vuh and similar sacred Mesoamerican traditions. The passages describing the death of Taríacuri's father, Pauácume II, and Tangáxoan's father, Aramen, for instance, read like the fatal wounding of deer who escape from their pursuers to die alone in the mountains (42, 62–63). This animal is mentioned in the *Relación de Michoacán* as a symbolic manifestation of the god Cupanzieeri (the old or dying sun), who is sacrificed by his "wife," a goddess named Achuri hirepe (the waxing or waning moon), after having been defeated at the sacred ball game. Cupanzieeri is later resurrected by his hunter son, Sirata táperi (the young or morning sun), who disinters his bones, which then metamorphose into a deer with a long, flowing mane and tail (241).

In this much-abridged version of the classic story line, the symbolic "death" of the evening sun in the west is hastened by the coming night just as its "resurrection" as morning star in the east signals the dawning of a new day. In order for the pattern of alternating day and night to be set in motion at the beginning of time, moreover, there must be a fusion or "marriage" of divine energies between sky and underworld. The role of the son in this cosmic drama is to fight against his maternal relatives, the forces of darkness, whose power must be harnessed before the father can be resurrected and a new solar deity installed to preside over a new creation.[37]

The narrative ambiguity in the *Relación de Michoacán* regarding which of the several "sons" is more directly responsible for reestablishing the sacred kingdom of their fathers is one of the distinguishing characteristics of this ritual celebration of the glories of gods and kings vis à vis related Mesoamerican oral histories.[38] As I argue in the final part of this chapter, at issue is not only the relative status of the various Uacúsecha lineages in 1538–41, but also the way differing interpretations of the lives of their forefathers tie in with the debate over the best location for the diocese as symbolic center for a new Christian era.

The double reading that I am proposing for part two of the *Relación de Michoacán*—its effectiveness both as political propaganda and as a blueprint for virtuous living—reaches a culmination in the petámuti's concluding sermon, with its strong prophetic overtones. Consider the following excerpt:

> oyd esto os digo vosotros que dezis que soys de michuacan como no soys adbene [. . .] zos donde an de benir mas chichimecas todos fueron a conquistar las fronteras y asy soys adbenediços de vna parte eres de tangachuran vn dios de los ysleños vosotros que dezis que soys de michuacan y soys de los pueblos conquistados que no dexaron de conquistar nyngund pueblo y soys en [sic] ençensados que asy hazian a los cativos y os dexamos por rrelleve de nuestra boca que no os sacrificamos ni comimos y mira que prometistes gran cosa que hariades las sementeras a nuestro dios curicaueri y prometiste el çyncho y hacha que fue que trayrias leña para sus cues y que estareis a las espaldas de sus batallones que le ayudareis en las batallas y que lleuareys sus rrelleues tras el que es que lleuareys su matalotaje a la guerra detras del y que acrecentareis sus arcos y flechas con el hayuda que le dareys y le defendereys en tienpo de neçesidad todo esto prometiste. (155–56)

> [Hear this [my lament], you who claim to be from Michoacán. What, are you not imposters? Where are more Chichimecs to be found? [Nay], they are all gone to conquer the borderlands, so you are imposters. You are from one side only, belonging to Tangáchuran, a god of the Islanders. You who say you are from Michoacán, [though] you are from the conquered peoples. For no town was left unconquered. [Thus] are you perfumed with incense (for that is how they prepared their captives). [Yea] we spared you as scraps for our mouth (which means, we did not sacrifice or eat you). Behold, you promised great things: That you would work the fields for our god Curícaueri. You promised the cinch and the ax (for bringing firewood to the temples); to be at the rear of his battalions (to help him in battle); and to carry the scraps of his offerings after him (that is, the war provisions), augmenting his bows and arrows (with the help you would provide); and defending him in time of need. All this you promised.]

There are at least two possible exegeses of the above passage, both of which are prefigured by the petámuti's reference to the god Tirípeme Curícaueri at the beginning of his performance (14).

Insofar as the petámuti is giving voice to the patron god of the Uacúsecha, his words read as an indictment of their allies and subject peoples. The charges brought against these "conquered peoples" are many, for they have failed to fulfill the many promises made in exchange for not being sacrificed as war captives: to till the fields used to support the religious infrastructure for the cult of Curícaueri; to maintain the fires burning in the temples and, by extension, to work diligently to produce tribute items destined for the royal treasury; to follow the military captains of their respective wards into battle, never deserting the cazonci in time of war or otherwise jeopardizing the security of the realm; to carry the "war provisions"; to increase the number of "bows and arrows" fighting on behalf of Curícaueri; to defend the cazonci, the earthly representative of the patron god of the Uacúsecha, and his emissaries whenever necessary. In this context the act of remaining faithful to tradition is tantamount to personal allegiance to the cazonci, which is incompatible with loyalty to any rival lord, including, presumably, the Spanish crown and its representatives, such as Christian missionaries and colonial administrators.

This is also a reading that puts a negative twist on the notion of being indebted. A recurrent metaphor in part two of the *Relación de Michoacán* is the reference to the acceptance of provisions dedicated to the gods, even from a relative, as equivalent to condemning one's descendants to the future status of "slaves." Thus, the fathers of Hiripan, Tangáxoan, and Hiquíngaje emphatically refuse to accept "war provisions" offered by friends and enemies alike, for they are convinced that the gods to whom this food and clothing is dedicated will seek retribution later (61–64). The mutual bonds of obligation between Uacúsecha lords and Purépecha commoners is thereby couched in terms of the relationship between master and slave, patron and beneficiary.[39]

On a more metaphysical level, however, the petámuti's words suggest that all human beings are purépecha; our existential condition is to serve as "food" for the gods. And if they decide to make us rich or famous or spare us a violent death, this good fortune only increases our obligation to repay our debt to them.[40] In accordance with this second interpretation of the above passage, when the petámuti states, "we spared you as scraps for our mouth," he can be understood to be referring to all the assembled peoples, including the Uacúsecha lords, and to be speaking not just for Curícaueri, but for all the gods of the heavens and earth, symbolically represented in the Tirípemencha, or gods of the center and four directions.⁴¹

According to this reading, those who are true "Chichimecs," who are destined to follow in the footsteps of Hiripan and Tangáxoan, are yet to be identified. All others are "imposters," especially those who make much of the outward symbols of their noble status: their "chairs" and precious "lip plugs" and fancy clothes and soft bodies:

> tu gente baxa de michuacan todos soys señores y os trahen vuestros asientos y sillas detras de vosotros todos os pareze que soys rreys avn asta los que tienen cargo de contar la gente llamados ocanbecha todos soys señores mira que curicaueri os ha hecho rreyes y señores por que no myrays a las espaldas al tienpo pasado quando erades esclauos. . . . y ahora sois caçiques con grandes beçotes que estendeis los ⩫\b/eços para que parescan mayores mejor seria que os pusiesedes mascaras pues que os contentays con tan grandes beçotes traheis todos bestidos pellejos y nunca los dexays ni os los desnudays mas andays enpellejados. . . . ya os aveys tornado todos ing\r/atos por que soys ya caçiques y señores y amays vuestros cuerpos por no trabajallos y yendo a la guerra os tornays del camino y venis mintiendo al caçonzi y le dezis señor desta y desta manera esta el pueblo que conquistaste y con lo que ꝺ\v/ienes mintiendo engañas al rrey que te rrepartio la gente y te hizo caçique ay ay esto es asy vosotras gentes que estays aqui. (156–57)

[O, commoners of Michoacán, you are all become lords, with your [high-backed] chairs and [three-legged] stools carried behind you. You all fancy yourselves kings, even those in charge of counting the people called ocánbecha, you are every one a king. Take heed that Curícaueri has made you kings and lords. Why not look behind you, at the past when you were slaves?. . . . [But] now you are caciques with great big lip plugs, [with which] you stretch out your lips so they appear bigger. [Truly] you would do better to wear masks, since you are so fond of big lip plugs. You dress all in skins and never go without them or take them off; [instead] you go about all skinned. . . . [Certainly] you have become most ungrateful, now that you are caciques and lords. You love your bodies, grown soft from lack of work. You turn back, on your way to war, and come lying to the cazonci, saying, "My Lord, the town you conquered is like this and this." With these lies you deceive the king who divided up the people and made you cacique. Alas, alas, I speak the truth, you peoples gathered here.]

Here the words of the petámuti give voice to the collective will of the gods, who lament the shortcomings of the people whose responsibility it is to provide for them. If he refers to Curícaueri in the third person in this passage, it is not only because he is speaking for the Uacúsecha (the Tzintzuntzanist position), but also because he is an embodiment of the entire pantheon of gods. As such, the petámuti takes care to reprimand the assembled "kings" (*irecha*), "lords" (*acháecha*), "caciques" (*caracha capacha*), "*ocánbecha*" (heads of units of twenty-five extended families), and "commoners" (*purépecha*), both separately and together.[42]

If the commoners are negligent in their responsibilities to their masters, he implies, the latter are even more culpable, for it is their responsibility to make sure there is sufficient "firewood" for the temples; that the fields are properly tended; the royal treasury well supplied in order to redistribute the surplus goods as necessary; and that the people are well fed and prospering. To "lie to the cazonci," by extension, is not only to betray a particular individual or dynasty, but to jeopardize the survival of the entire community kingdom and the very functioning of the cosmos.

In a different part of the *Relación de Michoacán*, the "gods of the fifth heaven" are addressed as follows: "you alone are kings and lords; you alone wipe away the tears of the poor" (188). In other words, the system of symbolic correspondences between earth and sky works in both directions: If the cazonci stands for Curícaueri, the opposite is also true. Thus, to speak in the name of the god is to give voice to his earthly representative (even if no such person exists at the moment of enunciation). Just as rulers stand in place of the gods, the gods are the prototypes for all who become "kings and lords." In this way myth functions as a "pattern for history" (López Austin [1990] 1993, 318).

Similarly, the reference to "the king who divided up the people" in the above passage is not just a fancy way of evoking the cazonci, but rather constitutes the very core of what the petámuti has been talking about throughout the entire performance. For the common thread that connects Taríacuri to those who ruled over the Lake Pátzcuaro Basin before him, those who ruled after him into the narrative present, and those who will rule in the future, is the act of dividing up the people, of symbolically reconstituting the iréchequa.

Taríacuri, as founder of the fourfold kingdom, may have been the first Uacúsecha leader to merit the title *cazonci*.[43] Tzintzicha Tangáxoan, executed by Nuño de Guzmán in 1530, may have been the last. But the possibility that someone will yet emerge to fulfill the role of "civilizer," to create a new iréchequa out of the ashes of preceding ones, is the hope implicit in the act of "remembering," of looking "behind . . . at the past" in order to draw lessons applicable to present circumstances.

On this more figurative level, the moral system exemplified in the petámuti's narrative is not entirely incompatible with Christian virtues, for many of the core values implicit in the mandate to burn "firewood" in the temples are capable of being translated into a colonial context. According to this reading, the petámuti is exhorting the assembled lords and caciques to make sure the places of worship are well maintained; to foment religious devotion among the people and punish transgressors; to oversee the collection of tribute and planting and harvesting of crops; to promote mutually beneficial exchanges with members of other groups; and to care for the commoners assigned to them, to figuratively "wipe away the tears of the poor."

On an even more universal level, his message to all the assembled peoples can be summarized in the mandate to fear the gods and, by so doing, to fulfill their personal destiny, to be who they "should be." Among the responsibilities entailed in this dynamic, they should burn tobacco and incense in prayer and otherwise faithfully perform the proper rituals at the appointed times; diligently practice their crafts; work the fields; defend the province in time of war; support their community leaders; marry and have children.

Respect for tradition is the sine qua non of all the above mandates. Like the nature of oral narratives themselves, however, which tend to be more flexible and adaptable to changing circumstances than written history, the tradition the petámuti is calling upon the assembled peoples to maintain is not fixed for all time, but rather a living, breathing expression of community values. This dialectical relationship of the petámuti with his listeners is exemplified by the audience's formulaic expression of approval at the end of the performance: "and they all [responded] it was well done" (157).[44] The "openness" of many oral narratives to audience participation is noted by its theorists (Lord [1960] 1965; Finnegan [1977] 1992, 231–35),[45] as are the tendency to "resemanticize" vocabulary borrowed from other traditions (Lienhard [1989] 1992, 108) and the importance accorded, not just the words themselves, but also the way they are delivered—the use of such variables as volume, tone, onomatopoeia, and gesture to cue the audience about how to interpret particular passages (Tedlock 1983, 3–155).

Another important association with the spoken, as opposed to written, word is its connection to the revelation of wisdom and to prophecy. In Plato's *Phaedrus* the privileging of speaking over writing is seen as the essence of the spiritual bond forged between teacher and pupil. The prophetic dimension of history is similarly highlighted in the work of many scholars who study the Spanish-American colonial period, whether their primary concern is with texts of European/Creole origin (Phelan [1956] 1970; Lafaye [1974] 1992), indigenous origin (López Austin [1973] 1989 and [1990] 1993; López-Baralt 1987; Florescano [1993] 1995 and 1999; León-Portilla 1992b), or some combination thereof (Bricker 1981; Gruzinski [1985] 1989 and [1988] 1993; MacCormack 1991; Baudot 1996).[46]

In this sense, the many lamentations expressed by Tirípeme Curícaueri through his ritual incarnation, the petámuti, take on the added significance of a call to the assembled peoples to find a way to make sense out of the unprecedented state of affairs brought on by the Spanish conquest. "Never before have we heard such a thing from our ancestors" (241), says the cazonci Zuangua upon receiving notice of a new, previously unheard-of people whose challenge to the hegemony of the Mexica could prove a threat to his own kingdom as well. The search for potential ways of inscribing these dangerously unfamiliar foreigners within indigenous tradition, of reinterpreting the prophecies and omens of the ancestors in order to account for the Spaniards' sudden appearance, comes across here as a primary motivating factor in the elaboration of the Escorial manuscript from the point of view of the petámuti and other indigenous participants.

For the prophets of the ancient Hebrews, the admission of personal culpability is the price to be paid for averting or overcoming calamity. In a similar fashion the petámuti returns incessantly to the notion that the assembled peoples have brought the wrath of the gods down upon themselves. "In this present year in which we find ourselves, Curícaueri bemoans his fate" (156), the petámuti proclaims, "alas, alas, I speak the truth" (157); all the "promises" you made have been broken, "thus are you most ungrateful" (155). In order to tame the power of the strange, to assimilate the previously unknowable, he insists, they must redouble their efforts to bring "firewood" for the temples, and the elders must take the initiative in searching the past for clues to help explain the displeasure of the gods.[47]

Nevertheless, one cannot fully appreciate the tenor of the petámuti's oral performance without understanding how the tone of lamentation that predominates in his concluding remarks is interspersed with humor. One example is the grotesque imagery of those lords excessively concerned with overt symbols of social status such as the turquoise lip plug, and who keep inserting bigger and bigger stones until they have enormous, distended lips (157). These exaggerated features are reminiscent of the petámuti's earlier description of that prototype of the debauched noble, Curátame II, about whom Tangáxoan indignantly remarks:

> enborrachese enborrachese y busque vna gran taça con que lo beua y sy no se hartare busca otra mayor taça y sy no se hartare que le alçen sus mugeres en alto y le zapuzen en vna tinaja de vino y que alli se hartara y que busque mas mugeres . . . y lleuadles las que tubieren grandes muslos y grandes asyentos y hynchira su casa dellas. (123)

> [Let him get drunk, let him get drunk. May he search for a huge cup in which to drink, and if he is not satisfied, look for an even bigger cup. And if he is [still] not satisfied, let his women lift him up high and submerge him headfirst in a vat of wine, [where] he will be sated. [Yea,] let him seek out even more women. . . . Bring those with great big thighs and enormous posteriors, [until] his house is stuffed with them.]⁴⁸

This sort of diatribe against drunkenness is a common motif in the petámuti's oral performance. As in the case of its moral antithesis—the mandate to "sacrifice the ears"—drunkenness serves here as a symbolic shorthand for a more general concept, that of licentious and sacrilegious behavior. The ideal Chichimec warrior, unlike Curátame, has a hard body and hands full of callouses; he does not adorn himself with rich robes, but rather covers his nakedness with only a loincloth and simple mantle; he does not overly indulge in the finer amenities of life, but practices ritual fasting and other forms of penance; he does not dilute the power of his divine life-force through indiscriminate sexual activity, but concentrates on founding a strong lineage with his principal wife.

The above characteristics, which make up the ideal attributes of the young adult male, do not necessarily apply with equal force to other categories of persons. This helps explain a certain ambivalence regarding the practice of polygamy in the pages of the *Relación de Michoacán*. Taríacuri, for example, eventually takes on more than one wife, but only after much soul-searching in response to the discovery of his first wife's infidelity (74–81). On the other hand, to have a large family and many women is repeatedly cited as one of the legitimate privileges of those who have the good fortune to become irecha, or king (44, 136).

The mandate not to dilute the sacred life-force also relates to marital rules promoting endogamy and discouraging the mixing of lineages (213).[49] In this regard Taríacuri, the son of a Uacúsecha lord and a woman from the island of Xaráquaro, has an innate disadvantage compared to Hiripan and Tangáxoan, for his dual ancestry makes him potentially susceptible to having "divided loyalties, rights, and powers" (López Austin [1990] 1993, 143). Nevertheless, once he becomes irecha, Taríacuri's mixed origin works to his advantage, providing him with a legitimate claim to the divine life-forces represented by the gods of both his paternal and maternal relatives, and thereby facilitating his reconstitution of the iréchequa centered on the Lake Pátzcuaro Basin. This combination of "male" and "female" attributes, although more "watered down" than the exclusively masculine virtue of the "purebred" Chichimec warrior, is also related to Taríacuri's success as a visionary and prophet.

Insofar as the principal characters in the petámuti's oral performance function as archetypes, they are able to transcend the limitations imposed by the life-spans of the historical individuals who embody them.[50] In the symbolic universe reenacted by the petámuti, Hiripan and Tangáxoan are always young, ever eager for the hunt, while Taríacuri is the prototypical cazonci, the wise and experienced ruler who lives to a ripe old age.[51] In the context of early colonial Michoacán, the questions become: Who will take the place of these archetypal characters? Who will metaphorically pick up the thread of sacred history temporarily lost in the crisis precipitated by the Spanish conquest and extend it into the future?

When the petámuti asks rhetorically in his concluding sermon, "Where are more Chichimecs to be found?" (155), he is thus inquiring as to the whereabouts of the symbolic successors of Hiripan and Tangáxoan. The unspoken corollaries to this question are: Who is destined to follow in the footsteps of Taríacuri? Who will serve to unite the powers of the solar god Curícaueri, in his various manifestations, with those of the goddess Xarátanga and other lunar deities? Who will have the power to symbolically reconstitute the iréchequa, to bring order out of chaos? And what signs could potentially serve as indications both that the time for a new foundation of the iréchequa might be drawing near and that a particular individual is the one destined to preside over the resettlement, the "dividing up," of the people?

In our search for the petámuti's implied answers to these questions, let us begin by analyzing the episode in his narrative that recounts the original "discovery" of the site for the temples to Curícaueri in Pátzcuaro.[52] I will then examine the pivotal role of this episode in light of other prophetic and foundational moments described in the *Relación de Michoacán* as well as in the context of additional documentary sources that suggest an incipient process of assimilating aspects of the colonial present into traditional mythico-historical categories.

SYMBOLIC LANDSCAPES

According to the literary theorist Michel de Certeau, all stories are symbolic languages of space ([1980] 1984, 115–30). This is especially true for narratives that trace their origin to oral traditions, for the multilayered symbolism of familiar places takes on special force in the presence of a live performer who can conjure up the spirits of the previous inhabitants by telling stories about them.

If one is to judge by the plethora of toponyms and demonstrative pronouns in part two of the *Relación de Michoacán*, the petámuti makes good use of the opportunity to point out the connections between the story he is recounting and the physical environment inhabited by him and his audience. Indeed, his entire performance can be read as a symbolic mapping of the landscape of the Lake Pátzcuaro Basin, in which important natural and humanmade structures—islands, mountains, springs, rocks, caves, forests, valleys, communities, pyramids, treasure houses, ruins—are mentioned in turn and associated with particular characters and events, often from widely divergent time periods.

Thus, in chapter seven, entitled "How [the Uacúsecha] found the place designated for their temples and how they accepted a challenge from those of Curínguaro" (34), the description of how Pátzcuaro came to get its name, many years before the Spanish conquest of the region, is interwoven with references to the efforts underway in 1538–39 regarding the transfer of the diocese from Tzintzuntzan. As the story begins, the Uacúsecha lords Uápeani II and Pauácume II are exploring the environs of their most recent settlement when they stumble upon a highly significant set of landmarks:

> veni aca aqui es donde dizen nuestros dioses que se llama çacapu hamucutin pazquaro veamos que lugar es y yendo siguiendo el agua no avia camino que estaua todo cerrado con arboles y con enzinas muy grandes y estaua todo escuro y hecho monte y llegaron a la fuente del patio del señor obispo que corre mas arriba donde esta la campana grande en vn cerrillo que se haze alli y llamose aquel lugar cuirisquataro y b\v/enieron deę\z/endiendo hasta la casa que

tiene ahora don pedro gouernador de la çibdad de michuacan a vn lugar que despues se llamo caropu hopansquaro andauan mirando las aguas que avia en el dicho lugar y como las viesen todas dixeron aqui es sin duda pazquaro ab\v/amos a ver los asyentos que auemos hallado de los cues y fueron aquel lugar donde a de ser la yglesia cathredal [sic] y hallaron alli los dichos peñascos llamados petazequa que quiere dezir [. . .] asyento de cu y esta alli vn alto y suuieron alli y llegaron aquel lugar y estauan alli ençima vnas piedras alçadas como ydolos por labrar y dixeron çiertamente aqui es aqui dizen los dioses que estos son los dioses de los chichimecas y aqui se llama pazquaro donde esta este asyento mirad que esta piedra es la que se deue llamar zirita cherengue y esta vacusecha que es su hermano mayor y esta tingarata y esta [. . .] mivequa ajeva pues mirad que son quatro estos dioses y fueron a otro lugar donde ay otros peñascos y conosçieron que era el lugar que dezian sus dioses y dixeron esconbremos este lugar y asy cortaron las enzinas y arboles que estauan por alli diziendo que abian allado el lugar que sus dioses les avian señalado. (34–35)

["Come here. This is the place our gods tell us is called Zacapu Hamúcutin Pátzquaro. Let us see what it is like." [So] they went along following the water, since there was no path, for it was all closed in with trees and huge oaks and was all dark and grown into wilderness. [Thus] did they arrive at the spring [the one in] the patio of the lord bishop that flows farther up, to where the large bell is, in a little hill that is formed there. That place was called Cuirís quataro. [From there], they continued descending to the house Don Pedro, governor of the city of Michoacán, has now, at a site later named Caropu hopánsquaro. They were walking along gazing at the waters there. Once they had seen them all, they [declared]: "This is surely Pátzquaro. Let us go see the foundations we have found for the temples." [Thereupon] they went to where the cathedral church is to be and found the said rocky outcrop called *petázequa*, which means base of a temple. [Indeed] there is a little elevation there. [When] they [had] climbed up and arrived [at] that place, standing there atop those protruding rocks, [which were] like idols not yet sculpted, they [proclaimed]: "Certainly, this is it, this is where the gods mean, for these are the deities of the Chichimecs and this spot, where lies this foundation, is called Pátzquaro. Look, this rock must be the one named Zirita cherengue and this one Uacúsecha, his elder brother;

this one [is] Tingárata and this [other] one Miueque Ajeua. Behold, these gods are four." [Then] they continued on to another location where there are other rocky outcrops. [Thus did they confirm] it was [indeed] the place about which their gods [had] told [them]. "Let us clear this site," they [determined]. So they cut down the oaks and [other] trees round about, saying they had found the place their gods had appointed for them.]

The symbolism of the natural springs and rocky outcrop with four protruding stones is similar to that of the eagle with a snake in its mouth perched on a flowering nopal cactus in the oral and pictographic traditions of the Aztecs or Mexica. That is, it functions as the definitive sign that the many years of pilgrimage endured by the Uacúsecha will soon come to an end, that they have arrived at the promised land described by the prophets, at the figurative center of their future kingdom. Moreover, as the analogy with the icon represented in the Mexican national flag suggests, this moment in the petámuti's narrative is pivotal in the formation of the collective identity of the inhabitants of the Lake Pátzcuaro Basin, in their construction of an "imagined community" à la Benedict Anderson (1983).[53]

In this sacred landscape oaks and other trees suggest the possibility of founding strong lineages, while natural springs and rocky protuberances mark the sites destined by the gods for human settlement.[54] The different kinds of "water" constitute figurative entrances to the watery underworld known as *pátzcuaro*. And the stone "foundation," called *petázequa*, whose rocky protuberances made of basalt (*tzacapu*) constitute a permeable boundary between earth and sky (*hamúcutin* is translated by Gilberti as "orilla generalmente," meaning "border"), is related to the veneration of the ancestors as gods.[55]

Thus, of the four distinctive rock formations that emerge from the base of the petázequa, one—the "elder brother"—is named Uacúsecha, like the ruling Chichimecs at the time of the Spanish conquest. Another—the "younger brother"—is identified as Zirita Cherengue—a name reminiscent of the title of the indigenous official (cherénguequauri) in charge of making cotton war doublets (177). As in other parts of the *Relación de Michoacán*, the coupling of an elder and younger brother here serves to unite two complementary concepts—in this case, bows and arrows (a Chichimec attribute) and cotton armor (associated with agriculture and textile production). The second pair of rocks—Tingárata and Miuequa Ajeua—may represent the brothers' female counterparts, as in the story of the creation of the first human beings from ash.[56] The fact that the four rocks are protruding, moreover, suggests an analogy with the legend of the four pillars holding up the universe. The number four can also be understood as a reference to the *tam hozqua*, the four stars of the Southern Cross evoked in an ancient song from Michoacán in connection with the ideas of pilgrimage and exile.[57]

The centrality of the above quote in my reading of part two of the *Relación de Michoacán* contrasts with the relatively marginal position accorded it in Francisco Miranda's editions of the Escorial manuscript. In the 1980 edition Miranda uses different typefaces to distinguish between those passages he attributes to the friar-compiler (standard type) and to the elders who provided the oral testimony (bold type). In the 2001 edition he sets off the friar's editorial commentaries as footnotes.

For the most part I agree with Miranda's attributions of particular utterances throughout the manuscript to either the friar or his indigenous informants. When it comes to those places in the text that do not fit comfortably within the Tzintzuntzanist interpretive tradition, however, like the references to the colonial present in the above description of the long-prophesied discovery of Pátzcuaro as center of the fourfold kingdom, Miranda tends to minimize their importance to oral tradition by marking them in whole or in part as interventions inserted by the friar at a later stage in the compilation process.

Thus, all references to Don Pedro and Quiroga in the above passage are presented by Miranda as originating with the friar-compiler, with the dialogue alone ascribed to the petámuti's oral narrative. The guiding thesis of my interpretation of the Escorial manuscript, in contrast, is based on the assumption that there is no such clear-cut distinction between prehispanic past and colonial present, no possibility of arriving at a presumably more "authentic" indigenous voice devoid of European cultural influences. As Dennis Tedlock explains, until recently the tendency among historians and ethnographers has been to "clip out what we judge to be truly aboriginal and cast aside anything that appears to us to be contaminated by the presence of Spanish missionaries" (1983, 333).

This approach has the unfortunate consequence, however, of de-emphasizing the agency of the indigenous peoples from colonial times to the present. If Christianity is assumed to be something imposed on the earliest inhabitants of the Americas without much active intervention on their part, then the value of post-conquest narratives in articulating an indigenous point of view declines in direct proportion to their degree of European influence. If, on the other hand, the process of cultural negotiation that took place during the colonial period is understood as a two-way dynamic, then texts such as the *Relación de Michoacán* are interesting precisely because of their "hybrid" nature, because they exemplify the way in which the principle of transculturation works in practice.[58]

To return to the analysis of the passage at hand, in the absence of corroborating evidence such as a transcription in the indigenous language of Michoacán of the petámuti's performance, it is doubtful we will ever be able to completely disentangle the friar's editorial commentary from the oral testimony. Judgments regarding the attribution of particular textual fragments are thus dependent on our ability as readers to come up with convincing arguments to explain their narrative significance.[59]

There are no easy criteria for determining how to go about this process, no rules of thumb that can be applied across the board without reference to narrative context. Once we discard the assumption that all references to the colonial present in the above quote necessarily originate with the friar-compiler, we are reduced to weighing the relative merits of attributing each sentence or sentence fragment to one contributor or another. Thus, the brief remark identifying Don Pedro [Cuiníarángari] as "governor of the city of Michoacán" stands out from the rest of the text, since presumably the assembled peoples would not need to be reminded of the status of one of their own leaders, and so it is a good bet for potential attribution to the friar-compiler. The same cannot be said, however, of other textual components. Why, for instance, would the friar bother to mention the "spring" located in the patio of Quiroga's episcopal residence, or the "large bell" on a nearby hill,[60] or Cuiníarángari's new house,[61] or the space set aside for construction of the diocesan cathedral? A more likely explanation is that these elements are included in the narrative not for the benefit of Mendoza or other European readers, but rather because of their symbolic significance for the petámuti and his indigenous audience.

Ironically, one of the keys to unlocking the traditional meaning of the oral performance is to concentrate on those aspects that are most innovative, that improvise on the standard story line in such a way as to fit it into a new context. Thus, the petámuti, by referring to concrete aspects of his surroundings as he metaphorically stands in place of the gods, is able to weave together the past of the ancestors, the colonial present, and the future heralded by the prophets. As Mircea Eliade observes, prophecy involves "the abolition of time through the imitation of archetypes and the repetition of paradigmatic gestures" ([1954] 1959, 35). We have already analyzed the symbolic significance of various details of dress and genealogy that help to elucidate some of these archetypal patterns.

What remains to be done is to explicate the way in which recurrent place-names mentioned by the petámuti function in a similar manner.

Throughout the petámuti's oral performance, the layering of symbolic meanings consistently occurs in connection with specific landmarks: the mountains where important visions and omens occur; the successive places where various peoples take up residence; the sites where Uacúsecha lords die and are buried; the forests where firewood is gathered and hunting expeditions are organized. The center of this metaphoric universe is the place where the petámuti himself is standing: in Pátzcuaro (42, 108), the location of the door to paradise through which [the] gods would descend and ascend (35).

The signs through which this symbolic door is made manifest to mortal eyes are described in the aforementioned paragraph: the natural springs and rock formations upon which Uápeani II and Pauácume II built their pyramids and which Quiroga also chose as the figurative center of his diocese; the very spot occupied today by the Museum of Popular Arts, intersection of the streets of Alcantarilla and Enseñanza, ex-Jesuit college with adjoining orchard, and atrium of the Jesuit church (Cárdenas García 1996, 29). Before performing a textual "excavation" on these historic Pátzcuaro locales, however, we need to spell out some of the patterns in the repetition of place-names in the *Relación de Michoacán*.

Consider the reference to Santa Fe (the pueblo-hospital founded by Quiroga on the northeastern shores of the lake in 1533–34) in the following account of an omen that occurred in the years preceding the birth of Taríacuri. Before the occurrence of this omen, which precipitated the uprooting of all the peoples settled in the Lake Pátzcuaro Basin, Tzintzuntzan served as the symbolic center of the iréchequa under the rule of the priests known as Uatárecha and their patron goddess, Xarátanga.[62] During a feast in the goddess's honor, they became inebriated and mocked certain aspects of the harvest ceremonies. The priests—especially two "brothers" named Quahuen and Camejan—put on wreaths made of red, green, and yellow chile peppers and bracelets of red and black beans. Meanwhile the priestesses, their "sisters"—named Pazímbane and Zucúraue—donned bracelets and necklaces made of kernels of red, spotted, white, and multicolored maize. Later, when the women went in search of fish to "cure" their brothers' hangovers, none were to be found, for the goddess had hid them all. Instead, they found a "large snake," which they skinned, cut into pieces, cooked, and ate with maize. At this point a magical transformation occurred:

ya que hera puesto el sol enpeçaronse a rrascar y arañar el cuerpo que se querian tornar culebras y siendo ya hazia la media noche tiniendo los pies junctos que se les avian tornado cola de culebra enpençaron a verter lagrimas y estando ya verdinegros de color de las culebras estavan ansi dentro de su casa todas quatro y saliendo de mañana entraron en la laguna vna tras otra y yvan derechas hazia vayameo cabe santa fee y yban hechando espuma hazia arriba y haziendo holas hazia donde estavan los chichimecas llamados hiyocan y dieronles bozes y ellas dieron la buelta y bolvieron hazia vn monte de la çibdad llamado tariacaherio y entraronse alli en la tierra todas quatro y donde entraron se llama quahuen ynchazequaro del nonbre de aquellos que se tornaron culebras y ansi desapareçieron y viendo esto los chichimecas llamados vacuseacha tuvieronlo por agüero. (25)

[Once the sun had set, they began to scratch and claw at their bodies, for they were turning into snakes. Round about midnight, with their feet together, [which were no longer feet but] a snake's tail, they began to shed tears. By now they were greenish black, the color of snakes. They were that way inside their house, all four of them. Leaving the house in the morning, they entered the lake one after another, heading straight toward Uayámeo near Santa Fe. They were spouting foam up high and making waves toward where the Chichimecs called Hiyocan were located. [Loudly] did they cry out to them, [whereupon the snakes] changed direction, heading back toward a mountain of the city [of Michoacán] named Taríacaherio. There they entered into the earth, all four of them. Where they entered is called Quahuen incházequaro, due to the name of those who turned into snakes. Thus they disappeared. The Uacúsecha Chichimecs, upon seeing this, held it to be an omen.][63]

Within Mesoamerican religious traditions, corn is typically considered a "male" food, while beans are encoded as "female" (López Austin [1990] 1993, 347). Thus, the sacrilegious nature of the above drunken parody of the harvest rituals dedicated to Xarátanga may involve the manner in which her priests and priestesses don jewelry associated with the opposite gender. This symbolic mixing of male and female elements—with its connotations of incest, given the way they address each other as siblings—is exacerbated by the brothers' request that their sisters go in search of fish for them to eat to cure their hangovers. Presumably, the cold, wet nature of fish also aligns it with the female aspect of things, a reading underscored by the sudden appearance of a "large snake," which is one of the animal incarnations of Xarátanga.[64]

The eating of the snake, in other words, is the metaphorical antithesis of the mandate to "feed" the gods that serves as the prototype for all virtuous conduct; and it results in the miraculous transformation of the Uatárecha into what they have just eaten. That is, they themselves become manifestations of Xarátanga and disappear into the earth on the side of Mount Taríacaherio (literally, "place of the great wind").[65]

The image of the four snakes "spouting foam up high and making waves" suggests that the Uatárecha were frightened away, forced to seek refuge in territory belonging to another dynasty, for "foam" is associated in another part of the text with canoes paddled vigorously for just this reason (118).[66] The union of the colors representing the center and four quarters of the world, moreover, suggests that the thematic focus of this episode involves the symbolic functioning of the iréchequa.[67]

What we have here, in short, is a figurative description of the disintegration of a once-powerful iréchequa centered in Tzintzuntzan around the cult of Xarátanga, an event that occurred several generations after the first Uacúsecha settlers arrived in the Lake Pátzcuaro Basin. This interpretation is reinforced by the petámuti's account of what happens immediately afterward. For the reaction of the peoples of the region to this omen is to metaphorically "scatter to the four winds," as in the local legend recounted by Maurice Boyd of the swallows that fly off in each of the four directions when a hawk pursuing them is struck by an arrow and falls to the ground (1969, 8).[68]

First, the Chichimec lord named Chánshori takes his god Huréndequauécara and settles in Curínguaro, followed by other Chichimec lords who take their respective patron deities and settle in the towns of Pichátaro, Irámuco, and Pareo. These four locations, not coincidentally, happen to be places where the Uacúsecha lords had previously organized hunting expeditions in the time of Curátame I (23). The subsequent rise to power of the Chichimec rivals of the Uacúsecha, including the lords of Curínguaro, is thereby encoded as destined to be of relatively short duration, for the Uacúsecha warriors had already symbolically laid claim to these locales through the principle of magic warfare.[69]

Even more extensive pilgrimages are undertaken by the gods Curícaueri and Xarátanga, who, along with their respective peoples, metaphorically "take to the mountains," a motif that recurs in various accounts of the years following the Spanish conquest of the region. Thus, the

Uátarecha priests move Xarátanga first to the slopes of Mount Taríacaherio, the place of prophecy where the four "snakes" entered the ground. From there she is brought to a place called Sipixo. These more or less temporary settlements are followed, in turn, by settlements at Uricho, Huiramangaro, Uacapu ("where Santángel is now constructed," notes the petámuti),[70] and finally to Taríaran and Acuézizan Arócutin.[71]

As for Curícaueri, the lords Uápeani and Pauácume take him from Uayámeo—site of the first Uacúsecha settlement in the Lake Pátzcuaro Basin near the future village-hospital of Santa Fe—to a large rock named Cápacuero, from there to Patamu angácarao, then to the side of Mount Ihuatzio zarauacuyo, subsequently to another place called Xénguaran, after that to Hónchequaro, and finally to Tarímichúndiro (this was a "neighborhood or subject town of Pátzcuaro" at the time the petámuti delivered his oral performance).[72] All these relocations transpire in the years preceding the definitive establishment of the Uacúsecha at Pátzcuaro, as prefigured in the quote cited at the beginning of this section.

One of the general principles that can be deduced from the recitation of all these toponyms is that the locales destined to serve as symbolic center of the iréchequa rotated over time, just as each of the major gods, in turn, was said to preside over a new "sun" or era (233–34). Part of the difficulty in interpreting indigenous testimonies from the early colonial period, such as those concerning the rivalry between the cities of Tzintzuntzan, Pátzcuaro, and Guayangareo-Valladolid (present-day Morelia),[73] is that it is often assumed the indigenous capital at the time of the Spanish conquest would continue as the preferred site of the local nobility.

The patterns exemplified in the petámuti's epic history, however, suggest that catastrophic events like the Spanish conquest, far from encouraging the ruling dynasties of the Lake Pátzcuaro Basin to remain in their current places of residence, would tend to precipitate the search for a new foundation for the iréchequa. This transitional period, moreover, would be characterized by heightened competition among those charged with discerning the will of the gods by interpreting the signs that transform everyday people and objects into divine presences.

The dynamic involved is similar to that in the description of the wanderings of the peoples of Curícaueri, Xarátanga, Huréndequauécara, and the other gods after the omen of the snake. Thus, one might anticipate that in 1538–39 (the time frame both for the transfer of the diocese and the transcription of many of the oral testimonies contained in the *Relación de Michoacán*) the petámuti and other prophets would be engaged in a search for clues from the past to help in determining the best site for the future foundation, destined to metaphorically unite all the "jewels" of the fourfold kingdom "in one place" (152).[74]

It is important to bear in mind, in this reading of the *Relación de Michoacán*, that one of the problems with prophecies is that their truth only becomes self-evident in retrospect. What seems inevitable from one point of view is not at all obvious from another. For the petámuti and his audience it is clear that the Uacúsecha are destined to become the next chosen people after the disbandings heralded by the omen of the snake. From the perspective of the characters in the story, however, many years must pass before they start to discern the shape of future events.

Indeed, when Taríacuri is a young man, hardly any of the other heads of dynasties see the Uacúsecha as potential rulers on a grand scale. Little by little, however, the eldest and wisest of them become impressed as Taríacuri systematically turns their best attempts at destroying him to his own people's advantage. Still, even after most of Taríacuri's contemporaries have correctly divined the will of the gods, they are nevertheless hard pressed to convince their "children"—figuratively, all the people under their care—to reform their decadent ways in time to avert imminent disaster.

As the moment for the consolidation of a new fourfold kingdom draws near, it is as if the mother goddess Cueráuaperi has gone mad. Everywhere, there are signs of the violation of the natural order of things: bulrushes and grasses grow in houses; bees make honeycombs in one night; saplings bear fruit before their time; tender maguey plants sprout thick stalks like wooden poles; little girls become pregnant before reaching puberty, laden with swollen breasts and children on their backs; old women give birth to obsidian blades—black, white, red, and yellow ones (110–11).

This excess of fertility is a terrible thing, a harbinger of imminent war, famine, death, and destruction. The weeds growing in houses signify the neglect of proper ritual, that is, of good "housekeeping." The frantic activity of the bees may be a metaphor for the idea that it is too late to prevent catastrophe, for no matter how hard they try, the bees cannot successfully complete the metamorphosis of their larvae in one night. The fruit of the saplings will not endure; neither will the immature maguey plants be able to produce wine for the religious ceremonies, nor the fragile prepubescent girls withstand the heavy responsibilities of motherhood before their time. And the multicolored obsidian blades are a clear reference to Tirípeme Curícaueri—the god in whose name the new iréchequa will be established through the sacrifice of those peoples who do not submit voluntarily.

Many of these same signs recur at the time the indigenous peoples of Michoacán first hear of the Spaniards, according to Don Pedro Cuiníarángari in part three of the *Relación de Michoacán* (242). Moreover, a few years previously, also during the reign of the cazonci Zuangua, an omen had occurred on Mount Xanóato hucazio that echoes many elements in the story of the earlier disintegration of the fourfold kingdom under the rule of the Uatárecha and their patron goddess, Xarátanga.[75] Once again there is an animal who represents a god, in this case a white eagle with large eyes and a wart on its forehead who is a manifestation of Curícaueri.[76] The references to the dismantling of the iréchequa are quite explicit in this prophecy, for the Tirípemencha are told by the messenger god Curita caheri to: put out the "hearth fires"; "break the wine vessels"; "leave off the human sacrifices"; and "destroy the drums [of war]" (234). In other words, to abandon their settlements and prepare for the dawning of a new Christian era.

The odd thing about these premonitions dating from shortly before the Spanish conquest, in comparison with the ones recounted by the petámuti from an earlier era, is that the eagle omen and the signs of nature gone berserk occur within a few years of each other. Perhaps that is the meaning of the enigmatic statement made by the god Curita caheri and his Tirípeme "brother" regarding the violation of the "determination [made] at the beginning . . . that no two gods walk together before the coming of the light, so we do not kill one another and lose our divinity" (233). The dispersion of the inhabitants of the Lake Pátzcuaro Basin triggered by the snake omen takes place while the Uacúsecha lords Uápeani II and Pauácume II are still young. And the reestablishment of the center of the iréchequa in Pátzcuaro does not occur until Pauácume's son Taríacuri is an old man. In other words, there is a relatively long transition period between the end of the reign of Xarátanga and the initiation of Curícaueri's supremacy.

One of the difficulties presented by the Spanish conquest, from the perspective of indigenous tradition, is the lack of the requisite number of generations to put the heads of competing dynasties to the test and thereby prepare for the symbolic foundation of a new era. As Alfredo López Austin observes: "violent changes or rapid innovations can overwhelm the processes of refunctionalization or remythification" ([1990] 1993, 308).

Still, the story told by Cuiníarángari in part three of the *Relación de Michoacán* provides some clues as to what must happen next in order to insure the dawning of a new "sun" under colonial rule. During the reign of Hiripan's son Ticátame in Ihuatzio, it turns out, there was a prophecy made by a poor old woman, a water seller, who claimed that the gods of the fourfold kingdom, the Tirípemencha, had told her:

> de aqui a poco tienpo nos lebantaremos de aqui de cuyuacan donde agora estamos y nos hiremos a mechuacan y estaremos alli algunos años y nos tornaremos a lebantar y nos yremos a nuestra primer morada llamada bayameo donde esta aora santa fee edificada. (242)

> ["Within a little while, we will rise up from here, from Ihuatzio, where we are at present, and will go to Tzintzuntzan. There we will be a few years, [before] we rise up again and go to our first dwelling place called Uayámeo," where Santa Fe is now constructed.]

The symbolic meaning of this passage is not difficult to interpret. First, a prophecy is made that had already been fulfilled at the time of the Spanish conquest: namely, the transfer of the Uacúsecha capital from Ihuatzio to Tzintzuntzan following the rule of Ticátame II (the move from Pátzcuaro to Ihuatzio had occurred upon the death of Taríacuri).[77] The most interesting prediction made by the old woman, however, is that, after Tzintzuntzan, the next capital of the fourfold kingdom will be Uayámeo— the site of the first Uacúsecha settlement in the area.

The way in which the old woman's prophecy is framed is also significant. In order to underscore its contemporary relevance, Cuiníarángari mentions that Uayámeo is the same spot where the pueblo-hospital of Santa Fe is now located.[78] Moreover, he attributes the recollection of this ancient prophecy to the cazonci Zuangua. In this way, Cuiníarángari is able to cast Zuangua in the role of the prototypically wise old ruler who foretells the end of the preeminence of his own people and, in so doing, manages to pass on to his descendants crucial information about what they will need to do once the fall of the iréchequa centered in Tzintzuntzan occurs.

Just as the role of the prototypical "son," whose task is to avenge the death of the "father" and thereby preside over a reconfiguration of the fourfold kingdom, is fulfilled by more than one character in the Escorial manuscript, there is an oscillation between: (1) the presentation of the founding of Santa Fe Uayámeo as precursor to the definitive establishment of the iréchequa at Pátzcuaro (following an analogous process to the appearance of the morning star as herald of the coming dawn); and (2) the notion that Santa Fe Uayámeo is itself destined to serve as the "sun," the symbolic center of a new moral and spiritual foundation.

Whichever position is highlighted, however, Quiroga's central role as both founder of the Christian community of Santa Fe and driving force behind the transfer of the diocese from Tzintzuntzan to Pátzcuaro marks him as likely to be the one predestined to bring the divine plan to fruition.

Another precondition for the fulfillment of the prophecy involves those who are the custodians of the ancient wisdom, who must also perform their role in the cosmic drama. Indeed, while the rise and fall of mortal kingdoms mimics the mathematical precision of the rising and setting of celestial bodies, this cycle is not divorced from human agency, for its regular recurrence depends upon events occurring on the surface of the earth. Interesting corroborative evidence for the active role of the indigenous nobles of Michoacán in determining the site for the future pueblo-hospital as a means of bringing their own prophecies to fruition can be gleaned from another document—the official record of the residencia that took place in 1536 upon completion of Quiroga's term as oidor for the Second Audiencia.

During this hearing several of the indigenous witnesses who testified on Quiroga's behalf mentioned that the determination of the site on which to found Santa Fe was left to the discretion of the nobles of Michoacán. Don Francisco, a lord of Ihuatzio, states that when Quiroga first arrived in Michoacán two and a half years previously:

> ... habló con los principales ... e les hizo entender que iba allí por mandado de su Majestad y que le fuesen leales y le obedeciesen por señor e se quitasen de muchas cosas malas e sacrificios que tenían porque Dios no se servía de ello ... que dejasen sus idolatrias y borracherias ... e que si querían que hiciese o mandase hacer un hospital como uno que había hecho en ... México que él trabajaría que se comenzase e hiciese, e ... pareció que Dios nuestro Señor inspiró en ellos porque luego buscaron un lugar para do se hiciese el dicho hospital y ellos fueron a enseñarle un barrio. ... e que ellos querían entender en ello. (Aguayo Spencer 1939, 430)

> [... he spoke with the nobles ... and gave them to understand that his going there was by order of his Majesty and that they be loyal to [the king] and obey him as their lord and give up many bad things and sacrifices that they had because God had no use for [such things] ... that they leave off their idolatries and drunken feasts ... and that if they wanted him to make or have made a hospital like the one he had built in ... Mexico, that he would undertake that it

be initiated and carried out, and . . . it was as if God Our Lord himself inspired them because they immediately searched for a place for the said hospital to be built and they went to show him a settlement [in the lake district]. . . and [told him] that they wanted to arrange for it.] (my trans.)

Don Francisco's testimony echoes many of the motifs central to the petámuti's oral performance: the trope of speaking in place of god and king; the implication that it is time for a new moral foundation; the idea of being inspired by the god destined to preside over the dawning of a new era; the search for the appointed place from which to begin to make the proper arrangements.

The testimonies of the other indigenous witnesses from Michoacán add more layers to this interpretation. Don Ramiro, an elder from Pátzcuaro who was over forty-seven years of age in 1536, emphasized the moral dimensions of Quiroga's activities: the bringing of order to a previously chaotic state of affairs in the region, especially with respect to the regulation of sexual behavior and the need to unify all peoples of the province under one spiritual authority. Don Alonso de Ávalos Acanysante, a lord of the *nahuatlatos* (Nahuatl speakers), stressed the concept of reciprocity—that the Spanish king was obliged to bestow favors upon the indigenous peoples of Michoacán because of their exemplary devotion to the Christian god. Another Don Francisco, a representative of the Huréndetiecha, used the metaphor of Santa Fe as a foundation (a translation of the term *petázequa*?) upon which to cement proper moral conduct in the region. Several of the indigenous witnesses, moreover, alluded to Quiroga's "civilizing" role in resettling those people who had "fled to the hills" (ibid., 429–30).[79]

So dramatic were the changes wrought by the founding of the pueblo-hospital of Santa Fe de la Laguna in Michoacán that the general consensus of the witnesses at Quiroga's residencia was that they must be due to "the hand of God" (ibid., 439, 444). The bishop of Mexico, Juan de Zumárraga, who was a Franciscan, went so far as to declare that the friars of his own order had been unable to make much progress in the evangelization of the area until Quiroga's arrival on the scene. Zumárraga also stated that Quiroga, who was a layman at the time, had so devoted himself to the work of God that he served as an "example, even a reproach, for the bishops of these parts" (ibid., 428–29). These glowing reports of Quiroga's accomplishments as oidor were a decisive factor in the crown's decision to propose him for first bishop of Michoacán later that same year.[80] And so the ground was prepared for the next stage in the symbolic rebirth of a territory that was still in the throughs of a devastating period of war, disease, famine, and political instability.

When Quiroga returned to Michoacán as bishop-elect in 1538, he set about making the arrangements for moving the majority of the residents of Tzintzuntzan to Pátzcuaro.[81] Why the determination was made to establish the diocese in Pátzcuaro, when the papal bull authorizing Quiroga to be consecrated as bishop specifically named the church of San Francisco in Tzintzuntzan as the diocesan see, has provoked a great deal of speculation over the years. With his training as a lawyer, Quiroga must have been well aware of the legal ramifications; he certainly went to some length to ward off potential challenges to the designation of Pátzcuaro as the spiritual and administrative capital of the province, albeit not entirely successfully.[82]

Territoriality, as Robert Sack observes, is always "socially constructed. It takes an act of will and involves multiple levels of reasons and meanings" (1986, 26). The official Spanish ceremonies marking the transfer of the diocese did not take place in a vacuum, but in a landscape inscribed with multiple layers of signs. Like the petámuti's oral narrative, these official ceremonies were performed with at least two audiences in mind. While the Spanish notary recorded the participation of Quiroga and other members of the clergy, the mayor, *regidores* (municipal councillors), and other Spanish residents of Tzintzuntzan, he likewise noted the presence of Don Pedro Cuiníarángari, Don Alonso, Don Ramiro, and the Purépecha commoners. The "great contentment and willingness of the natives" regarding the projected move is registered with particular care (León [1903] 1984, 265–70).

Clearly, the purpose was to conform to protocol according to the requirements of the Spanish legal system. At the same time these ceremonies provided a way of educating a recently converted populace regarding their place within the new hierarchy. Part of the genius of Quiroga, as James Krippner-Martínez has suggested, was that he offered a space for the indigenous people to exercise some control over their own inscription into the colonial system, despite his strong authoritarian and paternalistic tendencies (1993, 153–58, 2001, 71–106, 151–79). The passage concerning the founding of Pátzcuaro in the *Relación de Michoacán* provides evidence that the aforementioned approval of Cuiníarángari and the other indigenous participants was not just an empty formula. Rather, in the search for a meaningful way to integrate the traumatic experience of conquest within their cultural landscape, it marks the beginning of a dynamic process of transculturation.

Thus, the location for the new cathedral was chosen at the site of the ruins of the indigenous temples built on top of the strange rock formations representing the first human beings, who were godlike in their omniscience.[83] And the fountain at the bishop's residence was constructed over one of the natural springs that made up another component of the sign marking the end of the Uacúsecha's lengthy migration. This process of multiple coding continued throughout the colonial period with the dissemination of popular legends such as Quiroga's miraculous "discovery" of this very same spring by striking a rock with his "crosier—a ceremonial staff used by bishops" (León [1903] 1984, 209–10; Salas León [1941] 1956, 100–101). The spot where this event is said to have occurred is marked today by a modest stone plaque. Nearby, there is a monument containing a statue of the famous Virgen de la Salud, to whom Quiroga was allegedly praying when he struck the rock.[84]

Like the previously mentioned theme of Quiroga as a great "civilizer" who resettled those peoples who had fled to the mountains and brought order from chaos, this rediscovery of the sacred spring points to Quiroga as the chosen one charged with ushering in a new Christian era. Once more, a process begun in Uayámeo is brought to fruition in Pátzcuaro. Yet again, human agency is required in order to correctly identify and act upon the clues provided by the gods, but the general pattern of events is familiar. The spiral has advanced in one dimension, but not in the other.

I am not suggesting there was a consensus among all the indigenous peoples of the region at the time of compilation of the Escorial manuscript regarding Quiroga's role in the fulfilment of prophecy or the best site for locating the new Christian capital. On the contrary, just as "the struggle for the control of myth is part of the history of its functions" (López Austin [1990] 1993, 285), the championing of competing candidates is one of the hallmarks of the process described in part two of the *Relación de Michoacán*. The legal maneuvering manifested in other documents from the period over which city (Tzintzuntzan, Pátzcuaro, or Guayangareo-Valladolid) deserved the title "ciudad de Michoacán" can be similarly read as based on competing interpretations of indigenous history in the making.[85] Likewise, the longstanding debate regarding whether Quiroga or Fray Juan de San Miguel, one of the early Franciscan missionaries in Michoacán, deserves greater credit for founding hospitals in the region and dividing up craft specialties among the local communities can be understood as an expression of rivalry between different groups of Christian converts eager to promote one of their own foundational figures.[86] As has been observed by numerous commentators, neither of these colonial-era heroes invented the underlying relations of reciprocity upon which the economy of the region has depended since ancient times.[87] Their role is more akin to that of the prototypical cazonci who symbolically reinterprets traditional categories in the light of present circumstances.

Quiroga's philosophy, as expressed in his surviving writings, differs from that of Bartolomé de las Casas and other celebrated defenders of the rights of the indigenous peoples in that he lays a greater degree of blame for the sufferings of the indigenous peoples on their own resistance to Christian rule. The crux of my argument, however, is that this view is consistent with the prophetic vision articulated by the petámuti in his oral performance, as is Quiroga's emphasis on reordering indigenous society and government. As Quiroga put it, his goal:

> ... no hera quitárselo, sino hordenárselo, dárselo y confirmárselo, y trocárselo y conmutárselo todo en muy mejor sin comparación. (cited in Acuña 1988, 58)

> [... was not to take it from them, but to order it for them, return and confirm it for them, and exchange and commute it all into something incomparably better.] (my trans.)

The manner in which Quiroga was inspired by Thomas More's *Utopia* (Zavala [1937] 1965) and by contemporary Hispanic ideals regarding the founding of hospitals and cities (Warren 1963; Warren and Warren 1996) is not contradicted by this reading. Nevertheless, in terms of his symbolic presence within the pages of the *Relación de Michoacán*, Quiroga's importance is largely a function of the way in which he comes to occupy a similar space in the cultural geography of the Lake Pátzcuaro Basin to that of the great Uacúsecha hero Taríacuri.

CONCLUSION

As Helen Perlstein Pollard observes in her authoritative study of the prehispanic Tarascan state:

> Taríacuri, the great culture-hero and legendary founder of the Tarascan state, is no longer seen as the link between the people and their destiny. Rather, he was replaced by Bishop Vasco de Quiroga, "Tata Vasco," colonial administrator and cleric from 1538 to 1565, who is

extolled as the creator of the new social order. More recently, this founder of the colonial world is being increasingly replaced by Lázaro Cárdenas, ex-governor of the state of Michoacán, ex-president of the Mexican Republic, and hero of the latest new order, the modern Mexican state. (1993, 3)

One of the goals of this chapter has been to clarify the process whereby a symbolic bridge from Taríacuri to Quiroga began to be articulated in Michoacán circa 1538. If I have accorded a central role in the construction of such a link to the oral performance of the petámuti in the *Relación de Michoacán*, it is because the prophetic dimensions of his narrative suggest such a reading. In the vision voiced by the petámuti, there is no absolute boundary between the age of the ancestors, the moment of delivery of his performance, and those future dates when Taríacuri's true successors will become apparent. It is largely because of this dissolving of key aspects of his narration into a timeless present that the story he tells is still relevant today.

In the progressive transformation of the petámuti's words and gestures into an alphabetic text in Castilian, much was inevitably lost to posterity. Even more striking than what is unrecoverable, however, is what remains in plain view. The patterns, like constellations, suggested by the petámuti's use of symbolic language are there for all to see. The difficulty lies in temporarily setting aside the dominant Tzintzuntzanist interpretive tradition by finding a way to posit analogies with the better-known central Mexican and Maya mythologies without thereby losing the distinctive flavor of the petámuti's prophetic voice.

5

THE MANY FACES OF
DON PEDRO CUINÍARÁNGARI

The Indigenous Governor

> El rechazo del discurso europeo y su apropiación indígena coexisten
> ... las dos actitudes aparentemente antitéticas no son sino las dos
> caras de la misma moneda.
> —*Martín Lienhard*

The final drawing of the Escorial manuscript (plate 44, color section) captures the moment of the arrival in Tzintzuntzan in 1522 of the first Spanish military expedition to the region under the command of Cristóbal de Olid, a deputy of Hernán Cortés.[1] Don Pedro Cuiníarángari, whose testimony regarding the conquest in part three of the *Relación de Michoacán* is the primary source for our present-day understanding of this paradigmatic moment of cultural encounter,[2] is standing behind the cazonci Tzintzicha Tangáxoan, trying to get his attention. The cazonci, who is carrying a bow and arrow and wearing various adornments made of gold, feathers, jaguar pelt, and deerskin, is indecisive, caught between Cuiníarángari at his back (who is bringing him a message from the captain of the Spanish forces) and another indigenous noble named Timas. The latter's head is turned towards the cazonci, but his body and the index finger of his right hand are pointing in the direction of a priest wearing a uanduqua and another principal lord, who are heading in the opposite direction. Also depicted are porters carrying a variety of household objects, on both shores of the lake, as well as several people hiding behind maguey and other plants, carrying small children, animals, an earthenware vessel. On the waters of Lake Pátzcuaro, two canoes are visible, one filled with goods, the other empty.

The indecision of the cazonci in this picture echoes the famous vacillation of Moctezuma as described in the writings of Bernal Díaz del

Castillo and Francisco López de Gómara. But it is the characterization of Don Pedro Cuiníarángari that sheds the most light on the textual dynamics of this representative instance of the colonial genre defined by Miguel León-Portilla as "visions of the vanquished" ([1959] 1992). Like the anonymous *Anales de Tlatelolco* (1528) or book twelve of the *Florentine codex* (1577–80), Cuiníarángari's narrative, compiled circa 1538,[3] contains a mirror image of the heroic accounts written from the point of view of the Spanish conquistadors.[4]

Until recently the focus of scholars and popular readers alike has tended to remain fixed on the confrontations between Moctezuma and Cortés, Atahualpa and Pizarro, Tzintzicha Tangáxoan and Olid, and so forth. One of the disadvantages of this orientation, however, is that it deflects attention away from the processes of textual production and reception through which these prototypical stories of conquest have been passed down to us. As David Murray writes in his introduction to *Forked tongues: Speech, writing and representation in North American Indian texts*:

> By paying attention to the mediator or interpreter, rather than what he is pointing to, or in other words by concentrating on the various forms of cultural and linguistic mediation which are always taking place, we reduce the danger of making the space between the two sides into an unbridgeable chasm, or of turning differences into Otherness. Any temptation to imagine an archetypal pristine moment of confrontation between absolute others needs to be tempered by the almost ubiquitous presence on the scene of someone, usually an Indian, or . . . a mixed-blood, who had already made the connection, and who could act as mediator. (1991, 1–2)

In the interpretation of culturally hybrid texts such as the *Relación de Michoacán*, it is the figure of the intermediary that must guide the analysis if one is to avoid the temptation to either romanticize the "other" or, in the case of colonial-era chronicles and relaciones, engage in a knee-jerk condemnation of all things Spanish.[5]

If one looks closely at the image that Cuiníarángari projects of himself in the Escorial manuscript and the version he gives of events in Michoacán from 1519 to 1530, it becomes clear that shades of gray are more prevalent than black and white. He does not exalt his own position vis à vis the cazonci, nor does he come across as a puppet of the Spaniards. Rather, he portrays himself as a high government official faced with two often conflicting imperatives: to serve the cazonci and to keep his new masters, the Spanish colonial authorities, happy; fidelity to the past and survival in the present. His attempt to reconcile these two imperatives provides the dramatic tension that propels the story to its ultimately tragic conclusion. The subtext consists, on one hand, of information Cuiníarángari conceals about his own role in the death of the cazonci, and, on the other, of the possibility that Tzintzicha was not entirely innocent of charges brought against him by the Spaniards.

The image of the intermediary functions both as a metaphor for the role of Cuiníarángari within the text and also for the textual dynamics of the *Relación de Michoacán* as a whole, as we have seen in previous chapters. Compare the self-definition of the friar-compiler as "interpreter," the way he acts as a medium through which the elders are able to tell their story to the viceroy. The friar's appeal in the prologue to the authority of Jerome, patron saint of translators, likewise carries with it connotations of cultural mediation.

Regarding the other participants in the making of the *Relación de Michoacán*, similar cases can be made for their inscription within the text as cultural intermediaries. The anonymous caracha (scribes-painters) who, along with the copyists, were collectively responsible for the production of the text as artifact were trained in both Mesoamerican and European writing traditions. In the story told by the petámuti of the rise to power of the Uacúsecha, moreover, the role of messenger is highlighted through various motifs: the petámuti who serves as mouthpiece for the cazonci, who speaks, in turn, for the gods; the three elders Chupítani, Nuriuan, and Tecaqua—the ultimate repositories of moral authority—who shuttle back and forth between Taríacuri and the heads of rival lineages. In this sense, the role of the three elderly priests depicted in the frontispiece as informants for the friar-compiler is simply an extension of their traditional function as representatives of the cazonci and the Tirípemencha gods of the fourfold kingdom.

In the figure of Don Pedro Cuiníarángari these two threads of cultural mediation—interpretation and representation—come together as well. Like the friar-compiler, Cuiníarángari is positioned in the frontispiece between the elders and the viceroy. His role as indigenous governor is to interpret the commands of the Spaniards for the indigenous nobles and to serve as spokesman for the latter—to translate their needs and points of view into a language comprehensible to the colonial authorities. Even though Cuiníarángari never learned to speak Castilian, his role in the Escorial manuscript is that of a cultural interpreter.

As an official in the government of the cazonci, Cuiníarángari also serves as a messenger in the pages of the *Relación de Michoacán*. First, he is sent by Tzintzicha to round up warriors to fight against Cristóbal de Olid. Later, he is sent to surrender to Olid outside of Tzintzuntzan. Soon afterward, he is sent to Mexico City with one of the first shipments of gold and silver for Cortés.[6] Upon Cortés's replacement as highest colonial authority in New Spain by the members of the First Audiencia, Cuiníarángari is sent to search for more gold and silver to pay the ransom demanded for the cazonci by the Audiencia's president, Nuño de Guzmán. In all these instances Cuiníarángari reports the words of Tzintzicha to his subjects or to the Spaniards, and the words of the Spaniards and their interpreters to the cazonci. His duties are basically those of a go-between or emissary.

The way Cuiníarángari is dressed in the frontispiece marks him as an intermediary figure in another sense, that of a cultural hybrid. Unlike the friar and viceroy, who are in European clothing, or the three elderly priests, who are dressed exclusively in items of indigenous origin and symbolism, Cuiníarángari is situated at a crossroads between two different systems of signification. To begin with, he is wearing a turquoise lip plug known as an *angámequa*—an indigenous symbol of high office and nobility. The fish ornament on his hat, moreover, may constitute a reference to Michihuahcan as "place of the owners of fish" (Martínez Baracs 1997, 161–62) or perhaps to his Huréndetiecha heritage, which marks him as a descendant of those legendary fisherfolk considered the original inhabitants of the region. At the same time he is wearing a Spanish-style robe with belt, white ruff, hat, and black shoes; and, in the censored version of the frontispiece, he is praying.[7]

Even his name positions him on the boundary between indigenous and European cultural traditions. Thus, he is "Don"—a Spanish term designating an hidalgo, or person of noble birth[8]—and also Pedro, for Saint Peter—his baptismal name, which is appropriate given that the biblical Peter was both a fisherman and keeper of the keys. Still, he maintained his indigenous surname, which can be broken down into the components: *cuiní* (kwiní), bird; *harhá* (haṛá), pierced; and *nharhi* (ŋaṛi), face.[9] According to José Corona Núñez, the suffix *nharhi*—he spells it *ngari*—personifies the noun it modifies (1986, 110–11); thus, Cuiníarángari translates as both "bird with pierced face" and "pierced bird personified." In accordance with the conception of the *nagual*, or alter ego, references to humans of animal appearance evoke the principle of shamanic transformation.[10] And, since certain animals are symbolic representations of the gods, this name may simultaneously serve a totemic function.

In a similar way, the animals shown in plate 44 (color system) potentially stand for more than a literal reading of this drawing might lead one to assume. The horses upon which the conquistadors are riding are explicitly associated, in the accompanying prose narrative, with the "deer" who serve as manifestations of the solar deity Cupanzieeri (241). As for the animals being held in the lower register, one is a type of dog; the other, a bird. There is even a small fish lying on the ground.

On a literal level these pictorial animal references correlate with the account in the prose narrative of the food eaten by the conquistadors. Cuiníarángari mentions, for instance, that Olid's men ate a large quantity of "tortillas and partridges and eggs and fish" during the "six moons" they spent in Tzintzuntzan during the initial expedition (256). It is also possible, however, that the dog and bird stand for religious statues and other representations of the gods that were concealed at the time of the Spanish conquest. Or the dog may be a *uitzume*—the "perro de agua" famous in Mesoamerican mythology as the animal guide who leads the spirits of those who die by drowning to their final resting place. It is also conceivable that it functions as a name tag identifying the younger son of the cazonci, Huitziméngari.[11]

Given the ubiquitousness of the metaphor of "feeding" the gods analyzed in chapters three and four, the question arises: Are the animals in plate 44 destined to be eaten by the humans, or will the people serve to feed the animals, who stand for the gods of war? In accordance with my thesis regarding the multiple levels on which the metaphors of the Escorial manuscript tend to operate, I am inclined to see both interpretations as part of apparently antithetical readings that coexist, as Martín Lienhard puts it in the quote cited in the epigraph, like "two faces of the same coin." The first alternative suggests that the story told by Cuiníarángari should be taken at face value; the second, that it forms part of a vast symbolic universe made up of magical equivalences that can transform even the most commonplace of objects.

Another way of phrasing the same question, one that ties in with the notion of cannibalism featured in the work of Brazilian filmmakers of the '60s and '70s, is: Which of the human groups pictured—the Spaniards or the indigenous inhabitants of the Lake Pátzcuaro Basin—will eat the other?[12] That is: Does Cuiníarángari's narrative serve to inscribe the peoples of Michoacán within a European-based system of signs? Does it serve as a means for the indigenous peoples to symbolically "ingest" those aspects of colonial society they deem acceptable and "excrete" the rest? Or does it function in both ways at once, just as Cuiníarángari's appropriation of the discourse of Christianity implies a simultaneous rejection and affirmation of traditional indigenous values?

The emphasis on magical transformations in the Escorial manuscript, as in the common English expression "you are what you eat" (see discussion of the snake omen, chapter three), is accompanied by the necessity, on the part of the indigenous collaborators, to engage in a deliberate strategy of subterfuge. This form of doublespeak, a result of unequal power relationships institutionalized during the colonial period, is characterized by Lienhard as a type of "diglossia." While the conquered peoples are required to speak "Christian" before the colonial authorities, within their indigenous communities they continue speaking their ancestral languages ([1989] 1992, 107).

Another way of envisioning this dynamic is to picture the context of enunciation for those texts of indigenous origin that became part of the colonial record. The argument proposed in this chapter—that there is more than one way to interpret Cuiníarángari's words—should not be surprising given that he had more than one implied audience in mind. Like the petámuti's contribution to the *Relación de Michoacán*, Cuiníarángari's testimony was originally delivered in the form of an oral performance. Thus while he was addressing the friar-compiler and, through him, Viceroy Mendoza, the Holy Roman Emperor Charles V and, by extension, all other speakers of "Christian," Spanish and indigenous alike, he also delivered his account of the conquest in front of representatives from the major indigenous lineages of the Lake Pátzcuaro Basin and, above all, the elders who represented the living memory of the indigenous community.

Because the story he is telling is situated at a cultural crossroads, it follows that in order to be effective it must conform to more than one literary model. It has to be capable of being read as a Christian allegory and, at the same time, offer an interpretation of the conquest consistent with traditional indigenous values. Moreover, because the events he is recounting are still fresh in the minds of the members of his audience, the element of psychological trauma that lies just beneath the narrative surface should not be underestimated.

Cuiníarángari's "two faces" are a function of both political opportunism and genuine, even anguished, self-examination. The alternative voice represented by the writings of the caciques and principal lords of the early colonial period, as Lienhard observes, is not devoid of anxiety resulting from their precarious position in colonial society:

> Estos escritos revelan la doble preocupación de mostrarse adictos al nuevo poder y al cristianismo sin dejar de reivindicar ciertos valores antiguos.... Sin duda, los caciques-principales exorcizan, a través de esta práctica literaria, su mala conciencia de "colaboracionistas." ([1989] 1992, 66)
>
> [These writings reveal a double preoccupation: to demonstrate their allegiance to the new power and to Christianity without thereby neglecting to vindicate certain ancient values.... Without a doubt, the caciques and principal lords exorcize, through this literary practice, their guilty conscience as "collaborators."] (my trans.)

The prototype of all colonial-era collaborators is La Malinche—Cortés's interpreter and mistress, also referred to in sixteenth-century texts by her Christian name, Marina, preceded by Doña to indicate her noble origins, despite having been sold into slavery as a child.[13]

Like La Malinche, the reputation of Cuiníarángari has not fared well over the centuries. And, like her, his role in events that transpired from the time of the Spanish arrival on the scene until his death circa 1543 is due for a reevaluation.[14] Even La Malinche's gender, in certain respects, parallels that of Cuiníarángari, who is consistently encoded in the *Relación de Michoacán* as "female" because of his status as a descendant of the sedentary Huréndetiecha fisherfolk of Xaráquaro—those who represent the figurative antithesis of the nomadic Chichimec hunters.[15]

Among the Aztecs or Mexica, the symbolic female double of the *tlatoani* (supreme ruler) was named *cihuacoatl* (literally, "snake woman")— a position whose responsibilities included acting in lieu of the tlatoani in his absence, temporarily assuming power in the event of his death, and overseeing the administration of justice, religious ritual, and public works (León-Portilla 1980, 276–77). As a manifestation of the goddess Quilaztli— one of whose names was, precisely, Cihuacoatl—the occupant of this office was encoded as "female" in spite of the traditional requirement that he be both of the male gender and an outstanding warrior.[16]

The apparent contradiction between invisible female "essence" and male "covering" is resolved through recourse to the notions of divine possession and of all living things as combinations of contrary elements (López Austin [1990] 1993, 122–39). In accordance with this logic, the male priests of the goddess Cueráuaperi are referred to as "mothers" in the Escorial manuscript (236), and ice cream, in spite of its low temperature is encoded by the Nahuas as a "hot" food (López Austin [1990] 1993, 171–72).

As a cultural icon, La Malinche stands for both a particular historical individual and a generic archetype. It is this dual identity, as Margo Glantz observes, that renders her susceptible to the need for periodic reevaluations: "como cualquier personaje mítico y a la vez histórico—que desaparece y reaparece en forma cíclica en nuestra historia—, debe ser periódicamente revisado y quizá descifrado" (1994, 7). Because of Cuiníarángari's characterization as a male prototype of those who belong to the mother's line of descent,[17] he similarly functions on both levels: as an individual with distinctive positive and negative qualities, and also as a cipher upon whom the hopes and fears of those who judge him are projected.

Insofar as Cuiníarángari represents a person once made of flesh and bone, it is necessary to search the historical archives for clues to help contextualize the characterization he gives of himself in the pages of the Escorial manuscript. Insofar as his story forms part of an intertextual dialogue situated on the cusp of indigenous and European cultural traditions, however, it must be understood as more than just an important source of documentary evidence. Caught in a web of often contradictory signs, Cuiníarángari spins the stuff of legend using the tools of the traditional storyteller. His narrative, like the chronicles and relaciones of the colonial period in general, does not fit within the parameters established by modern canons of historiography. For this very reason it is not sufficient to judge it as "fact"; it must also be understood as "fiction."[18]

TEXT AND CONTEXT

The images of Don Pedro Cuiníarángari that can be gleaned from a perusal of colonial-era documents are quite disparate. Depending on the source, he comes across as an intelligent, persuasive negotiator; a portly buffoon; a proud and arrogant lord; a faithful emissary; or a cowardly traitor. Vasco de Quiroga described him as such an eloquent speaker that he brought tears to the eyes of those present at the court of the Second Audiencia (Aguayo Spencer 1970, 101). To the Spanish conquistadors and encomenderos, he was known, rather jocularly, as Pedro Panza—a reference, perhaps, to his well-endowed midsection.[19] When the deputy Gonzalo Juárez ordered him in 1529 to return the residents of Purúandiro and Guaricaro to their villages or be put to death, he responded scornfully "that he didn't want to return them and they should go ahead and execute him" (Escobar Olmedo 1997, 81; my trans.). And yet, when the cazonci was on trial a year later for the murder of Spaniards and for continuing to receive services from the towns given in encomienda, Cuiníarángari was the only indigenous noble to provide testimony against him, thereby originating the contemporary image of him as a treacherous opportunist who betrayed his lord (ibid., 72–73).[20]

Indeed, one of the most problematic facets of Cuiníarángari involves his participation in events that led up to the trial and execution of the cazonci in 1530. The circumstances surrounding this execution are telling and worth going into at length. For the sake of expediency, let us begin two years previously, in 1528, with the arrival in Michoacán of Juan de Ortega, the third in a series of inspectors sent to investigate the deaths of some sixty to seventy Spaniards at the hands of the indigenous population as well as other complaints brought by the Spanish authorities and encomenderos.[21]

In punishment Ortega enslaved most of the residents of Uruapan and Sevina, set dogs on several indigenous lords, and had others burned to death. He also encouraged the Spaniards to burn and plunder indigenous temples as a means of combating idolatry and obtaining slaves. At the same time he tried to prevent continued problems by warning Cuiníarángari under penalty of death not to take tribute from the encomiendas. He also reportedly declared that the cazonci deserved to die for his role in the killings, but was prevented from laying hands on him or other principal lords by a letter from the royal treasury official, Alonso de Estrada. Tzintzicha was under arrest in Mexico City by order of Estrada at the time. Although the punishments meted out by Ortega were heavily weighted in favor of the Spaniards, they were not entirely one-sided, for he also confiscated the encomiendas of Alonso de Mata and Juan de Sámano, whose mistreatment of the Indians under their authority he considered one of the underlying causes of indigenous unrest (Warren 1985, 124–36, 194–98, 207–208).

Ortega's intervention did not resolve matters, however. A year later, in 1529, Cuiníarángari and two of the cazonci's highest ranking Nahuatl interpreters—Don Francisco (his indigenous surname is not mentioned) and Gonzalo Juárez Cuycique—were accused by the comptroller Bernaldino de Albornoz of interfering with the control of the encomenderos over their towns. They were charged on several counts: depopulating villages; secretly using Indians granted in encomienda to cultivate maize and other crops; continuing to receive services from the said Indians and thereby preventing them from fully serving their new masters. Again, Cuiníarángari was threatened with death, but he responded scornfully. That year Tzintzicha was once more imprisoned in Mexico City, this time in the quarters of the president of the First Audiencia, Nuño de Guzmán.

Finally, in January of 1530, a trial was instituted against the cazonci by the encomendero of Uruapan, Juan de Villegas.[22] The charges against him included all the accusations that had been raised at various times since the official surrender to Olid in 1522. He was accused of ordering the deaths of Spaniards, of keeping the lords of the encomienda towns with him in Tzintzuntzan and thereby inhibiting their service to the Spaniards, of hiding the location of silver mines from the colonial authorities, and of practicing sodomy. Cuiníarángari is initially mentioned as codefendant, but after his testimony against the cazonci the charges against him were dropped. Previously, Cuiníarángari, Tzintzicha, and Gonzalo Xuárez Cuycique had been tortured by one of Guzmán's cronies, the chief law-enforcement officer in Tzintzuntzan, Antonio de Godoy, to get them to confess to the location of hidden treasure. Guzmán was organizing his first major expedition of conquest to Nueva Galicia (present-day Jalisco) and, in spite of the fact that the cazonci had already sent him several shipments of gold and silver, he was still desperate for funds to reimburse money he had borrowed from the royal treasury.

After the departure of the expedition from Tzintzuntzan, new charges were brought against the cazonci by Guzmán. He was accused of plotting to ambush the Spaniards at a place called Cuinao, of continuing to worship idols and practice human sacrifice, of dancing in the skins of Spaniards. In order to prove these charges, Tzintzicha was tortured. He was stripped naked and tied to a rack; his arms and legs were bound with cords, which were then tightened twice, on his right arm. The following day, Cuiníarángari was tortured. The ropes were tightened on his arms and legs six times; his entire body was stretched by the tightening of the *maestra* (main rope), and one pitcher of water was poured into his nose through a cloth. Don Alonso Vise and the Nahuatl-speakers Gonzalo Juárez Cuycique and Alonso de Ávalos Acanysante suffered even greater torments. On February 14, 1530, the cazonci was dragged through the camp by a horse, strangled, and then burned at the stake.

It is easy to condemn the testimony of Cuiníarángari against Tzintzicha when taken out of context; more difficult, if one takes into consideration the kinds of pressure that were being exerted on him at the time by Guzmán. Within a matter of months—from June–July 1529 to January 1530—Cuiníarángari underwent a transformation from an attitude of active defiance toward the Spanish authorities to one of, at least external, submission. It is not difficult to see why the figure of Guzmán occupies such a prominent place in the testimony of Cuiníarángari a decade or so later, at the time of compilation of the Escorial manuscript, nor why his depiction of Cortés, in comparison, is relatively benign.[23]

The documents that tell of Cuiníarángari's activities after the death of Tzintzicha are also revealing, both for what they say about Cuiníarángari and about his relationship with the other indigenous nobles of Michoacán. In late October 1532, for instance, Cuiníarángari traveled to Mexico City at the head of a delegation of nobles from Tzintzuntzan, including the two sons of the cazonci—Don Francisco Taríacuri and Don Antonio Huitziméngari—to plead for justice before the oidores of the Second Audiencia. One of these judges was Vasco de Quiroga. In his *Información en derecho*, written three years later, Quiroga recalls at length the impression that this visit gave him:

> ... que las lástimas y buenas razones que dixo y propuso, si yo las supiera aquí contar, por ventura holgara vuestra merced tanto aquí de las oír y tuviera tanta razón después de las alabar, como el razonamiento del Villano del Danubio, que una vez le vi mucho alabar yendo con la corte de camino de Burgos a Madrid, antes que se imprimiese, porque en la verdad parescía mucho a él y va cuasi por aquellos términos. (Aguayo Spencer 1970, 101)

> [... for the lamentations and sound reasoning that he expressed and put forth, if I knew how to tell them here, by chance Your Grace would receive as much pleasure in hearing them and have as much reason to praise them as the speech of the Villain of the Danube, which once I heard you praise greatly, when the court was on the road from Burgos to Madrid, before it was printed. For in truth he much resembled him and [his speech] was expressed in almost the same terms.] (my trans.)

Quiroga is referring here to Antonio de Guevara's popular book, *Libro aureo de Marco Aurelio*, which includes a speech given by the "rustic of the Danube" before the emperor Marcus Aurelius protesting the treatment of his people at the hands of Roman soldiers.[24] The moral lesson to be derived from this analogy is clear: The indigenous peoples may appear "barbaric" to the colonial authorities, but they are highly cultured and capable of expressing their refinement in unmistakable ways, despite the language barrier and the great depths to which they have fallen as a conquered people.

Based on his reading of the historical record, J. Benedict Warren concludes that Cuiníarángari was power hungry, a mysterious and sinister character always trying to be on the winning side.[25] There is no lack of direct and circumstantial evidence to support such a position. It is certainly possible that the death of the cazonci, in which Cuiníarángari played a role, led him to covet greater power for himself and his descendants. This interpretation, moreover, is consistent with the analysis outlined in chapter four regarding the way in which transitional periods between eras are traditionally characterized by heightened competition among rival dynasties. It also ties in with the systematic encouragement of divisions among the indigenous peoples by the colonial authorities as a means of consolidating Spanish rule.[26] And there is documentary evidence to the effect that in the 1550s Cuiníarángari's son Don Bartolomé was engaged in a power struggle with Don Antonio, the son of the cazonci.[27]

Nevertheless, if we are to take seriously the insight expressed by Quiroga in the above quote, it is not enough to take Cuiníarángari's appearance at face value. Whether or not he was a political opportunist, he was also a great orator capable of giving voice to the anguish of his people. And, by so doing, he provided a narrative context through which this suffering could be transformed into political action on the part of sympathetic colonial officials such as Quiroga, who used the anecdote about Cuiníarángari to argue, in his *Información en derecho*, against the continued exploitation of the indigenous population.

The friar-compiler of the *Relación de Michoacán* may cast doubt upon the depth of the indigenous peoples' conversion to Christianity in his prologue and intercalated commentary.[28] In the view of Don Pedro Cuiníarángari, however, it is the conquistadors who do not measure up to Christian standards. In his allegory of conquest Christ is the victor, not the Spaniards.

A pictorial equivalent of this position can be observed in plate 44 (color section), insofar as the spears held by Olid and his men as they ride into Tzintzuntzan are a reference to the Christian god they metaphorically carry with them. These spears are so huge that they dwarf the human figures who carry them. In the confrontation symbolically represented in this drawing, steel—a compound that can be shaped into weapons more powerful than indigenous knives—is destined to triumph over flint and obsidian, Jesus Christ over Curícaueri.[29] The story of the resulting mass conversions, however, does not focus on the initial bearers of the new religion, but rather on the largest figure in the drawing—the cazonci—who will prepare the way for the word of God to take root in the province.

In a similar manner the efforts of the Spaniards toward achieving the spiritual conquest of Michoacán are systematically de-emphasized in the story told by Cuiníarángari. Instead, he highlights the role of Tzintzicha in laying the groundwork for the conversion of all the peoples of the iréchequa, or fourfold kingdom. As in the petámuti's oral performance analyzed in chapter four, the symbolic dawning of a new "sun" rises from the ashes of preceding ones; in this case, out of the sacrifice entailed in the cazonci's symbolic martyrdom through fire.

THE SPANISH CONQUEST AS CHRISTIAN ALLEGORY

If one starts from the premise that Don Pedro Cuiníarángari was capable of great eloquence that could profoundly move those who heard him speak, one has to wonder: What rhetorical strategies did he use to achieve this effect? Or, to turn the above question on its head: How can a literary analysis of his narrative help to clarify the stance Cuiníarángari takes in relation to the Spanish conquest?

One of the characteristics of Cuiníarángari's account, according to Warren, is the tendency to "telescope" events—to present a number of similar occurrences as one incident (1985, 27). Thus, Tzintzicha's repeated visits to Cortés are condensed into one; the many times the cazonci was under house arrest in Mexico City (beginning with his imprisonment by Estrada) also become one, under the authority of Guzmán (Warren 1985, 132, 148–50). Although Cuiníarángari reports that Moctezuma sent messengers to Tzintzicha's father, Zuangua, he also suggests that this appeal for help took place while the Spaniards were in Tlaxcala, by which time Moctezuma was dead and Cuitláhuac was in command, and during the siege of México-Tenochtitlan, by which time both Zuangua and Cuitlahuac had died of smallpox or measles (ibid., 24–26). Again, it would appear that Cuiníarángari's account has condensed several embassies into one.[30]

Certainly, the story told by Cuiníarángari of the arrival of the Spaniards and death of the cazonci is more a passionate defense than a balanced presentation. His telescoping of events, although it violates modern canons of historiography, serves an important narrative function by adding to the overall dramatic effect.[31] In a few short years he witnessed the fall of a great empire and humiliation of a once powerful lord, the earthly representative of the god Curícaueri. "The sun these two realms used to gaze upon, that of Mexico and this one" (239), exclaims Zuangua at the beginning of Cuiníarángari's narrative.[32] By the end Zuangua's successor, Tzintzicha Tangáxoan, has been imprisoned, tortured, burned at the stake. "Behold, behold, you people, this man who was a scoundrel who wanted to kill us. . . . Behold him and take heed. Behold you commoners, for you are all scoundrels" (275), cries the Spaniard who announces the cazonci's death sentence to the indigenous warriors and prisoners in Guzman's camp. A rigorous historical narrative with attention to every detail would not produce such a strong impression in the listener/reader.[33]

Another rhetorical strategy used by Cuiníarángari is antithesis. Zuangua is portrayed as a wise and capable ruler, well versed in the ancient wisdom and interpretation of signs, shrewd in his dealings with the Mexica. He does not act in haste upon hearing of the arrival of the Spaniards, but sends messengers to Mexico to see what is happening for themselves. Concurrently, he calls a meeting of the council of elders to determine the significance of this new information. In making his decision he expresses distrust of his old enemies, whose trouble he ascribes to their inadequate manner of worshiping the gods,[34] but he does not underestimate the momentousness of what they have to say. And so he determines to remain vigilant, stoke the flames of religious fervor, and intensify preparations for war:

> pues aqui trabajemos mas como no suelen mudar el proposyto los dioses esforçemonos vn poco mas en traer leña para los ques quiça nos perdonaran. (244)
>
> [Let us work harder then, for do not the gods often change their plans? Let us exert ourselves a bit more in bringing wood to the temples. Perhaps they will forgive us.]

The metaphor of bringing firewood to the temples, as discussed previously, ties in with a whole series of symbolic equivalencies involving the proper functioning of the cosmos, the waging of war as a means of "feeding" the gods, the responsibilities of rulers in regards to their subjects and vice versa, and the human condition in general. In other words Zuangua's response is fully consistent with traditional expectations regarding the behavior of a cazonci. What Zuangua implies is that he will redouble efforts to ensure that all the peoples of the fourfold kingdom, including himself, fulfill their ritual obligations in an exemplary manner and, by so doing, he hopes to serve as an effective advocate for them in symbolic dialogue with the gods.[35]

If Zuangua comes across in Cuiníarángari's narrative as an exemplary ruler in both indigenous and European terms, the same cannot be said of Cuiniarángari's initial characterization of Zuangua's eldest son and successor, Tzintzicha Tangáxoan. Because of his father's untimely death,

Tzintzicha was not provided with the traditional opportunity to be coached in the proper behavior expected of a cazonci (219). Usually, when a cazonci became very old or sick, his successor was expected to begin shouldering many of his duties: "siendo muy biejo el que hera cazonçi en su bida enpezaba a mandar algun hijo suyo que le avia de subçeder en el rreyno" (219).

It should not be surprising, therefore, that in contrast to Zuangua he comes across at first as immature, uncertain, weak willed. He orders his three brothers killed for allegedly having slept with his women, then regrets having done so. He decides to fight the Spaniards to the death, then prepares to drown himself in Lake Pátzcuaro, then changes his mind and goes into hiding in Urapan. On the way to surrender to Cortés outside of Mexico City he begins to cry, afraid that Cuiníarángari and Tasháuaco have deceived him and he is going to be sacrificed.

At the turn of the century the historian Eduardo Ruiz characterized the cazonci, based on his portrayal in the *Relación de Michoacán*, as "a weak personality, reserved, hypocritical, and given to perverse sentiments" ([1891–1900] 1971, 416).[36] This wretched coward, capable of killing his own brothers but not of putting up a fight against an invading army, is contrasted with the young Mexica lord Cuauhtemoc, who valiantly defended his people against the Spaniards (ibid., 421–22).

This nineteenth-century reevaluation of the cazonci differs markedly from the dominant image of him that appears in the writings of colonial-era missionaries. The young king portrayed in Bartolomé de las Casas's *Brevísima relación de la destrucción de las Indias* (1542) is an innocent victim who, in spite of having voluntarily embraced the authority of the Spanish crown and the new faith, is brutally tortured and executed by Guzmán. The woodcut by Theodore de Bry that accompanied the 1597 German translation of the *Brevísima* depicts Tzintzicha with the soles of his feet being burned by a sadistic youth who pours oil over them, a vicious mastiff barely restrained by a Spaniard on one side, a third tormenter with primed crossbow on the other (Sebastián 1992, 133). As late as the 1940s this same current of Christian symbolism was tapped by Jesús Romero Flores in his rebuttal to Ruiz's negative characterization of the cazonci described above.[37]

The development of the pejorative image of the cazonci as an effeminate coward dates from shortly after the discovery and publication of the *Relación de Michoacán* in 1869, following centuries during which it lay forgotten in the Real Biblioteca del Escorial outside Madrid. What has generally escaped observation, however, is that the contrary image of the recently baptized cazonci as Christian martyr also draws much of its force from the version of the Spanish conquest articulated by Cuiníarángari and other nobles from Michoacán.

The root of the problem lies in the tendency of much Western scholarship to overlook the coexistence of oral and written traditions even in highly literate societies. This "tyranny of the alphabet" (Mignolo 1995; Lienhard [1989] 1992) is all the more problematic when applied retroactively to societies steeped in oral discourse. In spite of the highly legalistic mentality of missionaries and crown officials during the early colonial period, they had more in common with indigenous guardians of oral tradition than we sometimes choose to acknowledge today. Fray Bernardino de Sahagún's famous tribute to the rhetorical sophistication of the Nahuas in the prologue to book six of the *Florentine codex* is a case in point.

If one looks closely at Quiroga's description of the speech delivered by Cuiníarángari to the Second Audiencia in 1532, it can be seen to contain, in embryonic form, the same version of the conquest he later presented to the friar-compiler and indigenous audience circa 1538. The gist of Cuiníarángari's argument, according to Quiroga, was that the more the indigenous peoples humbled themselves before their masters, the worse they were treated; the more gold and silver they offered, the more they incited the Spaniards' greed (Aguayo Spencer 1970, 101–102).

It is not purely by chance that this viewpoint coincides with Las Casas's thesis regarding the exemplary gentleness and humility of the indigenous peoples as opposed to the overly choleric temperament of the Spaniards when inflamed by the sins of avarice and pride. Without necessarily constituting an instance of direct influence, this example illustrates how Cuiníarángari and other indigenous spokesmen were able to take advantage of a lack of unanimity among the Spanish colonial authorities with respect to the best way to govern the newly conquered territories, thereby laying the foundation for a legal defense of their people grounded in their model Christian behavior.

Ironically, the same presentation that struck a sympathetic chord in many missionaries and crown officials during the colonial period has tended to generate the opposite reaction in Mexican nationalists from Independence to the present, for whom humility in this context reads as cowardice, gentleness as weakness. The contrasting portraits of the cazonci in the sixteenth-century writings of Las Casas and La Rea, on one hand, and the nineteenth-century ones of Ruiz and Riva Palacio, on the other, are drawn from much the same sources; they simply cast the available evidence in a different light.[38]

As for Cuiníarángari's rationale for portraying the cazonci as he does in part three of the *Relación de Michoacán*, the apparent contradiction between the negative and positive images contained therein can be resolved by clarifying the dramatic and political exigencies that helped shape the story at the time of its inception. Essentially, Cuiníarángari was put in the position of having to account for the "bad" decisions made by Tzintzicha, most notably those that conflicted with Spanish interests, such as the decision to assemble warriors against Olid, or with Christian morality, such as the determination to have his brothers killed. Rather than ascribing these decisions to the cazonci alone, he attributes them to the evil influence of a certain noble named Timas and his followers who, according to Cuiníarángari, were only interested in stealing power from the cazonci. Through this operation Cuiníarángari is able to achieve two ends: he is able to avoid direct criticism of Tzintzicha; and he is able to position himself in the text as the opposite of Timas, as the "good" adviser who counsels the cazonci to receive the Spaniards in peace.

In order to achieve a sympathetic portrait in the eyes of the Spanish colonial authorities, Cuiníarángari also provides only partial or enigmatic information about some of the cazonci's actions. Did Tzintzicha intend to sacrifice the Spanish messengers sent by Cortés in 1521, as asserted by Francisco Montaño (Cervantes de Salazar [1566] 1985, 789–90)? Cuiníarángari says only that the cazonci:

> . . . hizo conponer los españoles como conpunian ellos sus dioses con vnas guirnaldas de oro y pusieronles rrodelas de oro al cuello y a cada vno le pusieron su ofrenda de vino delante en vnas taças grandes y ofrendas de pan de bledos y frutas dezia el cazonçi estos son dioses del çielo. (246)

> [. . . had the Spaniards adorned, the way they dressed their gods, with gold headdresses. Also, they put gold shields around their necks, and before each one they placed his offering of [maguey] wine, in large cups, and offerings of amaranth bread and fruit. The cazonci said: "These are gods from heaven."]

In the description given by Montaño, Tzintzicha's actions are characterized as preparations for the Spaniards' ritual sacrifice.[39] Cuiníarángari's testimony, on the other hand, remains open to several interpretations. On the surface he appears to be saying that the cazonci intended to honor the Spaniards, that he literally believed they were gods or messengers of the gods. For those familiar with indigenous symbolism, however, the treatment of the Spanish messengers as gods implies that Tzintzicha was considering the possibility of having them ritually sacrificed. Compare, for instance, plate 41, which shows the manner in which certain sacrificial victims were traditionally attired with headdresses and gold disks prior to their immolation.

Another inconsistency between Cuiníarángari's account and other sources has to do with whether or not some of the cazonci's warriors engaged in combat with the Spaniards under Olid. Legend has it that a general named Nanuma led the attack at Taximaroa, the border town between the Aztec and Tarascan empires, and also that in a neighborhood of Pátzcuaro, the so-called "barrio fuerte," a few hundred warriors under Timas and his daughter Eréndira held out against Olid before they were finally overpowered by the Spanish forces.[40]

Cuiníarángari's testimony regarding the events that took place at Taximaroa is enigmatic. On his way to round up warriors for the cazonci, he says he met a captain called Quézequaparé who told him that "all those of Taximaroa are dead" (249). Later, after Cuiníarángari had been "captured" by the Spaniards at Taximaroa (it is not clear whether he let himself be captured deliberately or not), his brother Tasháuaco (generally referred to in the text by his Nahuatl name—Huitzitziltzin)[41] asked him about the meaning of Quézequaparé's words, and Cuiníarángari replied: "I do not know; he refused to speak with me when I encountered him" (250). Tasháuaco's question is not answered, nor is an explanation provided for how the Spaniards captured Cuiníarángari. The possibility of an indigenous defeat at Taximaroa is hinted at, then passed over in silence.[42]

The scapegoating of Timas and use of ambiguous language goes some distance in explaining how Cuiníarángari shapes his presentation to the colonial authorities. But the dominant strategy used by Cuiníarángari to achieve a sympathetic portrait of the cazonci and, by extension, the indigenous peoples he represents is the aforementioned appeal to the notion that the essence of the conquest can be distilled into a parable about humility versus cholera, generosity versus avarice.

With the exception of a few brief appearances by Franciscan friars,[43] the Spaniards described in part three of the *Relación de Michoacán* are dominated by an insatiable hunger for gold. "These gods must eat it, they crave it so" (260), the cazonci remarks when faced with Olid's repeated demands for treasure. Another example of unadulterated greed and treachery is the Spanish interpreter García del Pilar, who takes his *mordida* (bribe) from each shipment of gold and silver sent to Guzmán without ever speaking to him on behalf of the cazonci.

By way of contrast the cazonci and other indigenous nobles do not hesitate to part with their worldly possessions:

> avn quedo vn poco de oro y plata \~~del pasado~~ que nos dexaron/ llebalo para que lo queremos nosotros del emperador es. (268).
>
> [There is still a little remaining of the gold and silver \bequeathed us ~~from the past~~/. Take it. What use is it to us? It belongs to the emperor.]

Whether the cazonci's reference to the Spaniards as gods who eat gold is meant to express wonder or contempt, there is no question that the conquistadors' behavior is at odds with Christian moral standards. In comparison, the comportment of the cazonci, after his surrender to Cortés and subsequent baptism, is exemplary according to these same standards.[44]

If, in the first part of Cuiníarángari's story (corresponding to the conquest of Michoacán by Cortés's deputies) the cazonci does not come across very well in comparison with his father Zuangua (237–64), in the second part of the story (which takes place during the presidency of Guzmán) Tzintzicha redeems himself by suffering with patience and dignity a plethora of unprovoked attacks and humiliations (267–77). More than his immaturity and weakness upon assuming command, it is this transformation that determines the cazonci's central narrative function. In other words, it is only after having been baptized Francisco, in honor of Saint Francis of Assisi, and having undergone a symbolic trial by fire under Spanish rule that he realizes his full potential. By the end of the story there is no question, moreover, that Tzintzicha has finally become "who he ought to be" (224) in accordance with indigenous tradition as well, the prototype of the good ruler: "he who carries the most sadness with him" (203).

The arrival of Guzmán as president of the First Audiencia functions as a pivotal moment in this reading of Cuiníarángari's narrative, for it provides the cazonci with an opportunity to prove his true capacity for leadership. Soon after coming to power, Guzmán orders the arrest of Tzintzicha and Cuiníarángari. From this inauspicious beginning, his behavior progresses from bad to worse. He issues impossible demands, treats the cazonci in a demeaning manner, makes false accusations, loses his temper, and resorts to physical violence. Each time they bring him what he has demanded he flies into a rage, insulting Tzintzicha, kicking the treasure with his foot, attacking Cuiníarángari with his sword. The cazonci is put in a double bind: Prohibited from continuing to exercise sovereignty over his subjects, he is nevertheless required to make constant demands on them for food, treasure, and services to satisfy the exaggerated expectations of Guzmán and his cronies.

Again, the most lucid observations regarding the situation are put in the mouth of Tzintzicha himself. On the contrast between Guzmán and Cortés, the cazonci notes: "He doesn't want to do this with us gently and little by little" (269).[45] On the impossibility of meeting all the demands made by Guzmán: "Sir, have your own people send to the towns [for eight thousand warriors to take part in the expedition to Nueva Galicia], for they belong to you" (273). On the agonizing contradictions of the situation in which he has been placed: "It would please me to die" (270).

If, in the first part of Cuiníarángari's narrative, Tzintzicha misses the opportunity to die a hero on the battlefield, in the concluding section he lives up to the even greater task of enduring with dignity an ignominious death at the hands of a brutal tyrant. Like the image of Cuiníarángari praying in the censored version of the frontispiece, the characterization of the martyred Don Francisco Tzintzicha Tangáxoan in part three of the *Relación de Michoacán* converts him into a symbolic rallying point for the recently baptized population of Michoacán, a metaphor for their spiritual superiority over the Spaniards according to both traditional Christian and indigenous definitions of virtue and vice.

CUINÍARÁNGARI VERSUS TIMAS

The above reading of Don Pedro Cuiníarángari's account of the conquest as a Christian allegory does not exhaust its interpretative possibilities. To use Lienhard's metaphor, Cuiníarángari is not only speaking a form of "Christian," but also his native tongue. Or, to put it another way, if there was disagreement among the Spanish colonial authorities regarding the best way to position themselves vis à vis the conquest, how can we expect there to have been consensus among the indigenous peoples towards such a traumatic event?

The way in which Cuiníarángari dramatizes this conflict among his own people—through a series of confrontations between himself and Timas—suggests that (1) he did not underestimate the potential appeal, for his indigenous listeners, of those with whom he disagreed; and (2) there is an undercurrent of self-doubt in Cuiníarángari's presentation that allows him to maintain a critical distance from the position he himself champions in the story: Namely, the decision to appropriate the spiritual power of the Christian god in order to gain certain rights, for himself and his people, within colonial society.

In the "Christian" reading of the above confrontation, Cuiníarángari unequivocally triumphs over Timas. My goal in the remainder of this chapter is to elucidate an alternate way of viewing this dynamic. The underlying question is where, along a spectrum arrayed between the two poles of collaboration (the standpoint represented by Cuiníarángari) and separatism (the stance championed by Timas), the indigenous peoples of Michoacán should position themselves. Far from unconditionally supporting his own representation of himself in this debate, Cuiníarángari, using Timas as mouthpiece, highlights the costs entailed in the decision to convert to Christianity. In this manner Cuiníarángari—as storyteller—symbolically exorcizes his bad conscience, and that of his audience as well, regarding their role in the cazonci's death.

In order to perceive this dimension of Cuiníarángari's narrative, it is necessary to pay close attention to those signs that point in more than one direction simultaneously. Consider, for instance, the way that Tzintzicha is dressed in plate 44 (color section). The bow, arrow, and quiver mark him as a Chichimec hunter. The deer hooves dangling from his calves convert him into a symbolic equivalent of the horses (i.e., large deer) that the conquistadors are riding. Like them, the cazonci is also a representation of the god Cupanzieeri, the one whose resurrection signals the dawning of a new era.[46]

The gold ear plugs and turquoise lip plug indicate that he is a *quangari*, or valiant man (178). The feather-decorated cotton armor is a sign of preparation for war (157). Other prototypically masculine attire includes the jaguar-skin headdress and armband (68).[47] The red sandals are an attribute of those who are of noble birth (81); the turquoise necklace, a privilege accorded those who are kings (44). Finally, the little gold bells he is wearing around his calves are associated both with prisoners prior to their ritual sacrifice (150) and with traditional burial ceremonies (219).

Indeed, the closest parallel with the way Tzintzicha is dressed in plate 44 (colored section) can be found in two other pictures and accompanying prose descriptions in the Escorial manuscript: the account of how a captain general was traditionally outfitted when leading troops into battle (192; plate 32), and the chapter on the burial ceremony of a cazonci (219–20; plate 39). All three descriptions mention the bow, arrow, and quiver; the lip and ear plugs; the jaguar-skin headdress with green plumes;

the jaguar-skin armband; and the gold bells. In short, Tzintzicha is attired, as Olid's expedition approaches Tzintzuntzan, in a way that suggests readiness for war, readiness for death.

In this context the figurative tug-of-war between Cuiníarángari and Timas for the cazonci's attention translates as a struggle over which side of the proverbial coin to emphasize: the need to make ready for victory, or the necessity of preparing for defeat. Ironically, at this point in the narrative Cuiníarángari is the one who comes across as the optimist, while the elder statesman Timas is of the opinion that the time has come to dispense with negotiations and make an all-out bid for maintaining political sovereignty.

But let us turn to a consideration of how this symbolic tug-of-war is manifested verbally, by listening to what the champions of these two opposing viewpoints say to Tzintzicha at that pivotal moment in the history of the Lake Pátzcuaro Basin depicted in plate 44 (color section):

> fue don pedro delante del cazonçi y dixole que nuevas ay de que manera bienen los españoles dixole don pedro señor no bienen enojados mas bienen paçificamente y contole lo que le avia dicho el capitan y que los saliese a rresçibir y dixole como avia visto a los españoles armados y que avian de llebar las maneras de mantas y pescado que esta dicho dixole aquel pre\i/nçipal que andaba por matar al cazonçi llamado timas que dizes mochacho mocoso alguna cosa les dixiste tu bamonos señor que ya estamos aparejados fueron por bentura tus agüelos y tus antepasados esclabos de alguno para querer tu ser esclabo queden vzizilzi y este que traen estas nuevas. (253)

[Don Pedro appeared before the cazonci and [the latter] asked him: "What news? How are the Spaniards advancing?" "Sir," Don Pedro replied, "they are not angry, but are coming peacefully." [Then] he recounted for him what the captain [Cristóbal de Olid] had said, that [the cazonci] was to go out to receive them. He told him how he had seen the armed Spaniards. And [he counseled the cazonci] to bring them the varieties of clothing and fish described above.[48] [Whereupon] the aforementioned principal lord named Timas, who was intent on killing the cazonci, said to [Don Pedro]: "What are you talking about, [you scoundrel, you] snotty-faced kid? Did you tell them anything? Let us go, My Lord, for we are ready. Were your grandfathers and ancestors slaves perchance, for you to want to be a slave? Let Huitzitziltzin and this one, who are bringing this news, remain behind."]

One of the first things that stands out from this verbal exchange is how poorly Cuiníarángari fares. Timas throws in his face that he and his brother Tashauaco/Huitzitziltzin are "slaves"—that is, descendants of a conquered people. He calls him a "scoundrel" and "snotty-faced kid" (both translations of the word *quatíngari* in Purépecha), thereby cuing the audience to be skeptical of Cuiniarángari's recommendations to the cazonci, given his obvious youth and inexperience. He suggests that he is a coward and, in general, treats him with such scorn that it might well evoke the audience's sympathy if Cuiníarángari had not just revealed himself to be extremely gullible in the way he informs the cazonci of the results of his "capture" by Olid.[49]

Cuiníarángari's reaction, moreover, is to go on the defensive. He defends his loyalty to the cazonci and then proceeds to modify his advice, first offering to go receive the Spaniards in Tzintzicha's place, then to die with him if he persists in following Timas's proposed course of action. Even though the cazonci is appreciative of Cuiníarángari when he speaks with him in private—"you have advised me well," he reassures him—he refuses to accept him into his confidence, to the point that Cuiníarángari ends up figuratively emasculated, lamenting in the company of Tzintzicha's women over what they imagine to be happening and wishing fervently for the return of his elder brother (254).

Which brings us to the question: What exactly is the advice Timas gives the cazonci? Timas says:

> señor haz traer cobre y pondremosnoslo a las espaldas y ahoguemonos en la laguna y llegaremos mas presto y alcançaremos a los que son muertos. (253)

> [My Lord, have them bring copper and we will take it upon our backs and drown ourselves in the lake. [In this manner] we shall make haste and overtake those who are dead.]

Taken at face value, the above passage seems to confirm the accusation made by Cuiníarángari that Timas and his followers were staging a palace coup of sorts by counseling Tzintzicha to drown himself in Lake Pátzcuaro. On a more symbolic level, however, its meaning is not so clear. Since Lake Pátzcuaro is described, in other parts of the text, as an axis mundi linking sky, earth, and underworld, to dress for war and plunge to the bottom of the lake can be interpreted, metaphorically, as preparing to fight against the forces of darkness. The reference to overtaking the recently deceased Zuangua and his predecessors also ties in with this reading, for only by following in the footsteps of the ancestors, in Mesoamerican mythology, can one attain to glory in both military and religious terms.

This more metaphorical twist on Timas's words is also consistent with the legends recounted by Ruiz at the turn of the past century involving the heroic defense led by Timas and his daughter Eréndira at the site of the main temple in Pátzcuaro ([1891-1900] 1971, 485-509).[50] The dual interpretation of the above passage hinges on an ambiguity in the word *pátzcuaro*, which refers both to the lake and to one of the principal indigenous cities at the time of the Spanish conquest.

What Timas was advocating, in other words, may well have been to organize a secret military plan to defend the fourfold kingdom, a plan predicated upon deceiving the Spaniards and their indigenous allies as to the whereabouts and intentions of the cazonci. Significantly, a few passages later in Cuiníarángari's narrative, Tzintzicha's alleged death in 1522 is presented much along these lines, suggesting it served as a pretext to stall for time and sound out the conquistadors regarding their motives:

> y llegaron diez mexicanos a la çibdad que enbiaba cristobal de oli y como b\v/ieron a toda la gente triste dixeron a los pre\i/nçipales por que estays tristes y dixeronle\s/ nuestro señor el cazonçi es ahogado en la laguna. . . . y bolbieronse los mexicanos y hiçieronselo saber a cristobal de oli como el cazonçi hera ahogado dixo cristobal de oli bien esta bien esta bamos que llegar thenemos a la çibdad. (255)

> [Whereupon ten Mexicans arrived in the city [of Tzintzuntzan], sent by Cristóbal de Olid. And, when they saw how dispirited all the people were, they asked the principal lords: "Why are you sad?" And they answered them: "Our Lord, the cazonci, has drowned in the lake." . . . [So] the Mexicans returned and informed Cristóbal de Olid that the cazonci was drowned. And Cristóbal de Olid said: "So be it. Let us go, we must hasten on into the city."]

Certainly Olid's response indicates, at the very least, that he did not much care whether the cazonci was dead or alive—not a very auspicious sign for those, like the young Cuiníarángari, who were advocating good-faith negotiations with the Spaniards over magical and/or literal warfare. The way this episode is recounted by Cuiníarángari circa 1538 also implies that Tzintzicha had spies in the Spanish camp who were close enough to overhear Olid's remarks.

In part two of the *Relación de Michoacán*, toward the beginning of the petámuti's epic history of the Uacúsecha, their enemies complain about the duplicity of these nomadic hunters (*chichimeca*, in Nahuatl), who, several generations after establishing themselves on the shores of Lake Pátzcuaro, undertake a series of marital alliances that bring them to the pinnacle of power. "These Chichimecs have two faces and speak in two ways" (38), their adversaries complain. In contrast to the largely pejorative connotations of being two-faced in the western European tradition, the context in which it is presented in the petámuti's oral performance, as an attribute of the ruling dynasty at the time of the Spanish conquest, converts it into an acceptable, even desirable, characteristic for those who seek the favor of the gods.

In plate 44 (color section) Tzintzicha is dressed for war; he is dressed for death. When the cazonci receives news of the Spaniards' arrival in Taximaroa, on the frontier between Mexica territory and his own, he declares: "Send messengers throughout the province and have the warriors gather here. Let us die [then]. Already the Mexicans are dead and now they are coming for us" (248). His initial response is to organize his people to fight against the Spaniards and their indigenous allies despite being outnumbered and ill equipped to prevail with bows and arrows against European firearms.[51]

The enduring mystery of Cuiníarángari's narrative is whether Tzintzicha changed his mind and decided to surrender peacefully (the Christian interpretation) or chose to pursue a two-pronged strategy of resistance, feigning submission on one hand and organizing covert attacks that allowed for the option of plausible denial on the other (a combination of both Cuiníarángari and Timas's advice). If Cuiníarángari's story is reevaluated in light of this second possibility, it becomes clear that his role, and that of his elder brother, was to distract the attention of the invading army from what was going on behind the scenes; to mount an elaborate ruse that had to be convincing enough to deceive not only the Spaniards, but also their Nahuatl-speaking interpreters.

This image of Don Pedro Cuiníarángari is markedly different from the one that predominates in most documents of Hispanic origin from the period. Even when he is derisively called Pedro Panza, the Spaniards inevitably refer to him as a brother of the cazonci and as the most prominent indigenous lord in Michoacán from 1530 to 1543, during the minority of Tzintzicha's sons.

Cuiníarángari's self-representation in part three of the *Relación de Michoacán*, in contrast, returns incessantly to the notion that he is not a blood relative of the cazonci. The priest known as *cúriti*, for instance, upon bringing a female relative of Tzintzicha to be the wife of Tasháuaco and Cuiníarángari,[52] reports the cazonci's words as follows: "He says you will be like brothers, in order to bring messages. Since the Spaniards have come, you will walk together like brothers in what he orders you to do" (208). Although the chapter in which this speech is contained is located in the section of the *Relación de Michoacán* dealing with marital ceremonies, it appears to have been extracted in its entirety from Cuiníarángari's account of the conquest.

In a kingdom composed of multiple ethnicities consolidated through marital alliances, to be a "brother" of the cazonci is the equivalent of being related to him by marriage. The cultural and linguistic ambivalence inherent in the use of kinship terms confers upon Tasháuaco and Cuiníarángari a certain strategic value for the cazonci and other ruling Uacúsecha.

Thus, Cortés writes in a letter to Charles V dated May 15, 1522, that a brother of the lord of Michoacán named Huitzitziltzin (that is, Tasháuaco) has just come to visit him outside of Mexico City with a gift of silver to pay homage to the emperor (1982, 184). Because it was also in Cortés's best interest to accept the more literal interpretation of the word "brother," it is easy to see how the Spaniards could have become invested in the peaceful submission version of events before they realized the full implications involved.

Another word whose meaning is notoriously slippery during the early colonial period is "Michoacán." The standard reference to Cuiníarángari as "governor of Michoacán" in documents from the period is often taken to mean that after the death of the cazonci he served as governor of the entire province (López Sarrelangue [1965] 1999). According to Cuiníarángari's own testimony in the Escorial manuscript, however, he was governor not of the province, but only of the city of Michoacán: that is, of Tzintzuntzan and, later, Pátzcuaro (277).

The resulting potential for misunderstanding was a double-edged sword from the point of view of both the Spaniards and the Uacúsecha. On one hand, it appears to have provided the cazonci and the ruling dynasty with the opportunity to organize an underground economic and political system under the noses of their "conquerors," as evidenced by the charges brought against Tzintzicha and other principal lords by the Spanish encomenderos in 1528–30. On the other, it planted the seeds for future claims by Cuiníarángari and his descendants to greater recognition by the colonial authorities than their status prior to the conquest probably warranted, as suggested by the lawsuits instigated by Cuiníarángari's son Don Bartolomé against Tzintzicha's son Don Antonio in the 1550s.

The haughty tone with which Timas addresses Cuiníarángari in the latter's account of the conquest implies both that Cuiníarángari was aware of criticism that he had overstepped his authority and that he felt the need to respond to this criticism on some level. Whatever his personal feelings on the subject, Cuiníarángari goes to great lengths at key moments in the narrative to underscore his lack of political ambition. The speech in which he responds to the cúriti, for instance, is a model of decorum and humility:

> ya os he oydo plega a los dioses que le podamos servir al rrey siendo los que devemos quiza no seremos los que avemos de ser y lo que a hecho agora el rrey no lo dize sino por la confiança que tiene en nosotros aqui esta mi hermano mayor y yo como nos abemos de apartar del de nosotros es el basallaje y hecharemos las espumas por las bocas para entender en lo que los españoles mandaren como sus sierbos como abemos de ser sus hermanos que nosotros en el prinçipio fuymos conquistados de sus antepasados y sus esclabos somos los ysleños y llevavamos sus comidas a los rreyes a cuestas y achas para yr al monte por leña y les llebabamos los jarros con que bebian y por esto nos enpezaron a dezir hermanos por ser sus governadores y entendiamos en lo que los rreyes nos mandavan donde es costunbre que los rreyes hablen por si solos y no tengan ofiçiales. (209)

[Now, I have heard you. May it please the gods for us to serve the king by being who we ought to be. Perhaps we will not be who we should. [Perhaps the message the king has sent] is only because of the confidence he has in us. Here are my elder brother and I. How can we abandon him? [Nay] it is our duty to be vassals and we will work to understand what the Spaniards demand of us until the foam comes from our mouths.[53] As his servants how can we be his brothers? Long ago we were conquered by his ancestors and we Islanders are his slaves. We brought the kings food upon our backs, and axes to climb the mountain for firewood. We carried the jars from which they drank. For this reason they began to call us brothers, because we were their governors and took care of what the kings commanded. Where is it customary for kings to speak for themselves without officials [to carry out their orders]?][54]

"Perhaps we will not be who we should," says Cuiníarángari. The anguish implicit in these words, the foreshadowing of a tragic end to the story, anticipates events that will occur in the wake of Cortés's return to Spain. For it is only then that the Uacúsecha strategy of feigning full capitulation while reserving part of their traditional privileges is put to a definitive test by the decision of Guzmán to pursue the legal case begun by the Spanish encomenderos against the lords of the Lake Pátzcuaro Basin.

The primary accusations—that Tzintzicha was still receiving tribute from towns the Spaniards had been granted in encomienda; that he had hidden other settlements from crown officials; that he had ordered the deaths of Spaniards—are well substantiated in the available documentary sources (Warren 1985, 239–41), including evidence from the Escorial manuscript regarding the persistence of indigenous religious and governmental structures as late as 1538.[55] In this sense, the trial of the cazonci in 1530 can be seen to result from a gradual recognition on the part of a certain sector of Spanish colonial society that they had been duped by the indigenous nobles of Michoacán. The execution itself, however, soon precipitated a counterattack by other, more farsighted colonial authorities who saw in it a sign of the danger of continuing the military conquest at the expense of efforts to win over the "hearts and minds" of the indigenous population.[56]

If Mendoza and the friar-compiler of the *Relación de Michoacán* endow Cuiníarángari with the authority to tell his version of the conquest, it is because it is in their interest to discredit Cortés, Mendoza's principal rival at the time of compilation of the Escorial manuscript. There was an even stronger incentive to contribute to disparaging the legacy of Guzmán, who was arrested with the tacit consent of Mendoza in 1537 and dispatched to Spain, where he led a relatively obscure existence until his death circa 1558–59 (Chipman 1967, 281; Adorno and Pautz 1999, 3:310–23).[57] Cuiníarángari's authority to tell his story from an indigenous point of view, however, is more problematic.

If one concentrates on the figurative tug-of-war between Cuiníarángari and Timas, the change in attitude precipitated among the indigenous inhabitants of the Lake Pátzcuaro Basin by the cazonci's death ushered in an anguished period of introspection in which those who advocated a policy of accommodation to Spanish rule, including conversion to

Christianity, played a leading role, albeit not necessarily one of which they were unequivocally proud.

Cuiníarángari's symbolic triumph over Timas, in this reading, is fraught with ambivalence. For, ultimately, Timas's dire prediction of the consequences of accepting Spanish rule comes closer to the truth than the initial optimism of Cuiníarángari, whose repeated assurances to Tzintzicha that everything will be all right eventually prove to be false.[58] As the cazonci tells his servants shortly before his execution by Guzmán:

> yd a dezir a los biejos y a mis mugeres que ya no me beran mas que las consuelen los biejos que no syento bien de mi echo que pienso que tengo de morir que miren por mis hijos y no los desamparen que como me a de ver aqui. (272)

> [Go inform the elders and my wives they will not see me again. Let the elders console them, for my deeds weigh heavily upon me. [Verily], I think I must die. Let them watch over my children and not abandon them. [Nay,], how can [my son] see me here?]

Having finally learned, through his own suffering, the true nature of the Spaniards, Tzintzicha can express only regret for his past actions, for not having chosen the option of death on the battlefield while it was still possible.[59] The message to the Spanish colonial authorities is clear: If you do not reward those who collaborate, you will incite the indigenous people to rebel. The message for Cuiníarángari's indigenous audience is more multilayered, suggesting both that they should pin their hopes on those who reward collaboration and also that it is a mistake to assume the interests of even the most sympathetic Spaniards fully coincide with their own.

Earlier in the narrative, when the potential benefits to be derived from collaboration with the Spaniards are at their peak, Tzintzicha summons Cuiníarángari and gives him a letter containing a death sentence against Timas. Although one might expect Cuiníarángari's tone at this moment to be self-congratulatory, given the insults previously heaped upon him by his rival, that is not the case. Instead, Cuiníarángari uses this episode as another opportunity to cast doubt upon his own legitimacy. As Timas puts it: "What, are you a valiant man? Where have you experienced the danger of battle, when enemies fight each other [in combat]? Where did you ever kill anyone?" (262). And then, when Cuiníarángari refuses to back down, Timas adds sarcastically that he really must be a valiant man (quangari), for everyone knows he conquered the province of Zacatula. To which Cuiníarángari replies that Timas is making fun of him, because everyone knows it was the Spaniards who conquered Zacatula (263).

Not content with impugning Cuiníarángari's manhood and, by extension, that of all who collaborated with the Spaniards, Timas also casts doubt upon the depth of their allegiance to both traditional indigenous and Christian values:

> seas bien benido pues que mi sobrino el cazonçi lo manda sea ansi yo poco falto que no le mate a el yos bosotros que no me aveys de matar yo me ahorcare mañana o hesotro dia que soys muy abarientos los que benis y codiçiosos los que me benis a matar. (262–63)

> [Make yourself welcome, since my nephew the cazonci orders it so. I came close to killing him myself. Begone, all of you, you're not up to taking my life. I'll hang myself tomorrow or some other day. You're only greedy, you who have come, and covetous, you who have come to slay me.]

Timas does not dispute, in this passage, that he must die, although Cuiníarángari attempts to undermine him by implying that Timas's haughty attitude is just a mask for his fear of death. Rather, his words suggest that Cuiníarángari's version of the conquest as Christian allegory, with the indigenous peoples of Michoacán embodying the virtues of charity and humility as opposed to the Spaniards' sinful pride and avarice, is a farce, for Cuiníarángari and his followers are no more than opportunists.

Significantly, Cuiníarángari's response, once again, is to go on the defensive, first reasserting his loyalty to the cazonci, then pointing out how he declined to enrich himself at the expense of Timas's widows. Still, he cannot have it both ways, for his refusal to sack Timas's home after carrying out the death sentence against him, although exemplary by Christian standards, is nevertheless a violation of indigenous tradition.

The issue of betrayal is at the core of this reading. In spite of the fact that Cuiníarángari remains silent about his own testimony against Tzintzicha, claiming that none of the indigenous nobles admitted the charges against him, not even under torture (275), his narrative as a whole reads as a partial recognition of culpability—an apology for not having been more astute, for not having counseled the cazonci more wisely, protected him more thoroughly, nor, ultimately, died along with him. Again, the use of foreshadowing stands out as one of the primary mechanisms by which Cuiníarángari exorcizes his bad conscience as a survivor. Toward the middle of the narrative, soon after the arrival of Guzmán on the scene, Cuiníarángari laments:

> como abemos de bibir segun las cosas que an ynbentado los españoles contra nosotros porque an traydo consigo los señores que agora tenemos prisiones y carçel y aperreamiento y enlardar con manteca con todo esto estamos esperando morir no nos apartaremos del mas juntamente moriremos con el si a el le matan. (209–10)

> [How are we to live given the things the Spaniards have invented against us? Because the lords who now rule over us have brought with them chains, and prison, and being thrown to the dogs, and torture by fire. With all this, we are awaiting death. Let us not abandon [the cazonci]; rather, let us perish together with him if they kill him.]

"How are we to live?" Cuiníarángari asks. And he answers that no matter what happens, he and his kin will not abandon Tzintzicha, but will die along with him if necessary. These two imperatives—survival and loyalty to the cazonci—are presented as one. In symbolic terms, since the cazonci represents his people, to protect him is also to further the interests of the community as a whole.

It is only when these two imperatives begin to diverge that the full scope of the tragedy the indigenous peoples are facing becomes apparent. In this retrospectively oriented reading, none of the characters in Cuiníarángari's story are entirely innocent. Not Timas, who admits to having tried to "kill" Tzintzicha through some sort of sinister endeavor.[60] Not even the cazonci himself, who, in the attempt to avoid the fate of Cuauhtemoc and the Mexica, nevertheless brings his people to the same tragic end.[61]

The Don Pedro Cuiníarángari who tells his story to the friar-compiler and indigenous nobles circa 1538 is not identical to the character of that name who appears in the pages of Escorial Ms. C.IV.5; nor are any of the members of his audience quite the same as they were before the death of the cazonci. The dramatic tension that structures his account derives from the impossibility of remaining fully faithful to indigenous tradition while adapting to the exigencies of colonial rule. The excessive adherence to the first mandate—the position represented by that proud old warrior Timas who obstinately refuses to accept the need to compromise—is portrayed as the equivalent of cultural suicide. At the opposite end of the spectrum, the overly optimistic assessment of the Spaniards' willingness to meet the indigenous peoples halfway—the posture of the young Cuiníarángari, that "snotty-faced kid" who thinks he can have it both ways—is unmasked as a form of cowardice and naïveté.

The Janus face of Don Pedro Cuiníarángari gazes in two directions. With one face, he seeks to inscribe himself and his people within a new political and religious system. To that end he describes his own behavior and that of the cazonci in terms evocative of Christian piety, humility, and suffering. He presents a convincing account of how he was personally involved in avoiding bloodshed. He underscores Tzintzicha's peaceful submission to Spanish rule and voluntary embrace of Christianity. And he insists on the cazonci's innocence regarding the charges brought against him. In short, insofar as Cuiníarángari looks to the friar and viceroy, his narrative is part of a strategy to gain tangible benefits from the colonial authorities in the form of greater recognition of indigenous rights and greater protection from mistreatment by unscrupulous crown officials.

Inasmuch as Cuiníarángari faces his indigenous audience, however, his narrative reads as a tragic story of the downfall of a once great empire, the humiliation of a proud and warlike people whose forced adoption of Christianity is a form of symbolic castration. "See how . . . they have dressed us all in women's skirts" (259), the Mexica tell Cuiníarángari as they take him on a tour of their ravaged capital. That this same fate is shared by the nobles of Tzintzuntzan is vividly captured in the image of the men grinding maize to make tortillas for the Spaniards in Olid's army, even "the lords and elders" (256).

The union of these two thematic strands produces a narrative that operates on multiple levels. Taken as a whole, Cuiníarángari's version of the conquest encourages his indigenous audience to embrace Christianity, but also to hold something back, to remember that they have been figuratively emasculated, that the Spaniards have turned them into *tarascue*—that is, Tarascans. The narrative function of the word "tarascue"—which literally means "child or parent-in-law" (Pollard 1993, 58)—converts it into a mark of humiliation for Cuiníarángari and his indigenous audience. As the friar-compiler observes: "they find [this name] offensive and say it originated . . . with those first women the Spaniards brought to Mexico City" (247).[62]

The issue is not whether this version of how the indigenous peoples of Michoacán came to be called Tarascans is etymologically correct. It may well be that the term predated the arrival of the Spaniards in the region and does not generally have pejorative connotations. As a literary critic, not a historian, however, I am interested in the implications of interpreting "tarascos" in this manner—the way in which its association with femaleness and political disenfranchisement ties in with other aspects of the *Relación de Michoacán* that similarly underscore the gender-based implications of the act of conquest.

If, in the petámuti's oral performance in part two, the indigenous peoples of Michoacán are the center of their own symbolic universe, in Cuiníarángari's account of the Spanish conquest in part three they have been displaced, transformed into second-class citizens who are no longer able to imagine history exclusively from their own point of view. In this sense it is fitting that the one chosen to tell the story is a descendant of the Islanders of Xaráquaro, those original inhabitants of the Lake Pátzcuaro Basin who were displaced by the Uacúsecha many years before—who became their in-laws, their symbolic other halves, much as female is figuratively encoded in the text in relation to male, farmer to hunter, fish to game, earth to sky, water to fire.

CONCLUSION

Don Pedro Cuiníarángari, the governor with the face of a pierced bird, is like a magician whose identity keeps changing the more one looks at him. He has been variously portrayed over the ages as a portly buffoon, a proud and arrogant lord, an eloquent orator, a skillful negotiator, an opportunist, a traitor to his people. In his own version of history, we see him progressively transformed as the smooth face of gullible youth gives way to the wrinkled brow of a prematurely aged veteran of some twenty-odd years of dealing with the contradictions and hardships of Spanish rule. It is a man's face, a woman's face. The face of one who believes in Christ, but does not fully trust Christ's messengers; of one who honors the ancestors, but preaches a new religion.

To return for a moment to the metaphor cited in the quote from David Murray at the beginning of this chapter, one of my goals has been to look beyond what Cuiníarángari is pointing to—the cazonci's voluntary submission to Christianity and subsequent martyrdom; or, conversely, his sacrifice on the crucifix formed by the disagreement among his people—to the acts of interpretation and cultural mediation that make this gesture possible. For the attempt to elucidate the contradictions embodied by "cultural brokers" like Cuiníarángari, as Eric Hinderaker observes (2002), is vital if we are to arrive at a fuller understanding of our pluralistic cultural heritage in the Americas.

The politics of conquest are such that survivors are always in the position of having to justify their actions. The case of Don Pedro Cuiníarángari speaks to the need to get beyond a facile celebration of multiculturalism or mestizaje that obscures the messy processes of bargaining and accommodation, physical coercion and betrayal that underlie all realignments of power relations. In a positive sense, Cuiníarángari symbolizes the effort to forge new collective identities that makes cultural survival possible. The negative side of this dynamic is the realization that, for those who make such an effort, there is an element of envy towards those who have died. The special burden of survivors is the imperative to continue struggling with the ghosts of the past as they move forward into an uncertain future.

Drawings of the Escorial Manuscript

Plate 2. Ceremony of Equata cónsquaro (Reprinted from Tudela [ca. 1541] 1956, 11.)

PLATE 4. Magical warfare by Taríacuri (Reprinted from Craine and Reindorp, plate 21.)

PLATE 9. Infidelity of Taríacuri's wife (Reprinted from Craine and Reindorp, plate 26.)

PLATE 10. Sacrifice of warriors from Curínguaro (Reprinted from Craine and Reindorp, plate 27.)

PLATE 11. Gift of the sacred arrows (Reprinted from Craine and Reindorp, plate 28.)

PLATE 12. Poverty of Hiripan and Tangáxoan (Reprinted from Tudela [ca. 1541] 1956, 91.)

PLATE 13. Immorality of Curátame II and virtue of Hiripan and Tangáxoan (Reprinted from Craine and Reindorp, plate 30.)

PLATE 14. Taríacuri's advice to Hiripan, Tangáxoan, and Hiquíngaje (Reprinted from Craine and Reindorp, plate 31.)

PLATE 15. Surrender of the islander Zapíuátame to Tangáxoan (Reprinted from Craine and Reindorp, plate 32.)

PLATE 16. Debauchery of Curátame II and penance of Hiripan, Tangáxoan, and Hiquíngaje (Reprinted from Craine and Reindorp, plate 33.)

PLATE 17. Gift of an obsidian blade representing the god Curícaueri (Reprinted from Craine and Reindorp, plate 34.)

PLATE 18. Execution of Curátame II by order of his father, Taríacuri (Reprinted from Craine and Reindorp, plate 35.)

PLATE 19. Dream apparitions of the gods Curícaueri and Xarátanga (Reprinted from Tudela [ca. 1541] 1956, 134.)

PLATE 20. Fall of the town of Itzíparámuco (Reprinted from Craine and Reindorp, plate 37.)

PLATE 21. Hiripan's fall from a rotten tree (Reprinted from Craine and Reindorp, plate 38.)

PLATE 22. Taríacuri's division of the future kingdom in three parts (Reprinted from Craine and Reindorp, plate 39.)

PLATE 23. Uniting all the "jewels" of the kingdom in one place (Reprinted from Craine and Reindorp, plate 40.)

Plate 25. Execution of Tamápucheca by order of his father, Taríacuri (Reprinted from Craine and Reindorp, plate 42.)

PLATE 26. Beheading of a lord of Curínguaro by a female relative of Taríacuri (Reprinted from Craine and Reindorp, plate 43.)

PLATE 28. Officials in the cazonci's government I (Reprinted from Tudela [ca. 1541] 1956, 171.)

PLATE 29. Officials in the cazonci's government II (Reprinted from Tudela [ca. 1541], 1956, 172.)

PLATE 30. Priests and guardians of the temples (Reprinted from Tudela [ca. 1541] 1956, 179.)

PLATE 31. Preparations for a surprise attack on an enemy village (Reprinted from Tudela [ca. 1541] 1956, 186.)

PLATE 32. Captain general's address to the assembled troops (Reprinted from Tudela [ca. 1541] 1956, 190.)

PLATE 34. Mourning those who die in war (Reprinted from Craine and Reindorp, plate 8.)

PLATE 35. Cazonci's administration of justice (Reprinted from Craine and Reindorp, plate 9.)

PLATE 36. Choosing a successor for a dead cacique (Reprinted from Tudela [ca. 1541] 1956, 202.)

PLATE 37. How the lords married among themselves (Reprinted from Tudela [ca. 1541] 1956, 207.)

do todos los otros grados heran ljcitos entrellos madre y hijo
nunca se casavan ni si consgº nj padre con hija ni sobrino con tia
esto abemos hablado por espirencia de una matrinjº e?

¶ tanbien casase uno con una muger strien al(?) hija y teniendo
he zical mjos yntencion de casarse con a otra muger si traen
les secusan con ella hasta que sea grande la hija la cual toma por mu
gier do desse(?) dad e dexa nla madrell̄

¶ no se casaban los hijos de padre no mas

¶ bien se casava el tio con su sobrina mas no el sobrino con su tia

¶ Vno tubo una muger en su ynfehjdad con la qual se a c͡curan tres
muriese prometio otra casamjento y tubo copula con ella
muriose su muger no se puede casar despues de xpiano con la que
prometio

¶ vno se caso en su ynfelidad con una muger y murio dexo una
hija nj muger no se puede casar con esta siendo fiel porque con
to afinj dad avnque sera en ynfiledad Ss

como murià del caçonçi y las çirimonjas con que le
enterravan

PLATE 39. Burial ceremony of a cazonci (Reprinted from Tudela [ca. 1541] 1956, 218.)

ban consigo como los a[...] enterrado en sus sepulturas. Estaban les dan[do]
[...] y van si todos a bañar todos los que abian elegido al señor
muerto y toda la gente porque no les pegase la enfermedad y y
ban todos los señores y toda la gente al paño del señor muerto
delante que estava y estaban alli vn dia comida obera del señor muerto
que lo vbiere[...] para entonces mayz cocido blanco y davan les a todos
un p[...] cocido todo y blanco con sal ny agua en los ojos dias y comyan to
dos y no[...] puede de comer por[...] ange todos cada vno por su estatuto ce[...]
[...] estos xinco dias y ancoa dias nyn[...]uno dela ciudad molia mayz [...] piedras
ny hazian lumbre [...] ny se fazer[...] [...]yn[...] no haga tian[...] ny[...] aq[...]
[...] dias ny merca[...]ba[...] ny andala nadie por la ciudad mas toda la gente
[...]taban tristes por que [...] y van todos los capitanes dela provincia y
los se[...] [...]niestre alas casas delos papas donde tenyan en[...] un ceybe[...]

Como hazian otro señor y los parlame[n]tos q[ue] ha[...]

PLATE 40. Choosing a new ruler (Reprinted from Tudela [ca. 1541] 1956, 223.)

PLATE 41. Inauguration ceremonies (Reprinted from Tudela [ca. 1541] 1956, 226.)

le a qual cansaran be que dixey otoy dan Pablo aldoso donde ma ya dos
rey Ohuaxi— truena todos su exerçito que desbaratan y tan gran que ya son
doze vezes que yason huidos y yason en gran duda lo que anda metida
en la tierra por todos los terminos esto le dixo al rey esto es que se la
que aca en todos esta en tierra caliente que muchos moria gold y todos dixos
a pues asi es ya que va se otra tirar y al pinuerines las en las d...
grande redondeas del señor pedraoso y con toda osa la que desia y an gran asi
para se el caçonci ynuerno §

·Dela benida de los españoles a esta provincia segun
melo conto don pedro que es agora gobernador y se
hallo en todo y como montezuma señor de mexico
ynbio a pedir socorro al caçonci § juan gua padre del que murio agora ————————————

PLATE 43. Mexica embassies to the cazonci Zuangua (Reprinted from Tudela [ca. 1541] 1956, 237.)

Beaumont "Maps"

PLATE 45. Transfer of the diocese from Tzintzuntzan to Pátzcuaro (Courtesy of The John Carter Brown Library at Brown University.)

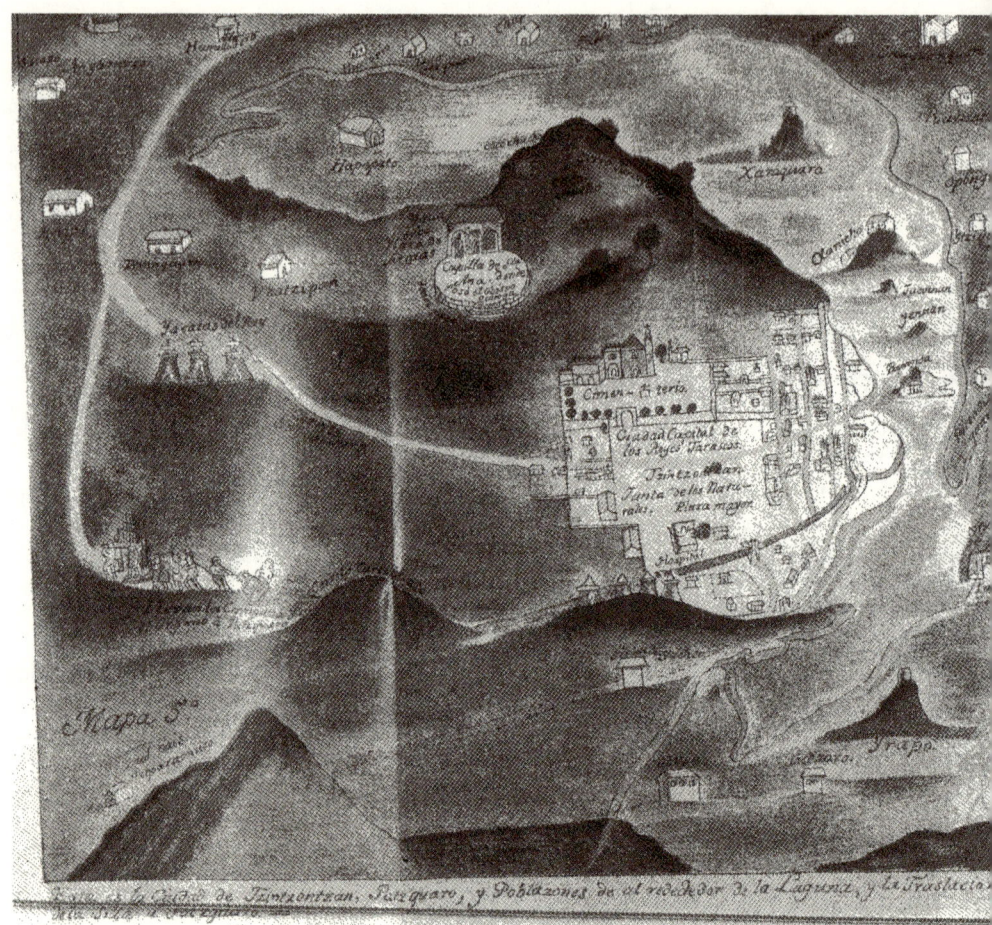

PLATE 46. Map of the Lake Pátzcuaro Basin (Courtesy of the Archivo General de la Nación, Mexico City; reprinted from Boehm de Lameiras 1994, 17.)

PLATE 47. Ceremony of Equata cónsquaro (Courtesy of the Archivo General de la Nación, Mexico City; reprinted from Boehm de Lameiras 1994, 150.)

Hands of the Escorial Manuscript

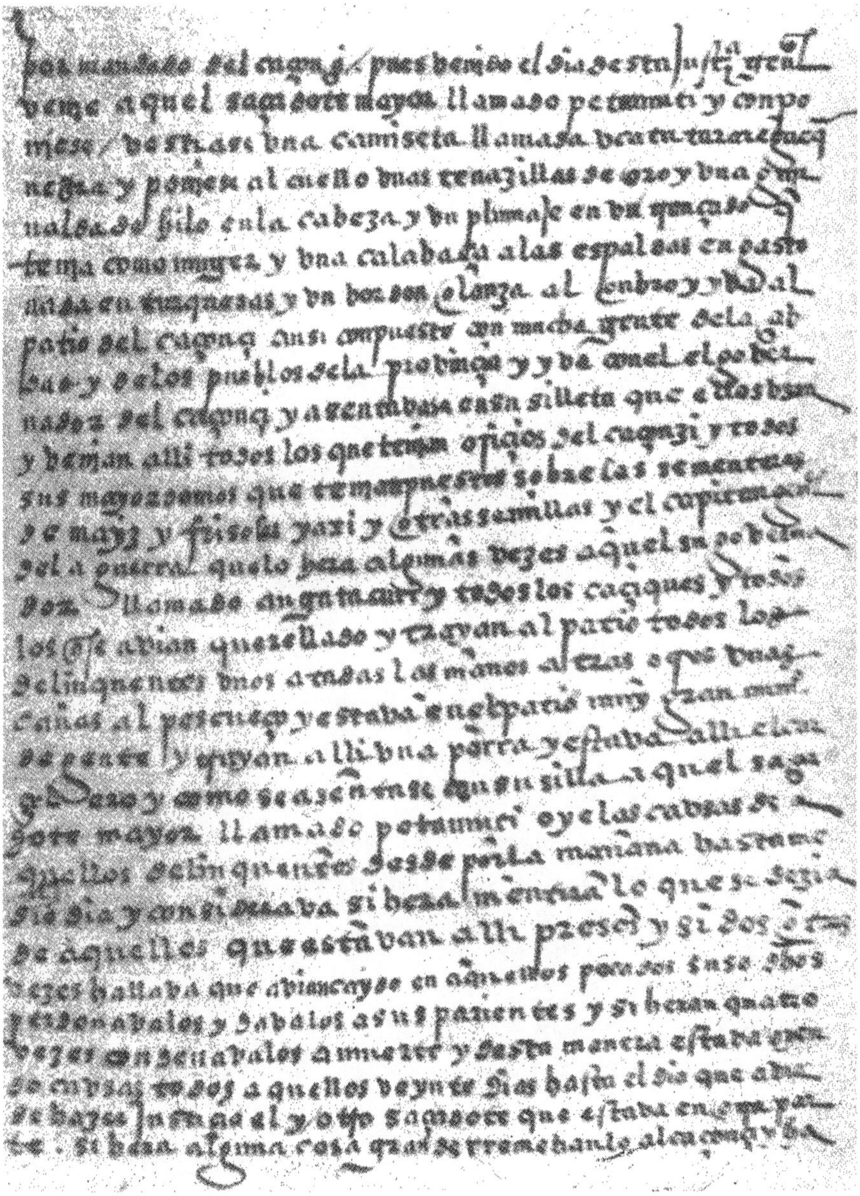

Plate 48. Hand 1, Prologue and first five chapters of part two (Reprinted from Tudela [ca. 1541] 1956, 13.)

echauan aquella sangre enlas dhas fuentes / y dspues dehecho el sacrificio salian aquellos dos llamados hauripicipecha q[ue] querie dz[ir] quita-
dores de cauellos y andauan tras la gente hombres y mugeres y criaturas
los cauellos con vnas nauajas de lançia / y estos andaua[n] todos enbi-
jados de colorado y vnas mantas delgadas enlas cabeças y tomaua[n] de aq[ue]ll[os]
cauellos [que] aui[a]n quitado y metia[n]los enla sangre delos q[ue] se aui[a]n
sacrificado y echaua[n]los al fuego. y desp[ue]s el siguiente dia baylauan
vestidos los pellejos delos esclauos sacrificados y enborrachaua[n]se cinco
dias y por el mes de haraspimpi lleuaua[n] ofrendas por los dhos sacrificados / y en otra fiesta llamada cahieriua pansquaro baylaua[n] con vn[as]
cañas de maiz alas espaldas / y u[n] esto vsaua[n] en estas fiestas con sus sacrificios [con] la q[ua]l se mishucen por la fiesta de cuingo y crei[a]n q[ue] te
les danan dos esclauos en ofrenda pa su sacrificio /

asi mesmo esta diosa cuerauaperi se vestia en al[gun] te[m]plo y iva y mayse a
meterlo y desp[ue]s viuase el mesmo a que sacrificasen y dauanle ahi
de su mucha sangre y beuiala / y entraua en hombres y mugeres y estos [que] auia tomado de estos otros pueblos de tarde en tarde delos sacrificaua[n]
diziendo q[ue] ella misma los auia escogido pa su sacrificio / esta tomara en
mucho en toda esta prouincia y nombrauan en todas sus fabulas y ora-
ciones y dezian q[ue] era madre de todos los dioses dela tierra / y q[ue] ella
enbiaua a[h]orcar alas tierras dandoles miedo y semillas q[ue] truxesen o
no se acordaua[n] de sus fabulas / tenia q[ue] fue al pueblo de vna to-
y otros pueblos y su ydolo principal en[c]una [que] esta es el pueblo de
cuchapequaro encima de vn cerro donde parece oy en dia derribado y
sopre la gente [que] esta diosa enbiaua los hambres a la tierra /

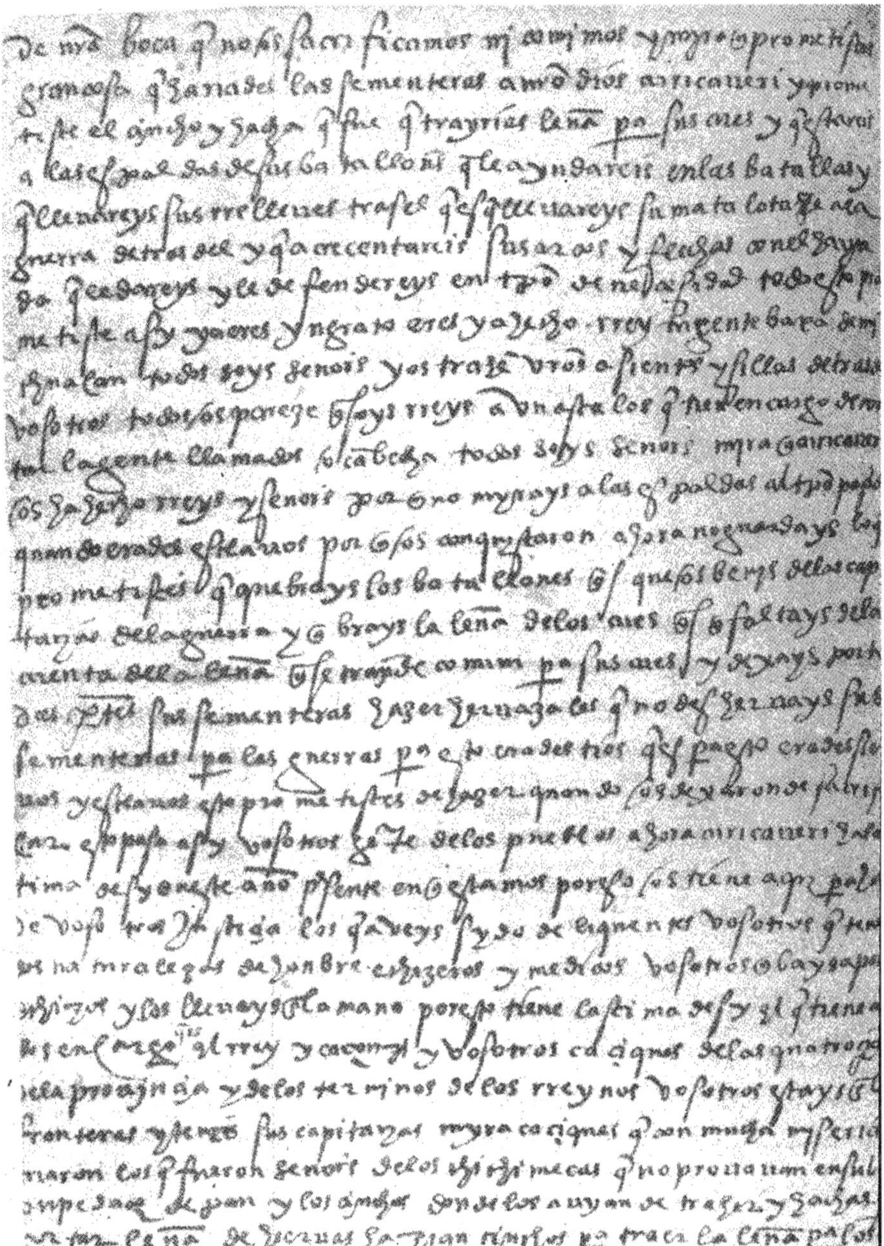

PLATE 50. Hand 3, Chapters six to thirty-five, part two (Reprinted from Tudela [ca. 1541] 1956, 156.)

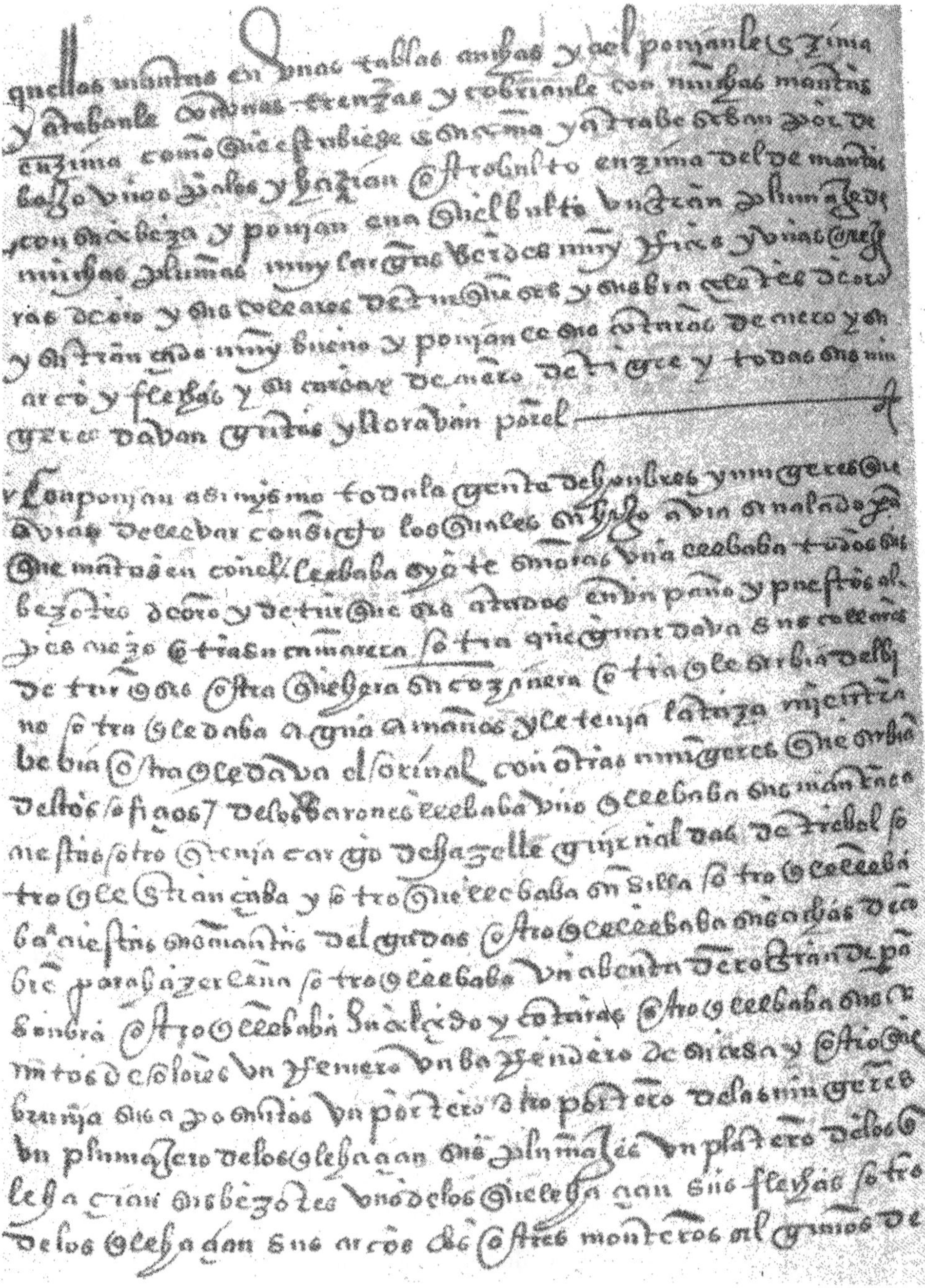

PLATE 51. Hand 4, All of part three (Reprinted from Tudela [ca. 1541] 1956, 220.)

equacazi xāon tien   satangel.   tyra

y del presente q trahian alcançar A nueuo   ynorarjo
                                                  persuasion
pa las guerras y ofrendas a sus dioses   oro y plata tinidad

ponese aqui como se caso don pedro q es a hora gouernador por q
desta manera se casaua todos.

bey siste yndios   esta relacion es de don pedro g[o]ynador

¶ Como tazcacuzi dio a sus sobrinos y hijo vna pte de sus dias cuzi
cauezi y como los q so flechaz por vnas cues q hiziezon y de la costu
bre q tenia los señores ctrefiales q muziesen:

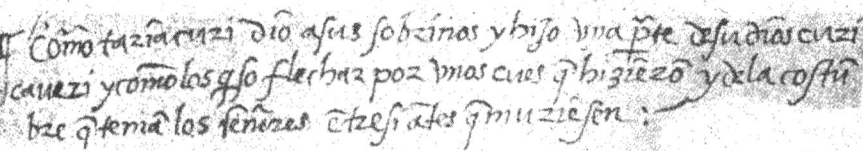

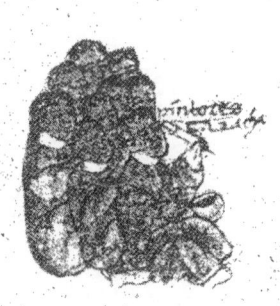

PLATE 52. Hand 5, The principal corrector (Reprinted from Tudela [1541] 1956, 32, 57, 86, 125, 171, 174, 207, 226, 250, 258, 266, 268.)

Glossary

ABBREVIATIONS

BL Juan Baptista de Lagunas
DG *Diccionario grande de la lengua de Michoacán*
ES Eduard Seler
FM Moisés Franco Mendoza, Pedro Márquez Joaquín and other contributors to the critical apparatus of the 2001 edition of the *Relación de Michoacán*
HT Antonio de Herrera y Tordesillas
LA Alfredo López Austin
MG Maturino Gilberti
MS Mauricio Swadesh
RM *Relación de Michoacán*

achá (ačá) n. pl. acháecha = lord, noble (DG, MG, MS, RM)
angámecha (aŋámeča) n. = official representatives (RM); those who wear lip plugs (BL)
angámequa (aŋámekwa) n. = lip plug (BL, DG, MG, MS)
angámucuracha (aŋámukurača) n. = mountain deities (RM); those who stand at the mouth or door (DG, ES, MG, MS)
angátacuri (aŋáhtakuri) n. pl. angátacucha = governor and captain general (RM); first inhabitant (MG, MS); first after the king (DG); one who stands at the cazonci's side (FM)
atari (atári) n. = tavern keeper, cup bearer (MG, RM); one who serves (MS)
auándaro (auándaṛho) n. = (in the) sky or heaven (G, S)
auita (auíta) n. = paternal uncle (BL, DG, MG, MS)
áxame (aášame) n. pl. áxamencha = sacrificer (MG, MS, RM); forked pole to support branches of trees (DG)
cacari (kakári) n. pl. cacacha or cacáriecha = stonemason, sculptor (DG, MG, MS, RM)
caracha capacha (karáča kapáča) n. = provincial caciques (RM); princes or principal lords (MG); administrators, those in charge of scribes (FM)
carani (karáni) v. = to write, paint (BL, MG); also, to draw (DG)
carari (karári) n. pl. caracha or carariecha = writer, painter, scribe (DG, MG); painter (RM)
cherénguequauri (čerégekwauri) n. = official in charge of making cotton war doublets (RM); cf. cherénguequa = cotton armor (MS); weapons (DG)
cumiechucuaro (kwumíehčukwaṛo) n. = hell (RM); underworld (MG, MS)

curá (kuṛá) n. pl. curáecha = grandfather elder(BL, DG, MG, RM); also, great uncle (MS)

cúriti (kúṛiti) n. pl. cúritiecha = preacher, pastor; also, those who wear gourds upon their backs and provide incense for the ceremonies (RM)

curízita (kuṛíh¢ita) n. pl. curízitacha = priest in charge of maintaining incense burners and pyres and bringing sedge and cypress branches (RM); cf. curíhtsitari = one in charge of stirring up the fire of the idols (DG); also referred to as curipe or cuiripe, pl. curípecha or cuirípecha(FM, RM)

curúhapindi (kwuṛúhapindi) n. = official in charge of hunting water fowl and game-birds (RM); one who prospers in hunting of ducks and pheasants (FM)

curúzetaro (kurú¢hetaṛo?) n. = map traced on the ground (RM); burnt ground (FM)

cuzuri (ku¢úri) n. = curer of hides (DG, MG, MS, RM)

echérendo (ečerendo) n. = (on the) surface of the earth (G)

hamúcutin (hamúkutini) n. = border, generally (MG, MS); at the door or shore (DG)

hirípati (hirípati) n. pl. hirípacha = priest of charge of ritual war preparations (RM); one who acts while hidden (FM)

hiuatsi (hiwá¢i) n. = coyote (DG, MS)

hozqua (hóskwa) n. pl. hózquaecha = star (DG, MG, MS)

huarache (kwaṛáče) n. = sandal (MS)

huréndetiecha (uṛéndetieča)-n. = those who are in first place (Seler); cf. uretiecha = the ancient ones (DG)

irecha (iréča) n. = king, sovereign (MG, MS); also, emperor, prince, and provincial deputy (DG); synonym for cazonci (FM)

iréchequaro (iréčekwaṛo) n. = royal court or palace (DG, MG, MS)

iréchequa (iréčekwa) n. = kingdom (MG, MS); group of towns under the jurisdiction of an irecha (FM)

ireri (iréri) n. = head wife of the cazonci(RM); cf. achá ireri = master of the house, uarhí ireri = mistress of the house (MG, MS)

ireta (iréta) n. pl. irétecha = town, community, residence (DG, FM, MG, MS)

ireti (iréti) n. = resident, citizen, settler, dweller (DG, FM, MG, MS)

ocánbeti (uhkámbeti) n. pl.ocánbecha = those in charge of counting the people and collecting tribute for public works RM); chief or foreman (DG); captain (MG, MS)

paricuti (paṛíkuti) n. = official in charge of canoe paddlers (RM); one who crosses over to the other side (MG); navigator (DG)

petámuti (petámuti) n. = high priest, head of the cúritiecha (RM); one who pronounces (FM)

petázequa (petá¢ekwa) n. = rocky outcrop or foundation serving as the base of a pyramid (RM); stiffness caused by remaining still over a long period of time (MG)

pirúuaqua uándari (piṛúwakwa wándari) n. = official in charge of textiles (RM); one who multiplies thread (FM) *pucúriquari* (phukúrikwari) n. = official in charge of woodcutters (RM); guardian of the mountains (MG)

purépecha (phuṛépeča) n. = commoners, language of the common people (MG, MS); also, people in general (DG, LA)

quangari (khwaŋári) n. pl. quangáriecha = warrior or brave, valiant man (DG, MG, MS, RM); also, morning star, the planet Venus (MG, MS); cf. quanguá paqua = your majesty (RM); quangah paqua = most powerful one (DG)

quatíngari (khwatíŋari) n. = scoundrel, snotty-faced kid (RM, MG, MS)

quengue (kéŋe) n. = guardian of ears of corn and other crops (RM); overseer (DG, MG, MS)

siranda (siránda) n. = book, paper, letter (DG, MG); also, thin sheet (MS)

siríhtaqua (siríhtakwa) n. = skirt (MG, MS)

sirúruqua (sirúrukwa) n. = leather band used by porters (BL); also, lineage (MS); cf. siruqua = lineage, caste, progeny (BL, DG)

tarascue (taṛáskwe) n. = misnomer for majority indigenous inhabitants of Michoacán (RM); father-in-law, mother-in-law, son-in-law, daughter-in-law (BL, DG, MS)

taríata (taṛíyata) n. = air, wind (DG, MG, MS)

tasta (tásta) n. = clothing, blanket, mantle (DG, MG, MS); also, canvas sheet (DG)

tatá (tatá) n. = father or father's brother (BL, DG, MG, MS)

thámbengarani (thámbeŋarani) n. = the four parts of the world (DG, MG, MS)

thamu (thámu) n. = four (BL, DG, MG, MS)

tharés (thaṛés) n. = idol (DG); cf. tharépeti = male elder, versus cutsímeti = female elder (MG)

tsiríquarequa (¢iríkwaṛekwa) n. = staff, scepter (DG, MG, MS)

tucúpachá (tukúpačá) n. = god (DG, HT, MG, MS)

tzacapu (¢akápu) n. = stone (MG, MS); also, crag (DG)

tzintzuni (¢hin¢úni) n. = hummingbird (MS)

uacús (wakús) n. pl. uacúsecha = eagle (DG, MG, MS); in plural, dominant group at the time of the Spanish conquest, descendents of Iréticátame (RM); also, maguey cactus (MS)

uandani (wandáni) v. = to speak (BL, DG, MG, MS)

uandaqua (wandákwa) n. = word (DG, MG); also, reason, saying, superstition (DG)

uandari (wandári) n. = poet (MS); speaker (MG); one in charge (DG)

uanduqua (wandúkwa) n. pl. uandúquecha = pectoral; pincers, tweezers (DG, FM, MG, MS)

uapátzequa (wapá¢ekwa) n. = neighborhood, precinct, tributary town (DG, MG, MS)

uaruri (waṛúri) n. pl. uarucha or uarúrecha = official in charge of those who fish with a net (RM); fisherman (DG)

uaxánoti (wašánoti) n. pl. uaxánocha or uaxánotiecha = messenger, letter carrier (MG, RM); one who is seated at court (ES)

uaxántsiqua (wašán¢ikwa) n. = chair (DG, MG, MS)

uázcata (wá¢kata?) n. = evildoer, one who is imprisoned after having been accused of a crime (RM)

uni (úni) v. = to make, do (MG, MS)

urani atari (uṛáni atári) n. = official in charge of painting pots and gourds (RM)

uri (úri) n. = one who makes or celebrates (MS)

usquarecuri (uskwarekúri) n. pl. usquarecucha = official in charge of feather workers (RM); cf. uzquarequa uri = official who makes images out of feathers (MG)

uuache (wuáče) n. pl. uuácheecha= brother's child (DG, MG, MS); also, paternal cousin (DG, MG); also, son or "my son" (BL, DG, MG, MS); also, child generally (MS)

yuriri (yuṛíri) n. = blood (DG, MG, MS); cf. yurítsqueri = maiden (DG, MG, MS)

Abbreviations

AGI	Archivo General de Indias.
AGN	Archivo General de la Nación.
CDHM	[1858–66] 1971. *Colección de documentos para la historia de México.* Ed. Joaquín García Icazbalceta. Reprint. 2 vols. Biblioteca Porrúa, 47–48. Mexico City: Editorial Porrúa.
CDIHE	1842–95. *Colección de documentos inéditos para la historia de España.* 112 vols. Madrid.
CDII	1864–84. *Colección de documentos inéditos relativos al descubrimiento, conquista y organización de las antiguas posesiones españolas de América y Oceanía.* 42 vols. Madrid.
CDIU	1885–1932. *Colección de documentos inéditos relativos al descubrimiento, conquista y organización de las antiguas posesiones españolas de ultramar.* 25 vols. 2d series. Madrid.
CEMCA	Centre d'Etudes Mésoaméricaines et Centreaméricaines.
CIASE	Centre for Indigenous American Studies and Exchange.
CIESAS	Centro de Investigaciones y Estudios Superiores en Antropología Social.
CNCA	Consejo Nacional para la Cultura y las Artes.
COLMEX	El Colegio de Mexico.
COLMICH	El Colegio de Michoacán.
CONACYT	Consejo Nacional de Ciencia y Tecnología.
CREFAL	Centro Regional de Educación de Adultos y Alfabetización Funcional.
FCE	Fondo de Cultura Económica.
HMAI	1964–76. *Handbook of Middle American Indians.* Gen ed., Robert Wauchope. 16 vols. Austin: Univ. of Texas Press.
IIA	Instituto de Investigaciones Antropológicas.
IIE	Instituto de Investigaciones Estéticas.
IIF	Instituto de Investigaciones Filológicas.
IIH	Instituto de Investigaciones Históricas.
IMC	Instituto Michoacano de Cultura.
INAH	Instituto Nacional de Antropología e Historia.
NCDHM	[1886–92] 1971. *Nueva colección de documentos para la historia de México.* Ed. Joaquín García Icazbalceta. Reprint. 3 vols. Nendeln/Liechtenstein: Kraus Thomson Organization.

ABBREVIATIONS

SEP	Secretaría de Educación Pública.
SUNY	State University of New York.
UMSNH	Universidad Michoacana de San Nicolás de Hidalgo.
UNAM	Universidad Nacional Autónoma de México.

Notes

INTRODUCTION: MAPPING IDENTITIES

1. Since Warren's well-documented article on the subject in 1971, most scholars have agreed that the evidence regarding the identity of the friar-compiler points to a relatively obscure Franciscan by the name of Jerónimo de Alcalá who was born in Vizcaya ca. 1580, arrived in New Spain in 1530, and is believed to have died in 1545. (For a revised version of this article in Spanish, see Franco Mendoza 2000, 37–56; an abbreviated Spanish version can also be found in Escobar Olmedo 2001, 89–100). Warren cites sources that place Alcalá in Tzintzuntzan and Pátzcuaro around the time of compilation of the *Relación de Michoacán* (i.e., the *Anales de Tarecuato* [1519–1666] 1951, 10–11) and name him as "the first to write and know the language of Michoacán" (Muñoz [ca.1583] 1965, 36). According to Alcalá's own testimony, he was about thirty-three years old in 1541, had spent most of the previous ten years in Michoacán, and was currently guardian of the Franciscan monastery in Pátzcuaro (Warren 1971, 322–25). One of Beaumont's "maps" (plate 45), which concerns events surrounding the transfer of the diocese in 1538–39, shows a young Franciscan identified as "Geronimo Alcala" who resembles the friar depicted in the frontispiece of the Escorial manuscript (plate 1, color section) except for the addition of beard and sideburns. This version of the Beaumont drawing, reproduced from the collection of the John Carter Brown Library at Brown University, may be from the original circa 1778 manuscript (HMAI 1975, 14:94; Roskamp 1998b, 9–10), as opposed to the more widely disseminated manuscript currently housed in the Archivo General de la Nación in Mexico City. In addition to the Escorial manuscript, Alcalá is believed to have produced several other works during his short life, an *Arte de la lengua michoacana* and a *Doctrina christiana en lengua de Mechuacán*, both of which are presumed lost. For additional information on Alcalá, see Miranda Godínez 1980, xxiii–xxv and 1981, 32–36; Chauvet 1983, 32–34; and Warren 1997, 30–32.

2. It is noteworthy that the friar-compiler of the *Relación de Michoacán* mentions Jerome, patron saint of translators, in his preface. Along the same lines, it bears mentioning that the famous Complutensian Polyglot Bible, edited at Alcalá de Henares from 1502 to 1517, ushered in a remarkable period of biblical and linguistic studies there (see Alvar Ezquerra 1996). The above time frame is consistent with the hypothesis that Alcalá may have studied at the university prior to his departure for the New World.

3. Alternate spellings for Cuiníarángari in colonial-era documents (excluding accents) include Cuinierangari, Cuiniharangari, Cuiniganihara, and Cuitamangari.

4. Any listing of scholars whose work centers on the notion of validating processes of cultural change as a potentially constructive, creative force rather than as a degradation of presumably "purer" forms of cultural expression must, of necessity, be incomplete. The following names should be understood as a representative sampling only of those whose work has directly influenced my own thoughts on the subject: Adorno, Bricker, Burkhart, Certeau, Farriss, Gruzinski, Lafaye, Lienhard, Mignolo, Murray, and Tedlock.

5. The Escorial manuscript was initially catalogued as IV.E.14 in a listing of the library's holdings dating from circa 1600 (the source for this information is a manuscript entitled "Catálogo de los libros en mano en romance" numbered H.15.). Changes to this catalogue in a later hand give the location as IV.N.11; it is currently classified as Ç.IV.5 or C.IV.5. All three call numbers can be observed on the frontispiece (pl. 1, color section). Zarco Cuevas states, erroneously, that the *Relación de Michoacán* arrived at the royal library in a shipment of books belonging to the Lic. D. Diego González, "prior de Roncesvalles" (1924, 2:106). A perusal of the manuscript from which he obtained this information—Ms. II.&.15—indicates that the work in question is actually a version of Motolinía's history of New Spain entitled *Ritos antiguos, sacrificios e idolatrías de los indios de la Nueua Hespaña* (catalogued as II.X.21). In other words, how the *Relación de Michoacán* came to be housed in the library of the Escorial is still a mystery. For those interested in exploring this topic further, several possible theories are summarized by Sánchez Díaz (2001, 209). The unrelated manuscript bound along with it is dated 1549 and bears the title *Calendario de toda la índica gente por donde han contado sus tiempos hasta oy, agora nueuamente puesto en forma de Rueda, para mejor ser entendido;* it is an incomplete version of a Mexican calendar wheel included in Motolinía's *Memoriales,* also known as Veytia Calendar Wheel no. 2 (HMAI 1975, 14:231). According to the bibliographic structure of Escorial Ms. C.IV.5 recreated by Hidalgo Brinquis (2001, 70–72), this calendar wheel was written on the same paper used for the drawing of the family tree of the cazonci (pl. 27, color section). The watermarks of Escorial Ms. C.IV.5, with the exception of the flyleafs added later, are four varieties of the "hand with star" type, commonly found in manuscripts from New Spain produced from 1525 to 1542 and beyond (Tudela de la Orden 1956, vii; Hidalgo Brinquis 2001, 58–59). Details regarding the binding can be found in Escobar Olmedo 2001, 17–21, and Hidalgo Brinquis 2001, 47–51.

6. My classification of the hands involved in the elaboration of the Escorial manuscript in plates 48–52 of this book differs from that of Tudela, who identifies the following hands and corresponding manuscript pages: 1. A1 (pp. 3–7); 2. A2 (pp. 11–30); 3. A3 (pp. 170–230); 4. A4 (pp. 231–77); 5. B (pp. 9–10); 6. C (pp. 31–167); 7. D (corrections throughout manuscript). See also Cortés Alonso 2001.

7. All quotes from the *Relación de Michoacán* in this book are based on my own paleographic interpretations of the facsimile edition by Tudela de la Orden, published by Aguilar in 1956, which was reprinted by Balsal Editores in 1977. In order to

give the readers as full a picture as possible of the ambiguities that characterize sixteenth-century written Castilian, I have endeavored to preserve the contractions and orthographic peculiarities of the original and have also refrained from providing punctuation, accents, and capitalization. I do, however, resolve abbreviations whenever possible in the interest of clarity. My interpretation of the final words in the title, for instance, is based on that of Miguelez (1917, 206), who observes that "majestad real católica imperial" (abbreviated in the Escorial manuscript as "mg. r. c i.") is a common form of address for Charles V encountered in documents from the period; he notes, moreover, that a line added above the *r* by a later hand has contributed to its confusion with the letter *e* by those who read the final letters as "ect"—an abbreviated form of etcetera.

8. All translations from the *Relación de Michoacán* are my own.

9. The most important information regarding the dates of compilation comes from the Escorial manuscript itself. First there is a comment, made by the friar-compiler in his prologue, to the effect that the project began in earnest soon after Mendoza's first visit to the region. This comment is often cited in support of a starting date of 1539—the year of Mendoza's first documented trip to Michoacán. Other evidence, however, suggests an earlier time frame. For instance, a remark inserted by the friar in part three states that the founding of the first Franciscan monastery in the city of Tzintzuntzan took place "about twelve years ago" (264). A marginal notation—"or xiii"—was added later in a different hand. Since the Franciscan monastery of Santa Ana is believed to have been constructed in 1526 (see plate 45, in which the year is written on the building), this particular passage may plausibly have been composed in 1538 and revised a year later, in 1539. Another passage, from part two, describes the construction underway in Pátzcuaro in preparation for the transfer of the diocese, a state of affairs that correlates with other documents from 1538 (León [1903] 1984, 265–71; Warren 1977, 439–57). A fourth passage, from part three chapter 28, refers to Antonio Godoy as "alguacil mayor" (chief law enforcement officer) of Tzintzuntzan. The dates in which Godoy served in this capacity are 1538–39 (my source for this information is Escobar Olmedo 2001, 353). Evidence that the manuscript was still under preparation in the early 1540s includes a remark from part three chapter 26, concerning an indigenous feast that took place on "November 14th of the present year" (262). According to Caso y Andrade, the feast referred to in this passage is Caheri uapánscuaro and it would have fallen on November 14th only in the years 1540–43 (1943, 27). Kirchhoff disagrees as to the festival referred to in the above passage, but not with the chronology proposed by Caso (1971, 215). See also Edmonson (1988). To summarize, the evidence suggests that the bulk of compilation work took place between 1538 and 1540, although it might have begun earlier. Perhaps Mendoza made an undocumented trip to Michoacán in 1537–38. On the other hand, it is possible that the friar-compiler neglected to take into consideration, when discussing the date for initiating the project, some of the preliminary gathering of materials on which the Escorial manuscript was based. The case for the date of completion is more clear-cut. On October 6, 1541, Mendoza mentioned that he was anticipating

receiving the manuscript shortly (Oviedo [1537–48] 1959, 4:252–53). Other important events that took place in 1541—the Mixtón War, the founding of the city of Valladolid—also suggest that the project had ended by that time, since they are nowhere mentioned in the narrative.

10. The inscription on folio 0'6 verso of the Escorial manuscript (according to the numbering system used by Hidalgo Brinquis) reads: "p sahagun o m"; that is, "P[adre] Sahagún [de la] O[rden] [de] M[enores]"/"Father Sahagún of the Order of Friars Minor."

11. For information regarding these manuscript copies, see Brand 1943, 2:37–108; HMAI 1975, 14:167–68; Graham 1977, 45–55; Brownrigg 1978; and Sánchez Díaz 2001, 210–14.

12. A pirated version of the 1869 edition of the *Relación de Michoacán* was published in Madrid in 1875.

13. See León 1927; Brand 1943; HMAI 1975, 14:167–68; and Sánchez Díaz 2001 for further information related to nineteenth- and early twentieth-century synopses of the contents of the *Relación de Michoacán*.

14. The sole English translation of the *Relación de Michoacán* is *The Chronicles of Michoacan* (Craine and Reindorp 1970), published by the University of Oklahoma Press as volume 98 of The Civilization of the American Indian series. Based on the Morelia edition (León 1903), which reverses the intended order of the two main sections of the text (as does the Escorial manuscript) and contains many paleographic errors, the English translation is of limited intelligibility, although the black-and-white photographs of the drawings by José de Prado Herranz are of good quality. The earliest facsimile edition is by Aguilar (Tudela 1956), with a preliminary study by Kirchhoff and a revision of words in the indigenous language of Michoacán by Corona Núñez; this deluxe edition of five hundred copies (the first hundred of which were hand painted) was reprinted by Balsal Editores in 1977, without notes and with a prologue by Corona Núñez, in a print run of two thousand copies. A more recent full-color facsimile and paleographic version, edited by Escobar Olmedo (2001) and published by Patrimonio Nacional de España, Testimonio Compañía Editorial and the Ayuntamiento de Morelia, puts the accent on reproducing the physical peculiarities of Escorial Ms. C.IV.5; as such, it is particularly valuable for scholars unable to consult the original. Indeed, the details of the manuscript are meticulously reproduced even to the binding, paper texture, watermarks, varying ink tints, precise color pigmentation, erasures, stains, inkblots, and other imperfections. An accompanying critical edition, with paleography and notes by Escobar Olmedo, includes previously unpublished essays by Hidalgo Brinquis of the Instituto del Patrimonio Histórico Español, Batalla Rosado of the Universidad Complutense de Madrid, Cortés Alonso of the Asociación Nacional de Archivos y Bibliotecas de España, Escobar Olmedo of the Academia Michoacana de Historia, Sánchez Díaz of IIH-UMSNH, and Miranda Godínez of COLMICH. The initial print run was 988 copies. The most widely disseminated non-facsimile editions have been by Miranda. His first, published in 1980, was initially issued by Fímax Publicistas in a print run of five hundred copies as volume 5 of the

Estudios Michoacanos series; it includes color plates of all forty-four drawings and differentiation between passages attributed to the friar and to the indigenous informants by means of roman versus bold type. In 1988, the complete 1980 Miranda edition, minus the illustrations, was reprinted in a print run of ten thousand copies by SEP as part of the Cien de México series. The 1980 Miranda edition also serves as the basis for the selections from part three of the *Relación de Michoacán* published by FCE in 1997 as part of the Fondo 2000 series with a print run of five thousand copies; this abridged version differs from the 1980 edition in that it lacks the illustrations and the contrast between roman and bold type. A more recent edition by Miranda, entitled *Monumentos literarios del Michoacán prehispánico* (2001), 1500 copies of which have been published to date, contains selections from the oral testimony of the indigenous informants, with the interpolated commentary by the friar-compiler included as footnotes, as well as reproductions of thirty-four of the forty-four miniatures. The most comprehensive non-facsimile critical edition to date was prepared by a team of researchers under the direction of Franco Mendoza, with paleography by Martínez Ibáñez and Molina Ruiz. Published jointly by COLMICH and the Gobierno del Estado de Michoacán in an initial print run of two thousand copies in the year 2000, it includes studies by Espejel Carvajal, Franco Mendoza, Jacinto Zavala, Pérez Martínez, Roskamp, Warren—all from COLMICH—as well as Terán Elizondo, Le Clézio, and León-Portilla, plus extensive glossaries and appendices by the editor, paleographers, Márquez Joaquín, Gómez Bravo, and Pérez Ramírez. A more modest Spanish edition was prepared in 1989 as volume 52 of the Crónicas de América series by Cabrero of the Universidad Complutense de Madrid. The French translation, by Le Clézio, was published by Gallimard in 1984; a Japanese translation, by Mochizuki Yoshirô, which is based on that of Le Clézio, was published by Shinchôsha in 1987 (for an in-depth study of these translations, see Jacinto Zavala 2001). Several Purépecha specialists at COLMICH's Centro de Estudios de las Tradiciones, including Franco Mendoza and Márquez Joaquín, are currently working on retranslating the Escorial manuscript into Purépecha (for a sample of this work-in-progress, see Franco Mendoza 2001, 265–83).

15. León completed an edition of the Escorial manuscript in 1903 as well as detailed commentary on it in *Los tarascos: notas históricas, étnicas y antropológicas.* The 1903 edition was based on a comparison between the 1875 reprint of the 1869 Madrid edition and a copy of the manuscript belonging to the Peter Force collection at the Library of Congress. A 1927 article by León provides an overview of additional bibliographic and critical information regarding the Escorial manuscript that supplements or corrects some of his earlier assumptions. Ruiz, for his part, draws extensively from the oral histories recounted by the petámuti and indigenous governor in his panoramic synthesis of colonial-era materials and nineteenth-century songs and legends entitled *Michoacán: Paisajes, tradiciones, leyendas,* originally published 1891–1900. One example of an ongoing debate rooted in the rivalry between León and Ruiz concerns the latter's speculations regarding the possible Andean origins of the indigenous inhabitants of Michoacán. See, for instance, Corona Núñez 1988, 7–8; Boyd 1969, 6–9; and Hurtado Mendoza 1986, 13–17. At present there is a growing body of archaeological

evidence that lends support to the notion of contact between western Mexico and northern South America, although the extent and nature of such contact is still unclear (for a summary of some of the issues involved, see Hosler 1994, 15–17, and Roskamp 1998a, 177–80).

16. Seler's most significant contribution to Michoacán studies, only recently available in English translation, is from volume 3 of his *Gesammelte abhandlungen zur amerikanischen sprach und altertumskunde*, originally published in 1908. For more information, see García Mora 1997, vol. 2, 367–77 (commentary by Sepúlveda y Herrera) and Franco Mendoza 2000, 139–46 (commentary by Miranda Godínez).

17. Several recent editions of the work of Corona Núñez (1986, 1988, 1992, 1993) are helpful in bringing together his numerous studies related to Michoacán, the majority of which were made public in diverse forums beginning in the 1950s. In spite of the continuing interest in his work evidenced by the above editions, Corona Núñez has been criticized for a variety of reasons. Although he is not mentioned by name, a critique of the assumption that the roots of all things Mesoamerican about the indigenous inhabitants of Michoacán are the product of Teotihuacan influence can be found in Williams and Novella (1994, 11–30). Roskamp, for his part, dismisses many of his theories as faulty or premature (1998a, 105–108, 234). See also Becker (1995), who argues that Corona Núñez's focus on prehispanic traditions led him to misread the deeply ingrained Catholicism of campesino culture in the 1920s to 1940s, when he served as a leading educator in the agrarian reform movement under the aegis of Lázaro Cárdenas—governor of Michoacán from 1928 to 1932 and president of Mexico from 1934 to 1940. Becker's revisionist view of Cardenismo has been challenged, in turn, by other recent scholarship that provides a more mixed evaluation of the legacy of the Cárdenas era (for an overview, see Spenser and Levinson 1999).

18. Other prominent advocates of the essential unity of Mesoamerican religious traditions include Caso and Kirchhoff. The latter, who tends to differ from Seler in his more socioeconomic focus, wrote the introduction to the 1956 Tudela edition of the *Relación de Michoacán* (reprinted in López Austin 1981), as well as a pan-Mesoamerican study of religious festivals (1971). The former is author of several studies on the calendrical system of the indigenous inhabitants of Michoacán (see, for instance, Caso y Andrade 1943 and 1971). For a brief biography of Caso by Beatriz Barba de Piña Chán, see García Mora 1997, vol. 2, 141–65.

19. I am especially indebted to Warren's research into the life of Alcalá (1971) as well as his definitive history of the conquest of Michoacán ([1977] 1985). His pioneering research into the early years of Quiroga's missionary work in the region ([1963] 1977) has also proven to be of much use for the purposes of this book. Warren's editorial efforts concerning the colonial-era dictionaries of Gilberti ([1558] 1987), Lagunas ([1574] 1983), and Basalenque ([1714] 1994), moreover, have contributed greatly to scholarly research in the areas of linguistics and ethnohistory, not to mention his discovery at the John Carter Brown Library, and subsequent publication in 1991, of an anonymous dictionary that includes a substantial number of terms

not found in other sources. For a summary of Warren's contributions to Michoacán studies over the past four decades, see Sánchez Díaz 1997.

20. Pollard's work has been instrumental in elucidating many of the ways in which Tarascan economic, political, and religious structures at the time of the Spanish conquest differed from the model of state formation in central Mexico. *Taríacuri's legacy* (1993), the fruit of decades of archaeological and related research in the Lake Pátzcuaro Basin, presents a comprehensive picture of the demographics, administrative centers, market networks, environmental zones, and primary markers of social status and ethnicity in Tzintzuntzan and nearby communities. Her systematic exploration of the ways in which archaeological and ethnohistorical evidence from the region complement each other makes her work particularly relevant to this study. See also Pollard 1980, 1982, 1991, 1994, and 2000.

21. See note 14 for information on Miranda's substantial editorial contributions vis à vis the *Relación de Michoacán*. Additional publications by Miranda concerning this text, as well as on Quiroga and other early religious figures from Michoacán, include Miranda Godínez 1981; and Briseño 1984, 2000, and 2001.

22. López Austin's principal area of specialization is the study of the Nahuatl-speaking peoples of central Mexico. Among his extensive contributions, special mention must be made of his ground-breaking 1973 study of the notion of sacred kingship among the Nahuas and 1980 analysis of the relations between cosmovision and the human body. In more recent publications he has undertaken exhaustive studies of particular mythic configurations from throughout Mesoamerica, such as those involving the opossum ([1990] 1993), as well as in-depth explorations of concepts relating to the afterlife among the Nahuas ([1994] 1997). His interpretations of the *Relación de Michoacán* include a 1976 article on the magical-religious foundations of power and a 1981 study entitled *Tarascos y mexicas*. Other major works, although centered on the Nahuas, include fairly extensive commentary on the Escorial manuscript (see, for instance: [1990] 1993, 137–38, 143, 145, 311–12, 314, 321, 368; 1994, 96–102; and 1999, 135–40).

23. Le Clézio, himself a writer by profession, has contributed to disseminating interest in the stories contained in the *Relación de Michoacán* throughout Europe and the Americas through several publications, including: his 1984 translation of the work into French; his 1985 synthesis of many of the core poetic components of the epic history told by the petámuti; and his insightful musings on the symbolic significance of the interplay between civilization and barbarism in a Mesoamerican context, with a focus on central and western Mexico (published originally in French in 1988; Spanish translation, 1992; English translation, 1993).

24. In the interest of brevity, I have left out of the above interdisciplinary list of post nineteenth-century interpreters of the *Relación de Michoacán* numerous historians and ethnohistorians, including Kirchhoff (1939; 1946); Jiménez Moreno (1947); López Sarrelangue ([1965] 1999); Dahlgren (1967); Baudot ([1976] 1983); García Alcaraz (1976); Herrejón Peredo (1978); Sánchez Díaz (1981; 2001); Martínez Baracs (1989); Krippner Martínez (1990; 2001); Beltrán (1994); Paredes Martínez (1996;

1997b); Navarrete Pellicer (1997); Pastrana Flores (1999); Verástique (2000); León-Portilla (2000); Escobar Olmedo (2001). Among linguists, special note must be made of Swadesh (1969); Alvarado Contreras (1985); Franco Mendoza (1999; 2000); Márquez Joaquín (2000). Among ethnologists and archaeologists, of Brand (1943; 1971); Tudela de la Orden (1952; 1956); Aguirre Beltrán (1953); Van Zantwijk (1967; 1985); Carrasco Pizana (1969; 1971; 1976; 1986); Sepúlveda y H. (1974; 1988); Jacinto Zavala (1981; 1999; 2000); Gorenstein (1983); Castro Leal (1986; 1989); Michelet (1989; and Arnauld 1991; 1995; 1996); Schöndube (1996); Espejel Carvajal (1992 and 2000); Roskamp (2000). Those who have approached the text from a mythicoliterary perspective, in addition to Corona Núñez ([1956] 1986; 1986; 1988; 1992), López Austin (1976; 1981), Miranda Godínez (1980; 2001), and Le Clézio (1984; 1985; [1988] 1993; 2000), include Hurtado Mendoza (1986), La Paz Hernández Aragón (1996), Franco Mendoza (2000), and Pérez Martínez (2000). Those who have studied the drawings include Toussaint (1937), Roskamp (2000), Salazar Simarro (2000), Batalla Rosado (2001), and Miranda Godínez (2001). There is also a comprehensive study of the bibliographic structure of Escorial Ms. C.IV.5 by Hidalgo Brinquis (2001). For a detailed listing of earlier scholars who utilized the *Relación de Michoacán* in their research, with specifics as to which editions they made use of, see Sánchez Díaz 2001.

25. For a discussion of evidence related to the correlation between the beginning and end of the rainy season in Mesoamerican latitudes and the extreme northern and southern apparitions of Venus as evening star, see Šprajc 1996.

26. Several recent studies propose recasting the nature of the debate to allow for a more pan-Mesomericanist definition of key cultural terms—such as Tula and Toltec—that have traditionally been assumed to refer to only one geographic location and ethnic group. Thus, López Austin and López Luján (1999) suggest using the related toponym Zuyuá as shorthand for a constellation of ideas that became politically ascendent towards the beginning of the Postclassic period in a number of different cultural centers in the Yucatan, Guatemala, Oaxaca, central Mexico, and Michoacán. Florescano (1999), for his part, is of the opinion that, in many prehispanic and colonial-era texts, Tula refers not to the city of that name in the present-day state of Hidalgo, but rather to the concept of the city as mirror of the cosmos, as evidenced most notably in the architecture of the ceremonial centers of La Venta and Teotihuacan.

27. The principal linguistic studies upon which I have based my interpretations of sixteenth-century indigenous terminology from the region derive the bulk of their information from an analysis of the works of Gilberti, Lagunas, and an anonymous dictionary recently published by Warren under the title *Diccionario grande de la lengua de Michoacán*. Franco Mendoza also refers to a seventeenth-century dictionary in the Newberry Library in Chicago.

28. Manuscripts or manuscript copies based on ethnographic materials believed to have been originally compiled by Olmos include: *Historia de los mexicanos por sus pinturas* (ca. 1535), *Codex Tudela* (ca. 1553), *Histoire du Mexique* (ca. 1543), *Arte para aprender la lengua mexicana* (1547). Surviving documents attributed to Motolinía

include *Historia de los indios de la Nueva España* and *Memoriales* (both compiled ca. 1536–43). The manuscripts compiled by Sahagún include: *Retórica y teología y filosofía moral de la gente mexicana* (1547); *De la conquista de la Nueva España que es la ciudad de México* (1547); *Primeros memoriales* (1558–60); *Memoriales complementarios, Segundos memoriales, Memoriales en tres columnas, Memoriales con escolios* (all compiled 1561–62); *Manuscrito de Tlatelolco* (1563–65); *Memoriales en castellano* (1568); *Breve compendio de los ritos idolátricos de Nueva España* (1570); *Manuscrito Enríquez* (1577); *Manuscrito Sequera* or *Florentine codex* (1578–80); *Calendario mexicano, latino y castellano* (1583–84); *Arte adivinatoria, Libro de la conquista, Vocabulario trilingüe* (all compiled 1585). Los Ríos provided the glosses for the *Codex Telleriano-Remensis* (1562–63), which is presumed to be a copy of a lost manuscript—the *Codex Huitzilopochtli*. Another related manuscript, the *Codex Vaticano A* (ca. 1566–89), appears to be a later copy of the same work. Durán, for his part, produced three compilations of indigenous traditions: *Libro de los ritos, fiestas y ceremonias* (1570–79), *Calendario antiguo* (1579), and *Ritos antiguos, sacrificios e idolatrías de los Indios de la Nueva España* or *Historia de los indios de Nueva España e Islas de Tierra Firme* (1581). This last manuscript formed the basis for Tovar's *Relación del origen de los indios que habitan en esta Nueva España según sus historias,* also known as the *Codex Ramírez* (1583–87).

29. See Ricard ([1933] 1982) for a discussion of patterns of evangelization among the religious orders of New Spain during the early colonial period.

30. The following quotes, from the friar-compiler's prologue, are representative of his point of view regarding the lack of "reason" evident in the traditions he himself contributed to preserving for posterity: "porque los rreligiosos tenemos otro yntento que es plantar la fee de cristo y pulir y adornar esta gente con nuevas costunbres y tornallos a fundir si posible fuese para hazellos onbres de rrazon despues de dios"/"for we religious have another mission, which is to implant faith in Christ, and polish and adorn this people with new customs, and fashion them anew if possible as men of reason following [in the way of] God" (3); "y en muchas cosas açertaran si se rre\y/gieran segun el dictamen de la rrazon mas como la tienen todos tan afascada con sus ydolatrias y viçios casi por hierro hazian alguna buena obra"/"thus, although they would have been correct in many things, had they governed themselves according to the dictates of reason, since [their reason] is so clouded with idolatries and vices, any good works they did were almost by accident" (4).

31. One of my goals in chapter three is to show that it is possible to establish analogies between certain features of the drawings of the *Relación de Michoacán* and colonial-era pictorial manuscripts from other regions within Mesoamerica. The rationale for this use of simile is that it provides a basis for reading the drawings as a parallel text to the prose portions of the manuscript. The burden of proof necessary to make such a claim, however, is not the same as that required in the case of arguing a literal equivalence between one thing and another. The drawings may be *like* other pictures that have been linked to formal writing systems without necessarily belonging to a formal writing system themselves.

CHAPTER 1. RECONSTRUCTING A MULTISTAGED PROJECT: THE ESCORIAL MANUSCRIPT

1. The quote cited in the epigraph is from book two of Bacon's *Advancement of learning*, first published in 1605 (1955, 234). It is also used as an epigraph in Reyman 1995.

2. Oviedo was named royal chronicler of the Indies by Charles V in 1532.

3. To my knowledge, I am the first to connect this 1541 letter from Mendoza to Oviedo with the *Relación de Michoacán*.

4. A recent essay by León-Portilla also analyzes the place of the *Relación de Michoacán* within the corpus of missionary ethnographic writings in sixteenth-century Mesoamerica (León-Portilla 2000). While we come to many of the same conclusions regarding the basic research model employed by these friar compilers, León-Portilla goes into greater detail vis à vis their various points of contact and differences. Regarding Fray Jerónimo de Alcalá, he stresses his exceptionality as the only one besides Fray Francisco de Bobadilla who wrote in direct response to a request from a secular official. He also makes special note of the comparatively large amount of space the Escorial devotes to historical, as opposed to religious, topics.

5. Motolinía's name upon arrival in New Spain was Fray Toribio de Benavente. He adopted the surname Motolinía when he observed the indigenous people pointing at his bare feet and meager habit and calling him *motolinia*, which means "poor one" in Nahuatl.

6. For a listing of manuscripts related to central Mexico compiled by Olmos, Motolinía, Sahagún, Los Ríos, Durán, and Tovar, see note 28 of the introduction to this book. Landa, for his part, compiled the famous *Relación de las cosas de Yucatán*, which has served as the starting point—albeit an imperfect one—for all subsequent discussions of Maya hieroglyphic writing and related topics.

7. According to García Icazbalceta, the *Historia de los mexicanos por sus pinturas* (ca. 1535) is a partial copy in Castilian of a manuscript compiled by Olmos and brought to Spain by Ramírez de Fuenleal in 1547. Wilkerson (1974), for his part, argues convincingly for the attribution of the *Codex Tudela* to Olmos. Another manuscript, the *Histoire du Mexique*, is probably a synthesis in French based on the works of Olmos and another Franciscan, Marcos de Niza (Garibay 1965, 14–16). See Maxwell and Hanson (1992) for English translations and concordances of the metaphors contained in Olmos's 1547 *Arte para aprender la lengua mexicana*.

8. See plates 48–52 of this book for examples of the hands of the Escorial manuscript. The prologue and the first five chapters of part two, including the title on the frontispiece (folios 1–4, 61–70), are written in a very even hand, with few embellishments or links between letters (hand 1). The two surviving pages of part one (folio 10) are in a more cursive style, with a distinctively large loop to the stem of the letter *y* and a pronounced lengthening of the letter *c* (hand 2). The remaining chapters of part two (folios 71–139) are in a less even and more elongated hand than the first,

with fewer links between letters than in hand 2; there is also a tendency to insert horizontal lines interlinearly (hand 3). The handwriting of the copyist responsible for part three (folios 6–59) is distinctive for its circular *q* and characteristic flourish at the end of each paragraph or chapter (hand 4). The hand of the principal corrector is noteworthy for its somewhat scratchy lettering and periodic use of an angular *r* that looks like a printed *z* (hand 5). For a different description of the varied hands of the copyists of Escorial Ms. C.IV.5, see Cortés Alonso 2001, 81–84. For information regarding the types of paper, ink, and pigments used in the manuscript, see Hidalgo Brinquis 2001, 58–66.

9. My hypothetical reconstruction of the procedure followed by the friar-compiler of the *Relación de Michoacán* in questioning his oral informants—in particular, the notion that the initial conversations were based on pictures that had been previously supplied to him by the indigenous elders—is similar to that followed by Sahagún during the making of the *Primeros memoriales* in 1558–60. This manuscript, one of the first compiled by Sahagún, entailed the production, first, of a number of paintings, which were then interpreted for him by his former students, who wrote their explanations in Nahuatl at the foot of the pictures (Sahagún [1577–80] 1982, 13:54). See also Baird 1993.

10. The variation between the usage of *o/u* and *e/i* in the Escorial manuscript is potentially significant, although not as a sign of the friar's linguistic limitations, but rather as an indication of the varied cultural origin of the informants and copyists. According to Friedrich (1971a, 164–87), the uses of these vowels still differ today in the regional dialects of different communities, with speakers from the Sierra farthest along the spectrum in a continuum favoring the raising of *o* to *u* and *e* to *i*.

11. This argument is largely conjectural, since plate 2 (on folio 61 of Ms. C.IV.5) derives from the same sheet of paper as folios 62, 67, and 68. Still, there is additional evidence supporting the hypothesis that some version of the picture of the festival of Equata cónsquaro was used to elicit the oral testimony rather than vice versa. First, the description of the ceremony in the accompanying prose chapter reads like a verbal commentary on the drawing, with explanations regarding the part played in it by each of the glossed figures. Second, it strikes me as more than coincidental that plate 2 is one of the few exceptions to the general pattern in part two according to which the pictures were added as an afterthought. Unlike plates 14, 21, 25, and 26 (which are squeezed into blank spaces at the ends of chapters) or plates 4–13, 15–20, 22, and 24 (color section) (which were added after the original chapter titles were whited out to make room for them), plate 2 was clearly anticipated by the copyist responsible for this section of the manuscript. The other exceptions to the above rule are plates 3 (color section) and 23. For a more detailed comparison of plates 2 and 47, see Roskamp 2000.

12. See Nader (1979) for a discussion of the central role of the Mendoza family in the Spanish Renaissance. The historiographical principles of the age were summarized by Cabrera de Córdoba in his famous dictum of 1611: "Yo digo, es la historia

narración de verdades por hombre sabio, para enseñar a bien vivir" (cited in Mignolo 1982, 77–78). Note both the emphasis on truthfulness and the stipulation that those who profess to write histories be learned men of good moral character.

13. Mendoza's hesitancy regarding the "truthfulness" of the *Relación de Michoacán* is echoed by a general ambivalence on the part of the Spanish crown towards the compilation of indigenous traditions. Thus, the famous royal mandate to "hacer entera relación"—that is, to give a complete account of the lands and peoples of the New World—was paralleled by equally insistent directives mandating the censorship of the information so obtained. The royal cedula of 1577 that ordered the confiscation of Sahagún's manuscripts and prohibited any further work of its kind is a watershed in this regard (NCDHM [1886–92] 1971, 2:267). Although the compilation of indigenous traditions did not come to a halt in the final years of the sixteenth century, there was a change of emphasis after 1577, with the active gathering of ethnohistorical information passing increasingly from the hands of the friars into those of colonial Spanish administrators and the descendants of the indigenous elite, with a consequent decrease in the amount of attention devoted to religious beliefs and practices.

14. For a detailed discussion of the rivalry between Mendoza and Cortés, see Adorno and Pautz 1999, 3:318–23.

15. Ironically, the potential benefits to be derived from the imposition of a pan-Indian identity by colonial officials such as Mendoza were tempered by the grave dangers it could pose in contexts beyond their control. Indeed, the incipient breaking down of boundaries among previously discrete indigenous groups is one of the primary characteristics not only of the Spaniard's indigenous allies, but also of those indigenous peoples who fought against them in the Mixtón War. As in the case of the alternate promotion and suppression of the recording of indigenous traditions by the Spanish crown, the decisive factor in determining whether such change was interpreted by the colonial authorities in a positive or negative light appears to be how much control they exercised over it.

16. In Mendoza's 1551 letter to his successor, he cautions him to maintain a critical attitude regarding prevailing stereotypes in Europe according to which the Spanish residents of the New World were considered disorderly and fractious and the Indians either guileless and fundamentally virtuous or lazy and deceitful. It all depends on how they are governed, he suggests, for both must be ruled with a strong hand or the differences among the various factions will endanger the well-being of the body politic (CDII 1866, 6:490, 498–99, 509–10).

17. With regard to the difficulties entailed in the prevailing tendency among scholars to view central Mexico as the norm for all Mesoamerica, see Michelet and Williams's critiques of the "marginal" or "secondary" status accorded western Mexico (Michelet 1995; Williams and Novella 1994) as well as Weigand's criticism of what he calls the "it doesn't exist" and "ceramic centered" tendencies of traditional approaches to Michoacán and related areas (Williams and Weigand 1995).

18. The etymology of these linguistic borrowings are as follows: *ají* (Taino, axí = chili); *areito* (Taino, areyto = song and dance); *cacalote* (Nahuatl cacalotl = crow; also

a two-pronged wooden device on which toasted maize is eaten); *cacao* (Nahuatl, cacahuatl = cocoa); *cacaxtle* (Nahuatl, cacaxtli = frame used to carry cargo); *cacique* (Taino, cacique = chief); *caimán* (Taino, caimáin = caiman); *canoa* (Taino, canoa = canoe); *charchuy* (Nahuatl, chalchihuitl = type of green jade or uncut emerald); *chichimeca* (Nahuatl, chichimecatl = Chichimecs, nomadic hunters with bow and arrow); *chontal* (Nahuatl, chontalli = foreigner); *ciuatlan* (Nahuatl, cihuatlan = place of women); *cu* (Mayan, also, possibly Taino = temple); *cuitlateca* (Nahuatl, cuitlateca = ethnic group); *cuyuacan* (Nahuatl, coyoacan = place of coyotes); *hamaca* (Taino, hamaca = hammock); *hibueras* (Taino, hibuera = type of gourd); *huzizilzi* (Nahuatl, huitzitziltzin = reverend hummingbird); *iguana* (Taino, higuana = iguana); *jalisco* (Nahuatl, xalixco = place above the sand); *jical* (Nahuatl, xicalli = gourd); *jicalan* (Nahuatl, xicallan = place of jicales); *macana* (Taino, macana = wooden club, sometimes lined with knives); *macegual* (Nahuatl, macehualli = commoner); *maguey* (Taino, maguey = cactus of the agave family); *maíz* (Taino, mahisi = maize); *mastil* (Nahuatl, maxtlatl = loincloth); *matlalzingas* (Nahuatl, matlatzinca = owners of nets); *mechuacan* (Nahuatl, michihuacan = place of the owners of fish); *naca* (Nahuatl, nacatl = flesh); *naguas* (Taino, nagua = cotton skirt); *naguatato* (Nahuatl, nahuatlato = Nahuatl speaker, used in the colonial period to refer to any translator or interpreter); *ocote* (Nahuatl, ocotl = pine torch); *otomí* (Nahuatl, otomitl = ethnic group); *papa* (Nahuatl, papatli = long matted hair; priest who serves as guardian of a temple); *patol* (Nahuatl, patolli = game of chance, played with pebbles and dried beans); *petaca* (Nahuatl, petlacalli= pouch for carrying things); *petate* (Nahuatl, petlatl = reed mat used for sleeping, sitting, etc.); *sabana* (Taino, sabana = plains, prairie); *tamal* (Nahuatl, tamalli = tamale); *tameme* (from Nahuatl, tlamama = to carry), *tianguis* (Nahuatl, tianquiztli = open air market); *tomate* (Nahuatl, xitomatl = tomato); *tototl* (Nahuatl, tótotl = bird); *tuza and tuzantlan* (Nahuatl, tuzan = type of pocket gopher); *yácata* (Nahuatl, yacatl = nose), *zacatula* (Nahuatl, zacatl = grass, pasture), *zapotlan* (Nahuatlo, tzapotlan = place of zapotes).

19. According to Bravo Ugarte, there were twenty-eight languages and dialects in Michoacán at the time of the Spanish conquest (cited in Dahlgren 1967, 13). The linguistic classification of Tarascan or Purépecha has yet to be established definitively, although distant affiliations have been suggested with languages such as Zuñi, Quechua, Chibcha and Sanskrit (for an overview, see Michelet 1995 and Sánchez Díaz 2001).

20. The existence of sizable communities of Nahuatl speakers in the Lake Pátzcuaro Basin can be inferred from several passages in the Escorial manuscript (22, 42, 151). For additional evidence, see: Scholes and Adams [1530] 1952; Warren 1994; Roskamp 1998a.

21. The question of what constitutes an autochthonous indigenous tradition in the case of Michoacán is taken up by Roskamp (1998a), who argues against what he calls the "p'urhépechización" or "tarasquización" of research into prehispanic antiquities—a state of affairs he equates with the dominant position of the *Relación de Michoacán* among colonial-era manuscripts from the region. I agree with Roskamp that more attention should be devoted to texts of non-Uacúsecha origin, but do not

share his view of the Escorial manuscript as oriented exclusively towards promoting the interests of the dominant indigenous group at the time of the Spanish conquest. On the contrary, I see the oral and pictorial narratives contained therein as adaptations by members of the colonial indigenous elite of long-standing mythical and conceptual categories shaped, in earlier manifestations, by non-Uacúsecha groups such as the Islanders of the Lake Pátzcuaro Basin and local Nahuatl speakers.

22. León cites two different sources for the etymology of *caltzontzin*: Brasseur de Bourbourg, who translates it as "gran jefe de muchas casas"; and Orozco y Berra, who is of the opinion that, while *cazonci* is a title of dignity, "los mexicanos, por encono y desprecio, jugando con la palabra, formaron *Caczoltzin*, introduciendo la radical de *cactli*, zapato, el diminutivo despreciativo; y el *tzin* reverencial" (León [1888–91] 1968, 1:161–62). The possibility that *cazonci* is a corruption of *caltzontzin* is also suggested by a *relación geográfica* compiled in Pátzcuaro in 1581, which similarly derives *cazonci* from the Nahuatl word for "old sandal" (Acuña 1987, 199). Corona Núñez agrees that *cazonci* is a derivative of *caltzontzin*, but believes that the true meaning is "great lord of innumerable houses or peoples" rather than "old sandal" (1957, 7–8). More recently, it has been suggested that *cazonci* may be a local Nahuatl equivalent of the Tarascan or Purépecha term *irecha*, meaning "lord of the seat/of the dwelling place" (Roskamp 1998a, 10 and Franco Mendoza 2000, 265).

23. The origin of the word *tarasco* given in the *Relación de Michoacán* is echoed by the indigenous informants of the *Relación de Pátzcuaro* (Acuña 1987, 198) and by Herrera in his *Historia general* (dec. 3, bk. 3, ch. 9). According to a slightly different version, the Spaniards began calling the indigenous peoples of Michoacán tarascos after a battle in which a man, searching for his son-in-law, cried out repeatedly "*tarascue, tarascue.*" This story is cited in the *Relación de Cuitzeo de la Laguna*, compiled in 1579 (Acuña 1987, 81–82), Lagunas [1574] 1983, 146, and Ciudad Real [1584–89] 1822, 520.

24. Those who propose a less pejorative definition for *tarasco* have traditionally based their opinion on information provided by Sahagún's informants, who were Nahuatl speakers: "The name of the god of these [people] was Taras; hence they are now called Tarascos. This Taras is known as Michoacatl [Mixcoatl] in the Nahuatl language. He is the god of the Chichimeca" ([1577–80] 1961, 11:189; bk. 10, ch. 29; trans. Anderson and Dibble). A growing body of scholarship traces the origin of the term to a similar word, *tharés*, which is found in several colonial-era dictionaries from Michoacán. Along these lines, Corona Núñez suggests a connection with the god Tharés úpeme ([1957] 1986, 25), whose name illustrates the way in which the concept of a religious image or statue made of wood or stone (*tharés*) could be attached to the evocation of a particular deity (Franco Mendoza 1999). López Austin, based on the correspondence between *tharés* (idol) and *tharé* [peti] (old man), derives *tarasco* from the name of an ancient fire deity, who was presumably the patron god of a prominent indigenous group from the region (1994, 96–102).

25. The more limited definition of *purépecha* is highlighted by Gilberti, who translates it as "maceguales" or "gente comun" and "villano, no escudero o cauallero" ([1559] 1989, 114, 549). He provides the following example of its usage: "Mayapechax

niquaesti yauanan vanaquareni, ca purepechax aqueaesti tareni. El officio de los mercadores es andar lexos a mercadear, y el de los maceueles es cauar y arar" (Gilberti [1558] 1987, 115). As Warren states, this usage implies that it was more or less equivalent to the present-day term *campesinos* (1991, 1:ix–x).

26. Swadesh translates *uandaqua* as "word" and *anapu* as "community" or "native of" (1969, 57, 148). In addition to the relaciones geográficas of Tiripetío and Cuitzeo, other sixteenth-century sources that give the autochthonous name as the province and language of Tzintzuntzan are: Lagunas [1574] 1983, 146 and Ciudad Real [1584–89] 1872, 520.

27. The 1559 edition of Gilberti's dictionary is entitled V*ocabulario en lengua de Mechuacan*; the 1574 grammar and vocabulary by Lagunas, *Arte y dictionario con otras obras en lengua michuacana*. Ramírez, for his part, observed: "casi en toda [la provincia] corre una misma lengua, que es la que llama el vulgo tarasca, que se dice de Mechoacán" ([1585] 1959, 2:492).

28. The accusations brought against Mendoza by Sandoval in 1546 include: his practice of giving "license to many natives to bear arms and ride horseback" in violation of a royal order prohibiting such behavior; that, in spite of the fact that he was in Jalisco at the time of the outbreak of the Mixtón War, he "returned to Mexico without ending the said revolt, which he could have accomplished with ease"; that he later "narrowly averted the loss of his entire force by not accepting [an] offer of surrender" from the rebels; "that after the capture of the *peñol* of Mixtón, many of the Indians . . . were put to death in his presence and by his orders. . . . Again, at other places Indians were thrown to the dogs in his presence"; that after the pacification of the land, "he left the branding iron of His Majesty in the hands of certain individuals who remained in the said province in order that they might capture and brand slaves, [many of which] were captured and taken from pueblos which were peaceful" (Aiton 1932, 13, 20–21). The judicial process against Mendoza began in 1544 with Sandoval's arrival in New Spain and interviewing of hostile witnesses (in collusion, it would appear, with Cortés, who was in Spain at the time). The entire affair was largely resolved by 1548, when the Council of the Indies ruled in Mendoza's favor, although Mendoza's son was still seeking additional injunctions arising from the residencia as late as 1555 (Aiton 1927, 158–71).

29. Tello (bk. 2, chs. 36–38) describes how thousands of rebels committed suicide during the Mixtón War, dashing themselves and their wives and children against the rocks, in order to escape death or enslavement at the hands of the Spaniards and their indigenous allies; the entire area of Cuiná was devastated, the population of that region almost completely destroyed. Even if one takes into consideration Tello's reputation for unreliability regarding events from the early colonial period (Brand 1971, 651–53; Adorno and Pautz 1999, 2:363), there is substantial evidence of cruelty provided by Mendoza himself, who admits that some excesses were committed, but nevertheless justifies the practices of enslavement and mass execution by arguing that an exemplary punishment was necessary in order to prevent the rebellion from spreading and to convince the other rebels to surrender without a fight (Pérez Bustamante 1928, 162–63).

30. In addition to the *Relación de Michoacán*, the *Codex Mendoza*, and Betanzos's *Suma y narración de los incas*, Mendoza probably had a hand in commissioning two anonymous manuscripts entitled *La orden que los indios tenían en su tiempo para hacerse tecutles* and *La orden que tenían los indios en suceder en las tierras y baldíos*, both compiled circa 1537 (published in Carrasco Pizana 1966, 134–38, and Paso y Troncoso 1939–42, 14:145–48). For evidence of the connection, see CDII 1864, 2:201–202.

31. The likelihood that Oviedo never received Mendoza's account of the things of New Spain, based on the *Relación de Michoacán* and other primary sources, can be deduced not only from the lack of inclusion of material from the relaciones commissioned by Mendoza in his general history, but also from his response to the viceroy, in a letter dated March 1, 1542, in which he expresses great interest in Mendoza's offer and pledges to immortalize his name by according a prominent place to the promised material (Oviedo [1542] 1959, 4:254; bk. 33, ch. 53).

32. The possibility that the memoriales and papers from Michoacán mentioned by Cervantes de Salazar were earlier drafts of the Escorial manuscript was first advanced in my doctoral dissertation (Stone 1992, 15–17). Significantly, Cervantes de Salazar refers to these papers immediately after his comments related to Huitziméngari ([1566] 1985, 809; bk. 6, ch. 28). For additional biographical information on Huitziméngari, see León [1884] 1980, 45–46, López Sarrelangue 1965, 169–78, and Kuthy-Saenger 1996, 255–67.

33. Huitziméngari is also said to have studied at the Colegio de San Nicolás founded, in 1540, by Quiroga (see León [1884] 1980).

34. In addition to the *Speculum coniugiorum*, a brief sixteenth-century Latin document entitled *Enchiridion baptismi adultorum et matrimonii baptisandorum*, written in Tzintzuntzan in 1544 by a Father Juan Focher (transcribed, translated, and commented by Pedro Carrasco), also discusses some of the same marital practices as the *Relación de Michoacán*. In particular, it clarifies the nature of those relationships considered to be incestuous. Namely: between parents and children; siblings—although exceptions could be made in the case of half brothers and sisters; and nephews and aunts—but not nieces and uncles (Carrasco Pizana 1969). The correct interpretation of the following passage in the Escorial manuscript—"nunca se casavan . . . sobrino con tia ~~con tia~~"—is thus "a nephew would never marry his [paternal] aunt [*uauá*] nor [maternal] aunt [*tsitsí*]" (218). What appears at first glance to be a copyist error crossed out during a subsequent perusal of the manuscript turns out to be a casualty of the translation process.

35. Based on his comparison of the passages on indigenous marital ceremonies in the Escorial manuscript and the *Speculum coniugiorum*, Noonan concludes that the similarities between the two works are best explained with reference to a common origin in oral tradition. In particular he cites the fact that Veracruz includes information not contained in the *Relación de Michoacán* and comes to different conclusions regarding the practices of incest, endogamy, and polygamy (Chiapelli 1976, 1:351–62). Noonan does not contemplate an alternate explanation, however; namely, the argument advanced in this book regarding the existence

of more than one written version of the work compiled by Alcalá, including a transcription in the indigenous language that Veracruz may have obtained from Huitziméngari.

36. An example of a divergence in interpretation between the Escorial manuscript and the *Speculum coniugiorum* concerns the admonition a father would traditionally give to his daughter about avoiding adultery. According to the Escorial manuscript, the penalty for such misconduct was the death of both the wife and her father—"y no solamente mataran a ti sino a mi tanbien contigo"—to which the friar-compiler adds the following observation: "porque ansy hera costunbre que por el malifiçio de vno muere\ian/ sus parientes o padres" (214). This same passage is translated by Veracruz, ostensibly with the help of Don Antonio Huitziméngari, in such a way as to suggest that the adultery will result in the deaths of both the wife and her father, but not necessarily by the arm of the law: "et non diu vives super terram si malum feceris, occidente simul et me, si adulterium commiseris" (Veracruz 1556, 317; pt. 2, art. 2). The latter translation is consistent with the notion, exemplified repeatedly in the petámuti's account of the rise to power of the cazonci's ancestors, that the gods reward those who are virtuous along with their kin and punish those who are bad.

37. Ramírez uses the first person only once to refer to the gathering of information related to indigenous antiquities: "como yo he sabido de algunos que le alcanzaron [a un gran sacerdote suio que decia que presto avía de venir la verdad], particularmente de uno que fue ministro suyo, que vive todavía" ([1585] 1959, 496). Rather than assume that Ramírez was responsible for compiling the material in question, I take this passage as evidence that he was copying verbatim from an earlier manuscript. There is an amusing example of this practice in Beaumont, who refers to an illness suffered by a previous Franciscan chronicler of Michoacán, Isidro Félix de Espinosa, as if it were his own (see Stone 1994).

38. In 1596, when Philip II appointed Herrera *cronista mayor de Indias*, he granted him access to all papers in the royal archives, as well as to those held by the king's secretary. Herrera cites among his sources relaciones sent to the Spanish crown by Ramírez de Fuenleal and by Mendoza, including the works of Zumárraga, Muñoz Camargo, Motolinía, "and many others" (dec. 6, bk. 3, ch. 19). He was also able to consult the relaciones geográficas that had been collected by Ovando and the writings of Las Casas, Acosta, and Cervantes de Salazar. See Ballesteros Gaibrois 1973.

39. The designation of these works as "official" chronicles of the Franciscan order in New Spain is based on the following characteristics: (1) they were written in response to direct orders from religious superiors; (2) the friars who wrote them were appointed official historians; and (3) the intention was to extol the virtues of their brethren and to record miracles, the founding of monasteries, literary accomplishments, extraordinary acts of charity, and other noteworthy events for each of the various provinces. Mendieta's instruction dates from 1571; that of Torquemada, from 1609; La Rea's from about 1637; Espinosa's from the mid-eighteenth century; and Beaumont's from the latter part of the eighteenth century.

40. Torquemada's chronicle was published in 1615, La Rea's in 1643. The others did not make it into print until the nineteenth century, but are nevertheless cited by many of their contemporaries. See Burrus 1973.

41. The rivalry between the different orders of mendicant friars in New Spain in the sixteenth century is amply documented by Ricard, who shows how the Franciscans, the first to arrive in force in 1524, laid claim to vast territories through the practice of mass baptisms. The Dominicans, who established themselves in the viceroyalty two years later, were already somewhat limited in their freedom of movement. The Augustinians, who did not start their evangelical activity until 1533, were forced to insert themselves into the gaps left by the other two orders ([1933] 1982, 61–82). The arrival of the Jesuits in 1572 marks another important stage of missionary expansion. In Michoacán post 1538, Bishop Quiroga favored the Augustinians over the Franciscans, in part because of a lengthy judicial controversy known as the *pleito grande*, initiated between Quiroga and his former ally, the first bishop of Mexico, who was a Franciscan (see León [1903] 1984, 136–63). During a visit to the Iberian peninsula, Quiroga subsequently recruited four Jesuits to bring back to Michoacán with him; they would have been the first to arrive in New Spain if they had not been forced to abandon the voyage due to illness in 1554.

42. According to the Jesuit Ramírez, Quiroga was the first to civilize ("poner en costumbres") the indigenous peoples of Michoacán—destroying their idols, fomenting monogamy, reforming what Ramírez believed to be the untenable Franciscan method of administering the rite of baptism, teaching them catechism. For this reason, he concludes, Quiroga deserves the title of "primero y verdadero padre de esta provincia" ([1585] 1959, 497–98).

43. A detailed examination of the successive reincarnations of the chapter on the burial ceremony of a cazonci in colonial-era writings, with a focus on the ever greater distance from an indigenous point of view, can be found in Stone 1994.

44. Ruiz was among the first to implicitly criticize the *Relación de Michoacán* for not living up to the standards of other early compilations of indigenous traditions, based in large part on "la falta de ilustración que se nota en el fraile" ([1891–1900] 1971, 6). Subsequently, Baudot ([1976] 1983, 387–430), following in the footsteps of Phelan's classic study of Mendieta, attempted to contextualize the work from the perspective of early Franciscan millenialism. In his study of the writings of Motolinía, Baudot convincingly establishes a link between the millennial beliefs of the early friars and an interest in indigenous antiquities. In the case of the *Relación de Michoacán*, however, it is not the friar-compiler—who Baudot erroneously identifies as Fray Martín Jesús de la Coruña—who is responsible for the prophetic dimensions of the narrative, but rather, as I argue in chapter 4, the indigenous high priest, or petámuti.

CHAPTER 2. TRANSPARENT SILENCES: THE FRIAR-COMPILER

1. The epigraph is from Barthes's famous article, "The death of the author" (1977, 142), translated from the original French by Stephen Heath.

2. The identification of the friar-compiler with La Coruña is criticized by León (1927), Bravo Ugarte (1962), and Warren (1971). The reasons they cite include: the manner in which Fray Martín is referred to in the third person in the Escorial manuscript and characterized as "muy buen rreligioso" (264); that he is not known to have learned the indigenous language of Michoacán; and that he was largely absent from the area from 1536 to 1541.

3. Tudela mentions Gilberti as probable author of the *Relación de Michoacán* in his 1956 edition. According to Glass (1958), the erroneous citation of 1539 as the date of publication of Gilberti's *Diálogo de doctrina cristiana*—an error that originally occurs in García Icazbalceta (1866, 98–100)—is partly responsible for this misattribution. The substitution of the date 1539 for 1559 is clearly a typographical error, since Gilberti did not arrive in New Spain until 1542.

4. See note 1 in the introduction to this book for more information related to Alcalá and a summary of the evidence for attributing to him the compilation of the *Relación de Michoacán*.

5. The original inspiration for the concept of silences used in this chapter comes from a book on the production of literary meaning by the French philosopher Pierre Macherey, who claims that "the work cannot speak of the more or less complex opposition which structures it; though it is its expression and embodiment. In its every particle, the work manifests, uncovers, what it cannot say. This silence gives it life" ([1966] 1978, 84; trans. Geoffrey Wall). My characterization of the Escorial manuscript as the product of multiple hands and voices—and thus an amalgam of competing agendas and viewpoints—has much in common with Macherey's theoretical model. In the attempt to weave these various parts into a cohesive whole, certain ideas and concepts (in general, those representing the values and prejudices of the friar-compiler) are privileged over others (those originating with the indigenous collaborators). I differ with Macherey on the nature of the relationship between these various textual levels, however. In the case of the *Relación de Michoacán*, I would argue that the modifications made to the final manuscript are not the result of unconscious forces, but rather of a deliberate editorial strategy or strategies.

6. The comparison with the *Florentine codex* is interesting in that it highlights the peculiarly hybrid nature of the Escorial manuscript. Unlike Sahagún, who separated the transcription in Nahuatl from the translation in Castilian and editorial commentary, the friar-compiler of the *Relación de Michoacán* weaves together the narrative voices corresponding to the three functions of informant, translator, and editor. Thus, his commentary is presented "lo mas al propio de su lengua y que se pueda entender"/"the closest to their language that can be understood" (14) and is often fused with the oral testimony in the same sentence. The end result both creates the impression of a more homogeneous text than is actually the case and makes the attribution of any particular utterance largely a matter of speculation.

7. *The Oxford dictionary of English etymology* derives barbarian from the Greek *bárbaros*, meaning "foreign," especially non-Greek speaking. The entry notes, moreover, that it probably referred originally to unintelligible speech and is related to the

Sanskrit word for "stuttering." For a discussion of this concept in colonial times, see Pagden 1986, 15–26. The notion of "stuttering" also ties in with Hulme's foregrounding of those moments in which a text "stutters in its articulation" (1986, 12).

8. By way of contrast with the frontispiece (plate 1, color section), several other drawings in the Escorial manuscript, more heavily indigenous in style and subject matter, do not associate written modes of communication exclusively with the Spaniards. Consider plate 35, which shows a messenger carrying a piece of crumpled or folded cloth or paper on which the crimes of the people being punished are presumably represented pictorially. A uaxánoti (messenger) is also pictured in plate 29 carrying something resembling a letter on a stick. Moreover, the foremost of the caracha, or scribes-painters, in plate 28 is shown holding a pen or brush, with a bowl of ink or paint by his side. The contrast between the frontispiece and these other pictures suggests that the absence of the scribes and painters corresponds to the initiative of the friar-compiler. In order to maintain a position of cultural superiority, he has symbolically erased, in those portions of the text over which he chose to exercise greatest control, evidence regarding the literacy, both alphabetic and pictorial, of his indigenous collaborators.

9. The work of these indigenous scholars is discussed by Garibay, who names over thirty individuals linked in some way with the Colegio de Santa Cruz, giving brief descriptions of their literary achievements ([1953–54] 1992, 707–31; pt. 2, ch. 7).

10. As chance would have it, a partial listing has survived of the books contained in the Franciscan monastery school in Tzintzuntzan in the late 1520s and '30s: four volumes of a Carthusian life of Christ in Castilian, a book on the conformities and another on the virtues and vices in Latin, a choir book, a collection of sermons, and some children's primers in Nahuatl. The source for this list is Alcalá, the compiler of the *Relación de Michoacán*, who taught Christian doctrine in Tzintzuntzan and Pátzcuaro during the late 1530s and early '40s (Warren 1971, 322–25 and 2000, 52–55).

11. The polemical nature of much of the work undertaken by Sahagún is underscored in his own descriptions of the Colegio de Santa Cruz. According to Sahagún: "The laity as well as the clergy, when they saw that this progressed and that [the boys] had even greater capabilities, therefore began to oppose this activity and to raise many objections against it to prevent it" (Sahagún [1577–80] 1950–82, 13:82; bk. 10, ch. 27; trans. Anderson and Dibble). One of these detractors was a regidor (municipal councillor) from Mexico City, Gerónimo López, who criticized the friars for providing the indigenous nobles with the skills to challenge the political and religious domination of the Spaniards (CDHM [1858–66] 1971, 2:148–50). As for the goal of forming an indigenous clergy, the initial enthusiasm for the idea among a select group of friars and colonial officials soon lost momentum. By 1555 the ordination of "indios, mestizos y negros" was officially prohibited (Kobayashi 1974, 324).

12. Sahagún saw his task as that of establishing the linguistic basis that would make later comparisons possible. Thus, his famous reference to laying the groundwork for those who would compose a dictionary in Nahuatl in the style of Ambrosio Calepino's Latin vocabulary (Sahagún [1577–80] 1950–82, 13:50–51; prologue to

bk. 1). Las Casas, for his part, grounded his comparisons of Amerindian and European societies, in his lengthy *Apologética historia sumaria* [1559], on such universal constructs as the nature of humans as social beings, the interaction between human societies and environmental factors, and the natural human inclination to worship the divine.

13. Martínez Baracs (1997, 144–45) observes that Gilberti's 1559 dictionary contains a number of fairly straightforward equivalences between Christian and indigenous virtues, such as charity towards others (*pampzperata*), chastity (*patzaquarequa hangua*), justice (*himangueon cez atsiperaqua*), humility (*cuhtzuquanisqua*), and temperance (*yangayangamahcuqua*). Franco Mendoza (1999) analyzes a passage from Gilberti's 1559 *Dialogo de doctrina christiana en lengua de Mechuacan* that attributes a series of virtues of prehispanic linguistic origin to the Christian God: *yamento cezequa* (power), *mimijiequa* (wisdom), *ambaquequa* (benevolence), *tzitzijequa* (beauty), *cuiripequa* (liberality), *harangenahperansqua* (compassion), *xaramequareta* (happiness), *nirahmapaquaca* (eternity), *teparaquaqua* (majesty).

14. According to Mendieta, Olmos was entrusted with producing a book about the "antigüedades de estos naturales indios, en especial de México, y Tezcuco, y Tlaxcala, para que de ello hubiese alguna memoria, y lo malo y fuera de tino se pudiese mejor refutar, y si algo bueno se hallase, se pudiese notar, como se notan y tienen en memoria muchas cosas de otros gentiles" ([1573–1604] 1997, 1:179; prologue to bk. 2).

15. The reference is to Jerome's letter to Paulinus, written in 394 A.D. and included in the prologue to the Latin Vulgate, where he speaks with admiration of the travels and quest for knowledge of wise pagans and also of that "most learned Christian," the Apostle Paul.

16. Regarding the role of religion in fomenting indigenous resistance to colonial rule, Viceroy Mendoza laid the blame for the outbreak of the Mixtón War on a group of Zacatec Indians who arrived in Nueva Galicia in the 1540s and began spreading the "word of the devil," which he refers to as *tlatol*, among the Christianized peoples of the region, prophesying the rebirth of the ancient gods and the destruction of the Spaniards. From the point of view of the Spaniards, the danger of this kind of rebellion was accentuated by the fact that the majority of the peoples involved were familiar with Christian and Spanish ways. The parodying of the Christian mass and the washing of the heads of the baptized to cleanse them of the influence of the friars are mentioned with horror by Mendoza. The possibility that these rebels might turn the "superior" technical and religious skills of the Spaniards against their masters was quite frightening to the conquistadors and missionaries, who relied on a certain amount of mystique, both military and religious, to maintain control over the indigenous population (Pérez Bustamante 1928, 154, 157, 161).

17. In addition to compilations of indigenous customs and beliefs, the early friars produced grammars, vocabularies, catechisms, collections of sermons, confessionals, plays, and histories in Nahuatl and other indigenous languages. Between 1524 and 1572, over a hundred manuscripts were written in the indigenous languages of New Spain alone, the majority by Franciscans (Ricard [1933] 1982, 39–60, 406–14).

A shift in emphasis away from the study of indigenous languages and toward the use of Castilian as the preferred vehicle for evangelization can be observed in the latter part of the century, as the more settled areas of New Spain came increasingly under the influence of the bishops and secular clergy and a preoccupation with religious orthodoxy and control grew in Europe in the wake of the Council of Trent.

18. See chapter one of this book for more information on Mendoza's role in commissioning compilations of indigenous traditions and using them as a source for making policy decisions.

19. MacCormack (1985) discusses a similar transition in early colonial Peru from a policy of "conversion by persuasion" using indigenous languages to conversion in Castilian based more overtly on the use of force.

20. The expression "hombres de razón" (men of reason) was often used in the colonial period as a shorthand for those of European descent, though it technically referred not to race, but to degree of Westernization/Hispanization, as the quote from the prologue of the *Relación de Michoacán* illustrates. Although conversion to Christianity is presented by the friar-compiler as a prerequisite for the title, he clearly does not consider baptism alone to be sufficient in the absence of an in-depth and long-standing immersion in the Christian faith.

21. Traces of the transfer from an oral to a written register in the Escorial manuscript remain, for instance, in the frequency with which the repetition of the conjunction "y" in Spanish is suppressed by the hand of the principal corrector. According to Franco Mendoza (2000, 25), the particle "ka" is used in spoken Purépecha to denote the end of an idea and the beginning of another, in addition to its use as a conjunction. In other words, it functions simultaneously as period, comma, and copulative.

22. The inconsistencies, between different hands, in the use of the letters *ç/z* (haçer/hazer), *b/v* (tanvien/tanbien), and *g/j/x* (megicana/mexicana) in the Escorial manuscript may be an indication that not all the copyists used by the friar-compiler were highly literate speakers of Castilian. Castilian of the late fifteenth and early sixteenth centuries was undergoing a transformation in the sounds represented by these letters. According to Lapesa, the differentiation between the following phonemes—/b/ and /v/, /z/ and /ʒ̂/, /z/ and /s/, /ž/ and /š/—was no longer common in the spoken language of the time (1981, 280–86). For a discussion of this dynamic in the context of colonial Peru, see Mannheim 1988, 168–208.

23. At the residencia of Quiroga in 1536, the first bishop of Mexico, Juan de Zumárraga, a Franciscan, attributed the sudden improvement in relations between the members of his order and the indigenous peoples of Michoacán to Quiroga. This view is reinforced by the testimony of several indigenous nobles, including a Don Ramiro from Pátzcuaro and a Don Francisco from Ihuatzio (Aguayo Spencer 1939, 409–54).

24. For a general discussion of the many European symbols, religious and secular, appropriated by the indigenous nobility of Michoacán, see López Sarrelangue 1965 and Kuthy-Saenger 1996.

25. Regarding the dynamic of indigenous appropriation of Christian symbols in early colonial Peru, see Adorno 1981.

26. Brown defines a "presentation miniature" as one "depicting the presentation of a book to its patron or donor. Strictly speaking, [it] appears only in the presentation copy of a text, but such images frequently entered into the decorative program and would be included in subsequent copies (in which case the term *dedication miniature* is preferable). Although encountered earlier, presentation miniatures became popular during the fifteenth century" (1994, 102). I am indebted to Francisco Gago-Jover for bringing to my attention a number of examples of such miniatures located in: (1) a 1370 French translation of Aristotle's *Ethics* currently housed in the Bibliothèque Royale in Brussels, MS 9505–6; (2) a circa 1371 *Bible Historiale* by Jean de Vandetar, The Hague, Rijksmuseum Meermanno-Westreenianm, MS 10.B.23; (3) a 1408 copy of Valerio Máximo translated by Fray Antonio Canals, Barcelona, Archivo Histórico de la Ciudad; (4) a circa 1480 translation of Boccaccio, *Des cas des nobles hommes et femmes malheureux*, Flanders (Bruges) Royal MS 14.E.V; (5) a 1485 copy of Hernando del Pulgar's *Claros varones de Castilla*, Madrid, Biblioteca Nacional, MS I-1569; and (6) a pre-1498 copy of Pierre de Valtan's *Credo fide militanti*, Lyons, MS 35320. Reproductions of the above miniatures can be found in: Avril 1978, 104, 110; Backhouse 1987, 71; and Brown 1994, 102.

27. The famous anecdote of Cortés kneeling before the twelve Franciscan "apostles" upon their arrival in New Spain in 1524 and kissing their hands (Mendieta bk. 3, ch. 12) is a good example of the importance attributed by Cortés and his successors to establishing the authority of the friars in the eyes of the indigenous peoples. Mendoza addresses this issue in his letter to Luis de Velasco, advising him to never castigate a friar in public (CDII 1866, 6:485).

28. By late 1538 or early 1539, Guzmán had returned to Spain and definitively fallen from royal favor, although his disgrace does not appear to have been as severe as some historians, such as Bancroft, supposed it to be (see Chipman 1967, 277–87). A useful overview of Cortés's rivalries with Guzmán and Mendoza can be found in Adorno and Pautz 1999, 3:310–23. A convincing case for the normative role of Guzmán within the colonial system, in spite of the way he was vilified by his contemporaries and continues to be represented today as an historical abberration, is presented by Krippner-Martínez (2001, 9–45).

29. The famous New Laws, proclaimed by Charles V in 1542, were meant to remedy the abuse of the indigenous population by the conquistadors and encomenderos. The extent and horror of these abuses are chronicled by Las Casas in his *Brevísima relación de la destruición de las Indias* and other writings. Las Casas was joined in this critique by other religious and by lay Spaniards concerned about the rapid demise of the indigenous population. Nevertheless, many missionaries (including prominent Franciscans in New Spain) preferred to emphasize the benefits conferred upon the indigenous population by evangelization rather than their suffering at the hands of the Spaniards. Motolinía, for instance, argued passionately against Las Casas's position in a famous letter of 1555 (included as an appendix in Motolinía [1541] 1979, 205–21). The comments by the friar-compiler of the Escorial manuscript regarding the lack of virtue of the indigenous peoples of Michoacán place him closer to Motolinía, who

preferred to emphasize the benefits of Spanish rule, than to Las Casas, with his emphasis on the denunciation of Spanish abuses.

30. The scribe's involuntary mistake is consistent with information provided on the indigenous system of justice in other parts of the Escorial manuscript. For common crimes such as adultery, sorcery, and theft, punishment (in the form of the death penalty) was reserved for those found guilty four times (13). Although this may strike some modern sensibilities as excessively rigorous, sixteenth-century European writers tended to favor harsh sentences. It would appear, moreover, that the indigenous nobles were held to a stricter code of ethics than the common people. Before accepting power, a new cazonci was wont to request: "si no nos supiere rregir rruegoos que no me mateys con alguna cosa mas pacificamente apartame del ofiçio y quitame el trançado ques ynsinia de señor"/"if I do not succeed in ruling us \you/, I beg you to not kill me with [a club or] some [such] thing, but rather to peacefully remove me from office and divest me of the braid that serves as the insignia of a [Chichimec] lord" (224). The *Relación de Michoacán* contains several examples of bad or ineffectual rulers who were killed for not living up to their responsibilities.

31. Don Francisco Taríacuri, the elder son of the cazonci, was about ten years old in 1531 (Warren 1994, 362), which would make him roughly seventeen to twenty at the time of compilation of the Escorial manuscript. Don Antonio Huitziméngari, for whom Viceroy Mendoza served as godfather and namesake, was a few years younger than his brother Don Francisco Taríacuri.

32. Two pioneering studies on the significance of position in pictorial space in colonial texts of indigenous origin are Adorno 1979 and López-Baralt 1979.

33. Examples of pictures in which the cultural hero Taríacuri, seated at right, issues commands that are executed at left include: (1) plate 18, in which he orders the death of his eldest son Curátame, who has proved to be a bad ruler; (2) plate 25, in which he orders the death of a virtuous son, Tamápucheca, because he has been captured by the enemy and thereby irrevocably destined to be sacrificed to the gods; and (3) plate 26, in which one of Taríacuri's female relatives brings him the head of an enemy lord whom she has enticed away from a dance and killed, in accordance with Taríacuri's instructions.

34. In plate 13 the two empty seats at far right signify a double power vacuum, for in the next room we see Curátame, who drinks to excess, attacking his father, Taríacuri, after the latter has abdicated to him the position of cazonci. In plate 40 the seat of power is temporarily empty due to the death of a cazonci, whose son, standing at the foot of the stairs leading to the palace, has been named to succeed him.

35. Examples of the appearance of a ruler seated on the left-hand side of the pictorial space as indicative of a reversal of the natural moral order include: plate 9, in which Taríacuri is shown at left praying on the mountain while his wife is at home, being fondled by two of her kinsmen; and plate 16, which shows this wife's son, Curátame, the bad ruler, seated in his palace on the wrong side of the pictorial space. The far right in plate 16 is reserved for the future rulers Hiripan, Tangáxoan, and Hiquíngaje, who attract the favor of the gods by doing penance in a cave. A variation on this

pattern occurs in plate 20, where, in addition to the inauspicious omen of the man at left shooting his wife with an arrow, the ruler in the palace at right is facing in the wrong direction, with the door of the palace ajar. This picture exemplifies the theme of a major transformation in the political and social order.

36. Other examples of the masking of the present tense when it suggests the continuation of idolatrous practices include: "y los otros dioses que t~~ienen~~\ian/ alli en la çibdad y por la provinçia"/"and the other gods they ~~have~~ \had/ there in the city and throughout the province" (197); and "avia otro diputado sobre toda la caza de patos y codorniçes llamado curuhape\i/ndi este rrecoge\ia/ todas estas dichas abes para los sacrifiçios de la diosa xaratanga"/"there was another in charge of hunting all the ducks and pheasants called *curúhapindi*; this [official] ~~gathers~~ \gathered/ together all the said birds for the sacrifices of the goddess ~~G~~ \X/arátanga" (175).

37. According to Cuiníarángari's testimony in part three of the *Relación de Michoacán*, both he and his brother Tasháuaco accompanied the Spaniards on numerous expeditions, including the conquests of Zacatula and Colima in 1522. Tasháuaco, who is also referred to by the Nahuatl version of his name, Huitzitziltzin, later accompanied Cristóbal de Olid to Pánuco in 1523 and to Honduras in 1524, where he died. Cuiníarángari and other indigenous nobles, moreover, were brought by force on Guzmán's conquest of Jalisco after the execution of the cazonci in 1530. Although, at the time of compilation of the Escorial manuscript, Mendoza had yet to take an active role in such military campaigns, by the end of the Mixtón War he could no longer claim to be free from charges of leading indigenous troops into battle and rewarding their service with slaves and other spoils of war.

38. The compiler of the *Relación de Michoacán* mentions two examples in which the violation of Christian marital precepts occurred before the arrival of the missionary friars. In the case of a man who promised to marry another woman while his first wife was still alive, he should be prohibited from marrying the second woman. In the case of a man who was married before the conquest to a woman who then died, he should be prohibited from marrying her sister, "porque contraxo afinidad avnque hera en ynfilidad"/"because he contracted affinity, albeit in [the time of] infidelity" (218).

39. In Michoacán the cazonci continued to have many wives until his death in 1530. In fact, one of the questions put to him by Guzmán under torture was to reveal the location of his "women" (Warren 1985, 220, 223, 241–42). The indigenous governor, Cuiníarángari, also continued to live with three or four wives until the arrival of Quiroga in 1533—more than a decade after the conquest of the region by Olid (Aguayo Spencer 1939, 450; León [1903] 1984, 132).

40. The citation from the Escorial manuscript is: "ansimismo en los casamientos que agora se casan clandestinamente nunca vsan de palabras de presente sino de futuro yo me casare contigo y su yntençion es de presente con copula porque tienen esta manera de hablar en su lengua"/"also in the clandestine marriages that occur nowadays, they never use words in the present, only in the future: 'I will marry you.' And their intention is in the present and with copulation, for they have this manner

of speaking in their language" (217). In this case the passage would not make sense if it were changed to the imperfect.

41. Regarding marriage among the indigenous nobles, the custom of keeping the lineages separate is likewise marked as problematic: "esta manera tienen\ian/ de casarse los señores entre si"/"in this manner the lords are \were/ wont to marry among themselves" (213). This passage may have been flagged at a later stage because of the similarity of this custom to Jewish marital practices, as the friar-compiler points out in his commentary. Even seemingly harmless practices, however, such as the custom whereby the parents of the prospective groom speak with the parents of the prospective bride, are marked as potentially problematic: "los parientes del que se avia de casar hablan\uan/ con los padres y parientes de la muger"/"the relatives of the one to be married \used to/ speak with the parents and relatives of the woman" (214). Perhaps in this case it was feared that the authority of the parents would somehow undermine that of the friars. The accounts of the evangelization of the peoples of Anahuac tell of parents who discouraged, even prohibited, their children from close contact with the Spanish friars. Another somewhat puzzling example, concerning the widows of men killed in war, reads: "esta bivda algunos dias mirando como va tu marido camino y no te cases esto le dice\zia/n a la muger para consollala"/"remain a widow for a few days watching over your husband as he begins his journey [to the underworld] and do not marry. This is what they \used to/ say to a woman to console her" (200). In this case the handwriting indicates that the change was made by the principal corrector. Perhaps the rationale had to do with the large number of widows resulting from epidemics and wars of conquest and the desire to have these women remarry as soon as possible.

42. Examples of officials described exclusively in the imperfect include those in charge of feeding the eagles, pumas, jaguars, coyotes, and wolves kept by the cazonci; and the tavern keeper, or *atari*, in charge of the maguey wine for religious festivals. As in most colonial-era texts, the translator uses Old World referents to describe several of these animals: "leones" (lions), "tigres" (tigers), "adives" (jackals).

43. *Uri* is an indigenous suffix meaning "maker of" (Swadesh 1969, 69). For a discussion of spelling changes such as $e>i$ and $\varsigma>z$, see chapter one, note 10; and chapter two, note 22.

44. An ordinance drafted by Mendoza and approved by Charles V in 1546 lists thirty-six prohibited activities, with the sanctions to be applied in each case (Paso y Troncoso 1953, 409–15). Although some reflect general assumptions about indigenous society on the part of the Spaniards—prohibitions regarding sorcery, cannibalism, sodomy—others are more specific. For instance there are entries forbidding the use of public baths except for those who are ill (since Europeans of the time considered such baths immodest) and the games known as *patol* and *batey*. *Patol* (the Hispanicized abbreviation of the Nahuatl *patolli*) is mentioned in the Escorial manuscript as one of the favorite games of the cazonci (261). Another entry prohibits indigenous nobles from receiving young girls in their homes with the understanding that they will raise and eventually marry them. This practice is described by Cuiníarángari in the

chapter entitled "de la manera que se casavan los señores"/"concerning the manner in which the lords would marry" (207–10) and by the petámuti in the chapters on the establishment of an alliance between the Uacúsecha and Huréndetiecha (26–33).

45. Examples of lack of censorship regarding the continuation of idolatrous practices under Cortés (Mendoza's most problematic rival at the time of compilation of the Escorial manuscript) and Guzmán (arrested with the tacit consent of Mendoza in 1537) include a reference to the way in which, after the initial conquest of the region, the indigenous peoples continued to carry their gods with them into war and sacrifice prisoners "y no les dezian nada los españoles"/"and the Spaniards said nothing to them" (264). Also, according to the *Relación de Michoacán*, after the execution of the cazonci by Guzmán in 1530, some of his ashes were carried away to be buried in the customary fashion, and one of the cazonci's women was secretly sacrificed and buried in a hidden grave (276). These passages serve both to disparage Mendoza'a rivals and also to establish the credibility of statements regarding the great strides made by the Franciscans and their new converts over a relatively short period of time.

CHAPTER 3. WRITING IN PICTURES: THE *CARACHA* (SCRIBES-PAINTERS)

1. The epigraph to this chapter, from the poem "Tahirassawichi en Washington" by Cardenal, is from his collection *Homenaje a los indios americanos* (1970). The poem evokes the words of a Pawnee chief on an 1898 visit to Washington, D.C.: his views on religion, cosmology, and the sacred dimensions of everyday life. See Le Clézio ([1988] 1993) for connections between the *Relación de Michoacán* and shamanic traditions among the Yaqui, Huichol, Cora, Opata, and Maya peoples.

2. Gilberti, in his dictionary of the indigenous language of Michoacán, translates the verb *carani* as "to write or to paint" ([1559] 1989, 42). He notes moreover, that the nominal form *carari* means "scribe or painter" as well as "escribano público"/ "public clerk" (362), "escribano de libros"/"writer of books" (362), and "yluminador de libros"/"illuminator of books" (406). There are two plural forms of *carari, caracha* and *carariecha*.

3. Traditional Mesoamerican books differ from the western European variety in that they typically consist of long sheets folded screen-fashion (like an accordion), with writing on both sides. In this sense the word "codex" is a misnomer, since it technically refers only to books "made up of leaves bound together at the side," as opposed to the papyrus or parchment rolls of ancient Rome (McMurtie [1943] 1989, 76). The use of "codex" has become so generalized with reference to preconquest and colonial pictorial manuscripts from Mesoamerica and is included in so many titles, however, that it is hard to avoid. The most common material used in prehispanic Mesoamerican screenfolds was a bark paper called *amatl* in Nahuatl, *hu'un* and *vuh* among the Maya peoples, and *siranda* in Michoacán. The screenfolds, which varied in size, were sometimes stored inside protective wooden or skin covers decorated with jaguar pelts. Other common writing materials included deerskin parchment and sheets of cotton cloth or maguey fiber. When sewn together to form screenfolds, rolls, or strips, they

were commonly referred to in Castilian as *tiras*. Other books were similar in format to a canvas and generally referred to as *lienzos* in Castilian. For discussion of these and related issues, see Glass 1975, 7–9; León-Portilla 1992a, 84; Boone and Mignolo 1994, 220–27. Some of the sacred connotations of Mesoamerican writing materials and traditional methods of making paper are detailed in Christensen and Martí 1971. Sandstrom and Sandstrom provide a thorough overview of the same, along with an in-depth analysis of the role of paper cult figures in present-day shamanic practices in the Huastec region of Mexico, with an emphasis on the way paper provides "a medium of communication between the human and spirit worlds" (1986, 12).

4. Interestingly, the custom of carrying letters on sticks is cited by colonial-era chroniclers as a European-inspired innovation (Tudela [1541] 1956, 172). In other words, the modification to this drawing appears to underscore the changing relationship of the indigenous messengers to the letters they were responsible for carrying after the Spanish conquest.

5. The three Beaumont "maps" in plates 45–47 were copied by him from a multisectional painted tira. He included a total of six of these "maps" in his eighteenth-century chronicle, including several depicting more than one pictorial scene. Roskamp refers to them collectively as the *Tzintzuntzan codex*, since they belonged to the Cuiní family of Tzintzuntzan (1998b; 1998b, 36–39, 263, 286; 2000, 244).

6. Roskamp acknowledges that his list is not definitive, since more colonial-era pictographic manuscripts may still be found in their communities of origin or in private collections. The ones he considers in his study are: the codices Carapan, Chilchota, Cuara, Cutzio I and II, Huapean, and Tzintzuntzan (copy by Beaumont); the lienzos of Arantza (erroneously referred to as Sevina by many commentators), Atapan, Carapan, Comachuén, Jucutacato, Nahuatzen, Pátzcuaro, and Puácuaro; the titles of Tócuaro and Xarácuaro; the coat of arms of Tzintzuntzan; the genealogy of the caciques of Carapan (copy by León); and the drawings of the Escorial manuscript. For those interested in viewing the aforementioned manuscripts, the reproductions provided by Roskamp are complemented by those available in Glass (1964); HMAI, vol. 14 (1975); Corona Núñez (1986); Florescano (1989); and Boehm de Lameiras (1994, 137).

7. To date scholars have tended either to cast doubt upon the existence of a pictographic writing system in Michoacán or to make passing mention of colonial-era pictorial manuscripts from the region without speculating about potential prehispanic prototypes. One reason for this reserve is the lack of explicit mention of such "picture books" by sixteenth-century commentators, especially since it is a silence that contrasts with the high praise generally accorded the indigenous artisans of the region in related areas such as painting with brushes, feather painting, and lacquering (see, for example, Sahagún [1577–80] 1950–82, 11:188–89; bk. 10, ch. 29; Acuña 1987, 202; La Rea [1643] 1996, 80; Escobar [1729] 1970, 49; Beaumont [ca. 1778] 1985, 2:56–57). Another reason for this reticence is the assumption on the part of many scholars that only proven phonetically based pictorial systems

can be considered writing (see, for instance, Batalla Rosado's analysis of the drawings of the Escorial manuscript).

8. No potentially prehispanic "picture books" have been found for the indigenous inhabitants of Michoacán similar to those preserved for the Maya (codices Dresden, Madrid, Paris, Grolier), Nahua (*Tonalamatl Aubin* and codices Borbonicus, Boturini, Moctezuma—all of which date from the early sixteenth century), and Mixtec (codices Vienna, Nuttall, Bodley, Colombino-Becker). The so-called Borgia group (codices Borgia, Féjérvary-Mayer, Laud, Vatican B, Cospi) may be either Mixtec or Nahua in origin.

9. Regarding studies of ceramic design style in the region, see Versluis 1994.

10. For a critique of the notion that alphabetic writing is the inevitable goal toward which other, presumably more primitive, writing systems naturally evolve, see Boone and Mignolo 1994, 3–49, and Mignolo 1989.

11. The definition of writing I am using in this chapter closely parallels the one formulated by Boone: "the communication of relatively specific ideas in a conventional manner by means of permanent, visible marks" (1994, 15). A similarly inclusive definition is proposed by Mignolo: "scratching on solid surfaces or using any kind of material meant to codify meaning" (1995, 119). In both cases the emphasis is on the function of writing as a codified form of communication rather than on the particular materials employed or the predominance of phonetic versus nonphonetic elements. An alternate definition provided by Mignolo underscores the biological basis of writing as a communicative behavior peculiar to *homo sapiens*, yet distinct from speech: "the use of hands and the extension of hands through a sharp instrument, brush, pen, fabric, or knotted strings, etc." (Boone and Mignolo 1994, 260).

12. For a discussion of the hypothesis that the Mixtec year glyph represents a solar observational device—a type of sundial—consisting of a pair of crossed trapezes mounted on a circular plate, see Aveni 1980, 20–21.

13. See chapter 2 for a critique of the friar-compiler's catalog of virtues and vices as they relate to the indigenous inhabitants of Michoacán. The supposed lack of abstract nouns in Purépecha is also directly challenged by linguists such as Franco Mendoza (1999), who notes the importance of metaphor *quaniéntsqua* (*khwaniéntskwa*) in understanding such abstractions (1999).

14. There are many associations with the term *chichimeca*—a word that does not connote any particular ethnic or linguistic origin. Among those cultural groups who tended to be especially proud of their Chichimec heritage, both the Mexica and Uacúsecha figure prominently. It is important to underscore that, in spite of the barbaric or uncivilized connotations of the term, in poetic contexts it generally refers to the ideal conception of the hunter-warrior as incarnation of the solar virtues of strength, bravery, skill, and self-sacrifice. It is in this sense that the bow and arrow and red deerskin braid function as symbols of nobility in the drawings of the *Relación de Michoacán*. Another defining Chichimec characteristic, that of being nomadic hunter/gatherers unfamiliar with agriculture and fishing, is not corroborated by the available

archaeological evidence regarding the origins of the Uacúsecha (Michelet 1989 and 1996). For further discussion of the centrality of this concept to the self-identity of the ruling dynasty of Michoacán at the time of the Spanish conquest, see Le Clézio [1988] 1993, 117–60.

15. Regarding the association between words, arrows, and magic in the *Relación de Michoacán*, compare the following belief among the present-day Moche peoples: "The Moche think words exist autonomously, as forces, after they have been spoken. They glide 'like an arrow through the air' and enter the body to which they are directed" (cited in López Austin [1990] 1993, 205). Among the Apaches, arrows are likewise associated with stories that derive their force from the interaction between speaker, listener, and the locus of enunciation: "All these places have stories. We shoot each other with them, like arrows" (cited in Basso 1996, 48). The moral and pedagogical function of such stories is augmented by their association with familiar landmarks that continue to haunt the imagination of the local inhabitants whenever they pass by them.

16. The *Cuauhtitlan codex* contains a similar example of an inauspicious rejection of everyday objects presented as precious gems and feathers. According to the story, Huemac, another name for Quetzalcoatl as king of Tula, belittled the gift the Tlaloque rain gods brought him in the form of tender kernels and husks of corn, thereby precipitating a terrible famine (analyzed in Florescano [1993] 1995, 157–58).

17. Figure 4 summarizes the information contained in the pages of the *Relación de Michoacán* regarding the male line of descent of the Uacúsecha dynasty founded by Iréticátame.

18. The motif of the tree as a symbol of political unity and authority, as well as of the connection between the different levels of the cosmos, is common in the Mesoamerican pictographic tradition. The specific type of tree varies, however. Among the Maya, the ceiba is the sacred dynastic tree, as in *La historia de los colores*, while in the *Relación de Michoacán* it is the oak.

19. Corona Núñez also mentions the analogy with an oak tree for plate 27 (color section) (1986, 123). In other parts of the text the cloverleaf garlands are associated with the goddess Cueráuaperi and those connected with her, such as certain gods who formed her escort, her priests, and those possessed by her spirit or destined to be ritually sacrificed (Tudela [1541] 1956, 158, 221, 232, 234–35).

20. For a discussion of the correspondence between this divine life-force and political authority in the *Relación de Michoacán*, as well as the various ways in which it can be strengthened—by prayer, self-sacrifice, and so forth, or dissipated—through intermarriage or unregulated sexual activity, see López Austin (1976). Roskamp discusses several examples of similar lines representing *cuerdas* (cords) in other surviving pictographic materials from Michoacán. His interpretation puts more emphasis on the notion of territoriality—through analogy with the indigenous method of measuring parcels of land—although he also notes a connection with the concepts of lineage and the order in which a text is meant to be read (1998a, 112, 239–40).

21. The terms used in the Escorial manuscript to characterize the relationship between Hiripan and Tangáxoan, on one hand, and Taríacuri, on the other, are "sobrino" (nephew) and "tío" (uncle). These appear to be translations, respectively, of the Purépecha kinship terms *uuache* and *auita*. The former translates variously as "son," "brother's child," "younger relative through the male line," or simply "youngster." Ditto for the latter which, depending on the context, can refer to a paternal uncle or any related kin in the second degree. In Western kinship terms, Hiripan and Tangáxoan are Taríacuri's first cousins once removed, since their fathers were Taríacuri's paternal cousins.

22. According to Beltrán (1994, 97), who bases his analysis on Swadesh (1969, 58), "el término bezote (*anha-me-kua*) tiene la misma raíz que muchas expresiones referentes a la nobleza, como arrogancia, honra, príncipe o capitán (*anha-ua-ta-nha-rhi*) y, muy significativamente, fundador de un linaje o bisabuelo (*anha-ndi-hpe-nsta-ni*)." Those who wore such lip plugs, which were typically of polished obsidian, in some cases inlaid with turquoise or rock crystal held in place by a band of gold, were called angámecha; in colonial-era documents, they are generally referred to as caciques or señores (Pollard 1993, 124, 129).

23. Even a cursory examination of the drawings suggests a fairly wide range of stylistic features and "signature motifs." The only speculation to date regarding the number of caracha responsible for the drawings of the Escorial manuscript has been by Salazar Simarro, who deduces the existence of at least five different painters, probably working as a team (2000, 300); and Batalla Rosado, who considers three sufficient to explain the degree of variation manifested in the drawings (2001, 159–60).

24. Although Robertson lists the use of "shading and modeling through variations in tone" ([1959] 1994, 2) as a pictorial convention of European as opposed to Mesoamerican origin, I wonder whether it may not have roots as well in the ancient Mesoamerican tradition of feather working, which put great emphasis on subtle gradations in color. Batalla Rosado notes especially the varying shades of green in many of the Escorial scenes incorporated into a landscape setting (2001, 151). Salazar Simarro does not speculate on this particular characteristic, but she does note several other potential examples of prehispanic pictorial influences in the Escorial manuscript: the predominant application of color in flat washes; the attention to consistency of line; the use of footprints to indicate paths; the hierarchizing of figures by size and location within the composition; the stylized representation of the human body, with large heads, slender torsos when standing, rounded when seated, and short limbs; the superimposition of heads in a more or less circular formation to create the idea of a multitude; and the use of indigenous markers of social status (2000, 301–302).

25. For a discussion of the technique of linear perspective as manifested in Italian Renaissance painting, see Edgerton (1975).

26. This multiple perspectivism is considered by Robertson one of the defining characteristics that distinguish Amerindian from European-influenced pictorial compositions during the colonial period ([1959] 1994). Mignolo also emphasizes its importance: "seen from an Amerindian perspective the world, more often than not, looks like

coexisting territories within the same space. Such a perspective is quite different from the Spanish (and European) one, in which either there is not such a thing as coexisting territorialities (like in López de Velasco) or, if there is, Amerindian cosmology and cosmography were reduced to the Christian ones" (1995, 246).

27. Roskamp similarly notes the prevalence of dual indigenous and European cultural symbolism in colonial-era pictorial manuscripts from Michoacán (1998a, 2000).

28. In one of the earliest descriptions of the indigenous "antiquities" of New Spain, Olmos' *Historia de los mexicanos por sus pinturas,* he is quite explicit regarding the religious significance of the painted Mexica screenfolds that he used as sources. Olmos notes that these "libros y figuras" were interpreted for him by former priests ("los que en tiempo de su infidelidad eran sacerdotes y papas") and principal lords, who were raised "en los templos." He takes care to observe, moreover, that they were evidently of great antiquity and that the majority were smeared with human blood: "según lo que demonstraban, eran antiguas y muchas de ellas teñidas, la mayor parte, untadas de sangre humana" (reproduced in Garibay 1965, 23). Landa, for his part, defends the burning of Maya books, in spite of his recognition of their worth as depositories of cultural knowledge, because of their idolatrous nature: "These people also made use of certain characters or letters, with which they wrote in their books their ancient matters and their sciences, and by these and by drawings and by certain signs in these drawings they understood their affairs and made others understand and taught them. We found a large number of these books in these characters and, as they contained nothing in which there was not to be seen superstition and lies of the devil, we burned them all, which they regretted to an amazing degree and which caused them great affliction" (cited in Clendinnen 1987, 70; trans. Alfred Tozzer).

29. The concept of sky-earth evoked in the captain general's remarks in the *Relación de Michoacán* (193) is similar to the Quiché Maya term *cahuleu,* which, according to Tedlock, "preserves the duality of what we call the 'world'. . . . To this day the Quiché Maya think of dualities in general as complementary rather than opposed, interpenetrating rather than mutually exclusive" (1985, 64–65). López Austin, in his discussion of the Nahuatl term *inamic,* also stresses the complementary nature of Mesoamerican dualities (1994, 120–27), as does Florescano (1999, 37, 51, 87).

30. The image of the body of the earth goddess projected onto the map of the world in the Ramírez littera annua ties in with the well-established correlation between the human body and cosmography among the Nahuas as formulated in López Austin [1980] 1989.

31. References to the four directions in Mesoamerica are generally conceived of in terms of the division of the solar year by the solstices and equinoxes rather than the cardinal points commonly used in European-style map making (Aveni 1980).

32. According to Le Clézio, "the ritual of a salve—the offering of the first hunt— to the gods on the hunting grounds evokes the most ancient of propitiatory rituals— practiced both by the nomads of the north (Comanches, Apaches, Sioux) and by the

semi-sedentary tribes of the Mayan plain—the survival of which among the Aztecs has been noted" ([1988] 1993, 124).

33. The way in which the ceremony of making a salve to the gods is described in the *Relación de Michoacán* suggests that the point of view is that of a solar god and/or an earth goddess. Regarding the first possibility, Aveni observes: "When the sun rises, he sees the north to his right, the south to his left; straight ahead is the region of the west where he will die each night" (1980, 156). As for the second hypothesis, see figure 1 for a visual demonstration of the correspondence between right and north, on one hand, and left and south, on the other, from the perspective of the earth goddess mentioned in the Ramírez letter.

34. Pollard's skepticism regarding the centrality of dualism as an organizing principle in prehispanic Michoacán stems in part from the lack of clear male/female counterparts for much of the indigenous pantheon (1991, 168).

35. Terán Elizondo identifies the key symbolic numbers in the *Relación de Michoacán* as four, five, and twenty, although she also notes the importance of the east-west and north-south axes—the former associated with the complementary dualities of red-white and morning star-evening star; the latter, yellow-black and ball court-sweat bath. Other key twentieth-century contributors to the subject of Tarascan cosmology include: León [1903] 1979; Seler [1908] 1993; Tudela 1956; Corona Núñez 1957, 1986, 1988, 1992, and 1993; Van Zantwijk 1967; Caso 1943 and 1971; Kirchhoff 1956 and 1971; Sepúlveda y H. 1974 and 1988; López Austin 1976, 1981, and [1990] 1993; Hurtado Mendoza 1986; Castro-Leal et al. 1989; and Verástique 2000.

36. Brotherston, in his encyclopedic study of indigenous literary traditions throughout the Americas, documents the widespread presence of the images of the quatrefoil and quincunx as visual equivalencies of the cosmos (1992, 82–102).

37. The rope appearing in plate 33 (color section) is reminiscent of the one described in the prose portions of the *Relación de Michoacán* as having been given to the god Curícaueri by his parents in the heavens, and which was used to tie the captives destined for ritual sacrifice (22–23). Nevertheless, as the metaphor of death as a process of "desatarse" (200) or becoming untied suggests, in a sense we are all captives, for our destiny is to "feed" or render homage to the gods. For other linguistic associations with the verb *cuerani* (to untie) during the colonial period, see Monzón García and Roth Seneff 1999.

38. The belief that those who die honorably are destined to "feed" the gods of the sky while those who die in disgrace "feed" the gods of the underworld explains the custom whereby those who were injured in battle would sprinkle their blood toward the heavens "por que no cayese en el suelo"/"so it would not fall upon the ground" (36). Another metaphor for the act of being dishonored is to have earth thrown in one's eyes (59, 216), for that is how the common people would fight, with rocks and clumps of earth (36). The preferred weapon of the nobility, in contrast, was the bow and arrow—associated with the sun, the golden eagle, and other birds of prey.

39. Franco Mendoza (1999) calls this principle of reciprocity a "pacto de coparticipación" between gods and mortals: "por el servicio religioso se coparticipa en el

establecimiento del orden divino-humano." He adds, moreover, that this pact exists on three levels: between gods; between humans; between gods and humans. Its centrality to other Mesoamerican religious traditions has been amply documented.

40. Further symbolic associations with the right- and left-hand sides of the cosmos are given in the following passage from the *Relación de Michoacán*, in which the goddess Xarátanga addresses Tangáxoan in a dream: "mira a la man [*sic*] derecha donde a de estar el juego de la pelota alli tengo de dar de comer a los dioses a medio dia" (136). At noon, when the moon is due to begin its ascent from underworld to sky, sacrifices are made to Xarátanga at her ball court, which is to the "right"—that is, the north or place of the noonday sun, as represented in figures 1–3.

41. Both Seler ([1908] 1993, 53–55) and Corona Núñez (1992, 33–34, 84) draw parallels between the gods of the right and left hands, as described in the Escorial manuscript, and the mythic encounter between the forces of day and night in central Mexican religious beliefs. As Aveni explains: "the sun is a celestial warrior who, on rising in the east, throws his arrows, or rays of light, at the stars, thus ending the night and establishing the day" (1980, 23). According to this symbolic system, the eagle and other birds of prey, envisioned as arrows or rays of light, engage in daily battle with the stars, who form the entourage of the moon. In the *Relación de Michoacán* the former are encoded as residing on the right-hand side of the cosmos; the latter, on the left-hand side.

42. Pollard describes Curícaueri as "both the messenger of the sun (the sun's rays), connecting the earth and sky, and the warmth of the hearth. As a sky force he was referred to in different terms for the rising, noon, and setting sun; as an earth force these phases of the sun were related to directions. As the original patron god of the Tarascan royal dynasty, he was a warrior and god of the hunt" (1991, 169). Franco Mendoza translates Curícaueri as "the essence of fire, he who makes fire possible": "el que origina o crea el fuego, o bien, el que se incendia, es decir, el que es fuego" (2000, 266).

43. It is, of course, impossible to know to what extent the arrangement of such complementary pairs on either side of an imaginary diagonal from pictorial lower left to upper right corresponds to a conscious strategy by the caracha. Nevertheless, if spatiotemporal organization is analogous to grammar, one would not expect its implementation to be conscious. There is ample evidence from the prose portions of the Escorial manuscript, moreover, to suggest that the specific dualities listed are not simply imaginative projections on my part. The female/male dichotomy ties in with the pairing of the gods Xarátanga and Curícaueri as well as their human counterparts—the Huréndetiecha and Uacúsecha—the former of whom are identified with the island of Xaráquaro; the latter, with the mainland. The subject/ruler opposition is also an important organizing principle in the petámuti's oral performance, whose main theme is the rise to power of the various ruling dynasties of the Lake Pátzcuaro Basin, culminating with the Uacúsecha. Ditto for the motif of the elder and younger brothers. The problem, as I see it, is the indiscriminate application of such dualities without reference to narrative and social context or their elevation over other equally important organizing principles, not their value per se in the making of structural analyses.

44. Seler translates Huréndetiecha as "people who are in first place" ([1908] 1993, 21). An alternate interpretation is provided by Márquez Joaquín (2000, 711): "los que son diestros"/"those who are skillful" (from *hurendi*, meaning "one who is wise or prudent").

45. Monzón García and Roth Seneff (1999) propose a related etymology for the present-day word *yurhixu*, which is used to refer to the hospitals established as charitable institutions during the colonial period under the aegis of the Virgin of the Immaculate Conception: *yurhítsirho* (place of the menstruating woman) > *yurhixo* or *yurhixu*.

46. In addition to plate 3 (color section), another drawing from the *Relación de Michoacán* that suggests an analogy between rivulets of blood on pyramid stairs and sacrifice is plate 10. Note the sacrificial victim at the base of the pyramid and also the explicit association between the pyramid and the god to whom it is dedicated (Curícaueri or a priest wearing his mask is literally peering out of the altar at the temple summit). Stairs can thus be seen to symbolize the possibility of communication between gods and mortals. Even when stairs appear alone (plate 40) or as ladders (plate 29), they still retain their significance as references to the principle of reciprocity that sustains the motion of the cosmos. The flip side of this dynamic is suggested by those drawings that show pyramid stairs without blood running down them, as in plates 4, 15, and 17. The absence of blood can here be interpreted as a negative sign of famine or neglect of human beings' ritual obligations to the gods.

47. Since each color is associated with a different direction (white with the west; yellow with the north; red with the east; black with the south; blue or green with the center), the use of all the colors together can be interpreted as a reference to the horizontal plane of the cosmos as quatrefoil/quincunx or one of its symbolic equivalents, such as the iréchequa, or fourfold kingdom. For a discussion of the traditional significance of color in Michoacán, see Corona Núñez (1992, 22, 75, 122), Hurtado Mendoza (1986, 87–88), and Pollard (1991, 169; 1994, 126) and Terán Elizondo (2000, 285–99).

48. A number of alternate translations for Pátzcuaro include: "donde se tiñen de negro"/"where things are dyed black" (from *pazcani*, "to dye black"); "lugar donde se guarda algo"/"place where things are stored" (from *patzáquaro*, "storage area"); or a derivation from the name of the rocky outcrop called *petázequa* (Roskamp 1998a, 158; Márquez Joaquín 2000, 713).

49. For a discussion of the multiple symbolic connotations of Tlalocan among the Nahuas, see López Austin [1994] 1997, 197–278.

50. See Pollard 1991, 175–77 and 1993, 178–80 for discussion of her hypothesis regarding the relatively recent reduction in the status of female symbols of power in Michoacán prior to the Spanish conquest. This state of affairs was especially pronounced among the elite, in spite of the importance accorded the female deities Xarátanga and Cueráuaperi in the official state religion. Such gender stratification contrasts with the more pronounced gender parallelism among commoners.

51. According to López Austin, among the most prevalent allegorical equivalencies in Mesoamerican mythology are analogies between the human body, house,

corn plant or cornfield, temple, town, surface of the earth, and cosmos ([1990] 1993, 161–62). The only one of these not featured in the drawings of the Escorial manuscript is the analogy with corn, whose central position in Nahua and Maya mythology is occupied instead, in the *Relación de Michoacán* at least, by the metaphorical system analyzed above related to trees and firewood. Again, we may be dealing with a belief system that correlates primarily with the indigenous nobility at the time of the Spanish conquest, as opposed to the commoners.

52. The association between writing and prayer is made explicit through comparison with another drawing, plate 31, which depicts the way in which the priest called *hirípati* would pray for success prior to the initiation of a military campaign. The priest is facing in the direction of the "sky," while the scene that will be played out on earth, if all goes in accordance with the blueprint outlined in the priest's prayer, is depicted at right. Just as a prayer seeks to bring about a desired effect, the pictorial representation of this prayer is accompanied by a concretization of the priest's request.

53. According to Corona Núñez, the spiral is associated with the conch-shell trumpet, whose sound represents the voice of the wind god Ehecatl-Quetzalcoatl in his role as creator deity; among the indigenous inhabitants of Michoacán, he is called "Taríacuri, Sacerdote del Viento, del Soplo Divino" (1986, 102–03; 1988, 21–22; 1992, 18). Westheim emphasizes the importance of the spiral in ancient Mesoamerican art as a symbol of fecundity, birth, and both female and male sexual organs ([1950] 1965, 112–19). For López Austin it stands for the circulation of divine energy through the sacred trees that are located at the center and four quadrants uniting earth and sky (see chapter three, note 56).

54. Mignolo defines the axis mundi as the place "where space and time meet; where the vertical and horizontal join forces with the movement of the skies and the changes of season" (1995, 231). According to Aveni the "layered-universe concept" of ancient Mesoamerica contrasts with "both the geocentric (earth-centered) and heliocentric (sun-centered) views of the universe which evolved in the classical Western world. . . . Instead, the hierarchical structure of the system becomes the basic theme of the picture" (1980, 15–17). For a discussion of the theological implications of a similar dynamic in Hindu cosmology, see Eck [1981] 1985, 25: "At times the ordering of the diverse parts of the whole seems best described as hierarchical; yet it is also true that the parts of the whole are knitted together in interrelations that seem more like a web than a ladder."

55. For a description of the massive wooden planks made from oak trees that formed the stockade perimeter of the fortress at Taximaroa, which marked the boundary between the lands of Michoacán and those of the Mexica at the time of the Spanish conquest, see Beaumont ([ca. 1778] 1985, 2:10; bk.3, ch.1).

56. Cf. López Austin's explanation of the Nahua concept of the circulation of divine energies through the cosmic trees at the center and four corners of the world ([1990] 1993, 60; [1994] 1997, 117, 269). The contrary forces descending from the sky and ascending from the underworld through these "tubes" come together in the

shape of a double helix or spiral, thereby initiating sexual activity and the process of change and decomposition over time. As in the story of the origin of colors cited in the preface to this book (Marcos [1994] 1999), these energies can also be conceived of as colors—indeed, as the very first colors—those that painted the world as we know it today, when they were flung by the gods from the top of the sacred tree. With the addition of the dynamic principle of motion to a previously static universe, the gods establish a mechanism for regular exchanges between the celestial and terrestrial realms, thereby inaugurating the process of reciprocity as a means of maintaining cosmic order.

57. Roskamp notes the analogy between caves and both ollas (cooking pots) and yácatas (pyramids) in the *Lienzo de Jucutacato* and *Genealogía de los caciques de Carapan* (1998a, 110, 217).

58. As is apparent in plate 16, Hiquíngaje was not as rigorous in his fasting as his two older cousins, who took pity on him and gave him most of the toasted corn they had brought to eat. As a consequence the fortunes of his descendants were correspondingly less distinguished.

59. Other sources consulted regarding the etymology of angámucuracha are: Tudela [1541] 1956, 16; Gilberti [1559] 1989, 57, 182; Warren 1991, 2:32; and Seler [1908] 1993, 19.

60. The visual metaphor of a man climbing a mountain in search of firewood as the equivalent of virtuous behavior is consistent with the admonition, found repeatedly in the *Relación de Michoacán*, not to "break the count of the firewood" (225, 228), for to do so is synonymous with failing to fulfill one's ritual obligations, thereby jeopardizing the fate of one's community and of the cosmos at large. This concept is connected with the idea of firewood as a symbolic shorthand for both tribute and squadrons of warriors (225, 228). The admonition not to "break the words of a superior" also occurs frequently as a metaphor for disobedience (196, 208, 228). León deserves recognition as one of the first scholars to suggest an analogy between references to firewood in the Escorial manuscript and concepts of both political authority and conquest ([1903] 1979).

61. There is a pun on the concept of sleep in the story of Carócomaco, who "slept" on the temple stairs in a literal sense, but not in the more metaphoric sense of undertaking a spiritual journey. The visions that come in dreams, not the act of sleeping per se, are what is essential to the shamanic experience.

62. In many parts of Mesoamerica the motif of a sudden reversal of fortune correlates with the reappearance of Venus as morning star after a period of disappearance during inferior conjunction (Aveni 1980, 26).

63. For further discussion of the concept of ollin as center, see Elzey 1976.

64. Additional information regarding manóuapa can be found in Pollard 1991, 170, and Corona Núñez 1992, 74–75, 124.

65. The symbolic meaning of the rock formation above the ojo de agua, or spring, in the Itzíparámuco drawing (plate 20) ties in with the notion in the *Relación de Michoacán* that to be old is to have deep roots. Thus, one knows that a population is

of ancient origin if its hearth stones "han hechado muy hondas rrayces" (139). A very old town was also said to have gray hair: "tiene canas de muy y antigua poblaçion" (139). It is also reminiscent of the Nahuatl term for community kingdom or city state, *altepetl*, which literally means "water-hill."

66. Corona Núñez equates the goddess Auícanime with the fearful Cihuateteo—giant female warriors who represented the souls of Nahua women who had died in childbirth and who haunted the crossroads (1988, 25–29). As maleficent spirits, or *tzitzime*, they were "the monsters destined to destroy this fifth world" (Clendinnen 1991, 174–205). Pollard describes Auícanime as a goddess of famine and sister to Cueráuaperi in that she converts the latter's characteristic associations with abundance and fertility into a sign of scarcity and death (1991, 170).

67. In the original version of plate 20 the goddess Auícanime is carrying the rodent mentioned in the accompanying prose chapter rather than a basket of eggs. Hurtado Mendoza mentions a present-day Michoacán legend that associates the descent of Auícanime to earth with the appearance of the new moon and with the mythical "La llorona," or crying woman who grieves over the loss of her children (1986, 73, 95–96).

68. The sweeping of the "good" wife is a reference to the notion of filth as moral aberration. See Burkhart [1986] 1989 for an in-depth discussion of this concept among the Nahuas. For some associations with this idea among the indigenous inhabitants of Michoacán, see Corona Núñez (1986, 108; 1992, 24).

69. To this day, women sweeping with brooms and heavy use of incense are still parts of the marriage ceremony in Tarascan indigenous communities (Pollard, personal communication).

70. A metaphor for the act of having sexual relations in the *Relación de Michoacán* is to exchange words, to speak to one another. Thus, the parents of a woman who has eloped reluctantly resolve to accept the man she has chosen, for "ya an mudado entranbos sus corazones y an hablado entre si" (216). The other metaphor in the above quote of the two hearts moving as one appears to be a reference to the state of being in love.

71. The pictorial critique of colonial society through representation of the ways in which it led to looser sexual mores among indigenous women can also be found in Guamán Poma, many of whose illustrations are quite graphic in this regard.

72. Corona Núñez draws an analogy between the image of the serpent-butterfly and the concept of ollin (1986, 97). Among the Nahuas, the snake was associated with water and the butterfly with fire (Seler [1908] 1993, 62). Together, they serve as a metaphor for war.

CHAPTER 4. REMAPPING THE LAKE PÁTZCUARO BASIN:
THE *PETÁMUTI* (HIGH PRIEST)

1. The source for the quote cited in the epigraph is one of Tedlock's poetic tributes to the Quiché Mayas, entitled *Breath on the mirror*, in which he weaves together

the traditional legends of the Popol Vuh and the living history transmitted to him by contemporary Maya day-keepers (1994, ix).

2. Cf. the following quote from Lévi-Strauss: "The first characteristic of a myth is that of operating on time as a totalizing action, one that folds—like an accordion—the present over the past and the future over the present" (cited in López Austin [1990] 1993, 207).

3. Regarding the etymology of Equata cónsquaro, also referred to as "feast of the arrows" in the Escorial manuscript, Franco Mendoza (1999) notes a possible correlation with the verb *equaquatan*, meaning "to place bundles (*haces*) on the ground."

4. Another translation for royal palace in the indigenous language of Michoacán is *iréchequaquahta* (Martínez Baracs 1997, 105).

5. Martínez Baracs provides a long list of words related to *ireta*, which is defined by Gilberti as "town of all together." These include *yrecha* (king); *yrechequa* (kingdom); *yrerucutsperi* (captain); *hima yreti* (native land); *yreri* (master or mistress of the house); *terungambo yreti* (citizen—*terungambo* refers to a head town); *çapi yreta* or *vmbamgandequa* (village or ward headed by a *çapi yrecha* or "little king"); *yreri yreti* (dweller); *yrequa* (dwelling place or inn). The root *iré*, he concludes, refers to both the act of settling and that of commanding, from the personal, familial level to the wider ones pertaining to lineage and kingdom (1997, 71, 104–109). Roskamp, for his part, observes that the term *cazonci*, if indeed it is a corruption of the Nahuatl *caltzontzin*, which combines the terms *calli* (house), *tzontli* (head), and *tzin* (a suffix indicating respect), is similar in meaning to the word *irecha*—from *iré* (seat or dwelling) and *achá* (lord) (1998a, 10). See also Swadesh, who adds the terms *iré-pi-ta* and *iré-pe-ti*, meaning "four hundred" (1969, 66)—a number related, in some Mesoamerican religious traditions, to the Pleiades (Tedlock 1985, 336).

6. Gilberti draws a partial analogy between the Purépecha term *tucúpachá* (supreme being) and the Christian concept of God, the difference being that there are many *tucúpacháecha* (Franco Mendoza, 1999).

7. The translation for *petámuti* in the *Relación de Michoacán* is "sacerdote mayor" (high priest). In Gilberti the verbal form *petámoni* is translated as "pronunciar"/"to pronounce" (484), suggesting that petámuti literally means "the one who pronounces" (i.e., the "orator"). Van Zantwijk claims that the modern equivalent of petámuti in the Lake Pátzcuaro Basin is the term *wandari* (literally, "speaker"), also spelled *uandari* (1967, 116).

8. Seler ([1908] 1993, 23) provides an alternate etymology for the name "Taríacuri," deriving it from a type of mockingbird called *tareácuri*, which points its beak into the wind when singing.

9. Mount Taríacuri is depicted in a copy of a map of the Lake Pátzcuaro Basin (plate 46) that was drawn around the time of the transfer of the diocese (note the varied spelling "Tariaquari" and the figures carrying an organ and large bell from Tzintzuntzan to Pátzcuaro).

10. The most important primary sources for information regarding the functioning of the pueblo-hospitals founded by Quiroga are his 1536 residencia (Aguayo

Spencer 1939, 409–54) and the *ordenanzas* (ordinances) he composed regarding their operation (ibid., 243–68; Warren [1977] 1990, 197–220; Hernández 1993, 277–96).

11. Regarding the use by the colonial authorities of regional rivalries in order to foreground the illegitimacy of the indigenous lords they themselves were supplanting, the Peruvian viceroy Francisco de Toledo stands out as a master of this strategy: "he organized an elaborate investigation of the Inca state whose objective was to enable him to present the Incas as tyrants and representatives of the devil who had taken all the lands and possessions of the people, and who had reduced the people to virtual slaves existing on the sufferance of their conquerors" (Spalding 1984, 248–49).

12. By way of contrast, the arrival of the Mexica in Anahuac is encoded in their own histories as a return to a place their ancestors had once inhabited. According to this view, although they may be the most recent of successive waves of immigrants from Aztlan, they are not usurpers (see, for instance, López Austin [1994] 1997, 56). The same holds true in the case of the Uacúsecha, for the petámuti notes that their ancestors spoke the same language and shared many of the same deities as the Huréndetiecha (original inhabitants) from the island of Xaráquaro in Lake Pátzcuaro (27–28).

13. The simultaneity of the different functions of myth is one of its primary characteristics. As López Austin explains: "Myth does not answer to a single law, but to many laws operating simultaneously . . . which is for the believer one more proof of the sanctity of the tale" ([1990] 1993, 297).

14. The indigenous informants of the *Relación de Cuizeo de la Laguna* noted in 1577 that a similar staff with multicolored feathers represented the power invested in a judge by the king: "denotaba el poder que tenía de su rey." They added, moreover, that such staffs were made from a dark wood called *tapintzirani* and that they had little pebbles inside that made a loud sound when shaken, thereby serving as a sign for people to leave their houses and accompany the one carrying the staff (Acuña 1987, 83).

15. For a discussion of the metaphysical rationale for the concept of divine possession in Mesoamerican religious traditions, see López Austin [1990] 1993, 122–37. For those interested in pursuing the connections between the magical thinking exemplified in the *Relación de Michoacán* and the shamanic basis of the indigenous religions of North America, see Le Clézio [1988] 1993. Le Clézio, who brings together references to messianic possession from a variety of sources, notes that "in most of the revealed religions of Indian America, the priest was more than an intermediary, he was himself a god. Through his body and voice it was the divinity itself which was present and spoke" (ibid., 152–53).

16. The final pictorial scene that depicts the tsiríquarequa is the upper right-hand register of plate 41. The accompanying prose narrative mentions ten high priests or bishops authorized to carry the feather-skirted staff or lance during the inauguration ceremonies (225). The number ten in this passage correlates with the five cúritiecha and five áxamencha who would traditionally participate in religious ceremonies prior to the departure of military expeditions (186–87).

17. With respect to the manner in which the petámuti functioned as a symbolic embodiment of the cazonci, consider the following quote from the *Relación de Michoacán*—"ya le abeys oydo lo que yo le mande dezir"/"Now you have heard what he has said by my command" (228)—which was how a newly elected cazonci was wont to address his people after the conclusion of a speech by the petámuti during the cazonci's inauguration ceremonies. The petámuti's status as head of the priests called cúritiecha, moreover, echoes that of the cazonci as head of the sacrificers called áxamencha. Additional evidence for the petámuti as symbolic double of the cazonci is provided by the way the brothers Uápeani II and Pauácume II were assigned the roles of "priest"—the elder—and "sacrificer"—the younger—by the Islanders of Xaráquaro (32).

18. The adviser named Nuriuan or Nuriban may traditionally have been recruited from among the Nahuatl-speaking nobility, for one of the cazonci's interpreters named "Nuritan" [*sic*] is mentioned by Don Pedro Cuiníarángari in his account of the Spanish conquest (238).

19. Although Pollard (1980) argues that Tzintzuntzan was the only prehispanic settlement in the Tarascan core to fully fit the definition of an urban center, Michelet (1996) is of the opinion that more archaeological evidence is necessary to make such a determination.

20. Franco Mendoza (1997; 1999) proposes the concept of "service" as a central theological principle in prehispanic Michoacán. He notes as well the key role of religious festivals in keeping intact the reciprocal relationship ("pacto de coparticipación") between gods and mortals, as well as between the members of each group separately.

21. The name of the god Curícaueri is generally translated as "the great fire," "the great burning" (Florescano 1989,2:180); or, alternately, "fire itself," "he who is fire" (Franco Mendoza 2001, 266). As such, he is not one of the visible manifestations of the sun, but rather the creative principle without which light and heat could not exist. See, for instance, the legend recounted by Boyd concerning the creation of the cosmos (1969, 2–5).

22. One of the passages from the *Relación de Michoacán* that can be read as providing a sacred basis for the establishment of reciprocal economic exchanges among the peoples of the Lake Pátzcuaro Basin tells how the Uacúsecha lords Uápeani II and Pauácume II were in the habit of gathering firewood for the goddess Xarátanga on Mount Yaguaro in Tzintzuntzan. Meanwhile, the Nahuatl-speaking Uatárecha under Lord Taríaran would gather firewood for Curícaueri in the forest called Atamataho on the outskirts of Uayámeo. And so, the story goes, as the two peoples went their respective ways, the firewood they were bringing to each others' gods would cross paths: "y la leña que trayan los vnos y llevavan los otros se encontrava en el camino" (24). Significantly, the pyramids to Curícaueri in Tzintzuntzan were later built on the slope of Mount Yaguaro (Pollard 1993, 45–49), while Quiroga's pueblo-hospital of Santa Fe was constructed near the forest of Atamataho outside Uayámeo (León [1903] 1984, 133).

23. The literal use of firewood as a major tributary item does not contradict its metonymic function as shorthand for "masculine" forms of tribute in general, as opposed to textiles, the prototypical "female" form of tribute.

24. The petámuti in plates 2, 24 (color section), and 30 is shown with streaks of red on his cheeks, as are several of the gods in plate 42 (color section). Although likely caused by face paint, this may constitute a reference to the custom of sacrificing the ears through penitential bloodletting. Another part of the text where this motif is featured is the chapter concerning the conquests undertaken by the Uacúsecha lords Hiripan, Tangáxoan, and Hiquíngare. When they are unable to defeat a town during their first attempt, Hiripan and Tangáxoan: "sacrificaronse las horejas y toda la gente para podellos vençer y avergonçabanse vnos a otros porque no heran mas esforçados"/"sacrificed their ears and all their people [did the same] so they could defeat them. [Verily] they shamed each other for not exerting themselves more" (151). Hiquíngaje is not mentioned in the above passage, which is consistent with his portrayal in the petámuti's narrative as less rigorous in the performance of ritual penance than Hiripan and Tangáxoan.

25. López Austin makes special note of the exceptional status of Taríacuri among legendary Mesoamerican rulers, since he never succeeds in having a personal encounter with either the patron god of his forefathers—Curícaueri—or the patron goddess of his maternal relatives—Xarátanga ([1990] 1993, 312).

26. Gilberti translates *uanduqua* as "tenazuelas para cejas"/"little eyebrow tweezers" (154), the same term used by the friar-compiler of the *Relación de Michoacán* to describe the pectoral worn by the petámuti.

27. A pentaphonic system predominated in the traditional music of Mesoamerica, consistent with the identification of the number five as symbol of the universe (Corona Nuñez 1992, 19–20; La Paz Hernández Aragón 1996, 141–43). Moreover, since the sounds of nature echo the voices of the gods, to play music is to metaphorically speak for the gods in their various manifestations. Thus, a rattle might represent the voice of the gods of rain; a drum, thunder; flutes, the songs of birds.

28. According to Pollard, the most common petroglyph motifs encountered in Michoacán are spirals, double spirals, bull's-eyes, and curving, meandering lines (1983, 159–62). A photograph of a pectoral similar to the one worn by the petámuti in the *Relación de Michoacán*, with spirals curling upward on both sides, is reproduced in Castro Leal et al. 1989, 273, and Schöndube 1996. Interestingly, one of the original features of the modern-day Basílica (conceived of by Quiroga as a cathedral with five naves, only one of which was ever completed) was a double spiral staircase, built in such a way that one person could climb up and another down at the same time without ever meeting (Toussaint 1942, 110).

29. Another reason for associating the Zacapu hireti lineage with the lords of Ihuatzio is that this town is physically located midway between Pátzcuaro and Tzintzuntzan (see map 2 and plate 46). This relative position is echoed in the description of the three mounds of earth made by Taríacuri as a symbolic representation of the iréchequa for the benefit of Hiquíngaje, Hiripan, and Tangáxoan (148). See plate 22,

where the above symbolic division of the fourfold kingdom in three parts is pictured at left.

30. The contents of some of the legal documents resulting from the disputes regarding the best site for the capital of the province between Quiroga, on one hand, and the Franciscans and Mendoza, on the other, are summarized in Escobar Olmedo 1989, 120–45.

31. The manner in which Hiripan and Tangáxoan are referred to as "orphans" in part two of the *Relación de Michoacán* (at a point in the narrative when their mother is described as still being alive) (92–93) can be explained by the Purépecha kinship term *naná*, which means both mother and maternal aunt. Perhaps the boys's fathers, Zétaco and Aramen, married two sisters, one of whom died or was sacrificed. Or perhaps they were cared for by some other maternal aunt after the deaths of both sets of parents.

32. The interpretation of Hiripan's fall from a tree as a negative sign suggests it may be related to the notion of Tamoanchan among the Nahuas as the mythic place where the gods first descended to earth and where sex and death came into existence. The broken branch of a tree, in this context, can have positive or negative connotations. It can symbolize the miraculous renewal of a people through the reestablishment of direct contact with their patron god, or it can refer to the notion of sexual transgression and resulting punishment (López Austin [1990] 1993, 64; [1994] 1997, 50–122). The latter interpretation is more likely in the case of Hiripan's accidental fall, given his strong negative reaction to it (145). As discussed in chapter 3, the encounter with the sacred does not always prove to be propitious, for the releasing of divine forces or energies can take the form of either a blessing or a curse.

33. One unfortunate corollary of the Tzintzuntzanist interpretation of the *Relación de Michoacán* is the tendency to discount the central role in the petámuti's oral narrative of the other towns that made up the triple alliance (namely, Pátzcuaro and Ihuatzio), as well as the prominent positions accorded the Huréndetiecha and Nahuatl-speaking nobility throughout the text. Such a reading highlights the ways in which the multiethnic character of the fourfold kingdom was perceived as a potential liability by the Uacúsecha, but not those ways in which it was encoded in their histories as a potential source of strength, depending on the narrative context.

34. According to Pollard, the available archaeological evidence indicates that "the ball game occupied a secondary role in Tarascan state religion" (1991, 173). Still, its presence in the region has been documented from prehispanic times to the present. For a summary see Pollard 1993, 154–55, and Borhegyi, 1969. Regarding the continuation of the practice into the twentieth century, Corona Núñez (1992, 86) describes how the Michoacán version of the game was played during his youth in the town of Cuitzeo, with a fiery ball made of maguey roots and wooden sticks in the shape of golf clubs.

35. See chapter 5 for discussion of how the mythic descent to the underworld to fight against the forces of darkness is articulated by Cuiníarángari in his account of the reaction of Zuangua's son Tzintzicha Tangáxoan to the Spaniards' arrival.

36. The great "beauty" of Hiripan and Tangáxoan is also commented upon by other characters in the petámuti's narrative (94).

37. As in the Popol Vuh, where the fathers of the hero twins must die in order to be reborn, the deaths of Taríacuri's father and uncle create the anticipation of the dawning of a new sun. According to Hurtado Mendoza, Achuri hirepe refers metaphorically to "the night who inspires or who gives breath to the spirit" (1986, 86). Márquez Joaquín translates the name as "el avergonzado humo" (2000, 701). Pollard notes that it "refers to either the waning sun or the moon"; she adds, moreover, that Cupanzieeri represents "the old sun who played the ball game and was associated with the west" and that their son, named Sirata táperi, is "the young or morning sun" (1991, 170). Seler draws a connection between the name Sirata táperi and the concept of "main root" or "trunk"; that is, the founder of a lineage or original human being ([1908] 1993, 54). Márquez Joaquín translates the name of this god as "the smoke [that hides its face for] shame " (2000, 717). Le Clézio observes that "the legend told in the *Chronicles of Michoacán* of Cupanzieeri, who was changed into a deer after his death, perhaps gives evidence of a cult of the deer ancestor identical to that of many barbarian nations of the north and northwest—Mayo, Yaqui, Pima, or Parras—as described by Father Pérez de Ribas, all of whom preached a cult of deer heads associated with peyote rituals" ([1988] 1993, 124–25).

38. Both the presence and absence of characteristics noted by López Austin and López Luján (1999) as evidence of a brief period of "zuyuanización" in fifteenth-century Michoacán may be attributable to the narrative fluctuation in the Escorial manuscript between the presentation of Taríacuri (who combines masculine and feminine traits) versus Tangáxoan (who is identified more exclusively with a Chichimec life-style) as the prototypical cultural hero for the region.

39. The concept of slavery among the indigenous peoples of Mesoamerica at the time of the Spanish conquest differed from its European form. Indeed, this is one of the main points made by Quiroga in a lengthy report composed in 1535 entitled *Información en derecho*, in which he denounces the enslavement of the indigenous population of New Spain (reproduced in Aguayo Spencer 1970, and Castañeda Delgado 1974).

40. See López Austin [1990] 1993, 152–53 for a discussion of the concept of *paga*, or payment, as a central component of Mesoamerican religious traditions.

41. The Tirípemencha gods appear to constitute a reference to the universe in its primarily masculine dimension. Their female counterparts are the cloud goddesses (also associated with the colors white, yellow, red, and black), who make up the retinue of the earth goddess Cueráuaperi (9). At times in the petámuti's oral performance, it appears that the female principle is meant to be subsumed under the dominant male paradigm, most notably in those passages where female rulers are censored as contrary to the natural order of things (114). At other times, however, the male and female appear as complementary aspects of each other, as in the notion that a cacique serves as "father and mother" of the people (205). Pollard has also noted this ambiguity regarding the importance accorded female deities in relation to masculine ones in Tarascan cosmology (1991, 176; 1993, 178–80).

42. The translations for these terms are derived primarily from the *Relación de Michoacán* and Gilberti. Thus, *irecha* is given for *rey*; *acháecha* is equated with *señores*; *caracha capacha* is provided as a translation for *caciques*; and *purépecha* is used to mean both people in general and commoners in particular. For further information regarding prehispanic and early colonial forms of government in Michoacán, see López Sarrelangue 1965, García Alcaraz 1976, Pollard 1980 and 1994, Beltrán 1994, Kuthy-Saenger 1996, and Paredes Martínez 1996.

43. Kirchhoff (1956) assumes that the use of the title cazonci pertains to the era of political dominance of Tzintzuntzan, which coincided with a diminution in the power of the triple alliance and a substantial increase in the size of the realm. My reading of the *Relación de Michoacán*, in contrast, highlights the concept of authority articulated by Franco Mendoza (1999), who notes that the power of the irecha or cazonci was conditional upon his recognition by the coalition of communities—a definition that emphasizes the importance of both a top-down hierarchy and a system of horizontal power sharing. According to this dynamic, the period when the Uacúsecha first attained hegemony over their neighbors, which coincided with the end of Taríacuri's rule, is at least as important a turning point in the intraregional power structure as the moment when the Uanácaze attained preeminence over the Zacapu hireti and Enéani during the reign of Tsitsíspandáquare.

44. The manuscript actually reads: "and they all *would respond* that it was well done" (my italics). The formulaic expression of approval by the audience, registered at the moment of transcription, is recast in the imperfect, presumably by the friar-compiler. As I analyzed in chapter two, this is a good example of the tendency to mix the contributions of the various participants in the making of the Escorial manuscript, even at the level of the individual utterance.

45. With regard to the openness of oral narratives to audience participation, Tedlock tells an amusing and edifying anecdote about how he, his wife Barbara, and another anthropologist were listening to a Maya day-keeper named Don Mateo recount the biblical tale of Adam and Eve as it had been passed down to him via oral tradition. Periodically, Don Mateo would stop and wait for input from the ethnographers, for this was a story he was fairly certain they should know something about. The latter, loath to "interfere" with and thereby "contaminate" their informant's testimony, kept resisting his efforts, until finally the exasperated Don Mateo drew his grandchildren into the narrative and was able to bring it to a satisfactory conclusion (1994, 143–66).

46. In addition to Corona Núñez, Le Clézio is the interpreter of the *Relación de Michoacán* who has most thoroughly and consistently focused on the prophetic dimensions of the text. For this reason his writings on the subject make for inspired reading (1985; [1988] 1993). Nevertheless, Le Clézio, a writer himself by profession, does not generally clarify for his readers the mechanisms employed by the petámuti to achieve this prophetic effect.

47. It is in the spirit of fulfillment of prophecy that the following testimony of the elders of the city of Pátzcuaro in the relación geográfica of 1581 should be understood: "the elders say that, in the time of their infidelity, there was less vice and there were

men thirty and forty years of age who had never known a woman, and they did not eat or drink as they do now, in which they are extremely degenerate. And it is to this that their illnesses can be attributed" (Acuña 1987, 201; my trans.). The sad irony, of course, is that the Spanish colonial authorities often interpreted such remarks as evidence that the indigenous peoples were leading relatively soft lives under colonial rule and that, as a result, there was room for additional taxation and other burdens.

48. Another grotesque image evoked in the petámuti's concluding remarks, that of the dissolute lords who "go about all skinned" (157), reads like a play on words suggesting both a luxurious life-style (i.e., the wearing of soft animal pelts) and the festival of Cuingo, when it was customary to flay captives who had been ritually sacrificed and to dance in their skins (158). The parody of the ceremonies dedicated to the gods is repeatedly invoked in part two of the *Relación de Michoacán* as a sacrilege that brings down upon its perpetrators and their subject peoples the wrath of the offended deity in the form of famine, war, sickness, and political instability (25, 110–15). The danger stems from the appeal of false prophets, those who are like "a wind that blinds the eyes and all the rejoicing is but one morning" (103). As the three elders explain to Taríacuri, the simple "breads" and "fruits" offered in sacrifice by those who are devout and lead virtuous lives is worth more than a lavish "party" thrown by a wealthy but dissolute potentate. A third grotesque image, the petámuti's ironic suggestion that those lords with big lip plugs might as well put on "masks" (157), similarly equates vanity with possession by the gods. Again, there is a contrast between the concepts of inside and outside, but in this case the external covering—that is, the mask—corresponds to the deity rather than to animal or human skin.

49. López Austin spells out the connections between sexual abstinence and rules concerning endogamy in a compelling article on the sacred nature of rulership in Michoacán (1976). Nevertheless, he neglects to provide a rationale for the ambivalence evidenced in the pages of the *Relación de Michoacán* regarding practices like polygamy and the union of masculine and feminine characteristics. My suspicion is that one of the relevant criteria at the root of this ambivalence is age: that, while young male nobles would be expected to abide by the rules described by López Austin, older heads of lineages were governed by a different set of imperatives.

50. With respect to the archetypal connotations of the role of cazonci in the *Relación de Michoacán*, compare Arguedas's definition of the supreme Andean ruler, the Inca, as "original model of all being" (cited in Pease 1990, 5).

51. Regarding the association between being a good ruler and old age, the friar-compiler of the *Relación de Michoacán* observes that the selection of a new cacique among the brothers and other relatives of a recently deceased one was traditionally made in accordance with the saying that the best candidate was the most experienced and discerning one or, as they put it: "el que tiene mas tristezas consigo"/"he who carries the most sadness with him" (203).

52. Several terms that imply a one-time occurrence, such as the concept of discovery, are consistently given in quotation marks in this chapter in order to underscore the manner in which all events recounted in the petámuti's performance are repetitions of archetypal patterns and, as such, never completely new.

53. My interpretation of the petámuti's description of the "discovery" of Pátzcuaro in part two of the *Relación de Michoacán* is consistent with van Zantwijk's intuition that the key to understanding this episode is through analogy with Mexica sources that detail the way in which their capital city was patterned on the symbolic structure of Aztlan (1967, 29). More recently, Michelet and Arnauld have expounded upon many of the connections between the ideologies of the ruling Uacúsecha and Mexica elite (Michelet 1989, 1995, 1996; Michelet and Arnauld 1991). While I agree with their hypothesis regarding the existence of some sort of connection between the two traditions, my reading of the primary sources suggests this may be due to the way both groups appropriated differing regional variations of widespread classical-era traditions in constructing their foundational narratives, rather than direct inspiration of the Uacúsecha origin story on central Mexican models.

54. Another early colonial manuscript from Michoacán that revolves around the notion of foundational moments is the enigmatic *Codex Plancarte*, with its enumerations of springs and other bodies of water, mountains, settlements, rocks, trees, animals, kings, and magical transformations (reproduced, with commentary, in Corona Núñez 1988, 41–90). See Roskamp 1998a for more extensive analysis and discussion of related pictorial manuscripts.

55. Based on his work among modern-day Purépecha, Carrasco Pizana (1971) notes similar symbolic connections between rock formations and ancestor deities, overlaid with associations between the two and the Virgin of Guadalupe.

56. The surviving portions of the Escorial manuscript contain only a brief reference to the creation of the first human beings from ash (212). The more extensive commentary on the subject, recounted by Ramírez, mentions four men and four women, for a total of eight ([1585] 1959, 492–94). The source used by Herrera, in contrast, mentions only one man and one woman (dec. 3, bk. 3, ch. 10). In the Popol Vuh the first humans numbered four and were "mother-fathers . . . with looks of the male kind" (Tedlock 1985, 165).

57. This ancient song was originally recorded and commented upon by Ruiz ([1891] 1979, 30, 48–49, 51–52). Corona Núñez provides the following Spanish translation: "Mi corazón muchas cosas recuerda/viendo las cuatro estrellas cuando cintilan/ellas siempre así saldrán, pero yo me estoy yendo,/de una vez acabaré y no volveré jamás,/Me estoy yendo, me estoy yendo" (1992, 23). The song is sometimes cited in support of the theory of a southern origin for the ancient inhabitants of Michoacán (see, for example: Boyd 1969, 6; Hurtado Mendoza 1986, 13–17).

58. The principle of transculturation was first formulated by Ortiz in *Contrapunteo cubano del tabaco y el azúcar* ([1940] 1973). It differs from the related concept

of acculturation in its emphasis on a two-way process of cultural change. Rama's *Transculturación narrativa en América Latina* ([1980] 1987) was instrumental in working out the applicability of the concept of transculturation to the field of literary studies. See Lienhard for a brief discussion of the history of these and related concepts from colonial times to the present ([1989] 1992, 92–94).

59. See chapter 2 for a detailed analysis of the editorial strategy pursued by the friar-compiler.

60. This bell is reproduced in several of the "maps" copied by Beaumont related to the transfer of the diocese (plates 45, 46). Its symbolic significance is further highlighted in Father Ramírez's description of the failed attempts of the colonial authorities to remove it from Pátzcuaro after Quiroga's death ([1585] 1959, 505). León mentions a popular sixteenth-century belief in the bell's efficacy in dissipating storms ([1903] 1984, 211).

61. Note that the upper part of the ceremonial center in Pátzcuaro, known as Cuirís quataro, is associated with Quiroga's episcopal residence, and the lower section, named Caropu hopánsquaro, with the indigenous governor's house.

62. The Uatárecha are cited in the *Relación de Michoacán* as lords or priests of Tzintzuntzan during the omen of the snake and as lords of Xaráquaro during the encounter of Uápeani II and Pauácume II with the fisherman with whom they forge a marital alliance. As such, they appear to function in a similar manner to the descendants of the ancient Toltecs in the oral and pictographic traditions of the Mexica. That is, they represent both ancient wisdom and moral decadence.

63. Cf. the tradition discussed by García Abarca (cited in the documentary appendix of Roskamp 1998a, 352), according to which certain emissaries of Lord Taríaran ate snakes, after which they became inebriated, were transformed into snakes themselves, and passed over to the "opuesta orilla" (opposite bank or shore), where they spoke with the gods, who told them to take their people and scatter to the four winds. Similar myths from the modern community of Tarerio involving the magical transformation of a man who eats a large snake are recounted in Castilleja González et al. 1993, 27–62. The snake may constitute an allusion to a hallucinogenic plant called *coatlxoxouqui* or "green snake" in Nahuatl (for information in this and other sacred plants, see Turo [1930] 1968).

64. Animal manifestations of the goddess Xarátanga include the snake, coyote, owl, vulture, and centipede. She is also sometimes represented as a half-moon or old woman (Hurtado Mendoza 1986, 72–77; Pollard 1991, 170).

65. Seler [1908] 1993, 21. Pollard equates the mountain named Taríacaherio in the *Relación de Michoacán* with the present-day Mount Taríacuri (1993, 149). Significantly, it not only serves in the petámuti's oral performance as the site of the disappearance of the four snakes into the earth's womb, but also as the place where Hiripan was later visited in his dreams by the god Curícaueri (134–35).

66. When the residents of the island of Xaráquaro make their escape from the Islanders of Pacandan in order to place themselves under the protection of the Uacúsecha, the petámuti describes how Taríacuri believes their story because of the foam caused by the frantic paddling of their canoes (118).

67. As in *La historia de los colores* (Marcos [1994] 1999), lovemaking is here associated with the mingling of the colors, which is linked, in turn, with the notion of the gods' descent to earth and the mixing of beans and corn.

68. Many of the legends compiled by Boyd (1969), although they tend to be framed in the style of nineteenth-century Romanticism, evidence parallels with themes and symbolic structures from the *Relación de Michoacán* analyzed in this book. Note, for instance, the metaphoric significance of color and references to the center and four directions, trees, arrows, deer, butterflies, and so forth, as well as the dynamic principle of the male elements of sky and fire (exemplified in the hunter-warrior) versus the female elements of earth and water (the terms in which female beauty tends to be described).

69. The principle of magic warfare is described in several passages from the *Relación de Michoacán*. Spies, for example, would secretly enter a community about to be attacked and hide eagle feathers, bloody arrows, and little balls of incense over which the priests called hirípacha had placed a spell (187–89). According to the petámuti, Taríacuri excelled at a similar type of symbolic warfare prior to becoming cazonci (45–46; plate 4). The act of organizing hunting expeditions likewise functions in the text as a promise to the gods regarding the future undertaking of mutually beneficial conquests in those places where deer have been ritually sacrificed (23). For a related discussion of the connections between arrows, territorial boundaries, and foundational acts in other pictorial manuscripts from the region, see Roskamp 1998a, 216–17, 225.

70. Tudela [1541] 1956, 26.

71. Espejel Carvajal (2000, 302–304) locates Taríaran slightly to the north of persent-day Cuitzitan.

72. Ibid., 31, 33, 34.

73. The city founded by Mendoza in 1541 did not come to be known as Valladolid until the seat of the diocese was moved there after Quiroga's death. At first it was referred to as City of Michoacán, as was Pátzcuaro and, previously, Tzintzuntzan. There was a lengthy legal battle over the name and coat of arms, which Quiroga won, although Tzintzuntzan was granted independence from Pátzcuaro and a new coat of arms in 1595 and Valladolid took over officially as center of the provincial government in 1578 (Warren, personal communication).

74. It is possible that the *Tzintzuntzan codex*, the only extant versions of which are the copy made by Beaumont in the eighteenth century and a map reproduced by Seler in 1908, represents a rival interpretative tradition to the one articulated by the petámuti in part two of the *Relación de Michoacán*. Roskamp (1998b) is of the opinion that this pictorial manuscript may have served as part of the 1567 "Información y probanza de la ciudad de Tzintzuntzan," which sought to recover the privileges of the indigenous capital at the time of the Spanish conquest vis à vis the new colonial ecclesiastical and administrative center constructed on the ruins of Taríacuri's old capital in Pátzcuaro.

75. Note that Mount Xanóato hucazio is also the place where Uápeani II and Pauácume II are shot with arrows by warriors from Curínguaro (Tudela [1541] 1956, 42).

76. See López Austin for a description of a similar white eagle representing the Mexica god Tetzauhtéotl as an example of the way in which divine possession often entailed a transfer of substance: "The god was the whiteness that possessed the body" ([1990] 1993, 236).

77. The move of the Uacúsecha capital from Ihuatzio to Tzintzuntzan is described in more prosaic terms in another passage from the *Relación de Michoacán*: "en tienpo de ticatame senor de cuyacan . . . pasose la cabeçera a michuacan que lleuo zizispandaquare a curícaueri a michuacan y todo el tesoro"/"in the time of Ticátame, lord of Ihuatzio . . . the capital was transferred to Tzintzuntzan. Thus did Tsitsíspandáquare bring Curícaueri and all the treasure to Tzintzuntzan" (166). The earlier decision to transfer the capital from Pátzcuaro to Ihuatzio is recounted in the final episode of the petámuti's performance, immediately prior to his concluding remarks (151–55).

78. The rationale for the attribution of this remark about Santa Fe to Cuiníarángari rather than to the friar-compiler is similar to the argument advanced earlier regarding the attribution to the petámuti of references to the colonial present in the passage describing the original "discovery" of Pátzcuaro.

79. I do not deny that the testimony of Don Alonso, Don Ramiro, and the two Don Franciscos at Quiroga's residencia—their exaltation of the exemplary Christian behavior of the people of Michoacán and acclamation of Quiroga in his role as "civilizer"—can be convincingly read as opportunism on their part—a means to curry favor with the colonial authorities. Certainly, these indigenous nobles were concerned to make themselves look as good as possible in the eyes of crown officials. In the same way that the Tzintzuntzanist reading does not fully exhaust the metaphorical connotations of the petámuti's oral performance in the *Relación de Michoacán*, however, the testimony of these nobles can also be understood as more than just a self-serving strategy, for it is equally significant as an expression of their world view and, as such, part of a genuine attempt to come to terms with their current circumstances in accordance with traditional indigenous values.

80. According to Hernández, Quiroga's name was proposed for first bishop of Michoacán on August 18, 1536, at a secret consistorial meeting in Rome that included discussion of the beneficial effects of Quiroga's visit to that province (1993, 189–90). Quiroga's residencia had taken place in April of the same year.

81. By January 9, 1534, Quiroga was back in Mexico City, where he continued to perform judicial services until July 1538 (Warren [1963] 1977, 117; Escobar Olmedo 1989, 114; León [1903] 1984, 134).

82. Several judicial documents were drawn up by order of Quiroga regarding the transfer of the diocese. One is entitled "La posesion que se tomo en Pazquaro para la translacion de la Iglesia" (AGI leg. 67–23, no. 5, ramo 47; it is included in the documentary appendix to León [1903] 1984). Regarding the move from Tzintzuntzan to Pátzcuaro, Quiroga argued that, since the latter was a subject-town of the former in 1538, the site he had chosen for the diocese was within the official boundaries of the "city of Michoacán" stipulated in the papal bull (Toussaint 1942, 39). The coincidences between this legal document and the passage from part two of the *Relación*

de Michoacán that describes the original "discovery" of Pátzcuaro by Uápeani II and Pauácume II are striking. All the aforementioned prophetic signs are noted: the abundant waters; the ruins of the platform that served as the base for the indigenous temples; the bell tower; the new living quarters for the indigenous governor and for Quiroga as bishop-elect, construction of which had already begun. The Spanish notary adds, moreover, that the entire area was marked by the remains of a high wall made of "dry stone" (a reference to the indigenous custom of building rubble-filled stone structures without benefit of mortar) that had enclosed the ancient plaza facing the main temples. See also the documentary appendix of Warren [1977] 1990 for a related document (AGI leg. 173, no. 1, ramo 2) that includes testimony by a number of indigenous nobles, including Cuiníarángari.

83. The inference regarding the godlike omniscience of the first human beings is made partly through analogy with the creation myth recounted in the Popol Vuh and partly based on remarks in the *Relación de Michoacán* suggesting the deification of the ancestors of the various inhabitants of the region (28, 34).

84. León includes a sketch of Quiroga's crosier in his biography ([1903] 1984). The venerated image of the Virgen de la Salud (presently housed in the Basílica) was made by an indigenous sculptor in 1538, at about the same time as the petámuti's oral performance and the transfer of the diocese to Pátzcuaro (ibid., 133).

85. According to Brand 1971, 653: "[when evaluating primary sources] between 1521 and the 1580s, we must be careful to decide whether Ciudad de Michoacan refers to Michoacan-Tzintzuntzan or Michoacan-Patzcuaro or Michoacan-Valladolid."

86. One legend, for example, tells of how Quiroga would spend long hours in "study, prayer, and penance" under the shade of a walnut tree, on more than one occasion "spattering it with his blood" (Salas León [1941] 1956, 96). This walnut tree sounds like a symbolic reference to Don Vasco's "lineage"—that is, the church founded by him. It was located, moreover, in an orchard adjoining what would become, after Quiroga's death, a Jesuit college, and where the ruins of the base of an indigenous temple are still visible (id.). This also happens to be adjacent to the site where Quiroga was buried in 1565, in the church of San Salvador which served as the first cathedral of Michoacán, and which was turned over to the Jesuits upon their arrival in 1573. In other words, Quiroga was buried in the same general area as Uápeani II and Pauácume II (Tudela [1541] 1956, 42–43, 151, 276).

87. Regarding the question of the origin of the extremely successful hospitals and artisan guilds of Michoacán, Beaumont, a Franciscan, tends to emphasize the role of Fray Juan de San Miguel, while the biographers of Quiroga, such as Moreno and León, give the latter the bulk of the credit. Chavero was one of the first to reframe the discussion by pointing out that these guilds did not originate during the colonial period (1882–83, 1:764). This opinion has since become widely accepted, as has the notion that the hospitals were based upon a prehispanic institution known as *huatápera*—"place of those who are injured"—or *yurhítsirho*—"place of the menstruating woman or maiden" (Monzón García and Roth Seneff 1999).

CHAPTER 5. THE MANY FACES OF DON PEDRO CUINÍARÁNGARI: THE INDIGENOUS GOVERNOR

1. Olid's expedition to Michoacán consisted of some two hundred Spaniards (estimates vary somewhat in the available primary sources) and tens of thousands of indigenous allies (the exact number is not specified). See Warren, *The conquest of Michoacán* (1985, 42–43). This work, which is an invaluable source of information for events in Michoacán from 1521 to 1530, is referred to extensively in this chapter. A more recent historical synthesis of the events leading up to the cazonci's death in 1530, also very good, is by Martínez Baracs (1989, 5–73). See also Adorno and Pautz 1999, 3:325–81 and Krippner-Martínez 2001, 9–45, for discussions of Guzman's activities in Michoacán.

2. The quote cited in the epigraph is from Lienhard's prizewinning book on the traces of oral discourse in Spanish American literature from colonial times to the present ([1989] 1992, 112): "The rejection of European discourse and its indigenous appropriation coexist . . . the two apparently antithetical attitudes are but two faces of the same coin" (my trans.).

3. There is a brief comment, inserted by the friar-compiler of the *Relación de Michoacán* toward the end of Cuiníarángari's narrative, that provides a clue to the date of compilation of this portion of the text. After mentioning the founding of the first Franciscan monastery in Tzintzuntzan, the friar remarks that this event took place "about twelve years ago" (264). A marginal notation—"or xiii"—was added later in the hand of the principal corrector. Since the first Franciscans established themselves in Michoacán toward the end of 1525 and beginning of 1526 (Ricard [1933] 1982, 37, 65), this would place the date of composition of this passage circa 1538 and its revision a year or so later, in about 1539. Another comment, in part three, chapter twenty-five, suggests that Don Pedro's testimony may have been transcribed in Pátzcuaro (Escobar Olmedo 2001, 339).

4. A complete translation into Spanish of the *Anales de Tlatelolco* can be found in Baudot and Todorov [1983] 1990, 184–206. The above anthology also contains a Spanish translation of the Nahuatl column of book twelve of the *Florentine codex*. For an English translation of the same by Anderson and Dibble, see Sahagún [1577–80] 1950–82, vol. 13.

5. In his popular account of cultural difference, *The conquest of America*, Todorov posits a number of polar oppositions (e.g., European linear time versus Amerindian circular time) to explain the seemingly impossible conquest of the Aztec empire by a few hundred Spanish soldiers. The problem with this approach is its dependence on a discourse of absolutes and consequent decontextualization of primary sources. The result is a thesis that shows remarkably little critical distance regarding the views of sixteenth-century Spaniards, essentially confirming stereotypes that have continued into the present of passive, noble Indians and active, daring conquistadors, as well as the flip side of this dynamic—the presentation of the indigenous peoples of the Americas as prototypical victims of the moral corruption at the core of European society.

6. Cervantes de Salazar gives a fairly detailed description of the treasure sent by Tzintzicha to Cortés ([1566] 1985, 802; bk. 6, ch. 25), as does Pietro Martire d'Anghiera ([1530] 1989, 537, 540–41; dec. 5, bk. 10), who saw a portion of the treasure that made it through to Spain in a private collection belonging to Juan de Ribera (for an overview, see Adorno and Pautz 1999, 3:301–02).

7. The toponym *michihuahcan* is of Nahuatl origin, as mentioned in chapter 1.

8. López Sarrelangue ([1965] 1999) documents the privileged position of the indigenous nobility of Michoacán during the early colonial period, a state of affairs she then shows to have rapidly given way to a progressive weakening of their position in colonial society. For further discussion of the special privileges many such nobles were accorded, including the right to use the title Don or Doña, wear European-style clothing, ride horses, and bear arms, see also Kuthy-Saenger 1996, 99–126.

9. See Swadesh 1969, 52, 74–75 and Friedrich 1971b, 140 for related concepts associated with the suffixes *hari* and *ŋari* in Purépecha.

10. For a discussion of the concept of the nagual, or animal alter ego, in Mesoamerican philosophy and theology, see López Austin [1980] 1989, 1:416–42.

11. According to Corona Núñez, the difference between the representation of the coyote and the uitzume, or "perro de agua" was that the latter was typically shown with his snout open and tongue hanging out. Corona Núñez also notes that the name Huitziméngari derives from the word for a statue consisting of a human body and dog's head (1992, 45).

12. Two of the most representative Brazilian films of the cannibalistic genre are *Macunaíma* (1969) by Joaquim Pedro de Andrade and *Como Era Gostoso Meu Française/ How Tasty Was My Frenchman* (1971) by Nelson Pereira dos Santos. See Stam 1989, 122–56 for a Bakhtin-inspired interpretation of the focus on cultural anthropophagy that grew out of the Brazilian modernist movement of the 1920s and that was later popularized through film.

13. The primary colonial-era source for biographical information on Doña Marina/La Malinche is Díaz del Castillo [1568] 1983, 58–62.

14. The available documentary evidence suggests that Cuiníarángari died in the epidemic of 1543 (López Sarrelangue [1965] 1999).

15. The classic study of the role of La Malinche in Mexican national consciousness is "Los hijos de la Malinche" in *El laberinto de la soledad* (Paz [1950] 1984). For Paz she represents both the symbolic mother of the mestizo nation and also the most despicable of traitors—the woman who betrays her own children in order to ingratiate herself with the man who has raped her. More recently, the figure of La Malinche has been rehabilitated in some Mexican and Chicana feminist fiction and scholarship. For a discussion of these trends, see Cypess 1991 and Glantz 1994.

16. Martínez Baracs draws an analogy between one of the translations for "governor" found in Gilberti's 1559 Michoacán dictionary—*uandátsperi*, literally, "he who speaks"—and the Nahuatl *tlatoani*, which means the same thing. He notes that, in the case of Michoacán, the act of speaking was associated not with the supreme ruler, but rather with his assistant (1997, 107). This line of reasoning ties in with the

notion discussed in chapter 4 that those who stand in place of the cazonci during important ritual functions, such as the petámuti during the ceremony of Equata cónsquaro, assume his identity, albeit temporarily, as if possessed by his spirit. Cuiníarángari, as indigenous governor, would presumably represent another instance of this symbolic equivalence between the supreme ruler and his various deputies when authorized to speak for him. This hypothesis is complicated, however, by the multiplicity of words for "governor" in the indigenous language of the time—the *Relación de Michoacán* gives the term *angátacuri* (see glossary for possible translations). Gilberti also translates "governor" as *camáhchacupeti*—from *camácaten*, "universal government" (Martínez Baracs 1997, 108). If the three terms *uandátsperi*, *angátacuri*, and *camáhchacupeti* refer to separate functions, then perhaps they indicate the existence of more than one individual who fulfilled the duties associated, in the European tradition, with the word "governor." On the other hand, they could refer to functions associated with groups rather than individuals, as in Paredes Martínez's hypothesis that several categories of high government officials were *angátacucha*, including the governor, captain general, and overseers of certain types of tribute (1996, 35).

17. According to Pollard, the analysis of kinship terms among the inhabitants of the Lake Pátzcuaro Basin around the time of the Spanish conquest suggest that bilateral kinship prevailed (1993, 55–59). Kuthy-Saenger notes, moreover, that "membership in [residential] wards was probably through the father's line . . . whereas the rules of marriage show a matrilineal and patrilineal mixture" (1996, 233).

18. I have placed quotation remarks around both "fact" and "fiction" to underscore: (1) the importance of White's ground-breaking demonstration of the way all historical accounts make use of literary strategies in order to produce the effect of verisimilitude (1973; 1978); and (2) the no less significant notion that, in spite of the nature of historical narratives as myths-in-the-making, they also constitute all that remains of flesh-and-blood people who lived, not in some sort of virtual reality, but in a world not too different from the one we inhabit today.

19. References to Don Pedro Cuiníarángari as Pedro (or Pero) Panza can be found in CDHM [1858–66] 1971, 2:83; Scholes and Adams [1530] 1952; and Escobar Olmedo 1997. An analogy with the humorous name given by Cervantes to Don Quixote's sidekick in the early 1600s (*panza* means "belly" or "paunch" in Spanish) is suggested by the way in which the honorific title "Don" is omitted whenever the indigenous governor of Michoacán is referred to in this manner. Moreover, in those documents in which he is presented as a powerful lord, such as the trial initiated by Albornoz (Scholes and Adams [1530] 1952; Escobar Olmedo 1997), or in which his presence is evoked in a respectful manner, such as the legal transcripts of the ceremonies in which bishop-elect Quiroga took possession of his diocese (León [1903] 1984, 264–71; Warren 1997, 439–57), he tends to be called Don Pedro rather than Pedro Panza. An alternate etymology for Panza derives it from the word *pantzin*, which means "reverend standard-bearer" in Nahuatl (López Sarrelangue [1965] 1999). In my opinion these two interpretations are not mutually exclusive, since it is not uncommon

for someone to be made fun of through the slight modification of the pronunciation of one of their names.

20. The translations of titles of colonial officials used in this chapter are derived from the glossary in Gibson [1964] 1983, 599–605, and the index of Adorno and Pautz 1999. *Alguacil mayor*, for example, is translated as "chief law enforcement officer"; *teniente*, as "deputy or assistant"; *visitador*, as "inspector"; *regidor*, as "municipal councillor"; *contador*, as "comptroller"; *tesorero* as "royal treasury official." Other useful definitions include *encomienda* as "grant of Indians, mainly as tribute payers, or the area of the Indians granted" and *encomendero* as "possessor of an *encomienda*."

21. Sixty to seventy Spaniards killed by the indigenous people of Michoacán is the number cited by the inspector Juan de Ortega in 1528. See Warren 1985, 133.

22. The official record of this trial (the original copy of which is located in AGI, ramo Justicia, legajo 108, no. 6) was published in 1952 by Scholes and Adams under the title *Proceso contra Tzintzicha Tangaxoan, el caltzontzin*. It includes both the charges against the cazonci and the transcripts of previous accusations made against the indigenous lords of Michoacán, including the 1529 investigation by Albornoz against Cuiníarángari, Don Francisco, and Gonzalo Juárez. An alternate version, based on AGI Justicia 227-5, has recently been edited by Escobar Olmedo (1997). For a thorough discussion of this legal case in light of other archival sources from the period, see Warren 1985, 211–36.

23. The presentation of Cortés in Cuiníarángari's story does not make him out to be a paragon of Christian virtue, but neither does it suggest that his behavior was excessive in terms of the generally accepted customs of the time. Cortés takes the cazonci to visit Cuauhtemoc, whose feet have been burned, and threatens him with torture if his orders are not obeyed: "Now you have seen what he looks like because of what he did. Do not follow his bad example" (261). Still, for the most part, Cortés treats the indigenous nobles well, entertaining them grandly and according the cazonci the respect due a king. Tzintzicha sums up his first visit to Cortés as follows: "Truly the Spaniards are most generous" (261). This favorable impression regarding Cortés's generosity ties in with the friar-compiler's emphasis on the virtue of liberality among the indigenous peoples of Michoacán: "for the lords consider it an affront to be stingy" (4, 185).

24. In a letter written to Charles V dated November 3, 1532, Bishop Ramírez de Fuenleal, president of the Second Audiencia, also refers to the favorable impression created in the oidores by Cuiníarángari and other nobles from Michoacán. He notes, moreover, that their visit to Mexico City had occurred "within the past ten days" (CDII 1864–84, 13:259–60).

25. See Warren 1985, 240: "The part played by Don Pedro during this whole last period of the Cazonci's life is mysterious and sinister. In the *Relación de Michoacán* he pictured himself as a devoted adopted brother of the Cazonci, always looking out for the sovereign's good. But the documents of the Guzmán period give us a quite different impression, leading us to think that perhaps here we have the Indian version of García del Pilar, always trying to stay on the winning side." Boyd also casts Cuiníarángari

in a negative light, describing him as a "spy, a shadowy Tarascan figure known in Spanish literature as Don Pedro Cuirananguari" [sic] (1969, xviii). A similar opinion was earlier voiced by Mateos Higuera, who refers to a "Ton [sic] Pedro, hermano [de Tzintzicha], quien intervino grande e infaustamente en la ruina de esa nación, por haber evitado la defensa de los Michoacanos contra Cristóbal de Olid" (1947, 166).

26. According to Gibson: "It was a deliberate viceregal policy in the sixteenth century to take advantage of [opportunities such as the minority of an indigenous lord] to introduce the desired Hispanic institution and simultaneously to reduce the powers of hereditary caciques" ([1964] 1983, 168).

27. See Escobar Olmedo 1989, 120–23 for summaries of several of these documents related to the rivalry between Cuiníarángari's son Don Bartolomé and Tzintzicha's son Don Antonio in the 1550s.

28. The contributions of the friar-compiler to the Escorial manuscript are analyzed in chapter 2. As regards the friar's perspective on whether or not the cazonci was guilty of the charges brought against him, one of his most lengthy intercalated commentaries to Cuiníarángari's version of the Spanish conquest provides the readers with some critical distance concerning this very matter (267). It is not the facts they report that differ, by and large; it is the spirit, the overall impression left by the two accounts, that contrasts markedly. While they both mention the same accusations—killing Christians, dancing in their skins, stealing from the towns given in encomienda, plotting to ambush the Spaniards in Cuinao—Cuiníarángari puts them in the mouth of Guzmán, in the context of his attempt to extort more and more gold and silver from the cazonci. Cuiníarángari further underscores the injustice of these accusations by implying that the only reason Tzintzicha continued to demand tribute and services from the towns was to satisfy the greed of Guzmán (270, 273). The comments by Jerónimo de Alcalá, on the other hand, suggest the existence of valid grievances and injustices on both sides, beginning well before the arrival of Guzmán. He implies Tzintzicha was guilty of at least one of the charges against him—continuing to receive service from the towns given in encomienda. And he allows for the possibility that the cazonci was involved in the deaths of the Spaniards. The other two accusations are passed over in a more cursory fashion. They also happen to be the ones Guzmán added to the list of grievances during the final phase of Tzintzicha's trial. Overall, the impression conveyed by the friar is that, although certain anonymous Spaniards (the only one named specifically is Guzmán) were in the wrong, the cazonci was also partly responsible for what happened to him.

29. The physical representation of the god Curícaueri that was kept in the main temple dedicated to him was a large piece of black obsidian (an extremely hard form of volcanic rock) from which shavings would periodically be taken so that additional temples could be founded in his honor in satellite communities (Tudela [1541] 1956, 108–09, 125–31; plate 17). A subsequent identification between Curícaueri and Christ crucified during colonial times is suggested by the placement of obsidian mirrors on representations of the cross. Quiroga, for example, is said to have taken an obsidian mirror originally placed on top of the main temple in Pátzcuaro "de manera que por

la tarde recogiese los últimos rayos del sol" and put it in the middle of a large cross in the neighborhood of San Francisco (Salas León [1941] 1956, 156–57).

30. The messengers sent to Michoacán from México-Tenochtitlan during the reign of the cazonci Zuangua are pictured in plate 43 of the Escorial manuscript, which also depicts some of the gifts of Hispanic origin brought by the Mexica ambassadors, including a sword and crossbow. Other gift items are of indigenous origin: precious green plumes, a feathered shield, two drums or gourds. In the lower register, four of Zuangua's sons are pictured. According to the accompanying prose narrative, Zuangua tells the messengers that his sons have gone on military expeditions to the four corners of the realm. This is simply a strategy to gain time to respond to their request, however, for the sons are actually in Tzintzuntzan, dressed in rags so the Mexica ambassadors will not recognize them (236–40).

31. It is important to note that the distance of Cuiníarángari's narrative from modern historiographical conventions does not imply that it is fully consonant with sixteenth-century Spanish norms. On the contrary, Cuiníarángari lacked the requisite literary and moral qualifications to be considered a "historian" from a Renaissance-European perspective. No matter how eloquent this illiterate indigenous governor, a recent convert to Christianity, may have been, he had no hope of entering the privileged category of "historian," reserved exclusively for highly educated men of letters with recognized prudence and Christian orthodoxy (see Mignolo 1982).

32. The idea of being "gazed upon" by the sun is here associated with favored status among the gods, especially success in military exploits.

33. If one compares Cuiníarángari's version of the death sentence given Tzintzicha with the transcription recorded by the Spanish scribe Hernando Sarmiento in 1530, the differences between indigenous conventions governing the telling of stories about the past and Hispanic legalistic protocol stand out clearly. According to Sarmiento, the crier's words were: "Esta es la justicia que manda hacer el emperador y reina nuestros señores y el muy magnífico señor Nuño de Guzmán, presidente de la Nueva España y capitán general de este ejército, en su nombre a este hombre por traidor, idolátrico, y porque ha muerto muchos españoles por su mandado, mándalo arrastrar y quemar por ello; quien tal hace que tal pague" (Scholes and Adams [1530] 1952, 67–68). Cuiníarángari's version of the same proclamation captures more accurately the intention underlying these words and the way they would have been interpreted by the indigenous peoples who witnessed the cazonci's death—that is, "you are all scoundrels"—than the words themselves in a literal sense.

34. Zuangua criticizes the Mexica for "not bringing wood to the temples, but rather . . . honoring their gods only with songs" (244). Regarding the derogatory opinion of the Uacúsecha concerning the ceremonies of the Nahuatl speakers of the Lake Pátzcuaro Basin, note also the following scornful comment made by Tangáxoan I to a lord of Taríaran named Hiuacha: "Who told you to count the days? We do not fight this way, counting the days. Rather, we fetch firewood for the temples. [Meanwhile], the priest name curí[ti] and the sacrificer take the smoke in prayer to the gods. Two nights we maintain a vigil to watch over the preparations among the people and

bid them farewell. Then we go to war" (143). The corresponding negative views held by the Mexica and related Nahuatl-speaking peoples regarding the indigenous inhabitants of Michoacán are summarized in Pollard 1993, 173.

35. Although many commentators have tended to emphasize the fatalistic undercurrents in the indigenous religions of Mesoamerica (see, for instance, note 5 above), the notion that Zuangua is able to engage in symbolic dialogue with the gods underscores the importance of human agency in determining the course of future events. As noted in chapter 4, the oral performance of the petámuti similarly suggests that our destiny may be written in the stars, but there is more than one way to "read" these patterns; in other words, it is up to us to take advantage of the opportunities we may be offered to help determine our own fate.

36. A similar opinion to that of Ruiz regarding the cazonci Tzintzicha was presented by Riva Palacio, also at the turn of the last century: "Tzintzicha se humilló tanto a Cortés, que más parecía un súbdito en presencia de su soberano, que un monarca delante de un capitán" (Chavero and Riva Palacio 1883, 2:29).

37. References to the death of Tzintzicha in colonial-era sources almost always contain a condemnation of Guzmán, independently of whether or not they convert the cazonci into a symbol of Christian martyrdom. Thus, Díaz del Castillo notes that his execution was one of the cruelest episodes that occurred during the entire conquest of New Spain: "fue una de las malas y feas cosas que presidente ni otras personas podían hacer, y todos los que iban en su compañía se lo tuvieron a mal y a crueldad" (*Historia verdadera*, ch. 197). Torquemada also characterizes it as one of the worst excesses committed by crown officials at the time: "pasó [Guzmán] por Mechuacan . . . donde tomó del rey Caczoltzin diez mil marcos de plata y mucho oro bajo y seis mil indios para carga y servicio de su ejército; y aún después de haberle quitado todo eso le quemó con otros muchos indios principales (caso el más cruel que decir se puede) y fue la causa porque no pudiese quejarse de estos tan manifiestos agravios que justificadamente se pueden llamar robos y tiranías" (*Monarquía indiana*, bk. 3, ch. 43). La Rea, for his part, emphasizes the spiritual dimensions of the story—the martyrdom of the newly baptized Tzintzicha, whose opportunity to confess before being executed is contrasted with Moctezuma's inability to attain eternal salvation: "aunque no se libró [el cazonci] de la tiranía de un ambicioso español, empero se bautizó y confesó al rey de los cielos, y murió con las esperanzas que no alcanzó Moctezuma" (*Crónica de Mechoacan*, ch. 15). Herrera is loath to condemn Guzmán too harshly, suggesting there were differences of opinion regarding his conduct in the matter; nevertheless, he implies that the available evidence supports the contention that Guzmán was led astray by excessive greed: "aunque pudo ser que Nuño de Guzmán lo justificase, para lo cual envió el proceso al Rey, muchos dijeron que lo hizo por tomarle [al cazonci] sus tesoros" (*Historia general*, dec. 4, bk. 8, ch. 1). Tello stresses the shock and horror of Charles V and the Spanish court upon hearing the news of the cazonci's death: "Todo el exército y los religiossos sintieron mal del hecho, y toda la Nueva España tuvo harto que hablar, y aun en España dio mucho que deçir, porque luego se supo, y el Emperador lo alcanzó a saber" (*Crónica*

miscelánea, ch. 27). The opinions of Oviedo and Gómara are discussed in Adorno and Pautz (1999, 3:349–51).

38. I am not suggesting that the accounts by Spanish friars, soldiers, and other firsthand participants in the events recounted by Cuiníarángari were not also instrumental in shaping the widely disseminated version of the conquest of Michoacán as a Christian allegory during the colonial period. My goal is simply to acknowledge the role the indigenous nobles of Michoacán played in helping to articulate this point of view.

39. Montaño's account, included by Cervantes de Salazar in his *Crónica de la Nueva España* (bk. 6, chs. 13–24), is quite long and detailed. The focus is the danger faced by Montaño and his three companions and the great service they performed for Cortés and the Spanish crown. For a critical assessment of this account in comparison with other documentary sources, see Warren 1985, 36–41. Although Cuiníarángari does not explicitly allude to Tzintzicha's intention of sacrificing the Spaniards, other details of his testimony coincide with that of Montaño, such as the staging of a hunt by the cazonci and the ritual sacrifice of a greyhound belonging to one of the Spaniards.

40. Although Ruiz and Romero Flores disagree about the character of Tzintzicha, they both combine oral and written sources in their respective histories of Michoacán. Ruiz, for example, provides a narrative reconstruction of the conquest by using nineteenth-century legends as a corrective to Cuiníarángari's version of events ([1891–1900] 1971). Romero Flores similarly weaves together aspects of oral and written traditions regarding indigenous resistance to the Spaniards, on one hand, and the cazonci's peaceful surrender to them, on the other (1946; [1971] 1978). Various pictorial documents from Michoacán include references to a general named Nanuma and a noble named Timas or Timaje (Roskamp 1998a and 1998b). In contrast to Ruiz, however, not all of these pictorial sources call into question the peaceful-submission version of events. There is also a tradition, based on documents belonging to Don Constantino Huitziméngari, a grandson of Tzintzicha, to the effect that the cazonci surrendered peacefuly to the Spaniards due to the miraculous resuscitation of a sister of his around the time of the Spanish conquest of México-Tenochtitlan. This sister is said to have advised him that "de ninguna manera convenía impedir la entrada de aquellas nuevas gentes que venían a plantar la ley del verdadero Dios" (Alva Ixtlilxochitl [ca. 1600–1640] 1975, 2:244).

41. Tasháuaco, Cuiníarángari's elder brother, is also called Huitzitziltzin—the Nahuatl version of his name—in the pages of the Escorial manuscript, for that is how Cortés and other conquistadors referred to him. He died while accompanying Olid's expedition to Honduras in 1524, which explains why he disappears from Cuiníarángari's narrative relatively early on (264).

42. Ruiz was struck by the enigmatic nature of the passage in Cuiníarángari's narrative concerning the events that took place at Taximaroa: "Muy confuso es el lenguaje de la Relación al referir este episodio. Parece que de intento se ha querido obscurecer el relato" ([1891–1900] 1971, 509). See also Schöndube B. 1996.

43. The three Franciscans mentioned by Cuiníarángari in his account are: Martín Jesús de la Coruña, one of the twelve "apostles" who arrived in New Spain in 1524 and founder of the Franciscan mission in Michoacán in 1525; Jacobo de Testera; and Francisco de Bolonia. Fray Martín is described as responsible for rescuing Cuiníarángari, Tzintzicha, and the Nahuatl-speaker Gonzalo Juárez Cuycique from being tortured by Antonio de Godoy at the behest of Guzmán (273). The other two friars are credited with securing the release in 1533 of Cuiníarángari, Don Alonso de Ávalos, and other principal lords, who were carried along as prisoners by Guzmán during his conquest of Nueva Galicia (277).

44. The one inconsistency with this portrait of Tzintzicha as an exemplary Christian in Cuiníarángari's account involves his order to kill Timas and other nobles who had counseled him against trusting the Spaniards. Cuiníarángari nevertheless contrives to use this opportunity to show how he himself had taken the Christian message to heart even at this early date. For although he carries out the cazonci's orders, he does not confiscate the belongings of Timas's wives as permitted by indigenous custom: "and [the men who had accompanied Don Pedro] began to take clothing and blankets from the women, because that was the custom when they killed someone. . . . And Don Pedro . . . ordered them to return their clothing and blankets. [Then] the women began to weep . . . and Don Pedro told them: 'Do not cry. Stay here. [Truly] we have only come to kill him. Do not go anywhere. Remain here with your children. Do not be afraid'" (263).

45. Regarding the unprecedented lack of transition time between eras represented by the Spanish conquest and the resulting difficulty in dealing with it from an indigenous point of view, see the analysis of the omens foretelling the conquest in chapter 4 of this book.

46. The word *tuytzen*, used in the *Relación de Michoacán* to describe the transformation of the god Cupanzieeri into a deer and also the horses of the Spanish conquistadors, refers in general to any animal that can be used to carry people or cargo (Roskamp 1998a, 221).

47. The contrast between masculine and feminine attire is detailed by Taríacuri's unfaithful first wife from Curínguaro in a parody of her husband's supposedly disrespectful behavior toward his in-laws. According to her, Taríacuri was wont to make fun of her father and brothers by equating their cloverleaf garlands with women's headbands, their gold ear plugs with women's earrings, their feather-decorated cotton armor with women's decorative capes, their tunics with women's shifts, their jaguar-skin armbands with women's bracelets, their loincloths with women's sashes and underskirts, their bows with women's looms, their arrows with women's shuttles and spindles (68). The complementarity between male and female principles—one of the keys to the structural analysis of the *Relación de Michoacán*—is here expressed in terms of the traditional indigenous vestimentary code.

48. The varieties of clothing and food that Olid, through interpreters, instructs Cuiníarángari to have the cazonci bring to a place named Quangaceo are: "rich mantles, those that are called *carángari, curize, zizupu,* and *echere atácata,* as well as other fine

cloths. [Also] partridges and eggs, [plus] ducks and fish of the varieties known as *huerepu, acúmara, urápeti,* and *thiró*" (249).

49. Regarding Cuiníarángari's gullibility in his initial dealings with the Spaniards, the anecdote in which he recounts how he was convinced that the priest who accompanied the Olid expedition was a sorcerer because of the way he celebrated mass is of particular interest (250). Again, taken at face value it reinforces the supposed childishness of the indigenous peoples, as affirmed by the friar-compiler (264–66). Conversely, however, it can be read as an indictment of that very position, if it is assumed that Cuiníarángari is casting himself in this episode in the role of a dupe. In this reading, it is not the childishness of the indigenous peoples in general that is being highlighted by Cuiníarángari, just the naïveté of his own youthful alter ego.

50. Eréndira, for example, is one of the most popular names for girls among speakers of Purépecha. Literally, it means "smiling one" (Gómez Bravo et al., 1992, 116).

51. Pollard estimates the population of Tzintzuntzan at the time of the Spanish conquest to have been approximately 25,000–35,000 and that of Ihuatzio and Pátzcuaro at about 4,000–6,000 each (1993, 33). If, as Beltrán argues, the cazonci's army was made up predominantly of members of the ruling lineages, with the commoners playing a supporting role (1994, 91–107), then it is unlikely the peoples of Michoacán could have matched the sheer numbers represented by the Spaniards' indigenous allies in 1522.

52. The way Tzintzicha's female relative is sent to both Tasháuaco and Cuiníarángari ties in with the practice of levirate marriages in Michoacán—the custom whereby a man would "inherit" his brother's wife or wives upon the brother's death.

53. Note the reference to "foam" in Cuiníarángari's reply to the cúriti. This metaphor echoes the image in the petámuti's narrative in part two of the *Relación de Michoacán* regarding the foam generated by the paddles of a people escaping by canoe from their enemies (25, 118). It also coincides with the scene depicted in plate 15, where Tangáxoan I, an ancestor of Tzintzicha, is shown grabbing Zapíuátame, an ancestor of Cuiníarángari, by the hair, in a symbolic gesture signifying capture. In other words, the historical explanation for why Cuiníarángari and his brother are symbolically encoded as "slaves" and "servants" of the cazonci in the pages of the Escorial manuscript is that their forebears placed themselves under the protective custody of the Uacúsecha.

54. The notion that it is the responsibility of Cuiníarángari as governor to speak for the cazonci ties in with his promise not to "break" the cazonci's words (248). To lie to the cazonci, in this sense, is the ultimate form of disobedience (157), as well as a grave threat to the legitimacy of a system based on the concept of delegating authority through ritual possession.

55. See, for instance, the opinion expressed by the friar-compiler of the *Relación de Michoacán* regarding the validity of certain charges against Tzintzicha (267), as well as references throughout Escorial Ms. C.IV.5 to the continuation into the narrative present of indigenous governmental and religious practices, many of which were later censored by the hand of the principal corrector (for a detailed discussion of this dynamic, see chapter 2 of this book).

56. "Hearts and minds" is a reference to the Vietnam-era policy formulated by Lyndon B. Johnson in 1967.

57. The conflict between the early Franciscans of New Spain and members of the First Audiencia, especially Guzmán, is well established (for a discussion of this dynamic in relation to Michoacán in particular, see Warren 1985, 86, 95). The roots of this animosity, however, differ from that harbored by Mendoza toward Guzmán; for, in the case of the Franciscans, they stem from their strong support for Cortés (see, for instance, Phelan [1956] 1970).

58. A representative instance of Cuiníarángari's repeated assurances to Tzintzicha that everything will be all right is the following remark, made in an effort to calm the cazonci's misgivings about the decision to go to Coyoacan (on the outskirts of México-Tenochtitlan) to meet with Cortés: "My Lord, we have not lied to you; we told you the truth [about the Spaniards]. What, will you not soon arrive [in Coyoacan] and see for yourself? They will be very pleased with your arrival" (261).

59. Other sources that refer to Tzintzicha's regret over having surrendered peacefully include the testimony of the Spanish interpreter García del Pilar against his former master Guzmán. Pilar recalled the cazonci's final words, addressed to his son-in-law Alonso Vise, as follows: "que vea el galardon que le dan los Christianos, y Nuño de Guzman en pago de los servicios que le hizo, y de el oro, y plata que le habia dado, y haviendo dado la tierra en paz, y sin guerra, que le mandaba que despues de quemado cojiese sus polvos, y cenizas de el, que quedasen, y las llevase á Mechoacan, y que alli hiciese juntar á todos los señores de la dicha Provincia, y que les contase lo que havia pasado, y que contase todo, y que viesen el galardon, que le daban los Christianos" (cited in Ramírez [1532] 1847, 269). These final words are evoked in a short story published recently by Martín del Campo (1996), which explains indigenous resistance to Christianity as a response to the un-Christian behavior of many of its supposed practitioners, as manifested in the treatment accorded Tzintzicha.

60. In the *Lienzo de Pátzcuaro*, Timaje (Timas) is portrayed holding a club, with which he appears to be menacing the irecha Tsintsicha (that is, Tzintzicha). Roskamp interprets this scene as reinforcing the view of Timas as the leader of a failed palace coup (1998a, 260; ill. 55). A more figurative reading is suggested by the location of Fray Martín Jesús de la Coruña, bearing a crucifix, immediately behind Timas, as well as by the significance of the club icon in other pictorial compositions from the region, where it refers to "feeding" the gods of the underworld. According to this reinterpretation of traditional indigenous categories through the prism of Christianity, by eluding the "club" wielded by Timas, Tzintzicha narrowly avoided burning for all eternity in hell.

61. The use of foreshadowing by Cuiníarángari also suggests that Tzintzicha suffered from a guilty conscience. At the time of his inauguration as cazonci, he is said to have accepted the position with trepidation, stating: "Let it be as you say, elders. It is my wish to obey you, [although] perhaps I will not do it well. [If so] I beg you not to harm me, but gently to remove me from command. May we not remain silent. Listen to what is being said about the people who are coming; for we do not know what

manner of people this may be. Perhaps I will have this office for only a few days" (246). Although these remarks are fully consistent with indigenous custom, according to testimony recorded in other passages from the Escorial manuscript (107–16, 224), their inclusion by Cuiníarángari in his account is significant as an indication of the message he was trying to convey to his indigenous audience about the Spanish conquest.

62. As a kinship term, *tarascue* refers to son's wife, daughter's husband, wife's father and mother, and husband's father and mother, but not wife's brother (*itsicue*), wife's sister (*iuscue*), husband's brother (*iuscue*), husband's sister (*tuuiscue*), sister's husband (*itsicue*, in the case of a male speaker; in the case of a female speaker, the translation is *iuscue* for an older sister's husband and *tuuiscue* for a younger sister's husband), or brother's wife (*iuscue*). In other words, *tarascue* only refers to kinship relationships with someone of a different generation than the speaker (Pollard 1993, 58). See chapter 1 for a brief overview of the modern debate over the use of the Hispanicized version *tarascos*—English, Tarascans—to refer to the indigenous peoples of Michoacán.

Works Cited

Acosta, José de. [1590] 1962. *Historia natural y moral de las Indias: En que se tratan de las cosas notables del cielo/elementos/metales/plantas y animales dellas/y los ritos/y ceremonias/leyes y gobierno de los indios.* Edited by Edmundo O'Gorman. Biblioteca Americana, Cronistas de Indias. Mexico City: FCE.
Acuña, René, ed. 1987. *Relaciones geográficas del siglo XVI: Michoacán.* Serie Antropológica, 74. Mexico City: UNAM-IIA.
———, ed. 1988. *Vasco de Quiroga: "De debellandis Indis" un tratado desconocido.* Vol. 1, Bibliotheca Hvmanistica Mexicana. Mexico City: UNAM.
Adorno, Rolena. 1979. Paradigms lost: A Peruvian surveys Spanish colonial society. *Studies in the Anthropology of Visual Communication* 5 (2):78–96.
———. 1981. On pictorial language and the typology of culture in a New World chronicle. *Semiotica* 36 (1–2):51–106.
———. 1986. *Guaman Poma: Writing and resistance in colonial Peru.* Austin: Univ. of Texas Press.
———. 1989. *Cronista y príncipe: La obra de don Felipe Guamán Poma de Ayala.* Lima: Univ. Católica del Perú.
———, and Patrick Charles Pautz. 1999. *Álvar Nuñez Cabeza de Vaca: His account, his life, and the expedition of Pánfilo de Narváez.* 3 vols. Lincoln: Univ. of Nebraska Press.
———. 2001. *Guaman Poma and his illustrated chronicle from colonial Peru: From a century of scholarship to a new era or reading.* English and Spanish. Copenhagen: Museum Tusculanum Press, Univ. of Copenhagen, and The Royal Library.
Aguayo Spencer, Rafael, ed. 1939. *Don Vasco de Quiroga: Documentos.* Mexico City: Editorial Polis.
———, ed. 1970. *Don Vasco de Quiroga: Taumaturgo de la organización social.* Mexico City: Ediciones Oasis.
Aguirre Beltrán, Gonzalo. 1953. *Formas de gobierno indígena.* Mexico City: Imprenta Universitaria.
Aiton, Arthur Scott. 1927. *Antonio de Mendoza.* Durham: Duke Univ. Press.
———. 1932. The secret visita against Viceroy Mendoza. In *New Spain and the Anglo-American West*, vol. 1, New Spain, ed. Charles W. Hackett et al., 1–22. Los Angeles: priv. print.
Alvar Ezquerra, Antonio. 1996. *La universidad de Alcalá de Henares a principios del siglo XVI.* Alcalá de Henares: Universidad de Alcalá de Henares.
Alva Ixtlilxochitl, Fernando de. [ca. 1600–1640] 1985. *Obras históricas.* 2 vols. Ed. Edmundo O'Gorman. Historiadores y cronistas de Indias, 4. Mexico City: IIH-UNAM.

Alvarado Contreras, Fernando. 1985. *El sánscrito en la lengua tarasca.* Mexico City: Manuel Porrúa.
Anales de Tarecuato [1519–1666] 1951. Colección Amatlacuilotl, 8. Mexico City: Editor Vargas Rea.
Anawalt, Patricia Rieff. 1981. *Indian clothing before Cortés: Mesoamerican costumes from the codices.* Norman: Univ. of Oklahoma Press.
Anders, Ferdinand, Maarten Jansen, and Luis Reyes García, eds. 1993a. *Manual del adivino: Libro explicativo del llamado Códice Vaticano B.* Facsimile. Códices mexicanos, 4. Madrid, Graz, and Mexico City: Sociedad Estatal Quinto Centenario, Akademische Druck-und Verlagsanstalt, FCE.
———. 1993b. *Los templos del cielo y de la oscuridad: Oráculos y liturgia: Libro explicativo del llamado Códice Borgia.* Facsimile. Códices mexicanos, 5. Madrid, Graz, and Mexico City: Sociedad Estatal Quinto Centenario, Akademische Druck-und Verlagsanstalt, FCE.
———. 1996. *Religión, costumbres e historia de los antiguos mexicanos: Libro explicativo del llamado Códice Vaticano A.* Facsimile. Códices mexicanos, 12. Madrid, Graz, and Mexico City: Sociedad Estatal Quinto Centenario, Akademische Druck-und Verlagsanstalt, FCE.
Anderson, Benedict R. 1983. *Imagined communities: Reflections on the origin and spread of nationalism.* London and New York: Verso.
Anghiera, Pietro Martire d'. [1530] 1989. *Décadas del Nuevo Mundo.* Trans. Agustín Millares Carlo. Ed. Edmundo O'Gorman. 2 vols. Santo Domingo: Sociedad Dominicana de Bibliófilos.
Aveni, Anthony F. 1980. *Skywatchers of ancient Mexico.* Austin: Univ. of Texas Press.
———, ed. 1975. *Archaeoastronomy in pre-Columbian America.* Austin: Univ. of Texas Press.
———, ed. 1977. *Native American astronomy.* Austin: Univ. of Texas Press.
Avril, François. 1978. *Manuscript painting at the court of France.* New York: George Braziller.
Backhouse, Janet. 1987. *The illuminated manuscript.* London: Phaidon.
Bacon, Francis. [1605] 1955. *Selected writings of Francis Bacon.* Modern Library. New York: Random House.
Baird, Ellen T. 1993. *The drawings of Sahagún's Primeros memoriales: Structure and style.* Norman: Univ. of Oklahoma Press.
Ballesteros Gaibrois, Manuel. 1973. Antonio de Herrera, 1549–1625. In *HMAI,* vol. 13, ed. Howard F. Cline, 240–55. Gen. ed. Robert Wauchope. Austin: Univ. of Texas Press.
Barthes, Roland. 1977. *Image, music, text.* Trans. Stephen Heath. New York: Hill and Wang.
Basalenque, Diego. [1673] 1963. *Historia de la provincia de San Nicolás Tolentino de Michoacán.* Ed. José Bravo Ugarte. México heroico, 18. Mexico City: Editorial Jus.
———. [1714] 1994. *Arte de la lengua tarasca.* Ed. J. Benedict Warren. Facsimile. Fuentes de la Lengua Tarasca o Purépecha, 6. Morelia: Fímax Publicistas.

Basso, Keith H. 1996. *Wisdom sits in places: Landscape and language among the western Apache*. Albuquerque: Univ. of New Mexico Press.
Batalla Rosado, Juan José. 2001. Una aproximación a la iconografía tarasca a través de las ilustraciones de la "Relación de Michoacán." In Escobar Olmedo [ca. 1541] 2001, 143–67.
Baudot, Georges. [1976] 1983. *Utopía e historia en México*. Trans. Vicente González Loscertales. Madrid: Editorial Espasa-Calpe.
———. 1996. *México y los albores del discurso colonial*. Mexico City: Editorial Patria.
———, and Tzvetan Todorov, eds. [1983] 1990. *Relatos aztecas de la conquista*. Translated by Guillermina Cuevas. Mexico City: Grijalbo.
Beaumont, Pablo. [ca. 1778] 1985–87. *Crónica de Michoacán*. 3 vols. Morelia: Balsal Editores.
Becker, Marjorie. 1995. *Setting the Virgin on fire: Lázaro Cárdenas, Michoacán peasants, and the redemption of the Mexican Revolution*. Berkeley and Los Angeles: Univ. of California Press.
Beltrán, Ulises. 1994. Estado y sociedad tarascos en la época prehispánica. In Boehm de Lameiras 1994, 31–163.
Benavente, Toribio de ("Motolinía"). [1541] 1979. *Historia de los indios de la Nueva España*. Edited by Edmundo O'Gorman. 3d ed. Sepan Cuántos, 129. Mexico City: Editorial Porrúa.
———. [ca. 1536–43] 1996. *Memoriales (Libro de Oro, MS JGI 31)*. Edited by Nancy Joe Dyer. Biblioteca Novohispana, 3. Mexico City: COLMEX.
Beristain de Souza, José Mariano. [1816–21] 1947. *Biblioteca hispanoamericana septentrional*. 3d ed. 5 vols. Mexico City: Ediciones Fuente Cultural.
Betanzos, Juan de. [1551] 1987. *Suma y narración de los incas*. Ed. María del Carmen Martín Rubio. Madrid: Ediciones Atlas.
Boehm de Lameiras, Brigitte, ed. 1994. *El Michoacán antiguo*. Zamora: COLMICH; Morelia: Gobierno del Estado.
Boone, Elizabeth Hill. 2000. *Stories in red and black: Pictorial histories of the Aztecs and Mixtecs*. Austin: Univ. of Texas Press.
Boone, Elizabeth Hill, and Walter D. Mignolo, eds. 1994. *Writing without words: Alternative literacies in Mesoamerica and the Andes*. Durham: Duke Univ. Press.
Borhegyi, Stephan F. de. 1969. The pre-Columbian ballgame: A pan-Mesoamerican tradition. In *Verhandlungen des XXXVIII Internationalen Amerikanistenkongresses*, vol. 1, 499–515. München: Kommissionsverlag Klaus Renner.
Boyd, Maurice. 1969. *Tarascan myths and legends: A rich and imaginative "history" of the Tarascans*. Monographs in History and Culture, 4. Fort Worth: Texas Christian Univ. Press.
Brand, Donald D. 1943. An historical sketch of anthropology and geography in the Tarascan region. *New Mexico Anthropologist* 6–7 (2):37–108.
———. 1971. Ethnohistoric synthesis of Western Mexico. In *HMAI*, vol. 11, edited by Gordon F. Ekolm and Ignacio Bernal, 632–56. Gen. ed. Robert Wauchope. Austin: Univ. of Texas Press.

Brasseur de Bourbourg, Charles Étienne. 1857–59. *Histoire des nations civilisées du Mexique et de l'Amérique Centrale.* 4 vols. Paris: n.p.
Bravo Ugarte, José. 1962. La Relación de Mechuacán: Análisis de la edición de Aguilar. *Historia Mexicana* 12 (45):13–25.
Bricker, Victoria Reifler. 1981. *The Indian christ, the Indian king: The historical substrate of Maya myth and ritual.* Austin: Univ. of Texas Press.
Brotherston, Gordon. 1992. *Book of the fourth world: Reading the native Americas through their literature.* Cambridge: Cambridge Univ. Press.
Brown, Michelle P. 1994. *Understanding illuminated manuscripts.* Malibu: J. Paul Getty Museum.
Brownrigg, Edwin Blake. 1978. *Colonial Latin American manuscripts and transcripts in the Obadiah Rich Collection: An inventory and index.* New York: New York Public Library, Readex Books.
Burkhart, Louise M. [1986] 1989. *The slippery earth: Nahua-Christian moral dialogue in sixteenth-century Mexico.* Tucson: Univ. of Arizona Press.
Burrus, Ernest J. 1961. Cristóbal Cabrera on the missionary methods of Vasco de Quiroga. *Manuscripta* 5 (1):17–27.
———. 1973. Religious chroniclers and historians: A summary with annotated bibliography. In *HMAI,* vol. 13, ed. Howard F. Cline, 138–85. Gen. ed. Robert Wauchope. Austin: Univ. of Texas Press.
Bustamante García, Jesús. 1990. *Fray Bernardino de Sahagún: Una revisión crítica de los manuscritos y de su proceso de composición.* Mexico City: UNAM.
Cabrero, Leoncio, ed. [ca. 1541] 1989. *Relación de Michoacán.* Crónicas de América, 52. Madrid: Historia 16.
Cardenal, Ernesto. 1970. *Homenaje a los indios americanos.* Letras de América, 30. Santiago, Chile: Editorial Universitaria. English translation by Monique and Carlos Altschul. Baltimore: Johns Hopkins Univ. Press.
Cárdenas García, Efraín. 1996. Pátzcuaro, Ihuatzio y Tzintzuntzan: Los centros de poder en el estado purépecha. *Arqueología Mexicana* 4 (19):28–33.
Carrasco Pizana, Pedro. 1966. Documentos sobre el rango de tecuhtli entre los nahuas tramontanos. *Tlalocan* 5 (2):134–38.
———. 1969. Parentesco y regulación del matrimonio entre los indios del antiguo Michoacán. *Revista Española de Antropología Americana* 4:219–22.
———. 1971. La importancia de las sobreviviencias prehispánicas en la religión tarasca: La lluvia. In *Verhandlungen des XXXVIII Internationalen Amerikanistenkongresses,* vol. 3, 265–73. München: Kommissionsverlag Klaus Renner.
———. 1976. *El catolicismo popular de los tarascos: Cristianismo y paganismo en la religión de los tarascos.* SepSetentas, 298. Mexico City: SEP.
——— et al., ed. 1986. *La sociedad indígena en el Centro y Occidente de México.* Zamora: COLMICH.
Casas, Bartolomé de las. [1542] 1977. *Brevísima relación de la destruición de las Indias.* Ed. Manuel Ballesteros Gaibrois. Madrid: Fundación Universitaria Española.

———. [1559] 1958. *Apologética historia sumaria*. Ed. J. Pérez de Tudela Bueso. 2 vols. Biblioteca de Autores Españoles, 105–106. Madrid: Ediciones Atlas.
Caso y Andrade, Alfonso. 1943. The calendar of the Tarascans. *American Antiquity* 9 (1):11–28.
———. 1971. ¿Religión o religiones mesoamericanas? In *Verhandlungen des XXXVIII Internationalen Amerikanistenkongresses*, vol. 3, 189–200. München: Kommissionsverlag Klaus Renner.
Castañeda Delgado, Paulino, ed. 1974. *Don Vasco de Quiroga y su "Información en derecho."* Chimalistac de Libros y Documentos acerca de la Nueva España, 39. Madrid: Ediciones José Porrúa Turanzas.
Castilleja González, Aída, and Víctor Hugo Valencia Valera, eds. 1993. *El Lago de Pátzcuaro: Su gente, su historia y sus fiestas*. Colección Divulgación. Mexico City: INAH.
Castro Gutiérrez, Felipe. 1998. Condición femenina y violencia conyugal entre los purépechas durante la época colonial. *Mexican Studies/Estudios Mexicanos* 14(1): 5–22.
———. 2002. Alborotos y siniestras relaciones: La república de indios de Pátzcuaro colonial. *Relaciones: Estudios de historia y sociedad* 23 (89):203–33. Zamora: COLMICH.
Castro Leal, Marcia. 1986. *Tzintzuntzan, capital de los tarascos*. Morelia: Gobierno del Estado de Michoacán.
———, Clara L. Díaz, and María Teresa García. 1989. Los tarascos. In Florescano 1989, vol. 1, 193–304.
Certeau, Michel de. [1980] 1984. *The practice of everyday life*. Trans. Steven F. Randall. Berkeley and Los Angeles: Univ. of California Press.
Cervantes de Salazar, Francisco. [1566] 1985. *Crónica de la Nueva España*. Ed. Juan Miralles Ostos. Biblioteca Porrúa, 84. Mexico City: Editorial Porrúa.
Chauvet, Fidel de Jesús. 1983. *Franciscanos memorables en México: Ensayo histórico (1523–1982)*. Mexico City: Centro de Estudios Bernardino de Sahagún.
Chavero, Alfredo, and Vicente Riva Palacio. 1882–83. *México a través de los siglos*. 2 vols. Mexico City: Ballescá Editores.
Chávez Cervantes, Felipe. 1997. Naturaleza, recursos naturales y cosmovisión p'urhépecha: Nota etnográficas para su estudio. In Paredes Martínez 1997a, 257–63.
Chiappelli, Fredi, ed. 1976. *First images of America*. Berkeley and Los Angeles: Univ. of California Press.
Chipman, Donald E. 1967. *Nuño de Guzmán and the province of Pánuco in New Spain, 1518–1533*. Spain in the West, 10. Glendale, Calif.: Arthur H. Clark.
Christensen, Bodil, and Samuel Martí. 1971. *Brujerías y papel precolombino/Witchcraft and pre-Columbian paper*. Mexico City: Ediciones Euroamericanas.
Clendinnen, Inga. 1987. *Ambivalent conquests: Maya and Spaniard in Yucatán, 1517–1570*. Cambridge: Cambridge Univ. Press.
———. 1991. *Aztecs: An interpretation*. Cambridge: Cambridge Univ. Press.

Clézio, Jean Marie G. le, 1985. *La conquista divina de Michoacán*. Translated by Aurelio Garzón del Camino. Cuadernos de la Gaceta, 4. Mexico City: FCE.

———. [1988] 1993. *The Mexican dream: Or, the uninterrupted thought of Amerindian civilizations*. Translated by Teresa Lavender Fagan. Chicago: Univ. of Chicago Press.

———. 2000. Universalidad de la "Relación de Michoacán." In Franco Mendoza [ca. 1541] 2000, 107–19.

———, trans. [ca. 1541] 1984. *Relation de Michoacan*. Paris: Editions Gallimard.

Ciudad Real, Antonio de. [1584–89] 1873. *Relación breve y verdadera de algunas cosas de las muchas que sucedieron al padre fray Alonso Ponce en las provincias de la Nueva España*. CDIHE, vol. 57.

Codex Mendoza. [ca. 1541–42] 1992. Edited by Frances Berdan and Patricia Rieff Anawalt. 4 vols. Berkeley and Los Angeles: Univ. of California Press.

Coe, Michael D. 1975. Native astronomy in Mesoamerica. In *Archaeoastronomy in pre-Columbian America*, ed. Anthony F. Aveni, 3–31. Austin: Univ. of Texas Press.

Corona Núñez, José. [1957] 1986. *Mitología tarasca*. Colección Cultural, 4. Morelia: SEP.

———. 1986. *Tres códices michoacanos*. Biblioteca de Nicolaitas Notables, 31. Morelia: UMSNH.

———. 1988. *Historia de los antiguos habitantes de Michoacán desde su origen hasta la conquista española*. Morelia: Balsal Editores.

———. 1992. *Estudios de antropología e historia*. Morelia: UMSNH.

———. 1993. *Diccionario geográfico tarasco-náhuatl*. Morelia: UMSNH.

Cortés, Hernán. [1519–1526] 1992. *Cartas de relación*. 16th ed. Sepan Cuántos, 7. Mexico City: Editorial Porrúa.

Cortés Alonso, Vicente. 2001. Un temprano testimonio de historia oral. In Escobar Olmedo [ca. 1541] 2001, 75–87.

Craine, Eugene R., and Reginald C. Reindorp, eds. and trans. [ca. 1541] 1970. *The chronicles of Michoacán*. The Civilization of the American Indian Series, 98. Norman: Univ. of Oklahoma Press.

Cypess, Sandra Messinger. 1991. *La Malinche in Mexican literature: From history to myth*. Texas Pan American series. Austin: Univ. of Texas Press.

Dahlgren, Barbro. 1967. *Los purépecha de Michoacán*. Historia prehispánica, 10. Mexico City: Museo Nacional de Antropología, INAH, SEP.

Díaz del Castillo, Bernal. [1568] 1983. *Historia verdadera de la conquista de la Nueva España*. 13th ed. Sepan Cuántos, 5. Mexico City: Editorial Porrúa.

Dibble, Charles E. 1971. Writing in central Mexico. In *HMAI*, vol. 10, edited by Robert Wauchope, Gordon Ekholm, and Ignacio Bernal, 322–32. Gen. ed. Robert Wauchope. Austin: Univ. of Texas Press.

Durán, Diego. [1579–81] 1995. *Historia de las Indias de Nueva España e islas de Tierra Firme*. 2 vols. Mexico City: Cien de México.

Eck, Diana L. [1981] 1985. *Darśan: Seeing the divine image in India*. Chambersburg, Pa.: Anima Books.

Edgerton, Samuel Y. 1975. *The renaissance rediscovery of linear perspective.* New York: Basic Books.

Edmonson, Munro S., ed. 1974. *Sixteenth century Mexico: The work of Sahagún.* School of American Research Advanced Seminar series. Albuquerque: Univ. of New Mexico Press.

———. 1988. *The Book of the Year: Middle American Calendrical Systems.* Salt Lake City: Univ. of Utah Press.

Eliade, Mircea. [1954] 1959. *Cosmos and history: The myth of the eternal return.* Trans. William R. Trask. New York: Harper and Row.

Elzey, Wayne. 1976. Some remarks on the space and time of the 'center' in Aztec religion. *Estudios de Cultura Náhuatl* 12:315–34.

Escobar, Matías de. [1729] 1970. *Americana thebaida.* Ed. Nicolás P. Navarrete. Documentos y Testimonios, 3. Morelia: Balsal Editores.

Escobar Olmedo, Armando M. 1989. *Catálogo de documentos michoacanos en archivos españoles.* Colección Catálogos. Morelia: UMSNH.

———, ed. 1997. *"Proceso, tormento y muerte del cazonzi, último gran señor de los tarascos" por Nuño de Guzmán, 1530.* Mexico City: Frente de Afirmación Hispanista.

———, ed. [ca. 1541] 2001. *Relación de Michoacán: Relaçión de las çerimonias y rrictos y población y governación de los yndios de la provincia de Mechuacan hecha al yllustrísimo señor don Antonio de Mendoza, virrey y governador desta Nueva España por su Majestad, ecétera.* Facsimile. Thesaurus Americae, 3. Madrid: Patrimonio Nacional and Testimonio Compañía Editorial; Morelia: Ayuntamiento de Morelia.

Espejel Carvajal, Claudia. 1992. *Caminos de Michoacán . . . y pueblos por los que voy pasando.* Colección Científica, 245. Mexico City: INAH.

———. 2000. Guía arqueológica y geográfica para la "Relación de Michoacán." In Franco Mendoza [ca. 1541] 2000, 301–312.

Espinosa, Isidro Félix de. [ca. 1752] 1945. *Crónica de la provincia franciscana de los apóstoles San Pedro y San Pablo de Michoacán.* Ed. José Ignacio Davila Garibi. Mexico City: Editorial Santiago.

Farriss, Nancy M. 1984. *Maya society under colonial rule: The collective enterprise of survival.* Princeton: Princeton Univ. Press.

Finnegan, Ruth. [1977] 1992. *Oral poetry: Its nature, significance and social context.* Bloomington: Indiana Univ. Press.

Florescano, Enrique, [1993] 1995. *El mito de Quetzalcóatl.* 2d rev. ed. Vol. 83, Cuadernos de La Gaceta. Mexico City: FCE.

———. 1999. *Memoria indígena.* Taurus Pensamiento series. Mexico City: Alfaguara.

———, ed. 1989. *Historia general de Michoacán.* 5 vols. Morelia: IMC, Gobierno del Estado.

Foucault, Michel. [1969] 1972. *The archaeology of knowledge and the discourse on language.* Trans. A. M. Sheridan Smith. New York: Pantheon Books.

Franco Mendoza, Moisés. 1997a. *La ley y la costumbre en la cañada de los once pueblos.* Colección Cultura purépecha. Zamora: COLMICH.

———. 1997b. Maturino Gilberti. In Paredes Martínez 1997a, 203–17.

———. 1999. *La religión prehispánica de los p'urhépecha*. Work in progress presented at El Centro de Estudios de las Tradiciones, COLMICH.

———, ed. [ca. 1541] 2000. *Relación de Michoacán: Relación de las cerimonias y rictos y población y gobernación de los indios de la provincia de Mechuacán*. Paleography by Clotilde Martínez Ibáñez and Carmen Molina Ruiz. Zamora: COLMICH; Morelia: Gobierno del Estado de Michoacán.

Friedrich, Paul. 1970. *Agrarian revolt in a Mexican village*. Englewood Cliffs: Prentice Hall.

———. 1971a. Dialectical variation in Tarascan phonology. *International Journal of American Linguistics* 37 (3):164–87.

———. 1971b. *The Tarascan suffixes of locative space: Meaning and morphosyntaxis*. Bloomington: Indiana Univ. Press.

Galarza, Joaquín. [1987] 1992. *In amoxtli, in tlacatl (el libro, el hombre): Códices y vivencias*. Códices Mesoamericanos, 3. Mexico City: TAVA Editorial.

———. 1997. Los códices mexicanos: Escribir pintando. *Arqueología Mexicana* 4 (23):6–13.

García Alcaraz, Agustín. 1976. Estratificación social entre los tarascos prehispánicos. In *Estratificación social en la Mesoamérica prehispánica*, edited by Pedro Carrasco and Johanna Broda, 221–44. Mexico City: INAH.

García Icazbalceta, Joaquín. 1886. *Apuntes para un catálogo de escritores en lenguas indígenas de América*. Mexico City: n.p.

———. [1886] 1954. *Bibliografía mexicana del siglo XVI*. Edited by Agustín Millares Carlo. Mexico City: FCE.

García Mora, Carlos, gen. ed. 1987–88. *La antropología en México*. 15 vols. Colección Biblioteca del INAH. Mexico City: INAH. A two-volume anthology of those sections pertaining to Michoacán, edited by Angelina Macías Goytia, was published by INAH as *La antropología en Michoacán* in 1997.

Garibay K., Ángel María. [1953–54] 1992. *Historia de la literatura náhuatl*. 2d ed. Vol. 626, Sepan Cuántos. Mexico City: Editorial Porrúa.

———. 1965. *Teogonía e historia de los mexicanos: Tres opúsculos del siglo XVI*. Sepan Cuántos, 37. Mexico City: Editorial Porrúa.

Gelb, I. J. [1950] 1963. *A study of writing*. 2d ed. Chicago: Univ. of Chicago Press.

Gibson, Charles. [1964] 1983. *The Aztecs under Spanish rule: A history of the Indians of the Valley of Mexico, 1519–1810*. Stanford: Stanford Univ. Press.

Gilberti, Maturino. [1558] 1987. *Arte de la lengua de Michuacan*. Edited by J. Benedict Warren. Facsimile. Fuentes de la Lengua Tarasca o Purépecha, 2. Morelia: Fímax Publicistas.

———. [1559] 1990. *Vocabulario en lengua de Mechuacan*. Edited by J. Benedict Warren. 2 vols. Facsimile. Fuentes de la Lengua Tarasca o Purépecha, 3. Morelia: Fímax Publicistas.

Glantz, Margo, ed. 1994. *La Malinche: Sus padres y sus hijos*. Colección Jornadas. Mexico City: UNAM.

Glass, John B. 1958. The Relación de Michoacán. *Hispanic American Historical Review* 38:550–51.
———. 1964. *Catálogo de la colección de códices: Museo Nacional de Antropología*. Mexico City: INAH.
———. 1975. A survey of native Middle American pictorial manuscripts. In *HMAI*, vol. 14, edited by Howard F. Cline, 3–80. Gen. ed. Robert Wauchope. Austin: Univ. of Texas Press.
———. 1978. *Sahagún: Reorganization of the Manuscrito de Tlatelolco, 1556–69*. Part 1. Mass: Lincoln Center; Mexico City: Contributions to the Ethnology of Mexico.
Gómara, Francisco López de. [1552] 1979. *Historia de la conquista de México*. Edited by Jorge Gurria Lacroix. Biblioteca Ayacucho, 65. Caracas: Editorial Ayacucho.
Gómez, Fernando. 2001. *Good places and non-places in colonial Mexico: The figure of Vasco de Quiroga (1470–1565)*. Lanham Md.: University Press of America.
Gómez Bravo, Lucas et al. 1992. *Uandakua michoakani anapu (el idioma de Michoacán)*. Morelia: Gobierno del Estado, IMC, UMSNH.
Gorenstein, Shirley, and Helen Perlstein Pollard. 1983. *The Tarascan civilization: A late Prehispanic cultural system*. Publications in Anthropology, 28. Nashville: Vanderbilt Univ.
Graham, Ian. 1977. Lord Kingsborough, Sir Thomas Phillips and Obadiah Rich: Some bibliographical notes. In *Social process in Maya prehistory*, edited by Norman Hammond, 45–55. New York: Academic Press.
Gruzinski, Serge. [1985] 1989. *Man-Gods in the Mexican highlands: Indian power and colonial society, 1520–1800*. Translated by Eileen Corrigan. Stanford: Stanford Univ. Press.
———. [1988] 1993. *The conquest of Mexico: The incorporation of Indian societies into the Western world, sixteenth-eighteenth centuries*. Translated by Eileen Corrigan. Cambridge, England: Polity Press.
Guamán Poma de Ayala, Felipe. [1615] 1980. *El primer nueva corónica y buen gobierno*. Edited by John V. Murra and Rolena Adorno. Translation and textual analysis of Quechua vocabulary by Jorge L. Urioste. América Nuestra, 31. Mexico City: Siglo Veintiuno Editores.
Hernández, Francisco Martín. 1993. *Don Vasco de Quiroga (protector de los indios)*. Bibliotheca Salmanticensis, 154. Salamanca: Univ. de Salamanca.
Hernández de León-Portilla, Ascensión, ed. 1990. *Bernardino de Sahagún: Diez estudios acerca de su obra*. Mexico City: FCE.
Herrejón Peredo, Carlos. 1978. La pugna entre mexicas y tarascos. *Cuadernos de Historia* 1:11–47.
———, ed. 1984. *Humanismo y ciencia en la formación de México: V coloquio de antropología e historia regionales*. Zamora: COLMICH; Mexico City: CONACYT.
———, ed. 1986. *Estudios michoacanos I and II*. Zamora: COLMICH; Morelia: Gobierno del Estado de Michoacán.
Herrera y Tordesillas, Antonio de. [1601–15] 1934–57. *Historia general de los hechos de los castellanos en las islas y tierra firme del mar océano*. 17 vols. Madrid: n.p.

Heyden, Doris. 1988. Black magic: Obsidian in symbolism and metaphor. In *Smoke and mist: Mesoamerican studies in memory of Thelma D. Sullivan*. J. Kathryn Josserand et al., eds. Oxford: B.A.R.

Hidalgo Brinquis, María del Carmen. 2001. Descripción material de la "Relación de Michoacán." In Escobar Olmedo [ca. 1541] 2001, 41–74.

Hinderaker, Eric. 2002. *Translation and cultural brokerage*. In *A companion to American Indian history*, 357–75. Eds. Philip J. Deloria and Neil Salisbury. Oxford: Blackwell Publishers.

Hosler, Dorothy. 1994. *The sound and colors of power: The sacred metallurgical technology of ancient West Mexico*. Cambridge: MIT Press.

Huerta, María Teresa, and Patricia Palacios, eds. 1976. *Rebeliones indígenas de la época colonial*. Mexico City: SEP, INAH.

Hulme, Peter. 1986. *Colonial encounters: Europe and the native Caribbean, 1492–1797*. London: Methuen.

Hurtado Mendoza, Francisco. 1986. *La religión prehispánica de los purhépechas: Un testimonio del pueblo tarasco*. Morelia: Linotipográfica "Omega."

Jacinto Zavala, Agustín. 1981. La visión del mundo y de la vida entre los purépecha. In Miranda Godínez 1981, 143–58.

———. 1999. ¿Cómo ser uandari? In Skinfill Nogal and Carrillo Cázares 1999, 67–84.

———. 2000. Tres traducciones de la "Relación de Michoacán." In Franco Mendoza [ca. 1541] 2000, 121–38.

Janer, Florencio, ed. [ca. 1541] 1869. Relación de las ceremonias, ritos, población y gobernación de los indios de la provincia de Michoacán. In *CDIHE* 53:5–295. Madrid: Academia de la Historia. Pirate reproduction, 1875.

Jansen, Maarten. 1997. Un viaje a la Casa del Sol: Códices mixtecos. *Arqueología Mexicana* 4 (23):44–49.

Jiménez Moreno, Wigberto. 1938. *Fray Bernardino de Sahagún y su obra*. Mexico City: P. Robredo.

———. 1947. Historia antigua de la zona tarasca. In *El occidente de México: Cuarta reunión de mesa redonda*, 146–57. Mexico City: Sociedad Mexicana de Antropología.

Kirchhoff, Paul. 1956. La "Relación de Michoacán" como fuente para la historia de la sociedad y cultura tarascas. In Tudela [ca. 1541] 1956, xix–xxxiii. Reprinted in López Austin 1981, 136–74.

———. 1971. Las 18 fiestas anuales en Mesoamérica: 6 fiestas sencillas y 6 fiestas dobles. In *Verhandlungen des XXXVIII Internationalen Amerikanistenkongresses*. Vol. 3, 207–21. München: Kommissionsverlag Klaus Renner.

Klor de Alva, J. Jorge, H. B. Nicholson, and Eloise Quiñones Keber, eds. 1988. *The work of Bernardino de Sahagún: Pioneer ethnographer of sixteenth-century Aztec Mexico*. Studies on Culture and Society, 2. Austin: Univ. of Texas Press.

Kobayashi, José María. 1974. *La educación como conquista (empresa franciscana en México)*. Centro de Estudios Históricos, 19. Mexico City: COLMEX.

Krippner-Martínez, James. 1990. The politics of conquest: An interpretation of the Relación de Michoacán. *The Americas* 47 (2):177–97.

———. 2001. *Rereading the conquest: Power, politics, and the history of early colonial Michoacán, Mexico, 1521–1565*. University Park: Penn State Univ. Press.
Kuthy-Saenger, María de Lourdes. 1996. Strategies of survival, accommodation and innovation: The Tarascan indigenous elite in sixteenth century Michoacán. Ph.D. diss, Michigan State Univ.
Lafaye, Jacques. [1974] 1992. *Quetzalcóatl y Guadalupe: La formación de la conciencia nacional en México*. Mexico City: FCE.
Lagunas, Juan Baptista de. [1574] 1983. *Arte y diccionario con otras obras en lengua michuacana*. Edited by J. Benedict Warren. Facsimile. Fuentes de la Lengua Tarasca o Purépecha, 1. Morelia: Fímax Publicistas.
Landa, Diego de. [1566] 1986. *Relación de las cosas de Yucatán*. Edited by Angel María Garibay K. 13th ed. Biblioteca Porrúa, 13. Mexico City: Editorial Porrúa.
La Paz Hernández Aragón, María de la. 1996. *Teatro indígena prehispánico*. Biblioteca del Pueblo, 6. Morelia: UMSNH.
Lapesa, Rafael. [1942] 1981. *Historia de la lengua española*. 9th rev. ed. Biblioteca Románica Hispánica, Manuales 45. Madrid: Editorial Gredos.
León, Nicolás. [1884] 1980. *Hombres ilustres y escritores michoacanos*. Biblioteca de Nicolaitas Notables, 2. Morelia: UMSNH, Gobierno del Estado.
———. [1903] 1979. *Los tarascos: notas históricas, étnicas y antropológicas*. Mexico City: Editorial Innovación.
———. [1903] 1984. *Don Vasco de Quiroga: Grandeza de su persona y de su obra*. Biblioteca de Nicolaitas Notables, 24. Morelia: UMSNH.
———. 1927. La Relacion de Michuacán: Nota bibliográfica y crítica. *Revista Mexicana de Estudios Históricos* 1:191–213.
———, ed. [ca. 1541] 1903. *Relación de las ceremonias y ritos y población y gobernación de los indios de la provincia de Mechuacán*. Morelia: n.p.
———, ed. [1888–91] 1968. *Anales del Museo Michoacano*. Biblioteca de Facsímiles Mexicanos, 1. Guadalajara: Edmundo Aviña Levy Editor.
León-Portilla, Miguel. [1956] 1963. *Aztec thought and culture: A study of the ancient Nahuatl Mind*. Translated by Jack Emory Davis. Norman: Univ. of Oklahoma Press.
———. [1961] 1977. *Los antiguos mexicanos a través de sus crónicas y cantares*. Colección Popular, 88. Mexico City: FCE.
———. 1980. *Totlecáyotl: aspectos de la cultura náhuatl*. Mexico City: FCE.
———. 1992a. *Literaturas indígenas de México*. Mexico City: Editorial MAPFRE, FCE.
———. 1992b. Las profecías del encuentro: Una apropiación mesoamericana del otro. In *De palabra y obra en el Nuevo Mundo*. Vol. 2, Encuentros interétnicos, edited by Manuel Gutiérrez Estévez, Miguel León-Portilla, Gary H. Gossen, and J. Jorge Klor de Alva, 225–48. Mexico City: Siglo Veintiuno Editores.
———. 1997. Grandes momentos en la historia de los códices. *Arqueología Mexicana* 4 (23):16–23.
———. 1999. Bernardino de Sahagún: Pionero de la antropología. *Arqueología Mexicana* 6 (36):8–13.

———. 2000. Jerónimo de Alcalá y los primeros frailes etnógrafos en Mesoamérica, siglo XVI. In Franco Mendoza [ca. 1541] 2000, 57–77.

———, ed. [1959] 1992. *Visión de los vencidos*. Biblioteca Americana, 8. Madrid: Historia 16.

Lienhard, Martín. [1989] 1992. *La voz y su huella: escritura y conflicto étnico-cultural en América Latina, 1492–1988*. 3d rev. ed. Crítica Literaria, 9. Lima: Editorial Horizonte.

López Austin, Alfredo. [1973] 1989. *Hombre-dios: Religión y política en el mundo náhuatl*. Cultura Náhuatl, 15. Mexico City: UNAM-IIH.

———. 1976. El fundamento mágico-religioso del poder. *Estudios de Cultura Náhuatl* 12:197–240.

———. [1980] 1989. *Cuerpo humano e ideología: Las concepciones de los antiguos nahuas*. 3d ed. 2 vols. Serie Antropológica, 39. Mexico City: UNAM-IIA. English translation by Bernard R. and Thelma Ortiz de Montellano. Salt Lake City: Univ. of Utah Press.

———. 1981. *Tarascos y mexicas*. Biblioteca SEP 80, 4. Mexico City: FCE.

———. [1990] 1993. *The myths of the opossum: Pathways of Mesoamerican mythology*. Translated by Bernard R. and Thelma Ortiz de Montellano. Albuquerque: Univ. of New Mexico Press.

———. 1994. *El conejo en la cara de la luna: Ensayos sobre mitología de la tradición mesoamericana*. Colección Presencias, 66. Mexico City: Instituto Nacional Indigenista. English translation by Bernard R. and Thelma Ortiz de Montellano. Salt Lake City: Univ. of Utah Press.

———. [1994] 1997. *Tamoanchan, Tlalocan: places of mist*. Translation by Bernard R. and Thelma Ortiz de Montellano. Mesoamerican Worlds series. Niwot: Univ. Press of Colorado.

———, and Leonardo López Luján. 1999. *Mito y realidad de Zuyuá*. Mexico City: FCE, COLMEX.

López-Baralt, Mercedes. 1979. La persistencia de las estructuras simbólicas andinas en los dibujos de Guamán Poma de Ayala. *Journal of Latin American Lore* 5 (1):83–116.

———. 1987. *El retorno del Inca rey: mito y profecía en el mundo andino*. Biblioteca de Autores de Puerto Rico. Madrid: Editorial Playor.

———. 1988. *Icono y conquista: Guamán Poma de Ayala*. Libros Hiperión, 102. Madrid: Ediciones Hiperión.

———, ed. 1990. *La iconografía política del Nuevo Mundo*. Río Piedras: Editorial de la Univ. de Puerto Rico.

López Sarrelangue, Delfina Esmeralda. [1965] 1999. *La nobleza indígena de Pátzcuaro en la época virreinal*. Edited by Felipe Castro Gutiérrez. Morelia: Morevallado Editores.

Lord, Albert B. [1960] 1965. *The singer of tales*. New York: Atheneum.

MacCormack, Sabine. 1985. The heart has its reasons: predicaments of missionary Christianity in early colonial Peru. *Hispanic American Historical Review* 65 (3): 443–66.

———. 1991. *Religion in the Andes: Vision and imagination in early colonial Peru.* Princeton: Princeton Univ. Press.
Macherey, Pierre. [1966] 1978. *A theory of literary production.* Translated by Geoffrey Wall. London: Routledge and Kegan Paul.
Mannheim, Bruce. 1988. On the sibilants of colonial southern Peruvian Quechua. *International Journal of American Linguistics* 54 (2):168–208.
Marcos, Subcomandante. [1994] 1999. *The story of colors/La historia de los colores.* Illustrated by Domitila Domínguez. Translated by Anne Bar Din. El Paso: Cinco Puntos Press.
Markman, Roberta H., and Peter T. Markman. 1989. *Masks of the spirit: Image and metaphor in Mesoamerica.* Berkeley and Los Angeles: Univ. of California Press.
Márquez Joaquín, Pedro. 1997. Problemas de traducción en textos del siglo XVI. In Paredes Martínez 1997a, 218–30.
———. 2000. El significado de las palabras p'urhépecha en la "Relación de Michoacán": Glosario de voces p'urhépecha. In Franco Mendoza [ca. 1541] 2000, 695–726.
Martín del Campo, Marisol. 1996. Con joyas, uñas y cabellos: Zincicha Tangaxoan. *Arqueología Mexicana* 4 (19):72.
Martínez Baracs, Rodrigo. 1989. La conquista; Los inicios de la colonización; Reorientaciones. In Florescano 1989, vol. 2, 5–122.
———. 1997. El Vocabulario en lengua de Mechuacán (1559) de fray Maturino Gilberti como fuente de información histórica. In Paredes Martínez 1997a, 67–162.
Mateos Higuera, Salvador. 1947. La pictografía tarasca. In *El occidente de México: Cuarta reunión de mesa redonda,* 160–74. Mexico City: Sociedad Mexicana de Antropología.
———. 1948. Códice de Arantza. *Tlalocan* 2 (4):374–75.
Maxwell, Judith M., and Craig A. Hanson. 1992. *Of the manners of speaking that the old ones had: The metaphors of Andrés de Olmos in the TULAL manuscript 'Arte para aprender la lengua mexicana.'* Salt Lake City: Univ. of Utah Press.
McMurtrie, Douglas C. [1943] 1989. *The book: The story of printing and bookmaking.* New York: Dorset Press.
Mendieta, Gerónimo de. [1573–1604] 1997. *Historia eclesiástica indiana.* Edited by Antonio Rubial García. 2 vols. Cien de México. Mexico City: CNCA.
Michelet, Dominique. 1989. Histoire, mythe et apologue: Notes de lecture sur la seconde partie de la Relación [...] de Michoacán. In *Enquêtes sur l'Amérique moyenne: Mélanges offerts à Guy Stresser-Péan,* edited by Dominique Michelet, 105–13. Études Mésoaméricaines, 16. Mexico City: INAH, CEMCA, CNCA.
———. 1995. La zona occidental en el Posclásico. In *Historia antigua de México,* vol. 3, edited by Linda Manzanilla and Leonardo López Luján, 153–88. Mexico City: INAH, UNAM, Miguel Angel Porrúa.
———. 1996. El origen del reino tarasco protohistórico: La cuenca de Zacapu. *Arqueología Mexicana* 4 (19):24–27.
———, and Marie-Charlotte Arnauld. 1991. Les migrations postclassiques au Michoacán et au Guatemala: Problèmes et perspectives. In *Vingt études sur le*

Mexique et le Guatemala réunies à la mémoire de Nicole Percheron, edited by Alain Breton et al., 67–92. Collection Hespérides. Toulouse: Presses Universitaires du Mirail.

Mignolo, Walter D. 1982. Cartas, crónicas y relaciones del descubrimiento y la conquista. In *Historia de la literatura hispanoamericana*, vol. 1, Época colonial, edited by Luis Íñigo Madrigal, 57–116. Madrid: Ediciones Cátedra.

———. 1989. Literacy and colonization. In *1492–1992: Re/discovering colonial writing*, edited by René Jara and Nicholas Spadaccini, 51–96. Hispanic Issues, 4. Minneapolis: Univ. of Minnesota Press.

———. 1995. *The darker side of the Renaissance.* Ann Arbor: Univ. of Michigan Press.

Miguélez, P. 1917. *Catálogo de los códices españoles de la Biblioteca de El Escorial.* Vol. 1, Relaciones históricas. Madrid: Imprenta Helénica.

Miranda Godínez, Francisco. 1984. Vasco de Quiroga, artífice humanista de la provincia de Michoacán. In Herrejón Peredo 1984, 131–49.

———. 2001. Las láminas de la "Relación de Michoacán." In Escobar Olmedo [ca. 1541] 2001, 173–203.

———, ed. [ca. 1541] 1980. La *Relación de Michoacán*. Estudios Michoacanos, 5. Morelia: Fímax Publicistas. Reprinted, without illustrations, 1988. Mexico City: SEP. Abridged version, 1997. Mexico City: FCE.

———, ed. 1981. *La cultura purhé: II coloquio de antropología e historia regionales.* Zamora: COLMICH, FONAPAS Michoacán.

———, ed. [1908] 2000. Los antiguos habitantes de Michoacán, by Eduard Seler. In Franco Mendoza [ca. 1541] 2000, 139–233.

———, ed. [ca. 1541] 2001. *Monumentos literarios del Michoacán prehispánico.* Nahuatzen: Ediciones palenque; Morelia: Morevallado Editores. Anthologized, without notes, in Escobar Olmedo [ca. 1541] 2001, 101–41.

———, and Gabriela Briseño, eds. 1984. *Vasco de Quiroga: Educador de adultos.* Retablo de Papel, 11. Pátzcuaro: CREFAL, COLMICH.

Mochizuki, Yoshirô, trans. [ca. 1541] 1987. *Chichimeka shinwa: Michoakan hôkokusho.* Tokyo: Shinchôsha.

Monzón García, Cristina, and Andrew Roth Seneff. 1999. Referentes religiosos en el siglo XVI: Acuñaciones y expresiones en lengua tarasca. In *La lengua de la cristianización en Latinoamérica: Catequización e instrucción en lenguas amerindias*, edited by Sabine Dedenbach-Salazar and Lindsey Crickmay, 169–81. Bonn Americanist Studies, 32. CIASE Occasional Papers, no. 29. Bonn: Verlag Anton Saurwein.

Muñoz, Diego. [ca. 1583] 1965. *Descripción de la provincia de San Pedro y San Pablo de Michoacán.* Serie de Historia, 8. Guadalajara: Instituto Jalisciense de Antropología e Historia.

Murray, David. 1991. *Forked tongues: Speech, writing and representation in North American Indian texts.* Bloomington: Indiana Univ. Press.

Nader, Helen. 1979. *The Mendoza family in the Spanish Renaissance 1350–1550.* New Brunswick: Rutgers Univ. Press.

Nava L., E. Fernando. 1999. *El campo semántico del sonido musical p'urhépecha*. Colección científica, 388. Mexico City: INAH.

Navarrete Pellicer, Sergio. 1997. Tecnología agrícola tarasca del siglo XVI. In Paredes Martínez 1997b, 74–142.

Nicolau d'Olwer, Luis. [1952] 1987. *Fray Bernardino de Sahagún*. Translated by Mauricio J. Mixco. Salt Lake City: Univ. of Utah Press.

Olmos, Andrés de. [1547] 1985. *Arte de la lengua mexicana y vocabulario*. Edited by René Acuña and Thelma Sullivan. Gramáticas y diccionarios, 4. Mexico City: UNAM-IIF.

Orozco y Berra, Manuel. [1880] 1960. *Historia antigua y de la conquista de México*. Edited by Angel María Garibay K. and Miguel León-Portilla. Biblioteca Porrúa, 18. Mexico City: Editorial Porrúa.

Ortiz, Fernando. [1940] 1973. *Contrapunteo cubano del tabaco y el azúcar*. Barcelona: Ariel.

Oviedo y Valdés, Gonzalo Fernández de. [1537–48] 1959. *Historia general y natural de las Indias*, edited by Juan Pérez de Tudela Bueso. 5 vols. Biblioteca de Autores Españoles, 117–21. Madrid: Ediciones Atlas.

Pagden, Anthony. [1982] 1986. *The fall of natural man: The American Indian and the origins of comparative ethnology*. Cambridge: Cambridge Univ. Press.

Panofsky, Erwin. 1955. *Meaning in the visual arts: Papers in and on art history*. Garden City, N.Y.: Doubleday.

Paredes Martínez, Carlos. 1996. La estratificación social de los tarascos: Cazonci, petámuti, angatácuri, purhepecha. *Arqueología Mexicana* 4 (19):34–39.

———, ed. 1997a. *Lengua y etnohistoria purépecha: Homenaje a Benedict Warren*. Encuentros, 2. Morelia: UMSNH-IIH; Mexico City: CIESAS.

———, ed. 1997b. *Historia y sociedad: Ensayos del seminario de historia colonial de Michoacán*. Encuentros, 3. Morelia: UMSNH-IIH; Mexico City: CIESAS.

Paso y Troncoso, Francisco del. [1887] 1888. Calendario de los tarascos. In León [1888–91] 1968, 85–96.

———. ed. 1939–42. *Epistolario de Nueva España, 1505–1818*. Biblioteca Historia Mexicana de Obras Inéditas. 2d series. 16 vols. Mexico City: Librería Robredo de J. Porrúa.

———, ed. 1953. *Tratado de las idolatrías, supersticiones, dioses, ritos, hechicerías y otras costumbres gentílicas de las razas aborígenes de México*. 2d ed. Biblioteca Navarro de Historia y Cultura Mexicana, 10. Mexico City: Ediciones Fuente Cultural.

Patrana Flores, Miguel. 1999. Los presagios de la conquista como forma de conciencia histórica. In Skinfill Nogal and Carrillo Cázares 1999, 127–42.

Payno, Manuel. 1869. Ensayo de una historia de Michoacán. *Boletín de la Sociedad Mexicana de Geografía y Estadística*, 2d series, 1: 619–32.

Paz, Octavio. [1950] 1984. *El laberinto de la soledad*. Colección Popular, 107. Mexico City: FCE.

Pease, Franklin. 1990. *Inka y kuraka: Relaciones de poder y representación histórica*. Working Papers, 8. College Park: Univ. of Maryland.

Pérez Bustamante, C. 1928. *Don Antonio de Mendoza.* Anales, 3. Santiago, Spain: Univ. de Santiago.

Pérez Martínez, Herón. 2000. El arte literario de la "Relación de Michoacán." In Franco Mendoza [ca. 1541] 2000, 79–105.

Phelan, John Leddy. [1956] 1970. *The millenial kingdom of the Franciscans in the New World.* 2d rev. ed. Berkeley and Los Angeles: Univ. of California Press.

Plancarte y Navarrete, Francisco. 1889. Los tecos. In León [1888–91] 1968, 16–26.

Pollard, Helen Perlstein. 1980. Central places and cities: A consideration of the protohistoric Tarascan state. *American Antiquity* 45 (4):677–96.

———. 1982. Ecological variation and economic exchange in the Tarascan state. *American Ethnologist* 9 (2):250–68.

———. 1991. The construction of ideology in the emergence of the prehispanic Tarascan state. *Ancient Mesoamerica* 2:167–79.

———. 1993. *Taríacuri's legacy: The prehispanic Tarascan state.* The Civilization of the American Indian Series, 209. Norman: Univ. of Oklahoma Press.

———. 1994. Factores de desarrollo en la formación del estado tarasco. In Boehm de Lameiras 1994, 187–246.

———. 2000. Tarascans and their ancestors: Prehistory of Michoacán; Tarascan External Relations. Chs. 5–6 of *Greater Mesoamerica: The Archaeology of West and Northwest Mexico*, eds. Michael S. Foster and Shirley Gorenstein, 59–80. Salt Lake City: Univ. of Utah Press.

Rama, Angel. [1980] 1987. *Transculturación narrativa en América Latina.* 3d ed. Mexico City: Siglo Veintiuno Editores.

Ramírez, Francisco. [1585] 1959. Relación sobre la residencia de Michoacán (Pátzcuaro). In *Monumenta mexicana*, 1581–1585, vol. 2, edited by Félix Zubillaga, 474–538. Rome: n.p.

Ramírez, José F., ed. [1532] 1847. Proceso contra Nuño de Guzmán. In *Proceso de residencia contra Pedro de Alvarado*, 259–76. Mexico City: n.p.

Rea, Alonso de la. [1643] 1996. *Crónica de la orden de N. Seráfico P. S. Francisco, provincia de S. Pedro y S. Pablo de Mechoacan en la Nueva España.* Edited by Patricia Escandón. Zamora: COLMICH, Fideicomiso Teixidor.

Recopilación de leyes de los reynos de las Indias. [1791] 1943. 4th ed. 3 vols. Madrid: Gráficas Ultra.

Reyes García, Luis. 1997. Dioses y escritura pictográfica: Lectura e interpretación. *Arqueología Mexicana* 4 (23):24–33.

Reyman, Jonathan E., ed. *The Gran Chichimeca: Essays on the archaeology and ethnohistory of northern Mesoamerica.* Worldwide Archaeology, 12. Brookfield, Vt.: Avebury Ashgate Publishing Company.

Ricard, Robert. [1933] 1982. *The spiritual conquest of Mexico: An essay on the apostolate and evangelizing methods of the mendicant orders in New Spain, 1523–1572.* Translated by Lesley Byrd Simpson. Berkeley and Los Angeles: Univ. of California Press.

Robertson, Donald. [1959] 1994. *Mexican manuscript painting of the early colonial period: The metropolitan schools.* Norman: Univ. of Oklahoma Press.

Romero Flores, Jesús. 1940. Tzimtzicha-Tangaxuan, el último cazonci michoacano. *Universidad Michoacana* 17 (3):55–63.

———. 1946. *Historia de Michoacán*. Mexico City: Imprenta Claridad.

———. [1971] 1978. *Michoacán histórico y legendario*. 2d ed. Mexico City: B. Costa-Amic Editor.

Roskamp, Hans. 1998a. *La historiografía indígena de Michoacán: El Lienzo de Jucutácato y los Títulos de Carapán*. CNWS Publications, 72. Leiden, The Netherlands: Research School CNWS, School of Asian, African, and Amerindian Studies.

———. 1998b. Pablo Beaumont y el Códice de Tzintzuntzan: Documento pictórico de Michoacán. *Tzintzun* 27:7–44.

———. 2000. El carari indígena y las láminas de la "Relación de Michoacán." In Franco Mendoza [ca. 1541] 2000, 235–64.

Ruiz, Eduardo. [1891–1900] 1971. *Michoacán: Paisajes, tradiciones y leyendas*. 2d ed. Documentos y Testimonios, 1. Morelia: Balsal Editores.

Sack, Robert David. 1986. *Human territoriality: Its theory and history*. Cambridge Studies in Historical Geography, 7. Cambridge: Cambridge Univ. Press.

Sahagún, Bernardino de. [1577–80] 1950–82. *General history of the things of New Spain: Florentine codex*. Edited and translated by Arthur Anderson and Charles Dibble. 13 vols. Monographs of The School of American Research, no. 14, pt. 1–13. Salt Lake City: Univ. of Utah Press.

Salas León, Antonio. [1941] 1956. *Pátzcuaro: Cosas de antaño y de hogaño*. 2d ed. Morelia: Talleres de la Editorial "Cantera."

Salazar Simarro, Nuria. 2000. Tres obras ilustradas del siglo XVI. In *Fray Bernardino de Sahagún y su tiempo*, 299–320. Jesús Paniagua Pérez and María Isabel Viforcos Marinas, eds. León: Universidad de León and Instituto Leonés de Cultura.

Sánchez Díaz, Gerardo. 1981. Tenencia de la tierra en el Michoacán prehispánica. In Miranda Godínez 1981, 201–209.

———. 1997. El Dr. J. Benedict Warren y la renovación de los estudios históricos sobre el Michoacán colonial. In Paredes Martínez 1997a, 15–23.

———. 2001. Las ediciones de la "Relación de Michoacán" y su impacto historiográfico. In Escobar Olmedo [ca. 1541] 2001, 205–27.

Sandstrom, Alan R., and Pamela Effrein Sandstrom. 1986. *Traditional papermaking and paper cult figures of Mexico*. Norman: Univ. of Oklahoma Press.

Scholes, France V., and Eleanor B. Adams. [1530] 1952. *Proceso contra Tzintzicha Tangaxoan, el caltzontzin*. Mexico City: Porrúa y Obregón.

Schöndube B., Otto. 1996. Los tarascos: pueblo rival de los mexicas. *Arqueología Mexicana* 4 (19):14–21.

Sebastián, Santiago. 1992. *Iconografía del indio americano*. Madrid: Ediciones Tuero.

Seler, Eduard. [1908] 1993. The ancient inhabitants of the Michuacan region. In *Collected works in Mesoamerican linguistics and archaeology*. 2d ed. Vol. 4, edited by J. Eric S. Thompson and Francis B. Richardson, translated by J. Eric S. Thompson, 3–66. Culver City, Calif.: Labyrinthos. Trans. into Spanish by Erika Kriegger, edited and with commentary by Miranda Godínez, in Franco Mendoza 2000, 139–233.

Sepúlveda y H., María Teresa. 1974. *Los cargos políticos y religiosos en la región del lago de Pátzcuaro*. Colección Científica, 19. Mexico City: INAH.

———. 1988. *La medicina entre los purépecha prehispánicos*. Serie Antropológica, 94. Mexico City: UNAM-IIA.

Skinfill Nogal, Bárbara, and Alberto Carrillo Cázares, eds. 1999. *Estudios michoacanos VIII*. Zamora: COLMICH; Morelia: IMC.

Spalding, Karen. 1984. *Huarochirí: An Andean society under Inca and Spanish rule*. Stanford: Stanford Univ. Press.

Spenser, Daniela, and Bradley A. Levinson. 1999. Linking state and society in discourse and action: Political and cultural studies of the Cárdenas era in Mexico. *Latin American Research Review* 34 (2):227–45.

Šprajc, Ivan. 1996. *Venus, lluvia y maíz: Simbolismo y astronomía en la cosmovisión mesoamericana*. Colección científica; Serie Arqueología, 318. Mexico City: INAH.

Stam, Robert. 1989. *Subversive pleasures: Bakhtin, cultural criticism, and film*. Baltimore: Johns Hopkins Univ. Press.

Stone, Cynthia L. 1992. A fragile coalition: The "Relación de Michoacán" and the compiling of indigenous traditions in sixteenth-century Mexico. Ph.D. diss., Univ. of Michigan.

———. 1994. Rewriting indigenous traditions: The burial ceremony of the cazonci. *Colonial Latin American Review* 3 (1–2):87–114.

———. 1995. Multiple authorship in a colonial Spanish-American text. In *Hacia un nuevo canon literario: Actas del XII Congreso de literatura latinoamericana*, edited by JoAnne Engelbert, 43–53. The Inca Garcilaso Series, 603. Hanover, N.H.: Ediciones del Norte.

Swadesh, Mauricio. 1969. *Elementos del tarasco antiguo*. Serie Antropología, 11. Mexico City: UNAM-IIH.

Tedlock, Dennis. 1983. *The spoken word and the work of interpretation*. Philadelphia: Univ. of Pennsylvania Press.

———. 1994. *Breath on the mirror: Mythic voices and visions of the living Maya*. San Francisco: Harper.

———, trans. 1985. *Popol vuh: The Mayan book of the dawn of life*. New York: Simon and Schuster.

Tello, Antonio. [ca. 1650] 1968. *Crónica miscelánea de la sancta provincia de Xalisco*. 3 vols. Serie de Historia, 9–11. Guadalajara: Univ. de Guadalajara, Gobierno del Estado.

Todorov, Tzvetan. [1982] 1984. *The conquest of America: The question of the other*. Translated by Richard Howard. New York: Harper and Row.

Toro, Alfonso. [1930] 1968. Las plantas sagradas de los aztecas y su influencia sobre el arte precortesiano. *Proceedings of the twenty-third International Congress of Americanists*, 101–21. Nendeln/Liechtenstein: Kraus Reprint.

Torquemada, Juan de. [1615] 1969. *Monarquía indiana*. Edited by Miguel León-Portilla. Facsimile of 1723 ed. 3 vols. Biblioteca Porrúa, 41–43. Mexico City: Editorial Porrúa.

Toussaint, Manuel. 1937. La "Relación de Michoacán": Su importancia artística. *Anales del Instituto de Investigaciones Históricas*, vol. 1. Mexico City: UNAM.

———. 1942. *Pátzcuaro*. Mexico City: UNAM-IIE.

Tovar, Juan de. [1583–87] 1987. Relación del origen de los indios. In *Origen de los mexicanos*, ed. Germán Vázquez, 33–195. Madrid: Historia 16.

Tudela de la Orden, José. 1952. Notas de etnología mejicana: Las clases sociales entre los tarascos. *Revista internacional de sociología*, vol. 10. Madrid.

———. ed. [ca. 1541] 1956. *Relación de las ceremonias y ritos y población y gobierno de los indios de la provincia de Michoacán*. Facsimile. Madrid: Aguilar. Reprinted, without notes, 1977. Morelia: Balsal Editores.

Uspensky, B. A. [1970] 1973. *A poetics of composition: The structure of the artistic text and typology of a compositional form*. Translated by Valentina Zavarin and Susan Wittig. Berkeley and Los Angeles: Univ. of California Press.

———. [1973] 1975. 'Left' and 'right' in icon painting. *Semiotica* 13:33–39.

———. 1976. The language of ancient painting. *Dispositio* 1 (3):219–46.

Veracruz, Alonso de la. 1556. *Speculum coniugiorum*. Mexico City: Juan Pablos. Scheide Library. Princeton University.

———. [1556] 1988. Textos del "Speculum coniugiorum" (o "Espejo de casamientos"). Translated by A. M. Garza and S. Castro. In *Antología de Fray Alonso de la Veracruz*, edited by Mauricio Beuchot, 277–312. Biblioteca Nicolaita de Filósofos Michoacanos, 1. Morelia: UMSNH.

Verástique, Bernardino. 2000. *Michoacán and Eden: Vasco de Quiroga and the evangelization of western Mexico*. Austin: Univ. of Texas Press.

Versluis, Vincent A. 1994. The iconography of the protohistoric Tarascan state of Western Mexico: The material expression of the state ideology. M.A. thesis, Michigan State Univ.

Warren, J. Benedict. 1963. *Vasco de Quiroga and his pueblo-hospitals of Santa Fe*. Washington, D.C.: Academy of American Franciscan History.

——— [1963] 1977. *Vasco de Quiroga y sus hospitales pueblo de Santa Fe*. Translated by Agustín García Alcaraz. Morelia: UMSNH.

———. 1971. Fray Jerónimo de Alcalá: Author of the "Relación de Michoacán"? *The Americas* 27 (3):307–26. Spanish translation with revisions in Franco Mendoza [ca. 1541] 2000, 37–56. Abbreviated version in Spanish in Escobar Olmedo [ca. 1541] 2001, 89–100.

———. 1977. *La conquista de Michoacán 1521–1530*. Translated by Agustín García Alcaraz. Estudios Michoacanos, 6. Morelia: Fímax Publicistas.

———. 1984. Los estudios lingüísticos en Michoacán en el siglo XVI: Una expresión del humanismo cristiano. In Herrejón Peredo 1984, 113–24.

———. 1985. *The conquest of Michoacán: The Spanish domination of the Tarascan kingdom in western Mexico, 1521–1530*. Norman: Univ. of Oklahoma Press.

———. 1997. Los estudios de la lengua de Michoacán: Cuestiones para investigación. In Paredes Martínez 1997a, 27–39.

———, ed. 1991. *Diccionario grande de la lengua de Michoacan por autor o autores desconocidos.* 2 vols. Fuentes de la Lengua Tarasca o Purépecha, 4–5. Morelia: Fímax Publicistas.

———, ed. 1994. Proceso contra Pedro de Arellano (1532–40). In Boehm de Lameiras 1994, 334–441.

———, and Patricia S. Warren. 1996. La evangelización de Michoacán: Las huellas de "Tata Vasco." *Arqueología Mexicana* 4 (19):40–45.

Weigand, Phil C. 1994. 'Rerum novarum': El mito de Mexcaltitán como Aztlán. In *Arqueología del occidente de México: Nuevas aportaciones,* edited by Eduardo Williams and Robert Novella, 363–81. Zamora: COLMICH.

Westheim, Paul. [1950] 1965. *The art of ancient Mexico.* Translated by Ursula Bernard. Garden City: Anchor Books.

White, Hayden. 1973. *Metahistory: The historical imagination in nineteenth-century Europe.* Baltimore: Johns Hopkins Univ. Press.

———. 1978. *Tropics of discourse: Essays in cultural criticism.* Baltimore: Johns Hopkins Univ. Press.

Wilkerson, Jeffrey K. 1974. The ethnographic works of Andrés de Olmos. In *Sixteenth-century Mexico: The work of Sahagún,* edited by Munro S. Edmonson, 27–77. School of American Research Advanced Seminar series. Albuquerque: Univ. of New Mexico Press.

Williams, Eduardo, and Robert Novella, eds. 1994. *Arqueología del occidente de México: Nuevas aportaciones.* Zamora: COLMICH.

———, and Phil C. Weigand, eds. 1995. *Arqueología del occidente y norte de México.* Zamora: COLMICH.

Zantwijk, R. A. M. van. [1965] 1967. *Servants of the saints: The social and cultural identity of a Tarascan community in Mexico.* Assen: Van Gorcum and Comp.

———. 1985. *The Aztec arrangement: The social history of pre-Spanish Mexico.* The Civilization of the American Indian Series, 167. Norman: Univ. of Oklahoma Press.

Zarco Cuevas, Julián. 1924–29. *Catálogo de los manuscritos castellanos de la Real Biblioteca de El Escorial.* 3 vols. Madrid: n.p.

Zavala, Silvio. [1937] 1965. La Utopía de Tomás Moro en la Nueva España. In *Recuerdo de Vasco de Quiroga,* 9–40. Mexico City: Editorial Porrúa.

———. [1941] 1995. *Ideario de Vasco de Quiroga.* 2d ed. Mexico City: COLMEX, Colegio Nacional.

Index

Note: All italicized words are of Purépecha origin unless otherwise noted.

Acanysante, Don Alonso de Ávalos (lord of Nahuatlatos), 149–50, 163, 278n.79, 288n.43
Acazitli, Don Francisco de Sandoval (lord of Chalco), 26
Achá (lord, noble; pl. *acháecha*). *See* Nobles, categories of indigenous
Achuri hirepe. *See* Gods and goddesses of Michoacán
Acosta, Father José de, 53, 245n.38
Adorno, Rolena, 90
Albornoz, Rodrigo de, 162, 282n.19, 283n.22
Alcalá, Fray Jerónimo de, 3, 31, 43, 229n.1, 234n.19, 238n.4, 245n.35, 247n.4, 248n.10, 284n.28. *See also* Escorial manuscript C.IV.5, friar-compiler of
Alcalá de Henares. *See* Spain, cities of
Alférez (Castilian, standard bearer). *See* Colonial authorities
Alguacil mayor (Castilian, chief law enforcement officer). *See* Colonial authorities
Allepetl (Nahuatl, town, community). *See* Territoriality, indigenous conceptions of
Alvarado, Pedro de, 31
Anahuac, towns of: Azcapotzalco, 47; Chalco, 26; Coyoacan, 290n.58; Huexotzinco, 79; México-Tenochtitlan, 17–19, 27, 32, 157, 162, 164, 166–68, 179, 185, 243n.28, 248n.11, 249n.14, 285n.30, 287n.40, 290n.58; Quauhtitlan, 47; Teotihuacan, 17, 115, 234n.17, 236n.26; Tepepulco, 47, 236n.26, 258n.16; Texcoco, 19, 249n.14; Tlatelolco, 19, 47; Tula, 115, 236n.26, 258n.16; Xochimilco, 47. *See also* Indigenous groups
Anales (Castilian, annals): Tarecuato, 229n.1; Tlatelolco, 155, 280n.4. *See also* Writing, Mesoamerican
Anapu (community, native of). *See* Territoriality, indigenous conceptions of
Angámecha (government officials), 23–24, 67–71, 84, 98, 109–10, 223, 254n.42, 259n.22, 282n.16; *angátacuri*, 179–81, 223; *atari*, 223, 254n.42; *cacari*, 68, 223; *carari*, 6, 13, 15, 22–25, 42, 46, 56, 59, 65, 74–110, 156, 223, 248n.8, 255–66; *cheréng̃uequauri*, 69, 138, 223; *curúhapindi*, 224, 253n.36; *cuzuri*, 68, 224; *ocánbeti*, 68, 72, 130–31, 224; *paricuti*, 68, 224; *pirúuaqua uándari*, 23–24, 68, 224; *pucúriquari*, 68, 225; *quengue*, 225; *tesorero mayor*, 70; *uaruri*, 69, 225; *uaxánoti*, 68, 76, 225, 248n.8, 256n.4; *urani atari*, 68, 226; *usquarecuri*, 69–70, 226. *See also* Government, indigenous forms of; Nobles, categories of indigenous; Tribute collection
Angámequa (lip plug). *See* Authority, indigenous symbols of. *See also* Escorial manuscript C.IV.5, vestimentary code in
Angámucuracha (mountain deities). *See* Gods and goddesses of Michoacán
Angándipenstani (great grandfather, founder of lineage). *See* Kinship terms in Purépecha
Angátacuri (pl. *angátacucha*) (governor). *See* Angámecha; Nobles, categories of indigenous. *See also* Camáhchacupeti; Uandátsperi
Angáuatangari (prince or captain). *See* Nobles, categories of indigenous
Anghiera, Pietro Martire d', 281n.6
Apaches. *See* Indigenous groups
Aramen (father of Tangáxoan I), 82, 123–24, 127, 271n.31
Artes y vocabularios (Castilian, grammars and dictionaries), 229n.1, 236–37n.28, 238n.7, 243n.27, 249n.17
Atahualpa (Inca lord), 155
Atamataho. *See* Lake Pátzcuaro Basin, forests of
Atari (overseer of alcoholic beverages). *See* Angámecha
Auándaro (sky). *See* Territoriality, indigenous conceptions of. *See also* Escorial manuscript C.IV.5, spatiotemporal organization of drawings
Audiencia: First, 72, 157, 162, 172; Second, 19, 148, 161, 164, 169, 283n.24, 290n.57
Augustine, Saint, 52
Auícanime. *See* Gods and goddesses of Michoacán
Auita (paternal uncle). *See* Kinship terms in Purépecha

Authority, indigenous symbols of: *angámequa*, 24, 84, 93, 97–98, 130, 157, 174, 223, 259n.22, 274n.48; *huarache*, 174, 224; *petate*, 23, 27, 241n.18; *tsiríquarequa*, 116–17, 225, 268nn.14,16; *uanduqua*, 122, 154, 225, 270nn.26,28; *uaxántsiqua*, 24, 61, 83–85, 103, 106, 130, 226, 252nn.33–35
Áxame (pl. *áxamencha*) (sacrificer). *See* Priests, categories of indigenous
Aztecs (from Nahuatl, *azteca*). *See* Indigenous groups
Aztlan, 268n.12, 275n.53

Bacon, Francis, 16, 238n.1
Barthes, Roland, 12, 43–44, 246n.1
Bartolomé, Don (son of Don Pedro Cuiníarángari), 165, 180, 284n.27
Basalenque, Fray Diego, 234n.19
Baudot, Georges, 43, 73, 246n.44
Beaumont, Fray Pablo, 16, 24, 39–40, 76–77, 87, 229n.1, 245nn.37,39, 256nn.5,6, 276n.60, 277n.74, 279n.87. *See also* Cuiní
Benavente, Fray Toribio de ("Motolinía"), 12, 19, 22, 39–41, 230n.5, 236n.28, 238nn.5,6, 245n.38, 246n.44, 251n.29
Betanzos, Juan de, 33, 244n.30
Bobadilla, Fray Francisco de, 238n.4
Bolonia, Fray Francisco de, 288n.43
Boone, Elizabeth Hill, 78–79, 257n.11
Bry, Theodore de, 168
Burgos. *See* Spain, cities of
Burial ceremonies, indigenous, 23, 39, 101, 122, 174, 246n.43, 255n.45

Caballeros tecles (colonial order of indigenous knights), 32
Cacari (pl. *cacacha*) (stonemason, sculptor). *See Angámecha*
Cacique (Taino, lord). *See* Nobles, categories of indigenous
Caheri uapánscuaro (Caheri upanscuaro). *See* Festivals of Michoacán, traditional
Cahuleu (Mayan, sky-earth). *See* Territoriality, indigenous conceptions of
Calendar of Michoacán, traditional, 234n.18
Calmecac (Nahuatl, school for future priests and rulers), 74
Caltzontzin. *See* Nobles, categories of indigenous. *See also* Tzintzicha Tangáxoar
Camáhchacupeti (governor). *See* Nobles, categories of indigenous.
Camejan (priest of Xarátanga), 141. *See also* Omens, of snake; Lake Pátzcuaro Basin, peoples of
Cando (lord of Curínguaro), 105
Capitán general (Castilian, captain general). *See* Nobles, categories of indigenous
Caracha capacha (regional administrators). *See* Nobles, categories of indigenous
Carani (to write, to paint), 77, 223. *See also* Writing, Mesoamerican

Carari (pl. *caracha* or *carariecha*) (scribe-painter). *See* Angámecha
Cardenal, Ernesto, 74, 89, 255n.1
Cárdenas, Lázaro, 8, 153, 234n.17
Carócomaco (lord of Queréquaro), 104, 265n.61
Caropu hopánsquaro. *See* Pátzcuaro, neighborhoods of
Cartero (Castilian, letter carrier), 76. *See also* Angámecha, *uaxánoti*
Casas, Fray Bartolomé de las, 15, 20, 40, 49, 152, 168–69, 245n.38, 249n.12, 251–52n.29
Caso y Andrade, Alfonso, 234n.18
Castañeda, Juan de Álvarez, 76
Castile. *See* Spain, regions of
Cazonci (supreme ruler). *See* Nobles, categories of indigenous. *See also* Tzintzicha Tangáxoan
Cedula, royal, 72, 240n.13
Certeau, Michel de, 136
Cervantes de Salazar, Francisco, 16, 33–34, 38, 244n.32, 245n.38, 281n.6, 287n.39
Chánshori (lord of Curínguaro), 80–81, 143
Charles III (king of Spain, 1759–88), 8
Charles V (holy Roman emperor 1519–58; king of Spain as Charles I, 1516–56), 7, 30, 40, 148–49, 159, 179, 231n.7, 238n.2, 251n.29, 254n.44, 284n.24, 286n.37
Cherénguequauri (maker of cotton war doublets). *See* Angámecha
Chichimecs (from Nahuatl, *chichimeca*). *See* Indigenous groups
Chupítani. *See* Council of elders
Cíbola, seven cities of, 26
Cihuacoatl. *See* Gods and goddesses of Anahuac; Nobles, categories of indigenous
Cihuateteo. *See* Gods and goddesses of Anahuac
Clergy: Augustinian friars, 12–13, 16, 34–37, 39, 237n.29, 246n.41; Dominican friars, 15, 20, 40, 49, 150, 237n.29, 246n.41; Franciscan friars, 3, 12–13, 16, 19, 39, 43–73, 125, 149, 151, 171, 229n.1, 231n.9, 232n.10, 237n.29, 245n.39, 246nn.40–44, 248n.10, 249n.17, 250n.23, 251nn.27,29, 255n.45, 279n.87; Jesuits, 12–13, 16, 19, 30, 37–39, 90, 237n.29, 246nn.41,42, 279n.86; rivalries between religious orders, 39, 41, 246n.41
Clézio, Jean Marie G. le, 9, 233n.14, 235n.23
Codices, 20, 74–75, 77, 82, 88–89, 95, 100, 255n.3; Bodley, 257n.8; Borbonicus, 257n.8; Borgia, 257n.8; Boturini, 79, 257n.8; Carapan, 256n.6, 265n.57; Chilchota, 256n.6; Colombino-Becker, 257n.8; Cospi, 257n.8; Cuara, 256n.6; Cuauhtitlan, 258n.16; Cutzio I and II, 256n.6; Dresden, 257n.8; Féjérvary-Mayer, 257n.8; Florentine, 47, 52–53, 97, 155, 237n.28, 247n.6, 280n.4; Grolier, 257n.8; Huapean, 256n.6;

Huitzilopochtli, 237n.28; Laud, 257n.8; Madrid, 257n.8; Mendoza (Mendocino), 32, 79, 97, 244n.30; Moctezuma, 257n.8; Nuttall, 96, 257n.8; Paris, 257n.8; Plancarte, 275n.54; Ramírez, 237n.28; Telleriano-Remensis, 237n.28; Tudela, 20, 236n.28, 238n.7; Tzintzuntzan, 24, 256nn.5,6, 277n.74; Vatican A, 237n.28; Vatican B, 257n.8; Vienna, 96, 257n.8. *See also* Writing, Mesoamerican

Colonial authorities: *alguacil mayor*, 163, 231n.9, 283n.20; *contador*, 162, 283n.20; *corregidor*, 30, 76; *Consejo de Indias*, 243n.28; *cronista mayor de Indias*, 17, 38, 238n.2, 245n.38; *oidor*, 55, 149, 164, 283n.24; *regidor*, 150, 248n.11, 283n.20; *teniente*, 283n.20; *tesorero*, 162, 283n.20; *visitador*, 162. *See also* Spanish crown

Commoners, indigenous. *See* Macegual; Purépecha

Conquests of, Spanish: Colima, 253n.27; Guiná, 31, 243n.29; Guatemala, 31; Honduras, 253n.37, 287n.41; Jalisco, 163, 243n.28, 253n.37; México-Tenochtitlan, 166–68, 185; Nochistlán, 31; Nueva Galicia, 66, 163, 173, 249n.16, 288n.43; Pánuco, 253n.37; Peru, 268n.11; Zacatula, 183

Consejo de Indias (Castilian, Council of the Indies). *See* Colonial authorities

Contador (Castilian, comptroller). *See* Colonial authorities

Coronado, Francisco Vásquez de, 26

Corona Núñez, José, 8, 97, 104, 113, 122, 157, 234n.17

Corregidor (Castilian, royal administrator). *See* Colonial authorities

Cortés, Hernán, 26, 32, 59, 61, 64, 154–55, 157, 160, 164, 166, 168, 170, 172–73, 179, 181, 283n.23, 287nn.39,41, 290n.57,58. *See also* Mendoza, Antonio de

Coruña, Fray Martín Jesús de la, 43, 246n.44, 247n.2, 288n.43, 290n.60

Cosmology, indigenous: 8, 10, 14, 37, 39, 83–85, 90–95, 98, 100, 110, 176–77, 235n.22, 255n.1, 258n.18, 260nn.26,30, 261n.35, 262n.43, 263–64nn.46,51, 265n.60, 269n.21, 272n.41, 279n.79; *axis mundi*, 90–91, 95, 98, 102, 108–10, 176–77, 264n.54; quincunx or quatrefoil (center and four directions), 90–94, 107–108, 260n.31, 261n.36, 262n.42, 263n.47, 264nn.53,56, 277n.68; right and left–hand sides, 91, 93–94, 98, 261n.33, 262nn.40,41, 264n.52. *See also* Territoriality, indigenous conceptions of

Council of elders: Chupítani,117, 126, 156, 167; Nuriuan, 117, 126, 156, 167, 269n.18; Tecaqua, 117, 126, 156, 167. *See also* Kinship terms in Purépecha, *curá*

Coyoacan (Cuyucan), 27, 241n.18. *See also* Anahuac, towns of; Ihuatzio

Cronista mayor de Indias (Castilian, royal chronicler of the Indies). *See* Colonial authorities

Cu (Mayan, pyramid), 27, 241n.18. *See also* Yácata

Cuauhtemoc (*tlatoani* of México-Tenochtitlan), 168, 184, 283n.23

Cueráuapari (mother of the gods). *See* Gods and goddesses of Michoacán

Cuicapicqui (Nahuatl, poet), 74

Cuingo. *See* Festivals of Michoacán, traditional

Cuiní (Beaumont informant), 17, 76, 256n.5

Cuiníarángari, Don Pedro (lord of Huréndetiecha; governor of city of Michoacán), 3, 9, 13–15, 24–25, 31, 42, 56–58, 70, 76, 86, 137, 139–40, 146–47, 150, 154–82, 230n.3, 233n.15, 253nn.37,39, 254n.44, 269n.18, 271n.35, 278n.78, 279n.82, 280n.3, 281n.14, 282–84nn.16,19,22–25, 27,28, 285n.31, 287–88nn.38,42–44, 289n.49,52–54, 290–91nn.58,61. *See also* Escorial manuscript C.IV.5, oral informants of; Panza, Pedro

Cuirípeti or *curízita* (pl. *cuirípecha*, *curízitacha*) (incense gatherer). *See* Priests, categories of indigenous

Cuirís quataro. *See* Pátzcuaro, neighborhoods of

Cuitlahuac (*tlatoani* of México-Tenochtitlan), 166

Cumiechucuaro (underworld). *See* Territoriality, indigenous conceptions of. *See also* Escorial manuscript C.IV.5, spatio-temporal organization of drawings

Cupanzieeri. *See* Gods and goddesses of Michoacán

Curá (pl. *curáecha* or *curacha*) (grandfather, elder). *See* Kinship terms in Purépecha. *See also* Council of elders; Escorial manuscript C.IV.5, oral informants of

Curátame I (successor of Uápeani I), 124, 143

Curátame II (son of Tariácuri), 82, 84, 87, 103, 120, 124–25, 134, 252nn.33–35

Curícaueri. *See* Gods and goddesses of Michoacán

Curínguaro (Coringuaro). *See* Lake Pátzcuaro Basin, towns of

Curípeti (pl. *curípecha*) (incense burner). *See* Priests, categories of indigenous

Curita caheri. *See* Gods and goddesses of Michoacán

Cúriti (pl. *cúritiecha*) (preacher, pastor). *See* Priests, categories of indigenous

Curúhapindi (overseer of game-birds). *See* Angámecha

Curúzetaro (map, sketch). *See* Territoriality, indigenous conceptions of. *See also* Escorial manuscript C.IV.5., spatiotemporal organization of drawings

316 INDEX

Cuycique, Gonzalo Juárez (lord of Nahuatlatos), 161–63, 283n.22, 288n.43

Cuzuri (curer of hides). *See Angámecha*

Díaz del Castillo, Bernal, 154, 281n.13

Diocese, transfer of, 113–14, 136–48, 150, 229n.1, 231n.9, 267n.9, 271n.30, 276n.60, 277nn.73,74, 278–79nn.77,82,84,85. *See also* Pátzcuaro; Tzintzuntzan

Durán, Fray Diego, 12, 19, 237n.28, 238n.6, 286n.37

Echérendo (surface of the earth). *See* Territoriality, indigenous conceptions of. *See also* Escorial manuscript C.IV.5., spatiotemporal organization of drawings

Equata cónsquaro. *See* Festivals of Michoacán, traditional

Enéani (Eneami). *See* Uacúsecha. *See also* Pátzcuaro

Eréndira (daughter of Timas), 171, 177

Escobar, Fray Matías de, 16, 35, 40

Escorial manuscript C.IV.5: bibliographic structure of, 21–25, 236n.24; binding of, 6, 38, 230n.5, 232n.14; correspondence between prose and pictures in, 22–25, 71, 77, 86, 237n.31, 239nn.9,11, 261n.37, 262n.43, 268n.16; dates of compilation of, 7, 21, 31–32, 231–32n.9, 280n.3; definition of moral values in, 12, 14, 26, 48–50, 55–62, 72, 79–81, 96, 103–107, 111–36, 143, 148–49, 171–73, 183–85, 245n.36, 247n.5, 251n.29, 252–53nn.33–35, 257n.13,14, 265n.60, 266n.68; dualism in, 91–102, 260n.29, 261nn.34,35, 262n.43; earlier drafts of, 17, 21–25, 33–40, 244–45nn.32,35; editions of, 8, 13, 18, 44, 230n.7, 232–34nn.12,14,15,17,18; friar–compiler of, 3, 7, 12–15, 43–73, 86, 165, 181, 184, 229nn.1,2, 231n.9, 233n.14, 237n.30, 239n.9, 245n.35, 246n.44, 247nn.2–6, 248nn.8,10, 250n.20–22, 251–52n.29, 253n.38, 254n.41, 257n.13, 270n.26, 273n.44, 274n.51, 276n.59, 284n.28; frontispiece of, 3, 7, 22, 46, 56–62, 86, 109, 117, 157, 238–39n.8, 248n.8; hands of, 6, 13, 21–24, 43–110, 230n.6, 238–39nn.8,11, 247n.5, 248n.8, 250n.21,22, 252n.30, 254n.41, 255n.2, 259n.23, 262n.43, 280n.3, 289n.55; missing parts of, 6, 21–22, 31, 37–38, 44; multiple authorship of, 3–4, 12–46, 73, 85, 247n.5; multiple perspectivism in, 41, 44, 87, 93, 101–102, 107, 259–60n.26; Nahuatl terminology in, 12, 27–30, 240–41n.18, 287n.41; nineteenth-century copies of, 7–8, 232n.11; oral informants of, 3, 9, 13–15, 18, 21–25, 30–31, 37, 42–46, 53–73, 76, 83, 86, 96, 98, 103, 105, 111–82, 185–186, 224, 233nn.14,15, 235n.23, 239nn.8,9,11, 245n.36, 246n.44, 247n.5, 250n.21, 268n.12, 269–70nn.17,18,22,24,26,28, 271n.35, 273–74nn.44,46,48, 275nn.52,53, 276n.59, 277nn.69, 74, 278n.77–79, 280n.3, 281n.14, 282–84nn.16,19,22– 25, 27,28, 285n.31, 287–88nn.38,42–44, 289nn.49,52–54, 290–91nn.58,61; references to cannibalism in, 65, 81, 93, 105; spatiotemporal organization of drawings, 14, 61–62, 78, 90–110, 252–53nn.33–35, 262n.43, 264n.52; translations of, 8, 232–33n.14, 235n.23; Tzintzuntzanist interpretation of, 124–26, 131, 139, 153, 271n.33, 278n.79; unrelated calendar wheel bound with, 16, 22, 40, 230n.5; use of color in, 86–87, 141, 143, 145, 174–75, 259n.24, 263n.47, 265n.56, 272n.41; use as a source, 13, 17–18, 21, 29, 33–42, 232n.13, 235–36n.24, 233n.15, 236n.24; vestimentary code in, 98, 111, 116, 134, 154, 157, 170–71, 174–75, 185, 288n.47; watermarks of, 230n.5, 232n.14, 239n.8; Western pictorial conventions in, 14, 46, 58, 86–87, 110, 259n.24, 260n.27

Escudos de armas (Castilian, coats of arms): 30, 256n.6, 277n.73

Espinosa, Fray Isidro Félix de, 39–40, 245nn.37,39

Estrada, Alonso de, 162, 166

Feather paintings, 76, 256n.7, 259n.24. *See also* Metaphorical systems related to; Writing, Mesoamerican

Festivals of Michoacán, traditional: Caheri uapánscuaro, 231n.9; Cuingo, 274n.48; Equata cónsquaro, 111, 116, 239n.11, 267n.3

Firstborn gods. *See* Gods and goddesses of Michoacán

Focher, Father Juan, 244n.34

Foucault, Michel, 12

Fourfold kingdom. *See* Territoriality, indigenous conceptions of, *iréchequa*

Four parts of the world. *See* Territoriality, indigenous conceptions of, *thámbengarani*

Francisco, Don: lord of Ihuatzio, 148, 250n.23, 278n.79; lord of Nahuatlatos, 162, 283n.22; lord of Xaráquaro, 149, 278n.79

Francis of Assisi, Saint, 19, 172

Franco Mendoza, Moisés, 223, 233n.14, 250n.21, 257n.13

Garcilaso de la Vega, El Inca, 35

Gilberti, Fray Maturino, 24, 30, 43, 77, 92, 116, 223, 234n.19, 236n.27, 242–43nn.25,27, 247n.2, 249n.13, 255n.2, 267nn.5–7, 270n.26, 272n.42, 281–82n.16

Godoy, Antonio de, 163, 231n.9, 288n.43

Gods and goddesses of Anahuac: Cihuacoatl (Quilaztli), 160; Cihuateteo, 266n.66;

INDEX 317

Ehecatl, 264n.53; Quetzalcoatl, 258n.16, 264n.53; Tetzalteotl, 278n.76, 287n.37; Tlaloque, 258n.16
Gods and goddesses of Michoacán: Achuri hirepe, 127, 272n.37; Angámucuracha, 103, 223, 265n.59; Auícanime, 105, 266nn.66,67; Celestial gods, 89, 92, 94, 96, 100, 170; Cloud goddesses, 272n.41; Cueráuaperi, 37, 97–98, 107, 145, 160, 258n.19, 263n.50, 266n.66, 272n.41; Cupanzieeri, 127, 158, 174, 272n.37, 288n.46; Curícaueri, 10, 65, 84, 92–93, 95–98, 104, 111, 113, 116–19, 123, 126, 128–31, 133, 135, 143–46, 165–66, 261–63nn.37,42,43,46, 269nn.21,22, 270n.25, 276n.65, 278n.77, 284n.29; Curita caheri, 108, 146; Earth goddess, 91, 94, 96, 99, 260n.30, 261n.33; Fifth heaven, gods of the, 131; Firstborn gods, 93–94; Huréndequauécara, 143–44; Manóuapa, 104–105, 265n.64; Miueque Ajeua, 138; Querenda angápeti, 104; Sea god, 91; Sirata táperi, 127, 272n.37; Tangáchuran, 128; Tharés úpeme, 242n.24; Tingárata, 138; Tirípeme, 107, 116–17, 119, 123, 129–30, 133, 145–47, 156, 272n.41; Tucúpachá, 38, 112, 225, 267n.6; Uacúsecha, 137–38; Uirámbanecha, 93–94; Underworld, gods of the, 92–94, 96; Xarátanga, 10, 65, 84, 92–93, 95–99, 104, 118, 121, 123, 135, 141–44, 146, 253n.36, 262nn.40,43, 263n.50, 269n.22, 270n.25, 277n.64; Zirita cherengue, 137–38
Gómara, Francisco López de, 40, 155, 278n.76, 287n.37
Government, indigenous forms of: continuation after Spanish conquest, 32, 55, 66–72, 179–81, 284n.28, 289n.55; craft specialties in Michoacán, 32, 67–71, 132, 151, 279n.87; *huatápera*, 279n.87; Mendoza's interest in, 22, 25–27, 32–33, 54, 68, 244n.30, 250n.18; succession in, 22, 61, 82–83, 117, 168, 252n.34, 268n.16, 269n.17, 290n.61. *See also* Angámecha
Gregory, Saint (the pope), 53–54
Guamán Poma de Ayala, Don Felipe, 90, 266n.71
Guatemala, Central America, 31, 77, 236n.26
Guayangareo (present-day Morelia). *See* Michoacán, towns of
Guevara, Antonio de, 164
Guzmán, Nuño Beltrán de, 55, 59, 64, 72, 82, 132, 157, 162–73, 167–68, 172–73, 181–82, 184, 251n.28, 253n.37, 255n.45, 280n.1, 283–86nn.25,28,33,37, 288n.43, 290nn.57,59. *See also* Mendoza, Antonio de

Hamúcutin (border, edge, shore). *See* Territoriality, indigenous conceptions of. *See also* Metaphorical systems related to, boundaries

Herrera y Tordesillas, Antonio de, 16, 38, 223, 242n.23, 245n.38, 275n.56, 286n.37
Hiquíngaje I (son of Taríacuri), 100, 103–104, 123–25, 129, 252n.35, 265n.58, 270nn.24,29
Hiquíngaje II (son of Hiquíngaje I), 124
Hiripan (son of Zétaco), 84, 100, 103–104, 123–24, 127, 129–30, 135, 147, 252n.35, 259n.21, 270nn.24,29, 271nn.31,32, 272n.36, 276n.65
Hirípati (pl. *hirípacha*). *See* Priests, categories of indigenous
Historias (Castilian, histories), 20, 38, 236–37n.28, 238n.7, 239–40n.12, 249nn.12,17, 285n.31
Hiuacha (lord of Taríaran), 285n.34
Huatsi (coyote), 28, 224, 281n.11
Hiyocan. *See* Lake Pátzcuaro Basin, peoples of. *See also* Indigenous groups, Chichimecs
Huarache (sandals). *See* Authority, indigenous symbols of. *See also* Escorial manuscript C.IV.5, vestimentary code in
Huatápera. *See* Government, indigenous forms of. *See also* Pueblo-hospital
Huastecs (from Nahuatl, *huaxteca*). *See* Indigenous groups
Huehuetlatolli (Nahuatl, ancient word), 20
Huemac (lord of Tula), 258n.16
Huexotzinco (Huejotzingo). *See* Anahuac, towns of
Huitziméngari: Don Antonio (son of Tzintzicha Tangáxoan), 13, 16, 34–37, 61, 117, 124, 158, 164–65, 179–80, 244nn.32,33, 245nn.35,36, 252n.31, 281n.11, 284n.27; Don Constantino (grandson of Tzintzicha Tangáxoan), 287n.40. *See also* Uitzume
Huitzitzilan (Uitzitzillan, Uchichila). *See* Tzintzuntzan
Huitzitziltzin, Don Francisco. *See* Tasháuaco
Huréndetiecha. *See* Lake Pátzcuaro Basin, peoples of
Huréndequauécara. *See* Gods and goddesses of Michoacán
Huresqua (lord of Curínguaro), 80

Ihuatzio (Coyoacan): association with Zacapu hireti lineage, 123, 270n.29. *See also* Lake Pátzcuaro Basin, towns of; Hiuatsi
Incas. *See* Indigenous groups
Indigenismo (Castilian, Nativism), 42
Indigenous groups: Apaches, 4, 258n.15, 260n.32; Arawaks, 27; Aztecs or Mexica, 9, 25, 74, 79, 115, 133, 138, 153, 160, 167–68, 171, 178, 184–85, 235n.22, 257n.14, 260n.28, 261n.32, 268n.12, 275n.53, 276n.62, 278n.76, 280n.5, 285–86nn.30,34; Chichimecs, 27–28, 80, 95–96, 98, 102, 106, 110, 115, 118, 122, 126, 128, 130, 134–35, 137–38, 142, 153, 160, 174, 177–78, 241n.18, 242n.24,

252n.30, 257–58n.14, 272n.38; Cuitlatecs, 27, 241n.18; Huastecs, 19, 256n.3; Incas, 33, 90, 268n.11; Matlatzincas, 27–28, 241n.18; Mayas, 10, 19, 27, 39, 79, 88, 126, 153, 238n.6, 255n.3, 257n.8, 258n.18, 260n.28, 261n.32, 264n.51, 266–67n.1, 273n.45; Mixtecs, 79, 88, 257nn.8,12; Moches, 258n.15; Nahuas, 8, 11–12, 17–20, 22, 25–31, 32, 39, 42, 47–48, 50–53, 74–79, 81, 88, 97, 114–15, 160, 169, 235nn.20,22, 240n.17, 255n.3, 257n.8, 260nn.29,30, 262n.41, 264nn.51,56, 266nn.65,66,68,72, 271n.32, 276n.63, 280n.4, 281nn.7,16, 282n.19, 286n.34; Otomis, 27, 241n.18; Pawnees, 255n.1; Toltecs, 236n.26; Zacatecs, 66, 249n.16, 276n.62. *See also* Lake Pátzcuaro Basin, peoples of

Irecha (king, sovereign). *See* Nobles, categories of indigenous

Iréchequa (fourfold kingdom). *See* Territoriality, indigenous conceptions of

Iréchequaro (royal court, palace) *See* Territoriality, indigenous conceptions of

Ireta (town, community). *See* Territoriality, indigenous conceptions of

Ireti (settler, dweller). *See* Territoriality, indigenous conceptions of

Iréticátame (Ticatame, Thicatame) (founder of Uacúsecha), 82–83, 86, 124, 258n.17. *See also* Kinship terms in Purépecha, angándipenstani

Itzíparámuco (Yziparamucu). *See* Lake Pátzcuaro Basin, towns of

Jerome, Saint, 3, 51, 156, 229n.2, 249n.15

Juárez, Gonzalo (Spanish deputy), 161. *See also* Cuycique, Gonzalo Juárez

Justice, indigenous forms of, 22, 24, 61, 76, 88, 96, 117, 183, 226, 245n.36, 248n.8, 249n.13, 252n.30, 268n.14, 288n.44

Kinship terms in Purépecha, 282n.17; *angándipenstani*, 259n.22; *auita*, 223, 259n.21; *curá*, 3, 24, 30, 37, 45–46, 55, 98, 103, 117–21, 139, 159, 182, 185, 224, 239n.9, 273n.47, 274n.48, 290n.61; *naná*, 271n.31; *tarascue*, 29, 185, 225, 242n.23, 291n.62; *tatá*, 152, 225; *tsitsí*, 244n.34; *uauá*, 244n.34; *uuache*, 225, 259n.21

Lagunas, Fray Juan Baptista de, 30, 39, 223, 234n.19, 236n.27, 243n.27

Lake Pátzcuaro Basin, forests of: Atamataho, 269n.22

Lake Pátzcuaro Basin, islands of: Pacandan, 5, 276n.66; Xanecho, 5; Xaráquaro, 5, 81, 96, 101, 118, 125, 135, 160, 186, 262n.43, 268n.12, 269n.17, 276n.62

Lake Pátzcuaro Basin, mountains of: Ihuatzio zarauacuyo, 144; Taríacaherio, 142–44; 276n.65; Taríacuri, 113, 267n.9, 276n.65; Xanóato hucazio, 146, 277n.75; Yaguaro, 269n.22

Lake Pátzcuaro Basin, peoples of: Hiyocan, 142; Huréndetiecha, 96–98, 101, 118, 122, 149, 157, 160, 180–81, 186, 224, 242n.21, 255n.44, 262n.43, 263n.44, 268n.12, 271n.33; Nahuatlatos, 28, 77, 149, 241n.18, 269nn.18,22, 271n.33, 285n.34, 289n.53; Purépecha, 29, 35, 66, 98, 115, 119, 129–32, 150, 166, 241–42nn.20,21, 252n.30, 261n.38, 263– 64nn.50,51, 285n.34, 289n.51; Uacúsecha, 10, 24, 62, 77, 80–83, 87, 92, 95–99, 101–102, 105–06, 112–13, 115, 119–20, 124–25, 127, 129, 131, 137, 142–47, 151–52, 156, 178–79, 181, 186, 241–42n.21, 255n.44, 257–58nn.14,17, 262nn.42,43, 268n.12, 269n.22, 271n.33, 273n.43, 275n.53, 285n.34, 289n.53; Uatárecha, 141, 143–44, 146, 269n.22, 276n.62

Lake Pátzcuaro Basin, towns of: Cuitzitan, 277n.71; Curínguaro (no longer in existence), 5, 80–81, 92, 102, 105–106, 118, 136, 143, 277n.75, 288n.47; Erongarícuaro, 2, 5; Huiramangaro, 144; Ihuatzio, 5, 28, 123, 147, 250n.23, 270n.29, 271n.33, 278n.77, 289n.51; Irámuco, 143; Itzíparámuco (no longer in existence), 5, 102, 104–105, 108, 120, 265n.65; Pareo, 5, 143; Pátzcuaro, 2, 5, 46, 111, 113–14, 123, 125, 135–39, 141, 144, 147– 51, 171, 177, 179, 229n.1, 231n.9, 248n.10, 250n.23, 267n.9, 270n.29, 271n.33, 273n.47, 275n.53, 276–79nn.60,61,73,74,78,82,85, 280n.3, 284n.29, 289n.51; Pichátaro, 143; Tarerio, 276n.63; Taríaran (no longer in existence), 5, 81, 144, 277n.71, 285n.34; Tzintzuntzan, 2, 5, 10, 24, 28, 48, 76, 113, 123–25, 136, 143–44, 147–48, 150–51, 154, 157, 175, 185, 229n.1, 231n.9, 235n.20, 243n.26, 244n.34, 248n.10, 256n.5, 267n.9, 269nn.19,22, 270n.29, 273n.43, 276–79nn.62,73,74,77,85, 280n.3, 285n.30, 289n.51; Uacapu, 144; Uayámeo, 5, 10, 113–14, 141–42, 144, 147, 269n.22, 278n.77; Uricho, 5, 144

Landa, Fray Diego de, 19, 39, 89, 238n.6, 260n.28

León, Nicolás, 8, 233n.15, 256n.6

León-Portilla, Miguel, 108, 155, 238n.4

Lienhard, Martín, 154, 158–59, 173, 280n.2

Lienzos (Castilian, painted sheets of cloth), 77, 256n.3; Arantza, 256n.6; Atapan, 256n.6; Carapan, 256n.6; Comachuen, 256n.6; Jucutacato, 256n.6, 265n.57; Nahuatzen, 256n.6; Pátzcuaro, 256n.6, 290n.60; Puácuaro, 256n.6. *See also* Writing, Mesoamerican

Littera annua (Latin, annual letter), 16, 37–38, 90, 290n.30

INDEX   319

López, Gerónimo, 248n.11
López Austin, Alfredo, 4, 9, 11, 85, 146, 223,
  235n.22

Macegual (from Nahuatl, *macehualli*, com-
  moner; pl. *macehualtin*), 29–30, 242n.25.
  See also Purépecha
Madrid. *See* Spain, cities of
Malinche, La, 15, 160–61, 281nn.13,15
Manóuapa. *See* Gods and goddesses of
  Michoacán
Marina, Doña. *See* Malinche, La
Marital customs, indigenous, 16, 23–25,
  35–37, 39, 65–66, 106–07, 117, 127, 132,
  134–135, 142, 179, 244–45nn.34–36,
  246n.42, 252n.30, 253–55nn.38–41,44,
  258n.20, 266nn.69–70, 274n.49, 282n.17,
  289n.52
Márquez Joaquín, Pedro, 223, 233n.14
Matlatzincas (from Nahuatl, *matlatzinca*). *See*
  Indigenous groups
Mayan (languages), 27, 241n.18
Mayas. *See* Indigenous groups
Memoriales (Castilian, rough drafts), 20,
  33–34, 39, 96, 230n.5, 237n.28, 239n.9,
  244n.32. *See also* Writing, Mesoamerican
Mendieta, Fray Jerónimo de, 20, 39–40,
  245n.39, 246n.44, 249n.14
Mendoza, Antonio de (first viceroy of New
  Spain), 3, 7, 17–18, 21, 25–27, 30–34, 37,
  40, 42, 45– 46, 54–62, 71–72, 86, 125, 140,
  156, 159, 181, 185, 231n.9, 238n.3,
  239n.12, 240nn.13–16, 243–44nn.28–31,
  245n.38, 249n.16, 251–54nn.27,28,31,37,44,
  271n.30, 277n.73; rivalry with Cortés and
  Guzmán, 26, 32, 41, 59–61, 64, 72, 181,
  240n.14, 243n.28, 251nn.27,28, 255n.45,
  290n.57
Mendoza, Diego Hurtado de (Renaissance
  poet), 26
Mendoza, Íñigo López de, Marqués de
  Santillana, 26
Mestizaje (Castilian, process of cultural
  mixing), 15, 187. *See also* Transculturation
Metaphorical systems related to: arrows,
  80–81, 87, 95, 104–105, 116, 128–29, 154,
  174; ashes, 38, 101, 132, 138, 255n.45,
  275n.56, 290n.59; ball game, 10, 126,
  261n.35, 262n.40, 272n.37; blood, 65, 75,
  87, 108, 156, 158, 170–71, 226, 260n.28,
  261n.38, 263nn.45,46, 270n.24, 277n.69,
  279nn.86,87; boundaries (caves, doors,
  fences, shores), 89, 102–104, 126,
  252–53n.35, 276n.63, 277n.69; clubs, 87,
  92–93, 100–101, 125, 252n.30, 264n.55,
  290n.60; crossroads, 104–109, 266n.66;
  dawning of a new sun, 127, 144, 146–47,
  149, 166, 174, 272n.37; debts, 129; deer,
  75, 98, 154, 158, 174, 252n.30, 255n.3,
  257n.14, 277nn.68,69, 288n.46; dreaming,
  83–84, 103–104, 121, 262n.40, 265n.61;
drunkenness, 103, 120, 134, 142, 148,
  252n.33, 274n.47; eagles, 89, 93–94,
  254n.42, 261n.38, 277n.69, 278n.76;
  feathers, 80, 116, 174, 258n.16, 262n.41,
  268nn.14,16, 277n.69, 288n.47; feeding,
  64, 84, 87, 93, 100–101, 108, 116–17,
  128–29, 143, 158, 167, 170, 258n.16,
  261nn.37,38, 265n.58, 266n.67, 274n.48,
  290n.60; female and male descent, 90,
  95–99, 103, 109–10, 118, 126, 135,
  161–62, 186, 282n.17, 274n.49; fire, 65,
  87, 95–97, 100, 186, 258n.17, 259n.21,
  262n.42, 266n.72, 277n.68; fishing, 96–98,
  141–42, 157, 160, 186, 276n.62; foam,
  143, 180, 276n.66, 289n.53; footprints,
  99–100, 259n.24; garlands, 83, 98, 122,
  258n.19, 288n.47; gems, 70, 80, 100, 116,
  119, 134, 141–42, 145, 157, 174, 258n.16,
  259n.22; gold and silver, 65, 80, 93, 118,
  154, 170–72, 259n.22, 288n.47; hallucinogenic plants, 272n.37, 276n.63; house-
  cleaning, 66, 106, 266nn.68,69; human
  body, 65, 82, 91, 93–94, 98, 105– 106, 154,
  259n.24, 266n.70; hunting, 98, 116, 126,
  135, 141, 143, 160, 174, 253n.36, 257n.14,
  262n.42, 277nn.68,69, 287n.39; jaguars,
  154, 174–75, 254n.42, 255n.3, 288n.47;
  masks, 130, 274n.48; music, 111, 174–75,
  264n.53, 267n.9, 268n.14, 270n.27; obsidian, 145, 165, 284n.29; paper, 75–76, 110,
  255–56n.3; rocks, 10, 14, 100, 105, 137–39,
  141, 261n.38, 265n.65; scents, 24, 63–64,
  91, 100–101, 105, 119–20, 128, 132,
  266n.69; settlements, 100, 105, 35, 138,
  141, 143–44, 267n.5, 275n.54; smoke,
  84–85, 97, 106, 119– 20, 272n.37, 285n.34;
  snakes, 138, 141–44, 160, 266n.72,
  276nn.63–65; speaking in place of, 111,
  114, 116–17, 131, 149, 180–81, 269n.17,
  281–82n.16, 289n.54; spirals, 101, 111,
  122, 151, 264n.53, 265n.56, 270n.28;
  stairs, 96–98, 101, 103–104, 252n.34,
  263n.46, 265n.61; standing in place of,
  103, 111, 114, 131, 140, 282n.16; sweat
  baths, 10, 261n.35; textiles, 23, 76, 116,
  225, 255n.3, 270n.23, 288nn.44,47; trees
  and firewood, 36–37, 85, 87, 99–100, 103,
  106, 118–19, 121, 125–26, 128, 131, 167,
  180, 258nn.18,19, 264–65nn.51,53,55,56,60,
  269nn.21,22, 270n.23, 271n.32, 275n.54,
  277n.68, 279n.86, 285n.34; water, 14,
  96–97, 100, 113, 137–38, 141, 151, 186,
  265n.65, 266n.72, 275n.54, 277n.68,
  279n.82; wind, 122, 143, 225, 264n.53,
  274n.48, 276n.63; women, 80, 99,
  105–108, 134, 252n.35, 263n.50, 272n.41
Mexica (ruling group in Anahuac at time of
  Spanish conquest). *See* Indigenous groups
México-Tenochtitlan. *See* Anahuac, towns of
Michoacán (Mechuacan) (from Nahuatl,
  michihuahcan): city of, 28, 30, 37, 45, 67,

179, 253n.36, 277n.73, 278nn.77,82, 279n.85; etymology of, 27–28, 157, 241n.18, 281n.7; province of, 28, 30, 179; *tierra caliente* (region of), 80, 91, 109, 116
Michoacán, *encomenderos* of: Alonso de Mata, 162; Juan de Sámano, 162; Juan de Villegas, 163
Michoacán, towns of: Guaricaro, 161; Guayangareo (Valladolid), 2, 144, 151, 232n.9, 277n.73, 279n.85; Puruándiro, 2, 161; Queréquaro, 104; Sevina, 162; Taximaroa, 2, 171, 178, 264n.55, 287n.42; Tiripetío, 2, 34–35; Urapan, 168; Uruapan, 2, 162; Zacapu, 2. *See also* Lake Pátzcuaro Basin, towns of
Mignolo, Walter D., 257n.11
Millenialism, 42, 73, 246n.44
Miranda Godínez, Francisco, 9, 46, 78, 139, 232–33n.14, 235n.21
Mixtecs (from Nahuatl, *mixteca*). *See* Indigenous groups
Mixtón War, 26, 31–32, 51, 66, 232n.9, 240n.15, 243nn.28,29, 249n.16, 253n.37
Moctezuma II (Montecuhzoma) (*tlatoani* of México-Tenochtitlan), 17–18, 26, 32, 286n.37
Montaño, Francisco, 33, 76, 170, 287n.39
Morelia. *See* Michoacár, Guayangareo
More, Saint Thomas, 152
Motolinía. *See* Benavente, Toribio de
Muñoz Camargo, Diego, 245n.38
Murray, David, 155, 186

Nagual (from Nahuatl, *nahualli*, animal guide, spiritual double), 157, 281n.10
Nahuas. *See* Indigenous groups
Nahuatl (language): historical presence in Michoacán, 28–29; use as a lingua franca, 12, 27, 48. *See also* Escorial manuscript C.IV.5; Lake Pátzcuaro Basin, peoples of, Nahuatlatos
Nahuatlatos (naguatatos). *See* Lake Pátzcuaro Basin, peoples of
Naná (mother, mother's sister). *See* Kinship terms in Purépecha
Nanuma (legendary general under Tzintzicha Tangáxoan), 287n.40
Niza, Fray Marcos de, 238n.7
Nobility, indigenous: appropriation of Christian symbols by, 55, 58, 159, 165–73, 183, 250nn.24,25, 287n.38, 288n.44; flattening of heads by, 126–27; privileges awarded in early colonial period, 32, 243n.28, 281n.8; rivalries among, 58, 81, 102, 143–65; 170–71, 173–78, 180, 268n.11; use of *don* by 157, 281n.8, 282n.19; use of tobacco pipes by, 24. *See also* Escorial manuscript C.IV.5, vestimentary code in
Nobles, categories of indigenous: *achá*, 68, 131, 223, 267n.5, 273n.42; *angátacuri*, 223, 282n.16; *angáuatangari*, 259n.22; *cacique*,
24, 27, 72, 130–32, 159–60, 241n.18, 259n.22, 272– 74nn.41,42,51, 284n.26; *caltzontzin*, 19, 29, 242n.22, 267n.5, 286n.37; *camáhchacupeti*, 282n.16; *capitán general*, 82, 89, 174, 260n.29, 282n.16; *caracha capacha*, 131, 223, 273n.42; *cazonci*, 23, 28–29, 61, 68–69, 72, 101, 109, 122, 131, 167, 242n.22, 252nn.30,34, 254n.42, 267n.5, 269n.17, 273n.43, 274n.50, 277n.69, 282n.16; *cihuacoatl*, 160; *inca*, 274n.50; *irecha*, 119, 130–31, 134–35, 242n.22, 267n.5, 273nn.42,43, 290n.60; *principal*, 72, 159–60, 177, 185, 260n.28; *quangari*, 126, 174, 182, 225; *rey*, 30, 72; *señor*, 49, 69, 72, 177, 259n.22, 273n.42, 290n.59; *tlatoani*, 160, 281n.16; *uandátsperi*, 281– 82n.16. *See also* Angámecha; *Macegual*; Purépecha
Nuriuan (Nuriban). *See* Council of elders

Oaxaca, Mexico, 77, 236n.26
Ocánbeti (pl. *ocánbecha*) (head of unit of twenty-five families). *See* Angámecha
Oidor (Castilian, royal judge). *See* Colonial authorities. *See also* Audiencia
Ojo de agua (Castilian, spring or watering hole), 105, 137–38, 141, 265n.65
Olid, Cristóbal de, 154–55, 157–58, 163, 165, 170–71, 175–78, 185, 253nn.37,39, 280n.1, 284n.25, 287–89nn.41, 48,49
Ollin (Nahuatl, movement), 104, 265n.63, 266n.72. *See also* Gods and goddesses of Michoacán, Manóuapa
Olmos, Fray Andrés de, 12, 18–20, 22, 39, 50–51, 53, 89, 236n.28, 238nn.6,7, 249n.14, 260n.28
Omens: of the eagle, 146; of the snake, 141–45, 159, 276n.62; of the water carrier, 146–47; prefiguring the Spanish conquest, 82, 107–109, 122, 144, 146–47, 288n.45
Ortega, Juan de, 67, 162, 283n.21
Otomís. *See* Indigenous groups
Ovando, Nicolás de, 245n.38
Oviedo y Valdés, Gonzalo Fernández de, 17–18, 25, 27, 33, 38, 238nn.2,3, 244n.31, 287n.37

Pacandan. *See* Lake Pátzcuaro Basin, islands of
Panza, Pedro, 161, 178, 282n.19. *See also* Cuiniarángari, Don Pedro
Papa (from Nahuatl, *papatli*, temple guardian). *See* Priests, categories of indigenous
Paquíngata (great grandson of Hiripan and lord of Ihuatzio), 124
Parícuti (canoe paddler). *See* Angámecha
Pátzcuaro (Zacapu Hamúcutin Pátzcuaro): as center of *iréchequa*, 103, 139, 141; association with Enéani lineage, 123, 270n.29; etymology of, 97, 263n.48; settlement of,

112, 118, 135–41; as site of petámuti's oral performance, 114, 141. *See also* Lake Pátzcuaro Basin, towns of; Diocese, transfer of
Pátzcuaro, neighborhoods of: Caropu hopánsquaro, 137, 276n.61; Cuirís quataro, 136–37, 276n.61; San Francisco, 285n.29; Tarímichúndiro, 144, 285n.29
Pauácume I (successor of Sicuírancha), 124, 144
Pauácume II (father of Taríacuri), 82, 118, 124, 127, 136, 141, 146, 269nn.17,22, 276n.62, 279nn.82,86
Paul, Saint (the apostle), 57, 249n.15
Pazímbane (priestess of Xarátanga), 141. *See also* Omens, of the snake; Lake Pátzcuaro Basin, peoples of, Uatárecha
Pérez de Ribas, Father Andrés, 272n.37
Petámuti (high priest). *See* Priests, categories of indigenous. *See also* Escorial manuscript C.IV.5, oral informants of
Petate (from Nahuatl, *petatl*, woven mat). *See* Authority, indigenous symbols of
Petázequa (rocky outcrop, foundation). *See* Territoriality, indigenous conceptions of
Peter, Saint, 157
Philip II (king of Spain, 1556–98), 6, 33, 245n.38
Pilar, García del, 171, 283n.25, 290n.59
Pirúuaqua uándari (overseer of textiles). *See* Angámecha
Pizarro, Francisco, 155
Pollard, Helen Perlstein, 9, 152, 235n.20
Popol Vuh, 10, 126–27, 267n.1, 272n.37, 275n.56, 279n.83
Priests, categories of indigenous, 23; *áxame*, 83, 107–108, 120, 223, 268n.16, 269n.17, 285n.34; *cuirípeti*, *curízita*, 63, 224; *curípeti*, 224; *cúriti*, 36, 117, 120, 179–80, 224, 268n.16, 269n.17, 285n.34, 289n.53; *hirípati*, 64, 100, 224, 264n.52; *papa*, 27, 64, 241n.18, 260n.28; *petámuti*, 24, 107–108, 112, 120, 224, 267n.7, 269n.17, 270n.26, 282n.16
Principal (Castilian, principal lord). *See* Nobles, categories of indigenous
Pucúriquari (overseer of firewood). *See* Angámecha
Pueblo–hospital (Castilian, town dedicated to charitable pursuits), 10, 148, 263n.45, 267n.10, 269n.22. *See also* Government, indigenous forms of, Huatápera; Lake Pátzcuaro Basin, towns of, Santa Fe de la Laguna
Purépecha (Phurhepecha, P'urhepecha) (majority language of Michoacán), 29–30, 225, 242–43n.25, 243nn.26,27, 281n.9, 289n.50; dialectical variations of, 239n.10; linguistic classification of, 241n.19, 257n.13. *See also* Macegual; Lake Pátzcuaro Basin, peoples of

Quahuen (priest of Xarátanga), 141–42. *See also* Omens, of the snake; Uatárecha
Quangari (warrior, brave). *See* Nobles, categories of indigenous
Quatíngari (scoundrel, snotty-faced kid),175–76, 185, 225, 285n.33
Quengue (overseer of corn and other crops). *See* Angámecha
Querenda angápeti. *See* Gods and goddesses of Michoacán
Quetzalcoatl. *See* Gods and goddesses of Anahuac
Quézequaparé (captain under Tzintzicha Tangáxoan), 171
Quiroga, Vasco de, 10, 39, 55, 76, 113–14, 125, 137, 139–41, 148–53, 164–65, 169, 234n.19, 235n.21, 244n.33, 246nn.41,42, 250n.23, 253n.39, 267n.10, 270n.28, 271n.30, 272n.39, 277n.73, 276nn.60,61, 277–78nn.79–82,84,86,87, 282n.19

Ramírez, Father Francisco, 16, 30, 37–39, 243n.27, 245n.37, 246n.42, 260n.30, 261n.33, 275n.56, 276n.60
Ramírez de Fuenleal, Fray Sebastián, 19, 238n.7, 245n.38, 283n.24
Ramiro, Don (lord of Pátzcuaro), 149–50, 250n.23, 278n.79
Rea, Fray Alonso de la, 39–40, 169, 245n.39, 246n.40, 286n.37
Reason, men of: use of expression by missionary compilers, 12, 50, 54, 237n.30, 250n.20
Regidor (Castilian, municipal counselor). *See* Colonial authorities
Relación de Michoacán. *See* Escorial manuscript C.IV.5
Relaciones (Castilian, transcripts of oral testimonies), 17–18, 25, 32, 45, 155, 161, 237n.28, 238n.6, 244n.31, 245n.38
Relaciones geográficas, 245n.38; Cuitzeo de la Laguna, 242n.23, 243n.26, 268n.14; Pátzcuaro, 242n.23, 273n.47; Tiripetío, 30, 243n.26
Residencia (Castilian, judicial review of tenure in office): of Mendoza, 32, 243n.28; of Quiroga, 148–49, 250n.23, 267n.10, 278n.79
Ricard, Robert, 237n.28, 246n.41
Ríos, Fray Pedro de los, 12, 19, 237n.28, 238n.6
Robertson, Donald, 86, 101
Roskamp, Hans, 24, 76–78, 241–42n.21, 256nn.5,6
Ruiz, Eduardo, 8, 168–69, 177, 233n.15, 246n.44

Sahagún, Fray Bernardino de, 7, 12, 19, 21–22, 39, 42–43, 47–49, 52–53, 73, 96, 169, 232n.10, 237n.28, 238n.6, 239n.9,

240n.13, 242n.24, 247n.6, 248nn.11,12, 280n.4; names of indigenous collaborators, 47
Sandoval, Francisco Tello de, 32, 243n.28
San Miguel, Fray Juan de, 151, 279n.87
San Nicolás, Colegio de, 244n.33
San Salvador (first cathedral in Pátzcuaro), 10, 279n.86
Santa Ana (first church and monastery in Tzintzuntzan), 48, 229n.1, 231n.9, 248n.10, 280n.3
Santa Cruz, Colegio de, 19, 47–48, 248nn.9,11
Santa Fe de la Laguna (Uayámeo). *See* Lake Pátzcuaro Basin, towns of. *See also* Pueblo-hospital
Screenfolds, 88, 255n.3, 260n.28
Seler, Eduard, 8, 223, 234nn.16,18, 277n.74
Señor (Castilian, lord). *See* Nobles, categories of indigenous
Shamanism, 9, 81, 157, 255n.1, 256n.3, 265n.61, 268n.15
Sicuírancha (successor of Iréticátame), 124, 157
Siranda (paper, sheet), 225, 255n.3. *See also* Writing, Mesoamerican
Sirata táperi. *See* Gods and goddesses of Michoacán
Siríhtaqua (wraparound skirt), 95, 225, 288n.47. *See also* Escorial manuscript C.IV.5, vestimentary code in
Soto, Fray Francisco de, 34
Spain, cities of: Alcalá de Henares, 3, 229n.2; Burgos, 164; Madrid, 4, 8, 164, 168
Spain, regions of: Castile, 3, 37, 90; Vizcaya, 229n.1
Spanish crown, 3, 19, 26, 32, 50, 55, 67, 72, 129, 149, 168–69, 181, 185, 240nn.13,15, 245n.38, 287n.39. *See also* Colonial authorities
Swadesh, Mauricio, 29, 223

Taino (language), 27, 240–41n.18. *See also* Indigenous groups, Arawaks
Tamápucheca (son of Tariácuri), 120, 252n.33
Tangáchuran. *See* Gods and goddesses of Michoacán
Tangáxoan I (son of Aramen), 84, 100, 103–104, 123, 127, 129–30, 134–35, 252n.35, 259n.21, 262n.40, 270–72nn.24,29,31,36,38, 285n.34, 289n.53
Tangáxoan II. *See* Tzintzicha Tangáxoan
Tarascan (language). *See* Purépecha
Tarascans, 88, 152, 235n.20, 266n.69; controversy with reference to majority indigenous population of Michoacán, 29, 185–86, 242nn.23,24, 291n.62. *See also* Purépecha
Tarascue (parent- or child-in-law). *See* Kinship terms in Purépecha

Tariácaherio. *See* Lake Pátzcuaro Basin, mountains of
Tariácuri, Don Francisco (son of Tzintzicha Tangáxoan), 117, 124, 164, 179, 252n.31
Tariácuri (Tariaqueri) (Uacúsecha founder of *iréchequa*), 61, 80–84, 96, 100, 103–06, 118–21, 123– 27, 131, 134–35, 141, 145, 147, 152–53, 156, 235n.20, 252n.33, 259n.21, 270nn.25,29, 272–74nn.37,38,43,48, 276–77nn.66,69,74, 288n.47. *See also* Lake Pátzcuaro Basin, mountains of
Tariáran (lord of Uatárecha), 269n.22, 276n.63. *See also* Lake Pátzcuaro Basin, towns of
Tariata (air, wind). *See* Metaphorical systems related to, wind
Tarímichúndiro. *See* Pátzcuaro, neighborhoods of
Tasháuaco (Huitzitziltzin) (lord of Huréndetiecha), 27, 168, 171, 175–76, 178–80, 241n.18, 253n.37, 287n.41, 289n.52
Tasta (mantle, measure of cloth). *See* Metaphorical systems related to, textiles
Tatá (father, father's brother). *See* Kinship terms in Purépecha
Taximaroa (Tajimaroa). *See* Michoacán, towns of
Tawantinsuyu (Tahuantisuyo) (Quechua, land of the four parts or corners), 90, 92
Tecaqua (Tecacua). *See* Council of elders
Tedlock, Dennis, 111–12, 139, 266n.1, 273n.45
Tello, Fray Antonio, 66, 243n.29, 286n.37
Teniente (Castilian, deputy). *See* Colonial authorities
Teotihuacan. *See* Anahuac, towns of
Territoriality, indigenous conceptions of, 88, 98, 102–103, 112, 150, 178, 258n.20; *altepetl*, 266n.65; *anapu*, 243n.26; *auándaro*, 91–92, 94–110, 186, 223, 261n.38, 264nn.52,53,56; *cahuleu*, 260n.29; *cumiechucuaro*, 91–110, 223, 254n.41, 261n.38, 264n.56, 271n.35, 290n.60; *curúzetaro*, 89, 99–100, 224; *echérendo*, 91–92, 99–110, 186, 224, 264nn.51-53; *hamúcutin*, 137–38, 224; *iréchequa*, 6, 10, 24, 95, 99, 109–10, 113–14, 116–17, 132, 139, 141, 143–47, 156, 166–67, 177, 224, 263n.47, 267n.5, 270–71nn.29,33; *iréchequaro*, 30, 69, 112, 117, 224, 252–53n.35, 267n.4; *ireta*, 224, 267n.5; *ireti*, 267n.5; *petázequa*, 137–38, 149, 151, 224, 263n.48; *terungambo*, 267n.5; *thámbengarani*, 92, 102, 107, 110, 112, 225; *uapátzequa*, 225; *umbamgandequa*, 267n.5. *See also* Cosmology, indigenous; Writing, Mesoamerican
Terungambo (head town). *See* Territoriality, indigenous conceptions of
Tesorero (Castilian, royal treasury official). *See* Angámecha; Colonial authorities
Testera, Fray Jacobo de, 288n.43

Tetzalteotl. *See* Gods and goddesses of Anahuac
Texcoco (Tezcoco). *See* Anahuac, towns of
Thámbengarani (four parts of the world). *See* Territoriality, indigenous conceptions of
Tharés (stone idol), 29, 137, 225, 242n.24
Tharés úpeme. *See* Gods and goddesses of Michoacán
Ticátame (son of Hiripan), 124, 147, 278n.77
Tierra caliente (Castilian, hot country). *See* Michoacán
Timas (Thimas), 76, 154, 170–71, 173–78, 180–84, 287n.40, 288n.44, 290n.60
Tingárata. *See* Gods and goddesses of Michoacán
Tiras (Castilian, long strips of cloth or paper, sometimes folded or rolled), 17, 24, 76, 255–56nn.3,5. *See also* Writing, Mesoamerican
Tirípeme (pl. Tirípemencha). *See* Gods and goddesses of Michoacán
Títulos (Castilian, titles): Tócuaro, 256n.6; Xaráquaro, 256n.6
Tlacuilo (Nahuatl, scribe–painter), 74, 78
Tlaloque. *See* Gods and goddesses of Anahuac
Tlatelolco (Tlatilulco). *See* Anahuac, towns of; *See also* Anales
Tlatoani (Nahuatl, supreme ruler). *See* Nobles, categories of indigenous. *See also* Uandátsperi
Tlaxcala, Mexico, 19, 166, 249n.14
Toledo, Francisco de (viceroy of Peru), 268n.11
Toltecs (from Nahuatl, *tolteca*). *See* Indigenous groups
Torquemada, Fray Juan de, 39–40, 245n.39, 246n.40, 286n.37
Tovar, Father Juan de, 12, 19, 237n.28, 238n.6
Transculturation, 140, 150, 275–76n.58
Treasure: 67, 69–70, 157, 163, 169, 171–72, 179–81, 278n.77, 281n.6, 284n.28, 286n.37, 290n.59
Tribute collection, 22–23, 32, 67–72, 80, 85, 96–97, 109–10, 119, 129, 132, 162, 181, 265n.60, 282n.16, 283n.20, 284n.28. *See also* Angámecha; Government, indigenous forms of
Triple Alliance in Michoacán, 100, 271n.33, 273n.43
Tsiríquarequa (staff, scepter) *See* Authority, indigenous symbols of
Tsitsí (maternal aunt). *See* Kinship terms in Purépecha
Tsitsíspandáquare (Tzitzispandaquare) (grandfather of Tzintzicha Tangáxoan), 124, 273n.43, 278n.77
Tucúpachá,. *See* Gods and goddesses of Michoacán
Tucúruan (grandson of Hiripan; lord of Ihuatzio), 124
Tula. *See* Anahuac, towns of. *See also* Zuyuá
Tzacapu (stone, basalt), 138, 225. *See also* Metaphorical systems related to rocks

Tzintzicha Tangáxoan, Don Francisco, 13, 17–18, 24, 26, 33–35, 55, 61–62, 67–70, 76, 82, 86, 104, 117, 124, 131, 154–57, 161–86, 245n.36, 252–53nn.31,37,39, 254–55nn.44,45, 269n.18, 271n.35, 280n.1, 281n.6, 283–84nn.22,23,25,27,28, 285n.33, 286–87nn.36,37,39,40, 288–90nn.44,51–55,58–61. *See also* Cazonci
Tzintzuni (hummingbird), 28, 38, 225
Tzintzuntzan (Zinzonza): capital of Uacúsecha in years preceding the Spanish conquest, 83, 141; capital of Uatárecha in years preceding the omen of the snake, 141–43; association with Uanácaze lineage, 123, 270n.29. *See also* Lake Pátzcuaro Basin, towns of

Uacapu (Santángel). *See* Michoacán, towns of
Uacús (eagle; pl. *uacúsecha*): 113, 225. *See also* Metaphorical systems related to, eagles
Uacúsecha: Enéani lineage, 123–24, 273n.43; Uanácaze lineage, 123–25, 273n.43; Zacapu hireti lineage, 123–25, 270n.29, 273n.43. *See also* Indigenous groups, Chichimecs; Gods and goddesses of Michoacán; Lake Pátzcuaro Basin, peoples of
Uanácaze. *See* Uacúsecha. *See also* Tzintzuntzan
Uandaqua (word), 30, 243n.26
Uandari (speaker, poet), 267n.7
Uandátsperi (governor). *See* Nobles, categories of indigenous. *See also* Angámecha, angátacuri
Uanduqua (pectoral, pincers). *See* Authority, indigenous symbols of
Uapátzequa (neighborhood). *See* Territoriality, indigenous conceptions of
Uápeani I (successor of Pauácume I), 124, 144
Uápeani II (father of Zétaco and Aramen), 82, 118, 124, 136, 141, 146, 269nn.17,22, 276n.62, 279nn.82,86
Uaruri (pl. *uarucha*) (overseer of fish). *See* Angámecha
Uatárecha. *See* Lake Pátzcuaro Basin, peoples of
Uauá (paternal aunt). *See* Kinship terms in Purépecha
Uaxánoti (messenger, letter carrier). *See* Angámecha
Uaxántsiqua (seat, stool). *See* Authority, indigenous symbols of
Uayámeo (Santa Fe de la Laguna). *See* Lake Pátzcuaro Basin, towns of. *See also* Pueblo–hospital
Uázcata (prisoner, accused), 24, 37, 118, 226. *See also* Festivals of Michoacán, traditional, Equata cónsquaro; Justice, indigenous forms of

Uirámbanecha (Uirauanecha) (gods of the left-hand side). *See* Gods and goddesses of Michoacán
Uitzume (water dog, spiritual guide of the dead), 158, 281n.11
Umbamgandequa (village). *See* Territoriality, indigenous conceptions of
Urani atari (painter of gourds). *See* Angámecha
Uricho (Urichu). *See* Lake Pátzcuaro Basin, towns of
Uruapan. *See* Michoacán, towns of
Usquarecuri (feather worker). *See* Angámecha
Uuache (son, youngster generally). *See* Kinship terms in Purépecha

Valencia, Fray Martín de, 19
Valladolid (present-day Morelia). *See* Michoacán, towns of, Guayangareo. *See also* Diocese, transfer of
Velasco, Luis de (second viceroy of New Spain), 27, 240n.16, 251n.27
Venus (morning and evening star), 104, 127, 147, 236n.25, 261n.35, 265n.62. *See also* Gods and goddesses of Michoacán, Manóuapa; Gods and goddesses of Anahuac, Quetzalcoatl
Veracruz, Fray Alonso de la, 16, 34–37, 244–45nn.35,36
Veytia calendar wheel. *See* Escorial manuscript C.IV.5
Virgen: de Guadalupe, 275n.55; de la Purísima Concepción, 263n.45; de la Salud, 151, 279n.84
Vise, Don Alonso (brother–in–law of Tzintzicha Tangáxoan), 163, 290n.59
Visitador (Castilian, inspector). *See* Colonial authorities
Vitoria, Fray Francisco de, 34
Vizcaya. *See* Spain, regions of

Warfare: indigenous conceptions of, 23, 64–65, 82, 87–89, 92, 99–102, 116, 118–20, 122–23, 128–30, 132, 135, 143, 145–46, 150, 158, 160, 167, 174–78, 182, 253n.37, 255n.45, 257n.14, 261n.38, 262n.41, 265n.60, 266n.72, 274n.48, 277nn.68,69,75, 285n.32, 286n.34, 289n.51
Warren, J. Benedict, 9, 43, 164, 166, 229n.1, 234–35n.19
Writing, Mesoamerican: clues to reading order in, 83, 99–102, 258n.20; connections to map making and judicial system, 88, 102, 248n.8; controversies surrounding, 46–54, 75–80, 87– 89, 109–10, 113, 169, 237n.31, 256–57nn.7,10,11; materials and formats used in, 75, 88, 255–56n.3; prehispanic examples of, 257n.8; sacred dimension of, 10, 14, 75–76, 89–110, 256n.3, 260n.28, 264n.52; terms related to in Purépecha, 77, 225, 255n.3. *See also* Anales; *Angámecha, carari*; Artes y vocabularios; Codices; *Escudos de armas*; Feather paintings; *Historias*; *Lienzos*, *Memoriales*; *Relaciones*; Screenfolds; *Tiras*; *Títulos*; *Tlacuilo*
Xanecho (Janitzio). *See* Lake Pátzcuaro Basin, islands of
Xanóata hucazio. *See* Lake Pátzcuaro Basin, mountains of
Xaráquaro (Jarácuaro). *See* Lake Pátzcuaro Basin, islands of
Xarátanga. *See* Gods and goddesses of Michoacán

Yácata (rectangular stone pyramid with circular extension), 27, 46, 101, 103–104, 241n.18, 263n.46, 265n.57. *See also* Cu
Yaguaro (Yauaro). *See* Lake Pátzcuaro Basin, mountains of
Yucatan (Peninsula), 19, 27, 77, 89

Zacapu. *See* Michoacán, towns of
Zacapu hireti. *See* Uacúsecha. *See also* Ihuatzio
Zacatecs (from Nahuatl, *zacateca*). *See* Indigenous groups
Zapíuátame (lord of Huréndetiecha; ancestor of Cuiníarángari and Tasháuaco), 289n.53
Zétaco (father of Hiripan), 82, 100, 123
Zirita cherengue. *See* Gods and goddesses of Michoacán
Zuangua (father of Tzintzicha Tangáxoan), 133, 146–47, 166–68, 172, 177, 271n.35, 285– 86nn.30,34,35
Zucúraue (priestess of Xarátanga), 141. *See also* Lake Pátzcuaro Basin, peoples of, Uatárecha; Omens, of the snake
Zumárraga, Fray Juan de, 48, 149, 245n.38, 246n.41, 250n.23
Zuyuá, 236n.26, 272n.38. *See also* Anahuac, towns of, Tula; Indigenous groups, Toltecs

www.ingramcontent.com/pod-product-compliance
Lightning Source LLC
Chambersburg PA
CBHW031427160426
43195CB00010BB/644